TRAILS

OF

THE

WHITE

SAVAGES

BY

Gary H. Wiles, B.A., J.D.
and Delores M. Brown

PHOTOSENSITIVE™
LAGUNA NIGUEL, CALIFORNIA

TRAILS OF THE WHITE SAVAGES
Copyright 1998 Gary H. Wiles and Delores M. Brown
All Rights Reserved.

This is Book 3* of our *HISTORY AS IT HAPPENS*™ Series.
It is an authoritative historical work based upon the
extensive research in its Bibliography, National Archives
documents, interviews of historians and 1,600 photographs
of artifacts and natural sites.

For Information write to:
PHOTOSENSITIVE™
P.O. Box 7408
Laguna Niguel, CA 92607
or
☎ or FAX (714) 495-8897

PRINTING HISTORY
First Printing 1998

ISBN: 1-889252-03-4

PRINTED IN THE UNITED STATES OF AMERICA.

Library of Congress Catalog Card Number [97-76332]

Other Books by these Authors

PONDER THE PATH [Book 1 of Same Series]
BEHOLD THE SHINING MOUNTAINS [Book 2 of Series]

***Please See Order Form Inside Back Cover To Order These
Other Exceptional Books**

TABLE OF CONTENTS	**CHRONOLOGY**	**PAGE**

INDEX TO 16 PINPOINT ACTION MAPS*

DIRECTORY FOR 11 ANCIENT [BLACK & WHITE] PORTRAITS

ACKNOWLEDGMENT

We thank the librarians of public, private, college and university libraries who unearthed books for us. The *University of California at Irvine* [where we have lectured] let us use their 1,200,000 books and access 16,000,000 more by MELVL® computer. Martha Utterback of the Daughters of the Republic of Texas Library at the Alamo provided names and land records. Gayle Ledford of *QB Boydstun Library* and Chris Morgan with Katie Rose of *Fort Gibson Historic Site* in Oklahoma furnished invaluable detailed area history.

We thank entertainment industry advisor Ray Glazner, Library Bibliographer Chuck Hamsa of the University of Southwestern Louisiana and Jodi Eldredge and Dr. Fred Gowans of Brigham Young University for reviewing *TRAILS*. Thanks to the State and National facility Historians providing vital information, like John Alden Reid of *Horseshoe Bend National Military Park* in Daviston, Alabama, whose articles with intimate military data [in bibliography] and maps drawn by Generals Andrew Jackson and John Coffee helped us draw our pinpoint action maps.

Thanks to Tod Butler and Michael Meier of the *National Archives* in Washington, D.C. and Bill Doty of the *National Archives* in Laguna Niguel, California for duplicate originals of Bonneville's letters in Chapter 34 and data for our Epilogue.

We still gratefully rely on data from our 10,000 mile 1992 sojourn with interviews of Dr. Fred Gowans of *BYU* of Provo, Utah, Archivist Lawrence Dodd at *Whitman College* in Walla Walla, Washington and taking 1,600 research photographs of original sites and artifacts in *Fort Hall Replica* at Pocatello, Idaho, *Museum of the Mountain Man* at Pinedale, Wyoming, *Buffalo Bill Historical Center* at Cody, Wyoming, *Museum of the Fur Trade* at Chadron, Nebraska [interviewing Dr. Charles Hansen, Jr.], *Fort Vancouver National Historical Site*, *Flagstaff Hill Interpretive Center* near Baker City, Oregon and Louisiana's *Chalmette Battlefield Visitor Center*.

We thank Park Rangers, Tribal Councils and Indian Schools, and forgive us for the many precious people we have omitted.

C

FOREWORD
by
Ray Glazner[1]

In *TRAILS OF THE WHITE SAVAGES* authors Gary Wiles and Delores Brown have created not only a fine work of history, but it is as readable as a novel.

Using their *history as it happens*™ methods, they have made famous and infamous historical figures live again in well researched, true life adventures so vivid and outlandish the rashest novelist could never risk portraying them as fiction.

As you read page after page of real history, you "hear" Andrew Jackson, Kit Carson, the Walkers, Sam Houston and many other legendary Americans "talking" in their own words. It affords an appreciation of history that is the next best thing to being there.

The book flows well. It illuminates actual humorous, frightening or deplorable incidents that are only hinted at in most history books. It is an in-depth study of an often overlooked era of American History intimately exploring the people and the pathways of westward expansion and the fur trade of the early 1800s.

Impressively researched, backed by a host of understandable maps, a pervasive bibliography and the intricate social and historical trappings of the times, this book should be required reading for everyone interested in the history of our country.

---

[1] Simi Valley, California's Ray Glazner is a distinguished educator, historian, historical re-enactor and consultant to state and national museums as well as the entertainment industry.

PROLOGUE

RAILS OF THE WHITE SAVAGES is Book Three of our nonfiction trilogy of true life adventures of legendary Americans on the frontier amid the wars and vital explorations of the early 1800s.

A brief word about the two earlier books of this **history as it happens™** series. Book One, Francis Parkman Award candidate *PONDER THE PATH*, profiles the Sublettes and other celebrated Mountain Men between 1808 and 1830. It's the human story of how William Sublette's grandfather Whitley inspired him as a boy to become the trailblazer who would stun the nation with his impossible journey opening the **Oregon Trail** to wagons.

Book Two, *BEHOLD THE SHINING MOUNTAINS* [1830 to 36] is *PONDER's* free-standing sequel. Considered for the Pulitzer Prize, it reveals America's march toward civil war, cholera epidemics and its wilderness so profoundly beautiful our ancestors were willing to die just to live there. The **Oregon Trail** is extended from the Rockies to Fort Boise by the most Quixotic wheeled explorers imaginable. [See the order blanks on this book's last page.]

TRAILS and our earlier works differ from traditional history books three ways. [1] They are **history as it happens™** in a high action documentary format. Dialogue evolves from diaries, journals, letters, newspapers interviews, autobiographies and quotes from authentic texts. Snippet quotes from these sources reveal the innermost thoughts of our forebearers. [2] A Table of Contents Chronology specifies every Chapter's precise historical period. With a historical time frame atop every page, the reader never guesses at dates. [3] Instead of focusing on a single person, these books put famous and infamous central figures together with their contemporaries embroiled in the local and national issues of their era, so it's like being there.

TRAILS OF THE WHITE SAVAGES appeals to readers from young adults through collegiate level. Excerpts from its 169 Bibliography references, diaries, journals and letters spice *TRAILS* into a luscious pudding of the antiquities for history lovers and general readers alike.

TRAILS stars fabled explorer and Mountain Man Joseph R.[2] Walker, his valiant brothers Joel and Big John with mysterious U.S. Army Captain Benjamin L.E. Bonneville, who'd have you believe he was only a fur trapper. Mountaineer and military heroes David Crockett, Sam Houston and Andrew Jackson are often center stage. All but Bonneville share secret bonds of ancient blood and battle.

TRAILS highlights others in supporting roles like celebrated sharpshooter Ewing Young, who will explore the history and development of the gun in Chapter 13. Kit Carson, pathfinders William Becknell, William Wolfskill and James Ohio Pattie will blaze new trails through the wilderness with you. *Apaches* will banish diabolical Old Bill Williams to trek hundreds of miles of desert naked without weapons, food or water.

Eleven ancient portraits portray central figures. Many other renowned souls live between these covers. You may find your relatives among the 326 real people [with identifying data] and 25 Indian Tribes in its 9,046 word Text Index.

Sixteen Pinpoint Action Maps put you in the battles and on legendary trails. Before land became a territory or state, old descriptions often used "Country," *e.g.* "Oregon Country." To avoid the confusion inherent in numerous undesignated areas, we have honored the "Country" custom in both maps and text. The book's 35 states with admission dates and pertinent geographical features are also described in the Text Index.

TRAILS OF THE WHITE SAVAGES explores America's wild youth from 1813 to 1836 with the complex, rugged Americans we've mentioned, and many other fascinating men and women, red and white, awaiting you. You'll fight the Creek Indian War with the Walker boys, Sam Houston and David Crockett serving under the General who rescued a

---

[2] Joseph's middle name was "Rutherford" after his great, great grandfather Reverend Samuel Rutherford but often appears as "Reddeford" because of an error in his November 4, 1876 obituary.

doomed nation and became a god in the eyes of all Americans -- except Joe Walker.

Explaining the *TRAILS* part of the title is easy. You'll open the **Santa Fe Trail** for business with Joe Walker in William Becknell's 1821 expedition, which they finish by flinging $10,000 in Mexican silver onto the streets of Franklin, Missouri.

You will share Becknell's harrowing 1822 ride through the *Jornada de Muerte* with Joe Walker, Ewing Young and a bedeviled crew in the first wagons over the **Santa Fe Trail,** risking Indian attacks and imprisonment in a Mexican dungeon for a share of Santa Fe's riches and delights.

In 1825 you'll survey the **Santa Fe Trail** with towering Walker brothers Joel, Joe and Big John carrying chain and transit through tribal lands of the *Osage, Comanche* and *Apache* with Old Bill Williams under command of Major George Sibley.

You'll search for the fabled **Old Spanish Trail** from Santa Fe to California with three expeditions led respectively by Sylvester Pattie, Ewing Young and William Wolfskill between fall 1827 and spring 1831.

Joseph Walker's much maligned[3] 1834 expedition with its *Paiute* battles will blaze the **California Emigrant Trail** back through the High Sierras, after a year long odyssey that shocked and baffled these Mountain Men who thought they'd seen it all. The 160 year brawl among historians over what Bonneville and Walker were up to in the West will end forever in the Epilogue.

TRAILS will also beguile you with the big river basins of the Missouri, Mississippi and the Platte and scale the majestic "snow-capped Towers of God" that we call the Rocky Mountains. You'll travel Tennessee, battle Indians in Alabama, fight the British, Spanish, and Seminoles in Florida, and run what's left of the invincible British Army back to their boats in Louisiana. No book about Sam Houston and David Crockett could omit the Homeric birth rites of Texas.

You may wonder who were the people branded *WHITE SAVAGES* and why? For that answer, we must revisit 1533 when Henry VIII, King of England, Ireland and Scotland,

---

[3] Joseph Walker's crucifixion over where he went and why is a travesty created and perpetuated by the ill informed, as the Epilogue proves.

divorced his first wife, getting himself excommunicated from the Catholic Church.

Henry retaliated by outlawing the Catholic religion in his realm and sanctifying the Church of England. Catholic since St. Patrick's arrival in 432 A.D., Ireland exploded in rebellion.

About 1610, King James I plucked the menacing Presbyterian Scots off England's northern border and "planted" them in the bogs of Ulster as pawns in his geopolitical chess game to checkmate the Irish Rebellion. Instead of going quietly into this good mud, the Scots created turmoil for the Lords of the Soil and displaced decent Irish farmers into city gutters. The resulting religious war between Protestant northern and Catholic southern Ireland still seethes *to this day*!

The late 1600s and early 1700s found the English driving their uncontrollable Scottish pawns from Ireland to the American Colonies by levying tyrannical taxes and outlawing their Presbyterian religion.

The Colonies, fearing catastrophic Indian wars on their western frontiers, beckoned these rugged Scots with promises of land. By 1720   50,000 rowdy Scottish pawns left Ulster for America -- where they became the "Scotch-Irish."

William Penn's Executive Secretary James Logan lured hordes of "Scotch-Irish" into orderly Dutch settled Pennsylvania. Later labeling them "bold indigents" when they squatted wherever they wanted to, Logan herded them with harsh taxes and legal flagellation into the Indian-infested forests of the Appalachian frontier.

America's coastal colonists could not conceive of being dismembered for the sake of owning a bit of dirt. But the burly "Scotch-Irish" farmed the Shenandoah and other remote valleys through the deadly land brawl called the Forest Wars. By 1770 nearly 10,000 whites and Indians had been murdered in ever worsening atrocities.

In 1772 Benjamin Franklin found the Irish brutes so revolting, he wrote: *"Was I ... to form my judgment of civil society by what I have seen lately, I should never advise a Nation of Savages to admit of Civilization:... I assure you, that ... compar'd to these People every Indian is a Gentleman."*

Under Franklin's pen name "Widow Dogood," he denounced these Scotch-Irish pawns as: *"White Savages under the influence of an ignorant and vicious [Presbyterian] clergy."*

Young poet Ralph Waldo Emerson wrote:

"Europe stretches to the Alleghenies; America lies beyond."

Did Emerson mean that all American frontiersmen were *WHITE SAVAGES*?

By the time the Revolution's first shot was fired at Concord in 1775, 250,000 *WHITE SAVAGES* had emigrated to America and were even less tolerant of British tyranny in America than in Ireland. Every third Continental soldier was a *WHITE SAVAGE.* By war's end 1,492 American officers and 26 generals were *WHITE SAVAGES.* Commodore Barry, father of the American Navy, who captured the first British vessel was also a *WHITE SAVAGE.*

Some said *WHITE SAVAGES* became the first real Americans by bursting the bonds of European autocracy binding a man be what his father was. An American was anything he had the guts to be!

As you shall see, several Ulster Scottish pawns soon fought their way to the king row in America, becoming our equivalent of Kings. Others became famous beyond anything they'd ever expected. *TRAILS* is about those *WHITE SAVAGES* and their legendary compatriots who were just plain good old American stock from here and the world over.

Come join us in the mists of the past outside Nashville's City Hotel. It's September 4, 1813. The War of 1812 rages. But that's not the feud on this quiet street awash in fury so barbaric, yet so trivial, only civilized men can understand it. The world's foremost *WHITE SAVAGE* is about to get shot down in a gunfight.

Gary H. Wiles, B.A., J.D. and Delores M. Brown

CHAPTER 1

PISTOL BALLS, BLOOD AND FURY   **SEPTEMBER 1813**

His heart fisting his ribs, skinny 46 year old General Andrew Jackson stalked past Nashville's City Hotel in step with hulking giant Colonel John Coffee. The General sensed that Tom and Jesse Benton lay in ambush in the morning shadows.

Eyes searching, General Jackson mused that soldiers who court death for a living crave her touch as much as they shun it. No man be more alive than him about to suffer the icy kiss of eternal darkness.

Lion-headed Tom Ben-

General Andrew Jackson - Age 46

ton filled the hotel doorway, hands hovering over the big bore dragoon pistols in his belt. Standing a muscular six feet, Colonel Benton did not turn his huge head, but swung his whole body to track Jackson and Coffee.

Colonel Coffee whispered down at Jackson, "Do you see that fellow?"

Through his frozen grin General Jackson grated, "I have my eye on him, but hold fast till we spy his brother Jesse. Walk toward the Post Office."

At 41, the black hair helmet swathing Colonel Coffee's head grayed about the muzzle. Pulse pounding, he walked on, wondering why every man who gambles his life is sure he'll win. As a cavalryman who swung his sabre from horseback, Coffee felt feeble plodding to battle in his battered thigh high boots. If Andrew Jackson's standing field orders be respected, every man's pistol packed double powder with a pair of bullets in the barrel. Business'd soon be brisk for Nashville's undertakers.

Colonel John Coffee Without His Usual Beard.

Jackson and Coffee picked up their mail in a brutally ordinary way, shoving it unopened in their inside coat pockets. They clopped along the walkway toward the City Hotel. Tom and Jesse Benton now crouched ever so slightly with coats pulled back to show braces of pistols in their belts.

"Have a plan for this, Andy?"

"Spanking boys doesn't require elaborate schemes."

Coming abreast of Colonel Thomas Hart Benton, General Jackson whirled brandishing his riding whip in his left fist and shrilled, "Now you crowing rascal, defend yourself!" General Jackson's right hand jammed his pistol into Benton's belly, backing him empty handed into the hotel hallway.

Jackson knew Jesse Benton hadn't fired for fear of striking his brother, but Jesse'd vanished! Jackson lashed Tom's head with his riding crop, yelling, "Kneel, damn you! Kneel!"

By the time Jackson saw Jesse in the side hall, it was too late. Jesse's double-loaded pistol boomed, deafening the three of them. Jackson reeled from the numbing blow of Jesse's ball ripping into his arm. Jackson unsheathed his small sword, but passed out before he could use it.

As Tom Benton fired into the frail General's fallen body,

he got shoved aside by Jesse trying to deliver the General's *coup de mort* with his other pistol.

But before Jesse could shoot, bystander James Sitler tackled his gun hand.

Having chosen the wrong doorway to head off Jesse Benton, Colonel Coffee bulled into the hall. Seeing his boyhood friend Andy Jackson in pooling blood on the floor, Coffee bellered and fired. But Tom Benton slipped inside Coffee's blast.

Clubbing his pistol, Coffee battered Tom Benton backward, sprawling him down the back stairs.

Hearing gunfire in the City Hotel, General Jackson's gigantic nephew Stockly Hays stormed in with his sword cane, but the point snapped off on Jesse's big bronze coat button. Dropping his blunted sword, Hays bulldogged Jesse Benton to the floor. Yanking a dirk from his boot, Hays stabbed Jesse in both arms.

Jesse pulled his hideout pistol to blow Hays through, but it misfired. Hays would have butchered Jesse, but for bystanders diving on to ruin the grandest brawl ever held at the City Hotel.

Tears streaming, towering Colonel Coffee carried his bloody little General all the way to the Nashville Inn, goring its floor like a slaughterhouse, as the manager gestured to get out. Coffee thundered, "If *every* doctor in Nashville's not in the General's room in two minutes, I'll slash you into cutlets!"

General Jackson's room was soon full of physicians trying to staunch the bleeding before Jackson's life ran into the mattress. One doctor said somberly, "General Jackson, we must amputate your arm if you are to live past sunset."

Jackson gasped, "I will keep my arm, sir. Dress my wounds with elm bark and hickory shavings as the *Muscogees* do. Colonel Coffee, will you see my orders are obeyed?"

Coffee snarled, "Sever his arm and lose yours in the doing. None here are so fleet with a blade as I -- and I do mine from horseback."

A townsman burst in. "Colonel, come wi' me!"

Coffee followed him to the hall. "What's this?"

"Bentons are in the plaza denouncin' General Jackson as an assassin."

As Colonel Coffee approached the plaza Thomas Benton boomed, "Your Old Hickory has bent and broken no more to strut and threaten the just who walk these streets in peace!" Benton brandished the small sword Jackson had lost in the brawl, then broke it in two, dropping the pieces at his brother Jesse's feet."

Coffee waved to Colonel Benton, "We must talk, sir."

Benton's hand dropped to the recharged pistol in his belt.

Coffee grated, "Come to the City Hotel bar. We'll talk like the gentlemen we once knew -- unless you'd rather babble till this crowd hangs you."

Both Bentons followed Coffee to the City Hotel, but all slipped into the Benton's room to avoid angry men in the bar.

Coffee grated, "Till this September 4th, we were a pair o' 41 year old Tennessee Militia Colonels standin' side by side agin the British in a desperate war to save our nation. What brought this foul business on?"

Jesse muttered, "Billy Carroll barges into our officer corps -- a loudmouth Pennsylvania squarehead -- promoted as Jackson's protégé though popular as pus. Littleton Johnston challenges Billy to a duel. Billy says he only fights *gentlemen*. I tell Billy I'm a *gentleman* and I'll bear the grievance."

Coffee squinted, "You butted into their fight?"

"I made it mine, but that treacherous snake Carroll crawled to the Hermitage and got Jackson for a second. Jackson pressured me into forgetting the duel. But other officers wanted Carroll called to account, so I challenged Billy again."

Tom tried to mask the disbelief in his eyes.

Coffee crooked his finger at Jesse to get the rest of it.

"Billy demanded the duel be at 10 feet instead of the gentleman's 30 and that we begin back to back like Frenchies, then wheel and fire. Jackson said we must wheel perfectly erect."

Tom sneered, "Never heard of anything so barbaric -- all to favor a fop!"

Coffee stilled Tom with his raised hand. "Talk, Jesse."

"Dueled June 14th. We wheeled. I shot Billy's thumb. He fired too quick nicking both cheeks of my butt as I wheeled. Jackson claimed I crouched and was neither correct nor honorable -- the claim itself dishonors all that be honorable!"

9

Tom snarled, "This chicanery transpired while I labored on Jackson's behalf in Washington getting the U.S. government to reimburse Jackson for money spent supporting our militia in Mississippi!"

"And learnin' o' this, you cursed General Jackson several times in public, didn't you Tom?"

"I railed at his disgracing my brother, but I never challenged Jackson. He knows that. We exchanged letters."

"Are you both blind?" Coffee bellered.

"What?" Jesse shouted back.

"The finest man we've ever known -- a man accepted as your house guest in North Carolina by your dead father -- bless his soul -- lies near death *over nothin'*! What's his crime?"

Jesse muttered, "He dishonored me!"

Colonel Coffee stood, towering over them. "You have safe passage from Nashville -- if you're gone by tomorrow's dawn. After that, I'll lead the mob that hangs you."

"What's our crime?" Tom Benton asked haughtily.

"Peevishness, Colonel -- befouled by vanity that reeks. Be gone by dawn or die," Coffee growled, storming out.

Kneeling by Jackson's bed after the doctors left the Nashville Inn, John Coffee prayed for Jackson to live. Moments after midnight, Jackson rasped, "John, had I two friends as true as you, I'd have no need of myself. Find precious Rachel's miniature in my shirt. If it's shattered, lie and say it's sound."

Coffee fished Rachel's miniature painted on ivory from the gory shirt on the floor. Blood caked on Rachel's image scrubbed off in the bedroom basin. Coffee marveled at how a man who'd been a Congressman, United States Senator, Judge and Major General could be so consumed with love of this plain

Miniature of Rachel Jackson

woman who looked like a chambermaid draped in lace.

He held Rachel's miniature before the General's ashen face. "She's unharmed, and she'll soon be here her lovin' self to tend you."

"You send those Benton snakes to their Maker, John?"

"Jist tromped their tails. They'll leave Nashville by sunup or stay here forever."

"Affair of honor made no sense, did it, John?"

"Do they ever? Doctors git all the bullets out o' you?"

"All but one strove to the bone in my left arm."

"You still carry Charles Dickinson's ball lodged agin your heart?"

The General nodded.

"Way I heard, Dickinson fired. You pretended he'd missed -- with his ball in your chest -- then shot him dead."

Jackson muttered, "That's the way it was."

"When Dickinson's bullet abscesses, your coughin' turns bloody with chills and fever."

"Over and over again," the General gasped.

"You keep this up, Andy, your pitiful little body won't know what to die of. I pray this was your last affair of honor."

"There's little honor in playing the fool."

"Pretty much what I told the Bentons."

Sergeant McNarney stood at ramrod attention beside General Jackson's Nashville Inn bed eyeing the wall. "I come fer the men -- Sir -- to say their piece. You didn't leave us to die in Mississippi -- Sir. By the living God, we'll not leave you."

"I'll stand good for their billets," General Jackson rasped.

"Been here two weeks. We'll forage fer ourse'ves -- Sir.

"As you wish, Sergeant McNarney."

"The men never told you how they felt, Sir -- with you and them other officers givin' up yer horses that the wounded might ride day after day on our return from hell -- buyin' our victuals with yer own money -- an' you spittin' blood. The men never said -- well Sir -- they never said how they --- how they..."

General Jackson groaned, "Sergeant McNarney, look down here. Tell them I know. Tell them I know I have received more from them than they had to give."

Seeing both men about to cry, Rachel Jackson wiped the

tears from her plump cheeks and said, "General Jackson must rest. Give my undying gratitude to the Tennessee Volunteers. Accept it yourself from the very bottom of my loving heart."

"Truly, Ma'm," McNarney grated, "General, your men be out there waitin' fer orders. Cain't march without you -- Sir. I'll be goin' now." McNarney saluted till the General's hand moved ever so slightly returning it.

General Andrew Jackson, who'd taken a sabre slash in the face as a Continental Soldier boy of 14 rather than clean the mud off a British officer's boots, was too choked to reply.

As Sergeant McNarney left, the local Public Safety Committee filed in, gawking to see if Andrew Jackson really had bled two mattresses full as rumor in the streets had it.

Sure General Andrew Jackson would die any moment, Colonel Coffee rose pointing toward the door.

The Methodist preacher, importuned, "General, you must hear this."

General Jackson coughed, "John, let the Minister speak. Might help me meet my Maker on better terms."

The Minister harangued theatrically, "On August 30th past, t'was muggy at Fort Mims. Men played devil's cards while young girls danced shamelessly. At the noon drum, 1,000 screeching devil Red Sticks fell upon the Fort, butchering Major Beasley and the other 553 -- save a few who fled to bear the news. Seized by the legs, babies was brained on stockade walls. Raped women was scalped alive and handed knives to kill theirselves. Bodies was mutilated to where a mother would not recognize her own issue. That Satanic *Shawnee Tecumseh* put the Creeks up to this. He bade them hurl the white man back into the sea from whence he came. General Jackson, unless your Militia marches to Alabama and annihilates them Red Sticks, Nashville and your wife here will share the fate of Fort Mims."

Coffee was astounded to see "dying" Andrew Jackson rise on his elbow, bullet wounds swollen like crimson volcanoes on his skeletal upper body. "Colonel Coffee, tie me on my horse. We're going to Alabama!"

CHAPTER 2

WILL THE WALKER BOYS FIGHT?   **DECEMBER 1813**

hough he'd only turned 15 on December 13th, Joseph Walker towered over most of the grown men in the Scotch-Irish clans of Houston, McClellan and Hays who'd trekked from Virginia's Shenandoah Valley to settle near Knoxville, Tennessee with the Walkers several decades ago. Looming over his mother Susan Willis Walker in her kitchen like a dark haired young bear, Joe eyed her nervously. He dearly wished he could just blurt his question to this delicate woman they called "Marm" because she was sweet and good as the marmalade she made.

Just as Joe had worked up his nerve to ask her, his fair haired 16 year old brother Joel, large as himself, strode in from their cabin's front room and said casually, "Marm, me and Joe wanta join the Volunteers and fight the Creeks. We ask your blessing."

"Joe and *I*," she corrected, smothering the anquish in her eyes. She brushed the crumbs from her apron as she tried to think what to say. "Time for schooling. Put some wood on the fire in the front room and be seated, gentlemen."

"Marm --" Joel began respectfully.

With her hand thoughtfully to her lips, Marm joined them saying, "A wise man doesn't gamble his life without knowing why."

"This's for the honor of the Walkers," dark complected young Joe muttered, trying to sound older than his 15 years.

Susan reeled from the thought of these callow boys butchering -- or being butchered by screaming Indians. Knowing she'd lose them for certain by citing their youth, she reasoned,

"Wars are not about honor, Joe. They're about land. Land is power. Rulers force their people to fight for land to increase their power. Today we'll skip Latin and discuss our own history. Now's the time you need to learn why you live near Knoxville, Tennessee instead of Wigton or Ulster."

Knowing Marm wouldn't hush till she'd said her say, both boys hunkered by the hearth. Joe asked, "Where's Wigton?"

"Scotland where your great grandparents, John and Katherine Walker had their first four children before they got *planted* in northern Ireland by the English."

"*Planted*? That mean buried?" Joel asked.

As the daughter of the wealthiest English planter in Goochland, Virginia, Susan'd grown up with talk of planting one tobacco crop after another. Her stern Father Willis had certainly never sullied their table with talk of the Scotch-Irish. He'd become apoplectic at her mention of marrying Joseph Walker -- whom he called a lout. She dried her clammy hands on her apron, careful not to soil her periwinkle linen dress.

Susan Willis Walker said, "Kings speak of *planting* ordinary men as we would of planting a crop."

Joe asked, "Why were the Walkers planted in Ireland?"

"That's a long story, Joe. It began when Henry the VIII, King of England, Ireland and Scotland got himself excommunicated from the Catholic Church by the Pope in 1533 for divorcing his first wife. Henry retaliated by outlawing the Catholic Church throughout his realm and sanctifying the Church of England. The Irish, who'd been Catholic for over a thousand years, revolted, bringing British armies to Ireland. Queen Elizabeth kept planting Englishmen in Ireland in the 1560s and 70s while her army reduced the nine counties of northern Ireland's Ulster Province to rubble."

"Hard to follow all that," young Joe complained, fingering his pinfeather whiskers.

"The English fight the long wars of this world. After Queen Elizabeth died in 1603, her successor King James I schemed to plant Scots in northern Ireland for a host of reasons -- mostly to smother the endless Catholic rebellion. King James shuffled your great grandparents and thousands of other Scots into Ulster, calling it *The Ulster Plantation*."

Joel launched a shower of sparks up the chimney with another log. "What's Ulster got ta do with us joining the Volunteers, Marm?"

"Shows how rulers exploit their people like pawns on a chessboard. The King seized all Ulster land and sold it to rich absentee Lords of the Soil in England, who rented it back to the Scots. When each Scottish tenant's lease ended, they put him on the rack."

"Tortured 'em?" Joe asked.

"Exactly. They knew new Irish tenants would pay double or triple the Scot's old rents. Wanting to banish the Scots, the Irish banded together to bid enormous new rents. Landlords wolfed down these fat bids, driving the Scots from land they'd farmed for decades. Rack-rents drove Scots to the American Colonies. Papist King James II defiling the Presbyterian Church, dislodged more Scots. Sheep rot, a seven year drought, famine and Queen Anne's Test Act requiring homage to the Church of England convinced thousands of Presbyterian Ulster Scots to pay the £9 it cost to sail to America. Those who couldn't raise passage money indentured themselves as slaves to come here."

"Did Walkers become slaves?" Joel asked in dismay.

"No, but by the time John and Kate Walker got to Pennsylvania in 1728, William Penn's Executive Secretary James Logan decided to *plant* Ulster Scots on the western frontier to protect his Quakers and Germans from the Indians."

"Marm, you gonna let us join the Volunteers and fight the Creeks in Alabama?" Joel asked pointedly. "You wouldn't have to teach us like this if Sam Houston hadn't closed his academy to join the Army. Sam's already a Ensign."

"You both need to know more before you decide to throw your lives away."

The boys exchanged suffering looks as their father Joseph stomped the snow off his boots outside their cabin, then burst in, dousing them with cold air. He hung up his bearskin coat, still cold-stiff, over its peg. "Schooling?" he asked, sitting down hard on the wooden bench to remove his soggy boots.

Wife Susan nodded. Young Joe rose and straddled his father's leg, grasping his boot.

"Latin today?" Joseph grunted pushing his son's backside

with his free boot to pop the other boot off.

She shook her head. "War." Susan paced as she got ready to beg for her boys' lives. Next thing her son Big John, only 12 and nearly tall as these boys, would be chafing to die with them.

"War?" Susan's great burly husband blurted.

"Our sons want to join the Volunteers to fight the Creeks, Joseph. I'm telling them how the Scotch-Irish have been exploited as pawns by one government after another in hopes these boys will get the gumption to watch this war instead of dying in it."

The elder Joseph took his old pipe from the mantle and packed it with tobacco. "I'll listen -- but speak my mind when I must."

"As I was saying, Secretary Logan bullied the Scotch-Irish onto the western frontier where they cleared trees and clawed their living from the ground till the French and Indian War in 1755. That English war with the French slopped over on people here -- just like this English war with the French has!"

His unlit pipe clenched in his teeth, Joseph asked, "What could they do when the French built Fort Duquesne on the Ohio and started paying Indians a bounty for colonist scalps?" Freed of his remaining boot, Joseph set a long splinter ablaze at the hearth to fire his pipe.

Her eyes begging for her husband's help, she rasped "War's are over land. When the land disputes settle, war goes away."

Susan's massive, bearded husband squinted at her. "Owning land gives a man freedom. Scots fought English rule from the days of William Wallace and Robert the Bruce for their freedom. Fighting the English and reading Chaucer became an honorable trade for Scottish lads. Scotland's motto was, *Nemo me impune lacessit* -- no one attacks me with impunity! English couriers carrying orders to the Scots were made to eat them. Wars falter when your enemy knows he can't win. With the French and English outpaying each other for scalps, what could the Scotch-Irish in America do but fight?"

"Refuse to fight like the Germans and the Quakers did," Susan replied.

"Germans ran like rabbits. So'd the Quakers. Scotch-Irish stood and fought." His splinter burnt to a curly black ember without reaching his pipe. Joseph ignited another splinter to burn yellow and blue and fired up his pipe. Its aromatic smoke laced his black beard.

"War's brutality feeds itself. One atrocity breeds a dozen more," Susan argued.

"What were the Scotch-Irish to do when the Indians ambushed a funeral party and even scalped a lady corpse for blood money?"

"Inhumanity's the very reason I warn these boys what will befall them. The French finally ended the war in 1763 by ceding Canada and all their forts to the English. But killing over land didn't stop. *Ottawa* Chief *Pontiac* goaded screaming heathens to drive Whites from Indian soil. Thousands on both sides died horribly before it stopped."

"It stopped because the Scotch-Irish made the Indians pay more for their killing than the land was worth to them," the elder Joseph concluded.

"And for all their trouble bigot Ben Franklin condemned the Scotch-Irish as *White Savages* who'd make any Indian seem a gentleman."

Elder Joseph Walker puffed his pipe and grated, "How that popinjay changed his tune when one of every three in the Continental Army turned out to be a *White Savage!*" He puffed his pipe as if he could see the past in its billows. "Susan, while you raised our family for ten long years in Virginia, those who came to Tennessee with me -- my brothers -- the Youngs, Donelsons, Crocketts, Houstons, McClellans -- even Andrew Jackson -- fought *Cherokees* with every breath to protect their clans. When Fort Loudoun fell, the *Cherokees* hacked Captain Demere's arms and legs off, scalped him alive and packed his mouth with dirt. The War Chief said 'You want land. We give it to you.' "

"Must these boys become barbarians? Haven't we taught them the worth of human life? Fifty thousand people have been slaughtered like cattle for this land we call America. The English now bribe the Indians to steal it back from us. Should our sons die over dirt?"

Joseph muttered, "You boys go hay the horses. Marm and I need to talk."

Joe and Joel donned their bearskin coats and headed for the barn. Their absence made the room feel hollow to Marm. She eyed her husband. "Joseph, did you ever watch young Joe move? He's just like our old herd dog Angus when he was a big, floppy puppy. Not a mean bone in his body. Joe just wants to go fight because Joel does. Surely, both boys needn't go."

"Since you brought up our old Collie, do you remember the day Angus died?"

"He came home with an arrow through his chest."

"Yes, but he herded all the cattle to our barn before he died. Joe has that same courage, and so does Joel. Can you doubt for a minute that those boys are going to fight after the Creek massacre of Fort Mims? Had I fewer mouths to feed, I'd volunteer myself!"

"Fort Mims is in southern Alabama. Why must our boys go down there?"

"Our whole country's at war. The Red Sticks are tools of the British like all the other tribes attacking settlers across this nation. Americans have yet to win a battle. We could lose this war. We don't have the French bolstering us as they did in the Revolution. You want to become a British subject, Susan?"

"Certainly not!"

"Neither do your sons, and I'll be long dead myself before the Union Jack flies over Tennessee."

"To Governor Blount:
Regardless of the whimpers of fireside patriots,... fawning sycophants or cowering poltroons, I shall not retreat -- though in finality, I man this post alone... Ignore the vile reptiles who would have England retake our blood-won soil! ... Popularity be damned. Save yr country, Sir.... If nothing else, send someone out here to bury me."

General Andrew Jackson

CHAPTER 3

FIRING SQUAD FOR A BOY   WINTER 1813-MARCH 1814

Andrew Jackson and John Coffee had beaten the Red Stick Creeks in every battle. But they were losing the war in Alabama to a supply system that would not feed their troops and mutinous militia men disappearing as their 90 day enlistments blew away like leaves in a tornado. Now Jackson sat his horse alone on the Fort Strother bridge across the Coosa River blocking the desertion of hundreds of infuriated infantrymen who'd become a mob. Bareheaded, his grizzled hair wafting in the wind, he tried to aim his rifle with one arm. Wrenching his crippled arm out of its sling to support his rifle, he screeched, "First man sets foot on this infernal bridge will take my bullet through his brain."

Hoofbeats hammered the bridge behind Jackson. He whirled to fire, but recognized loyal officers John Coffee and John Reid. Flanking their fierce General on clomping war horses with sabres drawn, they braced themselves to take the charge of once friendly men from Tennessee.

John Coffee recognized Jackson's furious look they called *shoot* back in Tennessee. That'd started when lout Russell

Bean on trial for slicin' his child's ears off in a drunken frolic, cursed the jury and Judge Andrew Jackson before stalkin' out of court. Andy'd ordered the sheriff to bring Bean back in irons, but him and his posse'd returned empty handed. Andy'd grabbed his own pistols and found Bean brandishin' two guns in the village square, braggin' he'd kill anybody who come fer him. Andy'd ordered Bean to surrender or get blown through. Bean'd looked into Andy's blazin' eyes and give up. When Bean was asked why he'd surrendered to a skinny Judge after standin' off a posse, Bean'd said, "I seen *shoot* in them eyes and knowed it was time to sing small --so I did."

Jackson croaked, "I'm privileged to die here with two men fine as you." But even as his body awaited the bullet shock it knew so well, he found his thoughts turning to John Coffee and what a force John'd been here in Alabama where they would die together.

Jackson remembered the evening he'd promoted John near the end of October. The sun had ovened his Command tent hot enough to roast an ox walking through it. He'd told John and Newt Cannon, "Our wrath must terrify the Creeks, or this war will wax eternal. When your enemy worships brutality, you'll not dissuade him with moderation." Then he'd wheezed, "John Coffee, I raise you to the rank of Brigadier General. Captain, you are now Colonel Newton Cannon." Jackson would never forget Coffee's quizzical look or the dazzling grin that followed his elevation to General.

Then on November 3rd, while Jackson'd built Fort Strother, General Coffee'd defeated the Red Stick Creeks brilliantly at nearby Tallusahatchee, killing every last warrior while he lost but five men.

With their own troops starving on November 8th, he and Coffee'd routed the 1,100 Red Sticks in their gaudy red body paint, saving the friendly Creeks besieged in Fort Talladega. They'd slain 299 of the enemy while losing 15 of their own. It was truly a signal honor to die with a soldier of John Coffee's calibre.

At that moment Coffee rose in his stirrups and slashed the air overhead noisily with his sabre.

But the mob's fury faltered at the bridge. Sullenly, they

eyed the three brave fools who blocked them from home. Seconds lingered into minutes. No man moved nor spoke.

Then marching feet whumped the bridge behind Jackson. Sergeant McNarney commanded, "Lep, Right, Lep! Companeeeee halt! Rifles at the ready!"

As the mob melted, Jackson shrilled, "Sergeant McNarney! Stand your men down. Resume sentry duties. Creek attack on this command is imminent."

"Yessir, General, Sir!"

The Creek attack on Fort Strother failed to materialize, but disasters did daily. In December 1813 General Cocke marched 1,500 men into Fort Strother amid joy and fanfare, but their enlistments were expired, and they had no winter clothing. Jackson begged the men to re-enlist, then moodily watched them march out like foxes slinking back to their holes.

Jackson's own men fled by night as their enlistments ended. Even the dispatch from his ally Governor Blount said he could not change the enlistment policy in Tennessee or the War Department. Its last line read, "*You are advised to abandon Ft. Strother and retreat to the Tennessee frontier.*"

On December 29, 1813, Jackson wrote Governor Blount: *"Is this campaign ended?...Was yr dispatch written on orders of the Sec'y of War or the whims of a peticoat populace?... Regardless of the whimpers of fireside patriots,... fawning sycophants or cowering poltroons, I shall not retreat -- though in finality, I man this post alone.... It is yr duty as governor to maintain 3,500 men in the field until the Creeks are exterminated or conqueored. The Creeks are wavering.... Arouse from yr lethargy. Ignore the vile reptiles who would have England retake our blood-won soil! ... Popularity be damned. Save yr country, Sir.... If nothing else, send someone out here to bury me."*

A cavalry Lieutenant reported to General Jackson the following week sans word from Governor Blount. He muttered, "Sir, the remainder of General Coffee's cavalry sent home for supplies defected after Coffee come down sick. Here's Coffee's letter and a dispatch from Georgia, Sir."

Jackson handed the young man his last slice of roast feral

pig and waved him from the tent.

The dispatch bemoaned the loss of 200 Georgia Militia troops to the Red Sticks on the Tallapoosa River. General John Floyd had ended Georgia's role in the Creek War by ignominious retreat.

Then came a tattered note from Mississippi's Territorial Command that General Ferdinand Claiborne's desertions and enlistment terminations had forced his withdrawal.

With the entire Creek campaign in his lap in mid-January 1814, General Jackson's Morning Report listed 130 men -- 22 unfit for duty. His regiment's enlistments were over. Tomorrow, he would sit alone sketching a petticoat coat of arms for the men who abandoned him.

Commotion swept Fort Strother. Certain the Creeks'd returned to annihilate his shirttail command, the emaciated Jackson strapped on his sabre and kissed Rachel's miniature goodbye.

Squealing fifes and drum rolls heralded 800 raw recruits straggling into Fort Strother on January 14, 1814. Jackson stiffened his frail body to attention and returned Tennessee Militia Colonel John Brown's salute. When Brown patted his shovel as his horse passed, General Jackson laughed uncontrollably, gleeful that Governor Blount actually read his letters and had dispatched a burial detail.

Marching in with the ragtag recruits beside his brother Joel, Joe Walker was amazed to see the famous General Andrew Jackson laughing like a regular feller.

The Officer of the Day welcomed the troops, then added, "You're arriving in the midst of a Creek Civil War where some swear allegiance to the British and some side with us. That muddles our task. You can't kill every Creek you see, because some are hostiles and some are friendlies. Learn the difference. Dismissed."

Cradling his rifle *Gunstocker John Walker*, made decades ago by its namesake, young Joe Walker railed, "We been at Fort Strother a week now, Joel. Must be something to do besides drill and clean our rifles. Mine's got too shiny to shoot."

The bugle call brought them loping to assembly. They

shook hands in ranks. "Joe, be careful. I don't wanta hafta tell Marm you're not coming home."

Eager to wring the most from his 800 men before they evaporated, Jackson marched them and a hundred friendly *Cherokees* out of Fort Strother hard and straight at Horseshoe Bend, the hostile Creek stronghold crouching in a loop of the Tallapoosa River.

On January 21, 1814 Jackson camped at Emuckfaw Creek half a day's march from Horseshoe Bend. He sent out his scouts. About midnight a scout reported, "Sticks bout three miles off, whoopin' like they's gonna tack us." As Jackson rolled his troops out and placed them in defensive positions, General Coffee rode in looking too sick to serve, but demanding troops to command in battle.

January 22nd's dawn was still dingy when the shadows around the Walker boys on the left wing turned to screaming Red Sticks. Both more excited than they'd ever been before, the Walkers loaded and fired, knocking Creeks down with their every ball for nearly an hour. While the Walkers were still choking on pungent powder smoke, the Creeks vanished. Joe pulled their long skinning knives out of the ground, startled at how his hand shook as he gave one of the heavy blades to Joel.

Joel muttered, "That was it."

"Was what?"

"You wanted something to do besides drill and clean your rifle. That was it."

After repulsing the Red Stick attack on Emuckfaw Creek, Jackson dispatched Coffee with 400 men with friendlies to track the Creeks into Horseshoe Bend and kill them. But one look at Hoseshoe Bend's tiers of logs like a beached man o' war told General Coffee his tiny force'd die in bloody tatters on its gunported wall. Seeing the Creeks were regrouping to attack, Coffee wheeled his troops, and thundered back as screeching Creeks ran at the right wing of Emuckfaw Creek's breastworks.

Dropping to rear guard his men, Coffee got cut off outside Jackson's perimeter. Sabre-hacking through flocks of Creeks, he took a bullet. Hugging his huge horse's neck, Coffee jumped the breastworks and tumbled to the wet grass unconscious. Jackson ordered, "Attend General Coffee."

In the center of his line, General Jackson saw Rachel's nephew Major Alexander Donelson's face blown off by a Red Stick's shotgun. Jackson fired at the killer, but missed him.
Joe Walker splattered the Red Stick shotgunner's head.

Moments later a torrent of Creeks hit Jackson's left flank with the all out assault he'd been expecting. He prayed his green recruits wouldn't quail.

"Joel, whatta you think God had in mind when he come up with war?" young Joe asked as he shot down a shrieking Creek.

"Punishment for our sins," Joel growled firing a ball into the skull of a naked Indian climbing the breastwork.

His reloading taking nearly a minute, Joe gasped, "He's makin' us look right into hell, so we'll behave better on earth."

"It's His way of getting us even for all the Walkers the Creeks have killed," Joel snarled, pointing his ramrod at two howling Red Sticks charging them. "You take the big-bellied one when you're loaded."

"You're bossing, Joel. Promised you wouldn't."

"Which one you want?"

"Both!" Joe shouted, firing his ball through the first Creek warrior's throat and into the face of the shorter one behind him.

Joel swung his sights onto another Creek brandishing a war club and flattened him with a smoky blast.

As they reloaded frantically, Joel grunted, "For somebody that don't want to hurt nobody, you're a natural born killer, Joe."

Whipping *Gunstocker John* to his shoulder to blow a Creek off the Emuckfaw breastworks, Joe fumed, "Foulest thing you ever said to me. Shut your mouth and shoot."

Joel blasted a lunging Creek with a moon-yellow face, then clubbed his rifle to drop another swinging a tomahawk at his head. "Sorry, Joe."

Their stubby Sergeant yelled, "Gotta fall back. Donchu Walkers know when you're licked?"

"We'll stick till the rest are out," Joe panted, amazed at how violently his own huge hands trembled.

Pleased the Creeks'd been repulsed on Emuckfaw's left, Jackson was angered by their tactic of firing and flopping behind logs to reload -- rolling the log closer and firing again. He called Colonel Billy Carroll, whose duel with Jesse Benton had sparked Jackson's Nashville gunfight. "Billy, if those Creeks won't stand up and fight like men, you'll have to stomp 'em like snakes!" Carroll's company stormed the logs, putting the Creeks to flight.

Proud of his men's stand at Emuckfaw, Jackson retreated toward Fort Strother to treat his wounded and get ammunition.

Chief Red Eagle, Christian-named William Weatherford, trailed Jackson, seeking an ambush to quiet his roiled Scotch-Irish blood after his disgrace at Emuckfaw. As Jackson's artillery pieces entered Enitachopco Creek, Red Eagle's warriors stormed from the shadows.

Fearing disaster if Creeks captured his cannon, Jackson had his rear guard engage them, ordering his left and right columns to wheel and recross Enitachopco Creek above and below to surround the Creek attackers.

But General Jackson's green troops fell back, leaving Billy Carroll and 25 stalwarts fighting to save the cannon amid fusillades of rifle balls. Cannoneers Constant Perkins and Cravan Jackson had no rammer or priming wire. Perkins rammed the grapeshot cartridge down the six pounder's muzzle with his musket butt. Jackson used his musket ramrod as a priming wire, tore a musket cartidge with his teeth to prime the vent and touched off the grapeshot blast with a lintstock match, flattening a horde of Creeks .

Lieutenant Armstrong sagged between the rifle swinging Walker brothers, rasping, "You must save the cannon!"

Screaming orders with rifle balls zipping past, General Jackson reformed his troops and hurled them against the ragged Creek lines.

Not willing to lose all his braves to this madman Jackson, Red Eagle arm-signaled retreat, leaving the battlefield to the dead. No doubt Jackson would attack Horseshoe Bend, but the entire Red Stick Nation would await him. To scalp such a fierce foe, would be one of the rare blessings of a war.

Jackson's troops buried 20 Americans and tended their

75 wounded, leaving 200 dead *Muscogees* sprawled along Enitachopco Creek.

On the march to Fort Strother, Jackson assessed his situation. Dear Rachel'd be devastated by her nephew's death. Coffee was wounded, but he was hard to kill. With little artistry, Jackson's reports would lure volunteers to share "the glory." In a war of dismal American defeats, Jackson's successful Creek campaign would acquit itself handsomely with the War Department -- perhaps annointing him with the U.S. Army Generalship all state Militia Generals hungered for. With more fine Tennessee boys like these, he could reduce the stronghold at Horseshoe Bend to rubble, saving one tree to hang Red Eagle -- who was anomalously both a red *and* a White Savage.

On February 6, 1814 the 39th U.S. Infantry Regiment marched smartly onto Fort Strother's nubby parade grounds, their banners billowing, drums booming and trumpets blaring.

General Jackson saluted Colonel John Williams who rode at its head. Veterans of two battles, the Walker lads were seasoned   enough not to wave at their brawny 6'5" kinsman Ensign Sam Houston, who dis-missed his company into the milling troops on the field.

Smartly uniformed in his blue woolen coatee, white linen trousers and tall black leather shako hat with its cords and tassels swinging, Sam Houston strode toward the Walkers, who suddenly felt shabby in their buckskins. Ensign Sam Houston obviously didn't know the protocol for an officer about to greet two enlisted cousins wearing dirty deerskins. Houston saluted, hoping they would understand.

Young Sam Houston

They saluted back, restarting the cycle of uncertainty. The situation resolved itself when they found themselves slapping each other's backs.

Eager to escape the field where his own soldiers might see him consorting with enlisted men, Sam Houston whispered, "Meet you by the Coosa bridge at dark."

A *Cherokee* officer walked between them, and Sam saluted and spoke to him in his native tongue. The *Cherokee* grinned and replied in English, "You couldn't have more than a thimble of Indian blood!" Then he finished with several stanzas in *Cherokee*.

Sure enough, at dusk the Walkers welcomed Sam's silhouette beside Fort Strother's bridge. They huddled in heavy coats to explore each other's lives for the past year in new moonlight that gilded their faces.

His words fogged by his breath, Joel said, "What'd you say to that Indian this afternoon, Sam?"

"Asked in *Cherokee* if he liked his duty here."

"What'd he say?"

"General Jackson pays him same's his Whites and listens to what *Cherokees* say."

Joe grinned, "You sounded more Indian than he did."

"Spent five years of my boyhood with the Western *Cherokees*. But I'd like to know if you completed *The Iliad* we started at my Maryville academy."

Finally Joe said, "After you told us we were ignorant till we read it, Marm drug us through Alexander Pope's book."

"*The Iliad* runs 24 books," Sam prompted.

"To be honest," Joe answered, "I got enough Homer with the one, Sam."

"Too bad. *The Iliad*'s Trojan War philosophy applies to all of us right here."

Joel scratched his head. "We've fought two battles. Poetry was the farthest thing from my mind."

"What was it like for you boys in the thick of the fight?"

"Like brawling in the gut bin after the hog slaughter," Joe blurted.

Trying to regain a measure of command, Sam said, "You boys are exceedingly young."

Joel countered, "How old're you, Sam?"

"Turning 21 in three weeks -- on March 2nd!"

Joe wondered, "How'd your mother take your coming

out here?"

Sam said, "Being in charge of our family since my father's death at Callighan's tavern -- my mother's become -- well -- resolute. When my father Colonel Houston died, she called him 'an improvident visionary.' When I asked permission to join the Army last March when the recruiters hit Maryville, mother said, 'My son, take this musket and never disgrace it. For remember, I had rather all my sons fill one honorable grave, than that one should run to save his own life. Go, Sam, remembering that while my cottage door is open to brave men, it is eternally shut against cowards.' She placed this ring on my finger with the word *Honor* engraved inside." Sam's voice choked with emotion. "Battle will be poetry and honor to me."

Near the end of February 1814 part of General Coffee's old cavalry brigade cantered in, followed by 2,200 dragoons in early March, swelling Jackson's Fort Strother rolls to nearly 5,000 men.

At last Jackson had the force he needed to capture Horseshoe Bend. Now he'd mold a fighting force. No more begging men to stay. Only with a professional army trained to act as one could Jackson hope to conquer the Creeks. The General's training regimen ran dawn till dark without rest.

Jackson discovered General John Cocke was sabotaging training, cutting sessions and coddling troops. Worse, General Isaac Roberts tried to force Jackson to release his men in three months. Jackson's runner summoned the weak-kneed Generals to his marquee. When they sauntered in, he screeched, "Hit a brace, Misters! I hereby arrest both of you. I order you to return as prisoners on your parole to Tennessee to present these written orders for your Courts Martial to Governor Blount's staff. Dismissed!"

The dazed Generals slumped before him. Jackson seized his metal-headed cane, shrilling, "Be gone from here now or depart this earth with your skulls cracked!" They left.

While Jackson arrested his Generals, 18 year old Private John Woods got the Officer of the Day's permission to leave his rainy sentry post to get a blanket. When the boy reached his tent, he found his comrades had left him some cold breakfast and began to wolf it down. The new Officer of the Day discovered his missing sentry in his tent and cursed him to a fare-thee-well.

A religious lad, Woods went wild, refusing to obey a direct order to resume his post, bringing another storm of profanity from the O.D.. Grabbing his rifle, Woods yelled, "I'll shoot the man who lays hands on me!"

Andrew Jackson was informed that Woods had mutinied. Jackson yelled, "Find that damned rascal and blow ten balls through him!"

By the time the guard detail stormed his tent, Woods had submitted to arrest. On March 12, 1814 Jackson had the boy Court Martialed, convicted in a trice and sentenced to die at dawn by firing squad two days hence.

Pleas from all quarters to commute the boy's sentence to dishonorable discharge or prison failed. Andrew Jackson ordered his entire command to witness the Woods execution.

At dawn March 14, 1814, the sky was swollen black with unspent rain. Young John Woods huddled against the stockade wall, tears streaking his cheeks and his hands trussed. The firing squad stood with their rifles to their shoulders in misting rain.

Standing in ranks, Joe Walker had never seen anything so wrong. This wasn't war with all these men ganged up on this boy. This was *murder*. Joe remembered the day he'd taken the token dollar off the drumhead sealing his enlistment. A wrinkled old man'd said, "Son, you got no idea what you're buyin' with that dollar."

"Ready -- Aim " echoed across Fort Strother. Joe Walker clamped his eyes shut. Marm had been right. When this Army hitch was over, he'd never kill another man. "Fire!"

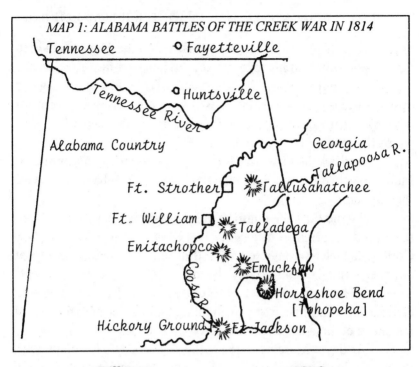

MAP 1: ALABAMA BATTLES OF THE CREEK WAR IN 1814

CHAPTER 4

HEROES OF HORSESHOE BEND   **SPRING 1814**

orning mists still shrouded Horseshoe Bend's colossal log ramparts at 10 o'clock on March 27, 1814. Andrew Jackson had never contemplated anything so formidable as Red Eagle's glowering fortress. He penned his observations of this Homeric bulwark in his journal: "*Horseshoe Bend -- or Tohepeka to the Creeks -- is a 100 acre wooded peninsula jutting into the Tallapoosa River. A 350 yard inward curved breastwork of large tree trunks laid horizontally atop one another to a height of 5 to 8 feet with a double row of artfully arranged portholes seals off this neck of land and gives its defenders a deadly crossfire upon any advancing army. It is a place well secured by nature and rendered more secure by art -- an engineering feat unequaled in my experience by white men -- let alone savages.*"

General Jackson's spies said Red Eagle had amassed over 1,000 wild warriors from the *Oakfusky, Newyouka, Hilla-bees,*

Fish Ponds and Eufaulas, exhorting them to a frenzy inside.

Jackson had 450 troops at Fort Strother and 450 securing Fort Williams to prevent severing of supply lines or getting surrounded. Today he led 2,200 soldiers and 300 *Cherokees.* Losing this battle was not an option with will-o-the-wisp enlistments where he mustered 130 men one day and 5,000 the next. If ever a field commander could see a war's victory in a single battle, it lay before him in the shifting mists, and by the eternal he would seize it!

Jackson's men dubbed him the "Iron General" after the mutineer's execution. With bone splinters -- which he sent home to Rachel -- piercing his left arm like porcupine quills and Benton's bullet against the bone, he could barely dress himself. Dickinson's ball abscessing his heart had him coughing blood. Dysentery cramped his entrails. He couldn't walk without his cane. "Iron General" indeed! To insure his men'd fight for him, he'd had "fight or die" orders read to them at dawn.

At 10:30 A.M. Jackson ordered his six pound and two pound cannon to breach the wall. Fifty feckless rounds fired from 80 yards barely knocked the bark off, so he had them lob twenty more at random into the compound without visible results. Sporadic musketry returned fire between cannon blasts.

Creek Medicine Men in bird plumage danced jerkily exhorting the sun to kill the invaders. Instead of having them shot, Jackson decided to put the fear o' God in them. He sent his interpreter to demand evacuation of women and children. When refugees fled the fortress, Jackson knew he had shattered their confidence with words, even if his shells had failed to batter down their wall. His aides wondered why he was smiling.

Preparing to attack the fortress from the rear, General Coffee ordered his *Cherokees* to build log breastworks along the Tallapoosa River bank. He pointed to the foggy Horseshoe Bend peninsula, motioning naked swimmers into the icy water to capture the Red Stick canoes, thwarting Red Stick escape from the rear of their fortress through the river.

Colonel Gideon Morgan and his men clambered into captured canoes led by *Cherokee* Dick Brown. Torch flaming in the bow of each canoe, they glided across the Tallapoosa, breaching the fortress's unprotected rear beach perimeter without firing a shot. Wending through the brush, they torched Creek wigwams.

Seeing black smoke over Morgan's diversionary force, Jackson ordered his cannoneers to roll their guns to the wall behind the infantry, then shrilled, "Storm the breastworks!"

The 39th Infantry charged, their battle cries smothered by murderous blasts from every gunport. Ramming their rifles through the gunports, they fired -- muzzle to muzzle -- with their enemy's balls welding to their bayonets. Bodies were blown back from both sides of the barrier.

Major Lemuel Montgomery climbed the wall shouting, "Follow..." but a skull-bursting bullet collapsed him onto Ensign Sam Houston scaling the breastworks. Sam lowered his dead comrade, then lunged among the Creeks. A long barbed arrow thunked into Houston's thigh. Young Sam yanked on the arrow till he nearly fainted from agony, but it hung fast.

Sam yelled to his Lieutenant, "Free me of this arrow!" Though the burly fellow pulled like a dray mule, the arrowhead clung in his flesh. Sam seized his sword, "Pull, damn you, or I'll run you through!" Thinking his Ensign mad, the Lieutenant ripped the arrow out. Sam's men hauled him over the wall to the surgeon's makeshift ward of strewn blankets.

General Jackson rode up as the surgeon stuffed rags into Sam's hemorrhaging gash, then bound it tightly. Never having seen the General at such close range, Sam was shocked at how fragile the prodigious warrior was -- like a fine China replica.

Jackson asked, "This officer fit for duty?"

"No!" the surgeon blurted, rushing to tend another.

Jackson peered down his thin nose. "What's your name?"

"Sam Houston, sir."

"Saw you breach that wall under fire. You got plenty o' sand. Press hard on your wound, you'll staunch it. Stay abed."

"Do we prevail?"

"Can't say yet, Ensign."

"Then I must respectfully disobey your order, Sir." Sam grabbed the General's stirrup, pulled himself to his feet and hobbled into the deafening battle.

Jackson marveled to himself, "Courage is all of it! Sam

Houston's one officer I'll never court martial for cowardice. Would to God I had an army of them!"

Staring at Horseshoe Bend's smoky barrier bristling rifles bothered Joe Walker far more than getting the order to attack it. Because of their enormous size and strength, the Walker boys vaulted the wall like flying shadows. Though Joe'd promised himself not to fight for the murderer of John Woods, his brother Joel and the Creeks left him no choice. Joel kept braining Red Sticks with his rifle butt. Joe, often back-to-back with his bearish brother, bashed Creeks senseless, astounded that such a brawl could endure all day.

Creeks in the brush unleashed swarms of arrows. When Joel caught one in his thigh, Joe bulled through the bushes after the archer, but he'd fled.

Returning, Joe shoved the arrow at an angle through Joel's massive thigh, then cut the head off and slipped the shaft back out. "Wanta see the surgeon?"

"Rip that corpse's shirt in strips, and bind my leg! I'll not let the surgeon cripple me when the Creeks can't," Joel growled.

Relentlessly, the Walkers among hundreds of other soldiers crowded the Creeks against cliffs snarled with fallen trees and brush, then awaited the order to burn them out.

Hand to hand battles surrounded Sam Houston. Staggering among them, Sam sabre-slashed one Creek after another.

Holed up under the part of their breastworks that roofed a ravine, Creeks directed murderous fire at their pursuers.

General Jackson yelled, "Lives of those who surrender will be spared," but begging no quarter, warriors replied with musketry. Jackson commanded, "Charge!" but no man headed into the holocaust.

Sam Houston seized a musket and limped toward them. Astonished that one cripple would charge, the Creeks allowed Sam within five yards of their barrier before blasting two rifle balls into him. Sam beckoned to his men with his musket as he fell. On hands and knees he crawled toward the enemy.

Jackson screamed, "See those heathens defile that young Houston? Burn them out! Take no prisoners!"

Rifle fire ripped the ravine. Where fierce braves had

stood scowling death down minutes before, painted corpses sprawled in swirling smoke.

Joe Walker seized Sam Houston, carrying him to an exhausted surgeon sitting numbly among his dead and dying in the growing darkness. Able to feel both rifle balls in Sam Houston's body, the surgeon clawed one out with his fingers. When he was sure Sam Houston could hear him, the surgeon mumbled, "No need to torture you with the scalpel. Your right arm and shoulder are shattered. You'll not live till morning."

Young Joe Walker grated, "Surgeon's flat wrong, Sam! You *were* poetry and honor on the battlefield, like you said you'd be. You will see sunrise tomorrow! You're too damn brave to die. I'll roost here with you."

With Joe Walker dozing beside him, Sam hung on through the night. Barely alive next morning, Sam Houston went with other litter cases to Fort Williams.

The Walkers couldn't see Sam off because of their unspeakable chore. The Iron General ordered his men to sever each Creek corpse's nose for an unimpeachable count of enemy dead. Joe'd heard of counting noses, but not like this.

By dusk March 28th, 557 noses were tallied, but at least 300 more uncounted Creeks had been shot in the Tallapoosa and washed down stream. Andrew Jackson was saddened to learn he had 49 dead soldiers, 23 dead friendlies and 154 wounded -- but still deemed Horseshoe Bend the crowning victory of his career. He ordered his dead weighted and sunk in the Tallapoosa, so the Creeks could not mutilate them. Somebody found dead Creek prophet *Monahee* shot in the mouth by grapeshot. Jackson noted that in his report, adding: *"...as if Heaven designed to chastise his impostures by an appropriate punishment. 300 captives were taken -- all but 4 women and children, but Red Eagle was neither found nor taken. I want his head as tribute for the massacre at Fort Mims."*

Perhaps Jackson would have to battle the Creeks again at their sacred Hickory Ground, but he'd rest his men beforehand.

While returning to Fort Williams, Jackson ordered Creek villages sacked and burnt, sending his once brazen enemies screaming in all directions. His scorched earth return from Horseshoe Bend forced starving Creeks to throw down their weapons. Joe Walker couldn't believe he was burning lodges of women and children, but orders were orders, and he was not going to stand in front of some wall to save the Red Sticks.

Warriors fled to Florida to join their British patrons, sure their vengeance would one day find this fiendish assassin of the Creek Nation.

On April 5th, after resting the troops for a few days, Jackson captured the sacred Hickory Ground of the Creeks at the fork of the Tallapoosa and Coosa Rivers, collapsing all Creek resistance.

On April 14, 1814, Andrew Jackson wrote his darling Rachel: *"I have burnt the Verse Town this day that has been the hot bed of the war and regained all scalps taken from Fort Mims...."*

Having brought every Creek tribe along his march to their knees, Jackson lofted the American Flag over the Hickory Ground on April 18, 1814. To dramatize their defeat, Jackson renamed their holy place Fort Jackson. Hostiles surrendered in swarms, accepting the Iron General's terms that they settle north of Fort Williams far from the British orbit in Florida.

On April 20th, Jackson refused to permit the last three Creek Chiefs peaceful surrender until they presented Red Eagle bound hand and foot. Fearing death, they fled Fort Jackson.

Next morning lithe, sad-eyed Red Eagle dressed as a farmer sauntered into Fort Jackson. Meeting Andrew Jackson, Red Eagle said quietly, "I am in your power. Do with me as you will. I am a soldier -- actually of the same blood as you when I am called William Weatherford."

Jackson growled, "Had you appeared trussed up, I'd have known how to treat you!"

"Treat me as a surrendering soldier. I fought bravely. Had I an army, I would yet fight. But I cannot animate the dead. Their bones are at Talladega, Tallusahatchee, Emuckfaw and Tohopeka. Had I been left to fight only the Georgia army, I could have raised my corn on one bank of the river while I fought them on the other. But you have destroyed my nation."

Jackson snarled, "Tell me why I should not provide you the same brutal death, you dealt our babies at Fort Mims!"

"Because you are a brave man, I rely upon your

generosity as victor over the vanquished. I will make my Chiefs obey you, granting you absolute power over my fallen nation."

Andrew Jackson's nod agreed his captive could prove useful. Grudgingly he admitted, "It took a cougar's courage to walk into this fort swarming with Americans whose only desire is to gut you. Since we're both Scotch-Irish, I remind you of our ancient Scottish prayer, *Lord, grant that I may always be right for Thou knowest I am hard to turn.* Though I'm amazed at myself, your eloquence has turned me. Return north with us tomorrow -- you'll be free to farm there. One sortie as a hostile will cost you your head."

"So be it," William Weatherford agreed.

Joe Walker watched in profound disbelief as Red Eagle strolled off down the dusty lane. How could Jackson kill a boy soldier over a petty dispute, then free the butcher of 500 men, women and babies?

Jackson marched his men with expiring enlistments home for discharge. Reaching Fayetteville, Tennessee in mid-May, Jackson addressed his soldiers in what was a well plowed field before they trampled it. "Your General salutes and compliments you! You deserve your country's undying gratitude, for within a few months you have annihilated a nation that for 20 years has scourged your peace and that of your people....The bravery you have displayed on the field of battle..."

Joseph Rutherford Walker eyed brother Joel's face aglow with the General's praise. But Joe knew two others should be in their ranks. One was bravest of the brave, Sam Houston, thrown away like a broken toy. The other was John Woods, murdered to make his fellows *well behaved* murderers. If Joel re-enlisted, that was his business. But Joe was going home. He'd fought the greatest battles of the Creek War, sharing a victory that gave him more questions than answers. He'd hug Marm, keep his mouth shut and try to live out his days without ever killing another man.

"Governor, muster all your food, water, gun powder, horses, wagons and criminals from New Orleans' prisons by Friday or you'll be serving this degenerate brandy as Admiral Cochrane's house boy."

Andrew Jackson

CHAPTER 5

FORTUNES OF WAR   **MAY 1814 - FEBRUARY 1815**

Joe and Joel Walker were elated to be free in Tennessee. Not having received their Army pay and having only a few coins between them, they traded Joel's rifle, their side knives and Army bullet pouches for a strapping 16 hand jack mule and rode him home bareback together.

Arriving at the run down Walker farm on their sore-backed jack, they gasped at its weed-grown fields and deserted corrals. Leaping off, Joe ran to the cabin, finding the front door bolted for the first time. He beat on the door yelling, "Marm! It's me! We're back from the war!"

Joel slid down from the mule and let it wander off. "Where you suppose they are, Joe?"

The sliding bolt jerked their heads toward the door. Aghast at the disheveled hair and sad eyes of the haggard woman peering through the cracked-open door, Joe whispered, "Marm, what's happened here?"

She creaked the door open and fell against Joe's chest sobbing, "Renegade Indians ran off our stock. They shot your father in the back. He's lain abed for months while the ground's gone fallow. You bring anything to eat?"

Joel rushed past Marm to see his father, while Joe answered, "Only half a jar of current jam and a couple cookies. I'll get 'em for you before I go hunting. I've still got *Gunstocker John* and he shoots plenty straight."

"Give the food to your father," Marm said fainting in Joe's arms.

Picking her up like a little girl, Joe carried Marm inside.

Joe could hear Joel and his father's faint voice from the bedroom, but he said dejectedly, "There's a lot to do here, Joel."

Old Hickory arrived in Nashville, Tennessee in mid-May 1814. Wherever he went, joyous mobs shouted their appreciation for crushing the Creek menace.

At his Banquet of State in Bell Tavern Jackson received a ceremonial sword while dear wife Rachel beamed. Jackson felt fate was returning the sword blackguard Tom Benton had broken after their fateful gunfight. How fickle Dame Fortune!

Jackson raised his glass. "Tennesseans who died fighting for you were true descendants of their sires of the Revolution and worthy of being called Americans." Approving roars seated the General and there, as throughout Tennessee, unstinted praise of Andrew Jackson flourished.

But next morning when Jackson met General Coffee in the Hermitage's lush garden, victory talk had vanished. Cadaverous in the brilliant sunlight, Jackson growled, "Madison's running this war in a petticoat. He's still cowed by the feeble congressional support his declaration of war got two years ago. It wouldn't pass at all today after all the whippings American forces have taken in all the campaigns but ours."

Having shaved away his great black beard and cut back his huge mop of raven hair, Coffee nodded nakedly, "Congress gives Madison neither the men nor the money to fight the war."

"They will after the British burn down Dowson's and Coyle's boardinghouses where they nest!"

"You mean you think the British'll attack Washington, D.C.?"

"Blockading us from New England to Georgia's but a prelude to landing Red Coats in Chesapeake Bay. Americans must strike decisively now or lose this war, John."

Young Sam Houston had misty memories of his miserable wagon trip from Fort Williams to his mother's home near Maryville, Tennessee. Seeing the horror on her face hurt him worse than his wounds. "I'd never have known this skeleton as you but for your kind eyes! What happened to my son?"

Sam rasped, "It's not me you see, Mother, but a shell with its former occupant evicted."

Elizabeth Paxton Houston was appalled by Sam's flaccid right arm, but she fell to her knees at sight of his running thigh wound. "Boy, your leg seethes with maggots! Hie yourself to a doctor!"

Carted to Knoxville, the leading surgeon declined to treat Sam, enunciating carefully, "Death will take you in three days."

Littered back to the surgeon's office a week later, Sam mumbled, "Unless you believe the dead can complain, you must admit my will to live has belittled your prognosis."

The surgeon retorted, "Can't imagine why a man wants treatment from somebody with such a poor grasp of his condition, but we'll start with laudanum."

"I must remain fully conscious to repel death from the threshold of my soul."

"Poetically put, but I'm about to kill your leg worms with corn liquor. However it may tease the tongue, it will be Dante's *Inferno* in the raw flesh of your thigh."

Sam laid his pistol on his chest and cocked it. "Doctor, if you plan severing my shattered arm in my torpor, prepare to die."

"Save your useless arm till gangrene comes for it."

Sam swallowed the laudanum, but still retched as the liquor hot-pokered his leg. Each time the doctor purged his thigh, Sam choked down the tincture of opium in its solution of alcohol, but the runny arrow-gouge refused to heal.

Sam squeezed his pistol handle each day till vestiges of strength returned to his shattered arm. But at night, he dreamt of other uses for the pistol -- such as blowing the roof off his skull.

During Sam's convalescence, newspapers alerted him to Andrew Jackson's June receipt of U.S. Army Major General's stars with command of the 7th Military District and how on August 9th, Jackson forced the Creeks to forfeit 23,000,000 acres in war reparations through the Treaty of Fort Jackson.

In a smoldering fury, Sam read that British troops sacked and burned the Capitol, the Presidential Palace and most of Washington, D.C. on August 24, 1814. Half delirious, he vowed to kill them all.

. Barely able to stay astride his horse in September 1814 as the British shelled Baltimore and Fort McHenry, Sam Houston rode to Washington. He arrived in October ready to fight as a cripple could be, but the British'd moved on.

Houston assessed Washington's rubble. It'd never been more than a roughhewn wilderness settlement with quagmire streets, a few taverns and seedy boardinghouses where Congress did the country's real business. But now Sam realized it was a mirror of himself -- defiled, broken and burnt out.

Books from the Library of Congress and furniture in the House and Senate wings, had been torched. Bits of scorched paper flitted in the stench of burnt books and charred wood. Most of the Presidential Palace remained, courtesy of a fierce thunderstorm that had doused the foe's incendiary efforts.

The Patent Office stood with broken windows and smoke tainted walls. The newspaper said Dr. William Thornton convinced the British officer that obliterating mankind's useful knowledge would brand him eternally infamous as the Turks who torched Alexandria's Library. Revolted by Washington's devastation, Houston penned: *"...In common with every true friend of my country, my blood boiled when I saw the ruin, and I experienced one of the keenest pangs of my life in the thought that my right arm should be disabled at such a moment, and while the foe was still prowling through the country."*

Reporting to Washington D.C.'s wretched Army detachment, Sam discovered he'd been promoted to 2nd Lieutenant May 20, 1814 because of General Jackson's report of his conspicuous gallantry, but Washington hadn't approved it yet.

Encouraged by a hundredfold, Houston accepted light Quartermaster duty. With his wounds hounding him to madness, Sam's canteen seldom held water. One day near 1814's end, Sam toppled off a wagon. His Sergeant squatted over him. "You've been lucky to ride so high and mighty this long -- you have -- Ensign. Drunk every day you are. I oughta put you on report."

"Please don't. They want any excuse to rid themselves of this broken soldier. Please don't give it to them."

Though David Crockett'd never read a newspaper, word

of Washington's burnin' had trickled through Tennessee's backwoods to his humble cabin.

He'd served under Gen'l Jackson early in the Alabama campaign agin the Red Sticks. His dander was up again, He told wife Mary, "I'm gonna teach them Red Coats howta act in another feller's country."

It wasn't Mary's pleas about being pregnant that kept David from riding east. Major William Russell called for all his ole Mounted Gunmen "to help Gen'l Jackson run them damfool Englishmen off our bare underbelly."

Young David Crockett

A shaky neighbor who'd been drafted offered David $100 to go as his substitute since they were both Scotch-Irish. Stocky 5'10", blue-eyed David Crockett gave him a smile that'd melt iron ingots and replied, "I's better raised than to hire myself out to git shot at. Save yer money an' we'll both go!"

Wind whipping her red-gold hair about her face, Mary Crockett stood tearfully in David's path on September 28, 1814. "Why can't them young single fellers go this time? They don't have a wife, a wee John Wesley and a little Billy countin' on 'em. You're 28 years old and you bin once a'ready. You leave me now, we'll never see each other agin."

"I'll not wait till them Red Coats comes aburnin' us out like they done back east. My rifle's itchin' fer that spot where them white belts crosses them Red Coats."

That afternoon, David Crockett became 3rd Sergeant for Captain John Cowan's 130 man company of Mounted Gunmen. Leaving Fayetteville as the town's breakfast woodsmoke tinged the dawn, they rode south to overtake General Jackson's Army on the march.

Since the British'd humbled the French, Jackson knew they'd soon redeploy their vast European army to conquer America. Getting wind of the impending British invasion of Mobile through his spies, Jackson made a frantic march down the Coosa and Alabama Rivers, reaching Mobile August 22nd after devouring 400 miles in 11 days.

Learning Jackson's army'd suddenly materialized in Mobile, British Admiral Cochrane withheld his invasion and called for warships to blast their way ashore.

Furious at Florida's Spanish Governor, *Don Matteo González Manrique,* Jackson dispatched a written demand to him: *"Refugee banditti from the creek nation ... drawing rations from your government and under drill of a British officer ... are crowding into Florida. They should be arrested, confined and tried for their crimes against the United States. ... The United States has retaliated and will do so again if further provoked. Be warned of my creed -- an Eye for an Eye, Toothe for Toothe and Scalp for Scalp...."*

Taking Jackson's letter as an invasionary declaration, Governor *González Manrique* aborted Spanish neutrality and welcomed British forces ashore at Pensacola.

On September 12, 1814 Admiral Sir William Percy sailed four British Men o' War into Mobile Bay. After landing Major Nicholls with his Marines and Indians on U.S. soil east of tiny Fort Bowyer, a scant 30 miles south of Mobile, Percy's 78 guns battered Fort Bowyer with broadsides.

Mindful of General Jackson's direct order to hold Fort Bowyer to his last man, stubby Major Bill Lawrence got his 20 heavy cannon so hot thundering at the British Men o' War he feared they'd explode with their next load. Lawrence also kept British Major Nicholls' invaders at bay on land with precise fire from two overheated long guns. Then Lawrence's cannon cut the anchor cable of Percy's flagship *Hermes,* drifting her aground under point blank bombardment from Fort Bowyer's gunners.

With blazes licking *Hermes'* powder magazines, Admiral Percy put his crew into longboats. *Hermes* exploded so deafeningly General Jackson jumped 30 miles away in Mobile. Having suffered 32 dead and 37 wounded at the hands of upstart Fort Bowyer, Percy's other riddled vessels slipped away in disgrace as black as the night that hid them.

After covering his four dead and stretchering his five wounded, Major Lawrence ordered, "Keep a sharp eye for that British shore party. After making flotsam of the king's warships by day, we'll not fall to his wharf rats by night!"

Abandoned by his fleet, Major Edward Nicholls led his Marines' miserable retreat to Pensacola through mosquito and snake-infested swamps.

Secretary of War James Monroe's communiqué found General Jackson at Mobile on October 10, 1814. Monroe confided that American Ministers negotiating at Ghent to end the war said a British invasionary expedition just left Ireland for New Orleans. Monroe's note ended: *"This invasion must be repelled. I have ordered the governors of Tennessee, Georgia and Kentucky to make 12,500 troops available to you immediately."*

Jackson spat, "Flapdoodle! My spies say the British'll invade from Florida. I'll not gallivant off to Louisiana just yet!" Adding Coffee's 2,000 Cavalry, hundreds more troops and Indians en route to Florida, Jackson's army swelled over 4,000. Jackson conferred with Coffee on how to legitimize this invasion, since Madison's minions never answered Jackson's June 27th letter requesting orders to invade Florida.

General Coffee mused, "Not often a lawyer asks an old Cavalryman for a horseback opinion on matters o' state. Write something you'd like read at your Court Martial."

So on October 26,1814, Jackson stuck his jaw out and wrote: *"As I act without the orders of the government, I deem it important to state ... my reasons for the measure I am about to adopt. First,...the safety of ...the union depends on it. The Hostility of the [Florida] Governor ... in permitting the place to [become] ... a British Territory. ... A[s] [he] ... declar[ed] to me that he had armed Indians and sent them into our Territory ... under command of a British officer. I feel a confidence that I shall stand Justified to my government for having undertaken the expedition. Should I not, I shall have the consolation of having done the only thing...which would give security to the*

*country by putting down a savage war, And what to me will be
an ample reward for the loss of my commission."*

On November 6, 1814 with his artillery trained on British warships in Pensacola harbor, Jackson sent written demands
under a white flag to Florida's Governor. But the British
foolishly fired on Jackson's flag of truce. Before Spanish
defenders could cock their muskets, 500 cavalry burst into
Pensacola from the west, while Jackson's main force of troops
and *Choctaws* stormed in from the east.

Herding Spanish soldiers like goats, Jackson prepared to
return fire from the anchored Men o' War. But British ships had
their guns trained in the wrong direction. The ten minute battle
was history before they could make sail and come about.

Appalled how swiftly Jackson had wolfed down his
town, Governor *González Manrique,* surrendered Pensacola
with its three forts. Forts St. Rose and St. Michael folded, but
Fort Barrancas, under British Command, remained defiant.

Enraged, Jackson unleashed Tennessee's Mounted Gunmen thundering on Fort Barrancas at first light. Sergeant David
Crockett's rifle was goin' to taste crossed white belts. But it
didn't. An earth bouncin' blast turned Fort Barrancas to grapeshot as the British detonated their own powder magazine.

Major Nicholls' Royal Marines with hundreds of Indian
allies, rowed gunwale deep boats through roiling smoke to their
waiting ships. Before sunset, every ship had fled, ending British
presence in Florida with their Spanish allies disillusioned and
New Orleans as their next likely port of call.

After dispatching General Coffee's 2,000 cavalry to
gather militias from Tennessee and Kentucky destined for Baton
Rouge, Jackson detailed men to guard Mobile. On the verge of
collapse, Jackson wrote Rachel to bring beds, tables, a carriage,
servants, Andrew Jr. and a nurse to New Orleans. Refusing help
to mount his horse, Jackson clambered onto it, riding for New
Orleans on November 22, 1814.

Left behind beating the bushes for Indians and renegades
around Pensacola, Sergeant David Crockett yearned to go to
New Orleans to show them Red Coats some Tennessee shootin'.

When Jackson hobbled into the outer office of Louisiana Governor W.C.C. Claiborne the morning of December 1, 1814, dismay settled over the delegation waiting for New Orleans' savior. Andrew Jackson looked like he'd climbed from his grave, gray straw hair splaying from his scuffed leather cap. His ragged uniform and muddy thigh-high boots disreputable, Jackson's scarecrow body wore the Spanish cape he'd received from Florida Governor *Manrique* like a death shroud. But once he rasped, "Announce me to the Governor!" his fierceness made them step back.

Governor Claiborne, wearing the good life's plumpness, waved Old Hickory into his private office where a deep chair waited with a small brandy reflecting itself in a gleaming French side table. Claiborne eyed Jackson gravely. "Before General James Wilkinson left here, he squandered what funds he hadn't stolen. Your war is unpopular with our French and Spanish residents, particularly since you mutilated Pensacola. They refuse to be marched. Most have declared themselves liege subjects of France. The banks will lend my government nothing."

"News is not all bad," Jackson grinned wryly. "As we rode in, your streets resounded with *Yankee Doodle, the Marseilles, the Chant du de Part* and other sprightly airs I didn't recognize."

Claiborne grated, "Is it true you've accepted those niggers under Colonel *Jean Baptiste Savary* into your force?"

"They are not *niggers.* They're able men honorably petitioning to serve a Louisiana lying prostrate -- and a faltering America humiliated by a multitude of defeats. I've welcomed every man who swears he can fire an 1808 Springfield musket."

"On behalf of the good white citizens of New Orleans, I deign to lodge a formal protest!"

Eyes slitted, Jackson asked, "These the same poltroons who've renounced allegiance to my nation? If so, tell them, we'll release a black man for every good white citizen who'll shoulder his musket. They'll no doubt take pleasure in fighting beside *Jean LaFitte* and his Baratarian pirates."

"You let those pirates you yourself called *hellish banditti* into your camp, they'll slit your throats before the British land."

Jackson locked his bony fingers behind his head of dirty hair. "I expect they'll give the British all the hell they can handle. Baratarians are the finest cannoneers in Louisiana, and there's no back bayou they haven't slipped through evading your posses."

"To what do you ascribe their new patriotism, General?"

"My pledge to dismiss pending piracy charges. Governor, I have 2,000 men of every stripe. Vice Admiral Cochrane's sailing 60 ships in here bearing 14,000 elite troops who humbled Napoleon at Waterloo. They lust for your women and booty, sir. Call up your militia. Enlist women to tend our wounded; Muster all your food, water, gunpowder, horses, wagons and criminals from New Orleans' prisons by Friday or you'll be serving this degenerate brandy as Admiral Cochrane's house boy."

On December 14, 1814, General Coffee sat his horse atop a hill at the head of his troops overlookin' a New Orleans helpless and divided under trees draped with Spanish moss. The day before, the British'd lowered 45 barges manned by 1,000 sailors into Lake Borgne to battle Andrew Jackson's five gunboats. It rankled Coffee how the British always made such a spectacle of an attack -- an unbroken front o' barges, red-shirted sailors bristlin' shiny muskets, dippin' their six oars to a side in perfect unison with a shiny black cannon in each bow.

Coffee watched, inwardly horrified, but outwardly impassive, as the British blasted all the American gunboats to the bottom of suddenly silent Lake Borgne. He prayed any American taken prisoner would swear Jackson had 20,000 men, instead of the 5,000 he led.

Swamp skirmishes with British regulars followed, but the grand battle began at daylight on Chalmette Plantation January 8, 1815. Jackson straddled his horse tensely in the fog behind his line. Dug in on the levee aiming over Rodriguez Canal, Jackson's cannon were double charged with canister, chain and horseshoes to fire point blank over the open ground. Huge cotton bales sheltered riflemen between his heavy guns. It wasn't the chill air that made his frail body shiver. The delay was unbearable.

New Orleans women waited behind Jackson's line to tend fallen Americans, but others knelt in their homes with *Hail Mary's* on their lips and hurricane shutters nailed over their windows.

Jackson espied pirate *Jean LaFitte* as the Congreve Rockets screeched red arcs over them in the fog. He hated what *LaFitte* was, but not the energetic Haitian born blacksmith himself, cunning as a robber baron and courageous as a bitch with pups. Jackson knew *LaFitte* was eager to fight, but was surprised to see him smiling while others looked so grim.

Jackson contemplated his opposing General, Sir Edward Michael Pakenham, 37 year old brother-in-law of famed Duke of Wellington. Barracks spies said Pakenham's neck wound at Santa Lucia had cocked his head to one side. A wound at Martinique had straightened it up. Jackson just wanted to blow it off.

Jackson had stationed 4,000 men here on his front line with 1,000 in reserve. He had the solid 7th Regiment along the Mississippi's east bank. *Plauché's* battalion, *Lacoste's* and *Daquin's* black soldiers anchored the middle flanked by the 44th Regiment and Billy Carroll's Tennesseans. Adair's Kentucky long rifles manned the left with General Coffee's cavalry out on the wing. *Choctaws* waited like serpents in the swamps.

Though separated from Jackson's main force, Jackson felt General David Morgan could hold the Mississippi's west bank with his 1,000 Louisiana and Kentucky militiamen.

Jackson heard British pipes and drums through the mist, then they fell silent. The biggest battle ever fought in North America was in the birth canal, and all he could hear was his own stomach growling. Why had the British halted?

Racing back through the dawn fog to retrieve their forgotten 16 ladders for scaling the levee and their bundles of sugar cane called facsines for filling Rodriguez Canal, the famed British 44th Regiment crashed into their own troops, tangling their advance to a confused halt.

Screaming Congreve rockets rainbowed through the mist overshooting Jackson's lines. Pipes and drums pummeled the fog again. Jackson's spies said the British still carried the short range .75 calibre smoothbore Brown Bess muskets they'd used in the Revolution. Well before the British 4th, 21st, 44th and 95th got close enough to hit anybody, Jackson ordered, "Long rifles commence firing!" His order echoed loud and faint along his line. Rifle balls butchered rank after rank of British Regulars. Rear ranks stumbled over their fallen wounded and dead.

As the Redcoats neared Rodriguez Canal, Jackson's cannons glutted the air with hot metal, blasting them backwards in bloody giblets. The Orleans Battalion band struck up *Yankee Doodle* over flying body parts, booming pistols and cracking rifles.

"Give it to 'em, boys. Let's finish this business, today," Jackson shrilled as he rode behind his battle line, mindless of the musket balls zipping by him.

Sharpshooters in dirty buckskins inflicted agonizing belly wounds right where the white belts crossed on the Red Coats.

Just when Jackson most admired these British iron men for marching into his maelstrom of metal, they broke and ran.

General Sir Edward Michael Pakenham spurred his horse into the melee where General Samuel Gibbs shrieked at retreating Regulars, "Reform! Reform!" Pakenham charged to lead his men, but a rifle ball shattered his sword arm and another collapsed his horse. Pakenham struggled up, yelling, "Reform and charge!" His Highlanders responded, advancing in ranks scythed as wheat stalks by withering fire. Gibbs and Pakenham fell, ripped by rifle fire. Leaderless, British soldiers panicked and fled.

Jackson stepped from his horse onto a cotton bale. "Battle's over, boys. Cease fire!"

Jackson tallied his casualties, reporting them to Monroe as 13 killed, 39 wounded and 19 missing in action. The battlefield held over 2,400 British killed and wounded.

The British had overrun General Morgan's American force on the Mississippi's west bank, but aborted their unopposed march to New Orleans, upon news of their slain Generals.

Andrew Jackson had General Sir Edward Michael Pakenham's body placed *bare and butt-up* in a hogshead of vintage rum and rolled him to the British for shipment home to England.

Admiral Cochrane sailed his fleet south, shelling Fort St. Phillip fecklessly from January 9th through the 12th. When heavy mortars from New Orleans reached American Major Overton, one salvo sent Cochrane scurrying for deep water.

On January 25, 1815 the British fleet with its ghoulish cargo of corpses and maimed sallied forth into the Gulf of Mexico. Thirsting for vengeance, Admiral Cochrane leveled Fort Bowyer near Mobile on February 11th, forcing American Major Bill Lawrence to surrender his 400 men.

Andrew Jackson strode into the plaza at New Orleans to shrieks of joy from people packed around him. Children crowned him with laurel wreaths. Fragrant flowers cascaded upon him. Wherever he walked bands invariably struck up *See the Conquering Hero Comes*. Booming artillery saluted him.

At the Ball of State, elegant Creole ladies eyed the General's 47 year old Rachel, plump and deeply tanned from running the Jackson plantation at the Hermitage. Lips hidden behind their fans, many muttered the French saying "She shows how far the skin can be stretched." But before the Ball ended Rachel won all but the haughtiest over with her honesty, sweetness and devotion to the greatest of the world's great Generals.

"Rule is -- root hog or die!"
David Crockett

 CHAPTER 6

With father Joseph Walker unable to do more than grouse about their shoddy management of the Tennessee farm, the Walker boys became prisoners of the plow, the seed and the scythe. Hunting trips to put meat on the table became furloughs from bondage.

Debts mounted. No matter how hard they labored, Joe and Joel could not capture a profit even with younger brother Big John's help. Samuel was too young to do more than tend the chickens and slop the hogs.

In their early twenties, sisters Lucy and Jane Walker, unable to work the fields like men, tried sewing for hire, but showed greater zeal for hunting husbands. Cherubic baby Susan fed barn cats and picked cucumbers for pickles.

Depressed by her husband's slide toward the grave and powerless to slow it, Marm shrank within herself and seldom schooled the Walker children. She left books for them to read. But Joel agonized over newspaper accounts of how the war dismembered the country. He longed to hear the Iron General's shrill commands -- instead of shucking corn and pitching hay.

The Walker family learned ever so painfully how poverty curdles life's milk and makes one forget there ever was such a thing as cream.

Joe seldom did more than scan Marm's books. He'd found the kindred spirit of his heritage in Scottish poet Robert Burns who'd died two years before Joe's birth. Joe committed many of the noble Scot's odes to memory, including the stanza of *Poet's Welcome* that reached into Joe's own life:

50

"God grant that thou mayest inherit
Thy mither's looks and gracefu' merit;
And thy poor worthless daddy's spirit,
Without his failens;
'Twill please me more to see thee heir it
Than a million mailens [farms].

Like a gold coin settling through layers of scum in a bog, Sam Houston sank deeper into obscurity each day. With leg and shoulder festering, Sam took indefinite leave before his Sergeant could report his drunken fall from grace and the supply wagon.

Drifting in a drunken haze among Lexington, Virginia's back alley saloons, Sam savored news of Andrew Jackson's triumphs over the British at New Orleans and the Washington bureaucracy with promotion to Commanding General of the Southern District of the Army.

Perhaps the Army was Houston's only hope, fading each day as more expendable heroes hit the streets. On March 1, 1815, the day before his 22nd birthday, Sam sobered up and wrote the Hon. James Monroe, Secretary of War, citing his promotions and seeking retention in the service.

With no reply, Sam sent letters to Tennessee Congressman John Rhea, General Jackson and startled friends who thought Sam Houston'd been killed in the Creek War. Perhaps the real Sam Houston had been. Eyeing his loaded pistol, he croaked, "Somebody's got to listen!"

David Crockett's outfit'd finally got orders to go home. David hoped he'd never hear another copperhead slitherin' in the dark or git woke up to kill somebody. They marched north from Florida's northern border swamps.

Not all Creeks knowed the war was done, but David was used to arrows streakin' from the shadows and musket balls kickin' dirt on him. His meanest enemy was a heap closer -- his belly. His outfit hadn't tasted bread in months. David eyed the other starvin' men, then grated, "Rule is -- root hog er die!"

David got Captain Cowans' permission for him and two other hunters to light out at daybreak and shoot game afore the army's noises run everthin' off. Crockett was so famished, he shinnied up a 30 foot dead pine with no limbs to knife a gray squirrel out of its treehole and gobble it raw but for head and tail. This left him bad ashamed cause he allas give his first kill to the sick.

Two days later Crockett and a hunter named Vanzant come to a grassy plain. Even in dawn's dim light, Crockett spied animal trails, whispering, "This's the Promised Land."

"What's that?" Vanzant grunted.

"Canaan, that God promised to Abraham."

"What's zat mean?"

"Means our outfit ain't gonna starve, you knothead. Foller me an' don't walk on nothin' but yer own big feet."

They slipped up on a gang o' turkeys in the low trees and headshot four before the rest got smart enough to fly off. By the time David's outfit caught up they'd also bagged a hawk, a copperhead and four toads. They come on a bee tree, smoked the bees stupid with a fire, then tomahawked the trunk open. They clawed honeycomb out and stuffed it in their faces, bees and all.

When the Mounted Gunmen caught up, they spent the day fillin' the air with cookin' smells and their guts with food. By nightfall David'd give away the rest of his meat and honey to the sick in other outfits.

Havin' made friends with his belly agin, David lay on his blanket and belched. To nobody in particular David muttered, "Hunger's like what the Irish say about hangin' -- ain't turble, but it's turble hard ta git used to."

A soldier retorted, "So's the Army!"

David replied, "Puts me in mind o' how I found out what the Army was all about from Gen'l Jackson hisself. My Cap'n dragged me to the Gen'l claimin' I's disrespectful. Gen'l tole the Cap'n, "Don't make orders to yer men without maturin' 'em, then carry 'em out no matter the cost.' I tuck that to mean *Be sure you're right, then go ahead.* Bin doin' that ever since."

Crockett's outfit couldn't outmarch starvation. Every time they reached an Indian settlement, David'd offer a farmer a dollar fer a hatfull o' corn. Most refused, but would trade a hatfull for ten bullets and another for ten charges o' powder.

At the Hickory Ground, they found no food. The men voted for a forced march through the 49 miles of wilderness to

Fort Williams. All went to bed hungry, but at noon next day they received enough pork and flour to get them to Fort Strother.

Two more bony horses died, got cooked and chewed as stringy meat on the way to Fort Talladega.

David drifted from his outfit to wander Talladega's grassy ruins where he'd fought agin 1,100 Red Sticks two year ago. He saw the black remains of the house 46 Creeks had run into. A squaw in the doorway'd drew back her arrow, bracing her bow with her feet. That arrow spitted Lieutenant Moore's skull beside Crockett, drivin' the men plumb crazy. The squaw'd got blown through by 20 balls. Then Crockett and the others'd shot the warriors down like dogs, before firin' their house. Three days later Gen'l Coffee'd brought 'em back foragin' for food. The stink made a few men vomit. Some charred bodies had been et by rovin' hounds. Under the house where they'd burnt the Creeks, David'd dug into the potato cellar. Fat rendered from the Indians dripped on the spuds. Men'd wolfed the greasy flame-baked potatoes. David'd et too, findin' these devil servin's less evil than the moldy beef hides he'd chewed for days.

Now it was all a ghost's gourd patch o' skulls layin' around black house ruins. He had the odd feelin' men of another time would do it all over agin right here and still be hungry jist like him. He ran and caught up with his outfit.

Hunger gnawed Crockett skinny before he got home. At sight of his cabin, David forgot his belly wonderin' if Mary was all right. Though she'd said he'd never see her agin, there she stood, holdin' a baby with a tousled boy at each side. Next thing David knowed, they was all in a pile, laughin', squealin' and squallin'. Wasn't long after their ruckus, David figured sumpthin' was bad wrong with his gray-faced wife.

"When did this little un come?" David asked as Mary scrubbed the supper dishes.

"Case you ain't figured it out, Margaret's a girl. I nick-named her Polly. She's strong, but I'm poorly."

"Mary, I reckon we love as hard in the backwoods as anybody in the whole o' creation. Love o' me and the boys'll pull you through whatever's ailin' you."

Mary Crockett rallied, and the color came back to her cheeks. Heartened, David harnessed the mule and soon turned the plow's rusted blade shiny in the dark Tennessee dirt. His soul told him, this was the Promised Land fer sure.

On May 21, 1815, David Crockett's friends and neighbors elected him Lieutenant in the 32nd Regiment of the Tennessee Militia to thank him for savin' 'em from the Creeks.

But the joy o' the warm days slipped away. Before the summer of 1815's shadows grew long, Mary Crockett died in her bed. David dug her grave, and lowered her into it inside a new-sawed coffin. He held baby Polly, the last treasure from the cold body in the ground. With John Wesley and little Billy huggin' his legs, David stood head bowed unable to speak.

At last David uttered, "Death entered my humble cottage and tore from my children an affectionate good mother -- and from me a tender lovin' wife. The ways of the Almighty falls heavy upon us, but these ways is right, and we gotta accept 'em an go about our lives."

John Wesley looked up through his tears, "Good thing you come home, Pap. Me an' li'l Billy couldn't dig Ma's grave."

David peered through his tears at the stern faced little feller, "John Wesley -- a man kin allas do what's gotta be done. I see a man in you, John Wesley -- a real man."

Together they shoved the dirt into Mary Crockett's unmarked grave, then walked into the dusk, hopin' their sobs'd be mistook fer night birds.

Having pondered newspaper accounts of the Army's discharge of Colonel Thomas Hart Benton and Sam's arch enemy Colonel John Williams, Sam Houston was astounded to receive orders approved by Andrew Jackson to report to the First Infantry in New Orleans.

When Sam stopped at the Hermitage outside Nashville to pay his respects, Andrew Jackson invited him into the study. After Sam's shabby hotel rooms, he was thunderstruck by the study's elegance.

"There's no guesswork with me, young man. The two big bills I admire most in a man's spiritual wallet are loyalty and bravery. All else is small change. You, sir, are rich in my currency."

"I must rid myself of these Creek bullets, General."

"Lieutenant Houston, I'm an expert at hoarding bullets. Got one by my heart and a spare in my shoulder. Some day I'll get mine removed. Write me when the surgeons have purged yours." Jackson saluted, "Dismissed."

Sam saluted back, about-faced and left the Hermitage.

Feeling like a frail Christ resurrected, Sam stopped at his Maryville home. Packing his Bible, Pope's *The Iliad,* some *Shakespeare, Akenside's poems, Robinson Crusoe, Pilgrim's Progress* and *The Vicar of Wakefield,* he headed south.

Arriving in sweltering, fever-ridden New Orleans in 1815's early summer, Sam witnessed the launching of the Mississippi's first steamboat before reporting to his barracks.

Sam was surprised at how quickly his shoulder surgery came on, till he reflected on it. His doctors could remove but few fragments from his shoulder and furloughed him to New York's better medical facilities. Before summer's end brusque New York surgeons extracted his musket ball and bone chips, ordering indefinite medical leave to recuperate at home. But the proud flesh of his thigh wound resisted all ministrations.

Sam wrote General Jackson that his "*strong right arm was ready for duty.*" Just before Christmas 1815, his astonishing orders arrived in Maryville. He was to join *General Jackson's Staff* at the Hermitage. Sam bought new uniforms and the finest white horse he could afford, arriving flat broke in splendor at the Hermitage.

The first Jackson staff member Sam met early in 1816 was stocky John H. Eaton, who radiated confidence and occasionally even disagreed mildly with Jackson. Though polite, Eaton barely acknowledged his existence, except to say Sam [at 6'5"] was "taller than the flagpole."

Soft spoken John Overton talked about land specula-

John H. Eaton

55

tion and legal matters. Jackson called Overton "Judge," because he'd taken Andy's old Tennessee Superior Court seat. John's brother Samuel was a staff member with a very direct look, but always deferred to John's views.

It didn't take Sam long to decide that Jackson's staff were mediocre military men, but powerful political protégés. Many lived in the Hermitage or its lavish outbuildings. All had been at Andrew Jackson's side for years. The enormity of the honor of his inclusion in this elite group silenced Sam, but he memorized virtually every single word they said.

Burly General John Coffee, was tall enough to see eye to eye with Sam, but Coffee seldom spoke except on cavalry issues.

Jackson's Nephew and private secretary Andrew Jackson Donelson made Sam's acceptance obvious to the others. Other staffers were South Carolina's James Gadsden and Robert Butler with random visits by Billy Carroll and Tennessee's Governor Joseph McMinn.

Sam couldn't believe he'd risen from being a penniless saloon cripple to earning $30 a month and allowances at the vortex of Tennessee's political power and perhaps the nation's.

Rooming at the Nashville Inn, Sam conversed nightly in the bar with ascendant politicians James K. Polk and James

Andrew Jackson Donelson

Buchanan. The moment Sam felt drunk, he went to bed muttering, "Only a fool drinks his way out of the Promised Land."

The task of Jackson's staff in early July 1816 was to thwart Article IX of the Treaty of Ghent. Gaunt as ever in the bright sunlight of the Hermitage terrace, Jackson grew livid as he read it aloud: *"The United States agrees to end hostilities with the Indians ...and forthwith restore to such tribes ... all possessions ... which ...they were entitled to in 1811 prior to such hostilities.* This infernal thing nullifies the war we fought with the Creeks, returning the 23,000,000 acres we got to pay for that war by my Treaty of Fort Jackson. I'll not stand for it!"

Judge Overton postulated, "Seems to me the Creek came to terms with the United States four months before the Treaty of Ghent, and were thus exempted from Article IX's operation."

Jackson turned to young Donelson. "Exactly the way I see it. Andrew you write Monroe and tell him that. The British can blather till the ocean dries up, and I'll not return one clod of dirt to those Creek devils who brained babies at Fort Mims."

Having lived with the *Cherokee* and been an advocate of Indian rights, Sam Houston had to choke down a glass of water to keep from yelling his way out of the Promised Land.

John Eaton tapped the table. "That may well be for the Creeks whose Chiefs signed the Treaty of Fort Jackson, but what about those who fled to Florida and fought us?"

Sam couldn't believe he heard his own voice saying, "Those in Florida were not within the jurisdiction of the United States and neither gained nor lost property under any treaties."

Jackson cooed, "Brilliant, Sam! Put that in my reply to Monroe's order to return the Creek land, Andrew. Mention in a side note the British are more interested in our profitable commerce than enfeoffing the Creeks with a place to hunt squirrels."

"Uncle, you realize as a General in the United States Army you are refusing to obey the direct order of the Secretary of War?"

"Andrew, you have a profound grasp of the obvious. Write what I've told you in your most innocuous prose and dispatch it. Just who will Monroe send to arrest me? All the men brave enough in this country are right here on this veranda."

Diaperin' a infant was no job fer a feller with hands like pitchforks. David Crockett invited his brother and wife Birdie to live in his cabin. Twelve days of that forced David to announce over Birdie's pitiful supper vittles, "You folks'll be happy ta know I'm gittin' hitched, so you kin go back ta the good life."

Birdie sighed her relief, "Who's the lucky lady?"

David grinned, "Ain't met 'er yet!"

David felt a neighbor six mile away was a Godsend, but

one within sound of his ax was a nuisance. Still there was that young widder Elizabeth Patton within a day's ride.

David spruced up at a spring near her tidy little farm, wettin' his hair down so it didn't stand like a rooster's comb. All he knowed fer sure was this Elizabeth had lost her husband in the Creek War and she had two little uns.

Almost like she'd got wind he was comin', portly 27 year old Elizabeth Patton was purtied up shellin' peas into a blue bucket on her front porch, when David rode up. "You the folks sellin' the Guernsey heifer?" he asked politely.

"No, I'm Elizabeth Patton born May 22, 1788 in Buncombe County, North Carolina with a son named George and girl Margaret Ann. I'd make a fine mother for your young uns, and I thought you'd never git here, Lieutenant David Crockett -- that I voted for after hearin' you tell us voters what a heller you was."

"Well, yer way smarter'n a Guernsey heifer and lookin' purty as a brindle pup. Guess I'll git down and set a spell."

"I'm hopin' you'll do way more'n that!"

Three months later in the midst of 1816's summer, everbody who was anybody in Franklin County Tennessee and quite a few nobodies was gathered in Elizabeth Patton's livin' room for her weddin' to David Crockett. David and the minister waited in the center o' the room. All eyes was fixed on the front door awaitin' the bride's grand entrance. Guttural grunts sounded outside the door, followed by a large nonchalant pig enterin' in the bride's place to titters o' laughter.

David bent over the pig, "Old Hook, from now on, I'll do the gruntin' around here." He grabbed the pig's ear and ushered it out, returnin' in time to wed the real bride.

"I have sanguine hope we will be fully successful with the chikesaws and once more regain by tribute what I ... fairly purchased with the sword."

Andrew Jackson

CHAPTER 7

LAND EATERS AND THE SEMINOLES   FALL 1816 - SPRING 1818

After the torment left the elder Joseph Walker's body in the fall of 1816, he was buried on their farm's highest hill overlooking the fields he cherished. His inflexible pride having gone into the grave with him, 19 year old Joel and his 18 year old brother Joe accepted financing for a crop from their sister Jane's husband, Abraham McClellan. The Walkers avoided the most vile shame of the Scotch-Irish -- bankruptcy. But Marm, more bitter than ever, railed against those she blamed for her husband's death.

The Walkers and their McClellan guests stared into their congealing supper plates while Marm ranted, "I told you boys that war was over land. Now that the Indians have yielded, Land Eaters gorge on their ground. They've stripped millions of acres from beneath the Creeks, leaving them homeless nomads. Now they rob the rest. Wasn't for the Land Eaters' colossal greed, your father would still sit in that chair. You boys wouldn't have gone to war over dirt, and he never would have been shot in the back behind his own plow."

Joe rose, took his dishes, and left the table, but Joel locked eyes with Marm. "We did not kill our father! You'd have had the British and their Indian henchmen at this table tonight if General Jackson hadn't saved our farms and our nation. What Old Hickory does now, he does for our good, and takes not a handful of land for himself."

Disbelief widening her eyes, Marm gasped, "You think those Indians will not fight again? You honestly believe they will allow their tribal lands to be traded willy-nilly among land speculators?"

Joel leaned forward, "You weren't there, Marm. Indians call the General *Sharp Knife*. They quake in his path. They will not fight him. They will take our government's money and live peaceably in the West."

From the shadows behind Marm, Joe retorted, "I was there! Not all will bow down, Joel. Hundreds have fled to Florida to join the runaway slaves they call the *Seminoles*. When the Indians find a leader, they will rise again!"

Joel growled, "And so will I. Unlike you, I never leave a job half done!"

Joe lunged into the kitchen table lamp light. "Well I won't. I'll stay home to care for Marm and this farm like I should have last time! I'll not come home to find our mother dying!"

Abraham McClellan stood up, steeling his blue eyes first on one, then the other of the young Walker men who were near a foot taller and 40 pounds heavier than himself. "It hasn't come to another war yet, Gentlemen, and most likely it won't. If war comes again, each man must decide for himself what's proper to do about it. Our task now is to labor long and prosper -- to set ourselves apart from those who'll never be more than slaves on their own land. Jane, we must go home before this rain turns these quagmire roads to rivers."

General Jackson's elation over James Monroe's Presidential landslide revealed his every tooth to the men of his staff gathered around a long table on the Hermitage terrace. "Our stellar good fortune to have a military man elected to that chair! His closest friends call him *Cocked Hat* in deference to his exemplary Revolutionary War service. Monroe feels about Florida as we do. After he negotiated the Louisiana Purchase, Monroe spent 18 months in Madrid striving vainly to get them to sell Florida to us."

Sam Houston asked, "How old a man is Monroe, General?"

"Nine years senior to myself -- I'm 49."

As Sam waved the flies off his raspberry tart, General Jackson added, "Houston, we need your help."

"You have it, sir. Task me."

"*Cherokees* ceded 1.3 million Tennessee acres by treaty in exchange for land west of the Mississippi and cash annuities. Now they balk. You resided among them. We're recommending you for Indian Subagent at a salary of $1,000 per annum and expenses, triple your current wage. We think you can persuade them to honor their treaty and save them from perdition."

Woefully sorry he'd agreed in advance, Sam Houston said weakly, "I'll apply for the Subagent position, General."

Jackson's September 18, 1816 letter to Rachel confided: "*I have sanquine hope we will be fully successful with the chikesaws and once more regain by tribute what I ... fairly purchased with the sword.*"

Choctaws and *Chickasaws* vowed to die before surrendering their lands. But one by one, each tribe quailed before Sharp Knife. By late October 1816, vast tribal realms were ceded to the U. States by treaty.

Sharp Knife wrote to President Monroe on October 23, 1816: "*...the sooner this country is bought in the market, the better. White settlers will flood into the territory and give us a population capable of defending [this] frontier....*"

Sam Houston convinced himself moving west was necessary to keep his lifelong *Cherokee* friends from being trampled by hordes of land-hungry Whites.

After receiving his October 21, 1817 appointment as Subagent, Houston took indefinite Army leave, donned his buckskins and became the "Raven" of his youth. In November 1817 he reached the lodge of his foster father Chief *Oo-loo-te-ka,* who also called himself John Jolly. Though deeply touched at seeing Sam, the Chief was anything but *Jolly.* The treaty exchanging land treasured by the tribe for centuries for smoke in the West was being spat upon by *Cherokee* tribal elders.

Calling a council, the Raven towered over them. Speaking their tongue and gazing into the eyes of one tribal elder after another, he said, "Sharp Knife swears the U. States will pay all it has promised and let me lead you west where you will be safe from Land Eaters. To make certain, I have become

Indian Subagent and will lead your High Council to Washington to have the Great Father lay his solemn hand upon this paper to put stone into its words."

Amid yells of "Cheat" and "Thief," Sam readied himself for a riot. But John Jolly stilled them with a raised hand. "Raven will lead us from the horrors of this place. We leave with him for Washington at daybreak."

But dawn found Sam convulsing in his blankets, his eyes too full of scalding sweat to open. Some said his ague arose from lies rather than Swamp Fever. Having given his word, John Jolly left for Washington with the *Cherokee* delegation.

When Sam's fever subsided, he rode to Nashville and convinced his friend Governor Joe McMinn, to pass out blankets so no *Cherokee* would freeze in the winter wind. Sam promised McMinn the U. States would stand good for the tribal blankets, then relapsed into fevered dreams of being shot to dog meat at Horseshoe Bend.

In late September 1817, with a decent start on his second family with Elizabeth, David had moved family, dogs, Old Hook the pig, and all the furniture two wagons could hold to Giles County, Tennessee. Surprised he was sorta famous there, David "bout had hisself a stroke" when folks elected him Justice of the Peace on November 25, 1817.

Havin' never opened a law book and barely able to scrawl his name, David had his Constable write warrants and writs. At the Constable's suggestion, David farmed lots o' the court's business to referees who was seldom lawyers. David kept cases on wolf scalp bounties and "things he knowed bettern' the next feller."

One night after all the lamps was blowed out in their cabin, Elizabeth whispered, "Don't ya feel uneasy sittin' up there, decidin' cases you don't know nothin' about?"

David grinned, "Them other judges been doin' zactly that fer years and plumb broke the trail fer me. Difference between me an' them is, nobody appeals from my judgments cause I decide by what's right stead o' what's legal."

John Jolly saw new Secretary of War John C. Calhoun as

a serpent saying snake's words through a man's mouth. His most vile word was "Wait," which sank its fangs in every request.

In his most expansive moments after several three-finger bourbons, John C. Calhoun was barely civil to white colleagues. But since the *Seminole* War had erupted in Florida, he distrusted these lazy blanket draggers so, he often met their delegation grasping a pistol in his coat pocket. Who could tell a *Cherokee* from a *Seminole* -- or for that matter -- who wanted to? Since the Indian Bureau was under his War Department's jurisdiction, he could not foist them off on other agencies, so he stalled them.

In January 1818, John Jolly left his delegation in Brown's Indian Queen Hotel and led the 341 men, women and children of his *Cherokee* band west to Arkansas Territory. Because of Sam Houston's haranguing, Jolly's people made the trip warmly clothed, supplied with blankets, kettles, traps and other gear. Each of Jolly's 109 warriors carried a new government issue musket, angering Whites inflamed by Florida war news.

In Washington in native regalia, Sam was accosted by the Indian Queen Hotel's imperious desk clerk, "When's the government gonna pay our bill?"

Sam confided, "I disembowel people who annoy me. If you're not careful, I'll mount your head over the front entrance with our unpaid bill between your teeth."

Two days later, in buckskin warshirt, breechclout and leather leggings, Sam lead his *Cherokees* into the office of Secretary of War John C. Calhoun. Discovering that Houston was the Subagent he'd expected to meet as an officer and a gentleman, Calhoun's eyes bugged, his face twitched, and he nearly fired his concealed pistol. "Get out!" he shouted.

As startled *Cherokees* fled, the emaciated Calhoun leaped to his whiplike six feet, bellowing at Sam, "Not you!! In all my years in public office, no subordinate has ever come before me at an official meeting as a savage in stinking raiments! And you, Mr. Samuel Houston, shall never do it again. Now hie yourself back to the dung heap you so cruelly abandoned to come here!"

Sam scurried back to the Indian Queen and his wide-eyed *Cherokee* delegation. "I'm not quite sure what the Secretary meant. Please remain in Washington -- but use the Hotel's back door. The clerk's rabid over our bill."

Sam scrubbed his skeletal body till it glowed, then brought himself to that state of sartorial elegance his entire three months pay would buy and waited. He received the summons to Calhoun's office in early February 1818. Sam thought by now, Calhoun had learned that Sam'd served on General Jackson's personal staff and would begin with a half hearted apology.

Sam had barely shut the door when Calhoun shouted, "Get in here and sit right there! I'm serving you this statement of charges. You will answer each charge right now!"

Sam read page after page of calumny in profound disbelief.

Calhoun snarled, "Did you, as charged, sell whiskey to the *Cherokees*?"

Sam tried to answer, but found himself mentally cursing Calhoun as the political assassin he'd been warned of.

"Well did you sell them whiskey? And did you prevent a *Cherokee* force from marching to the relief of U.S. Army units?"

"I did *not,* sir! I am a recognized war hero of Horse-shoe Bend, while I doubt that a paper shuffling tyrant such as yourself has ever risked mortal combat. Were it not for that pistol you keep waving in my face, I would feed you these charges, page by page."

Calhoun snarled, "Your response to each charge is due in 20 days! Get out of my sight!"

Sam reeled into the street. Man was safer in a war than being ambushed by words in Washington. No wonder the British had sacked and burned this place!

At his hotel, Houston composed his nine page reply to the charge that he kept *Cherokees* from aiding U.S. troops under *Seminole* engagement. Suddenly he realized he'd threatened a cabinet officer, subjecting himself to a firing squad. But he wouldn't run. He'd attack.

Next day, Sam got body-searched by a hoary Colonel with bad breath, before being admitted to the office of James Monroe, President of the United States. Houston laid the written charges against him on the President's glistening desk, then placed his reply on top of them. "I am Indian Subagent Samuel Houston, a Lieutenant on leave from General Andrew Jackson's staff. Are you familiar with the calumnious charges lodged against me, Mr. President?"

While Monroe perused his papers, Sam sized him up -- a slender fellow with a receding M-shaped hairline, light blue eyes and a cleft chin. His neck ruffle threatened strangulation, but the President didn't seem to mind it.

Monroe's voice was calm, but forceful. "I am familiar that you are an insubordinate who appeared before your superior in savage regalia. You are on the thinnest of thin ice here, Houston. Trod lightly, lest you drown in dark waters. Since some of these charges carry a death sentence, I shall investigate them myself. Don't bother chasing down General Jackson. He's marching through Georgia. That will be all."

"Mr. President, I shall heed your advice Biblically. But my concern's more with the whereabouts of Senator John Williams, once my commanding officer in the 39th Regiment, who has devoted much of his life to initiating specious charges against me. Perhaps Senator Williams, who was a mouse at the Battle of Horseshoe Bend, where I was thrice wounded and given a field promotion to Lieutenant, still strives to embarrass me -- or General Jackson whom he regards even more uncivilly than myself."

"Consider yourself under house arrest." Monroe pointed to the door. Sam left.

On the final day of February 1818, Houston received a note from Secretary of War John C. Calhoun. His heart pumping loud like cannon fire, he ripped it open. *"After thorough investigation, Subagent Samuel Houston has been exonerated of all wrong doing as to the charges presented against him."*

Feeling vulgarly diminished by blowhard bureaucrats, Sam Houston picked up his pen on March 1, 1818, the day before his 25th birthday, and scratched his reply -- to neither Calhoun nor Monroe -- but to General David Parker at the War Department, it read: *"Sir, you will please accept this as my resignation to take effect from this date."*

Having thus resigned from both the Indian Bureau and the U.S. Army five years to the day after picking up the Army's dollar from the drumhead, Sam found his loyal *Cherokee* friend *Tah-lhon-tusky,* and together they began their sad retreat from

Washington.

Two weeks later, they reined up at the Hiwasse River. *Tah-lhon-tusky* said in *Cherokee*, "Raven, why don't you come live with us. These white people are too damn mean!"

"Nothing would give my heart more joy, but my debts crush me, I have no job, no prospects of work, and I eat more each day than I own."

"Those are white man diseases. Come with me into the forest and be free of them."

Sam eyed his companion wistfully. "The worst disease of *Cherokee* or white man is honor. We both suffer from it. Be careful, Old Friend." Sam spurred his horse toward Nashville.

"The minds which electrify the world, generate their own fire. ..."

Sam Houston

 **CHAPTER 8**

THE FLORIDA WARS   **SPRING 1818-MARCH 1819**

Joel Walker locked eyes with his brother near the Walker farm's woodpile. "Joe, the farm'll support our family now, and Marm's herself again. We went into battle in Alabama together in '14. Why won't you back Old Hickory now?"

"Farm can't run itself. Big John's 17 -- Samson's size with a boy's brains. I'm 20 now Joel. Gotta do something with my life. We're owed our wages from the Creek war."

"This isn't about wages, Joe! It's about fugitives and Indians killing people!"

"You're going back to a war over the *Seminoles* ambushing a boat?"

"It's not just one attack, Joe! Butchers slip over our border nightly, scalp settlers, burn barns, steal stock then beat it back to Florida. It's up to men like us to stop 'em!"

"How? General Gaines went down there and blew up their Negro Fort on the Gulf, and that didn't even slow 'em down. The *Seminoles* will raid into Alabama and Georgia for decades. You gonna fight 'em for the rest o' your life?"

"The Iron General will stop 'em! He crushed the Creeks in Alabama and blasted the British to bits in New Orleans. He'll smash these *Seminoles!*"

"Joel, when we were boys, we saw as two eyes in the same head. Now we see for ourselves."

"Joe, you were a boy among men but you fought like a man among boys."

"Man's not measured only by how he kills. Jackson

destroys his enemies by murder. I destroy mine by making friends."

"You sound like Marm. You know her way won't ever stop these border raids!"

"Joel, even Jackson can't solve the *Seminole* problem without taking Florida. Newspaper said Britain's minister warns that the U. States invading Florida will bring Britain into a war as Spain's ally. British don't bluff about going to war!"

"They damn well might after losing two of 'em over here. You gonna soldier with me er not?"

"Fight the *Seminoles* if you have to, Joel. I'll take care o' the Walkers right here in Tennessee and teach Big John how to coax corn outa tired dirt."

Badly burdened by debts, Sam Houston paused in Maryville in the spring of 1818 to confer with his puzzled brother James. "You say you wanta sell your inheritance? Sam, that doesn't even exist till after our Mother passes on."

"Way I see it, James, I own one eighth of this family's assets. I'm a cripple without a farthing owing a fortune. If I starve before the reaper harvests her, I'll miss my share, won't I? Will you buy my share or not?"

"All right, Sam! Whatever I can lay hands on will fix the price."

Sam shook hands feebly before heading for Nashville. "Send me whatever you can, James. Don't let mother know I'm begging alms. She'll have me horsewhipped."

Houston rented the Nashville Inn's garret. Though his Army commission was gone, Sam knew he was commissioned by God for leadership. He wrote of himself: "*Those men who borrow their lights from others, never lead the human race through great crises -- they who depend on the strength they gather from books or men, are never equal to lofty achievements. The minds which electrify the world, generate their own fire; ... .*" Then he penned a terse demand for his back pay to imperious John C. Calhoun at the War Department.

The nominal sum arriving from his brother James went for surcease, but his creditors still chewed him like wolves downing a wounded stag.

He consulted his relative Judge James Trimble to throw them off his scent. But the balding Judge with his penny sized glasses answered, "You can't afford a lawyer, so why not become one and defend yourself? You could study here in my office. Major Lemuel Montgomery was killed at Horseshoe Bend. His books lay before you. Might pass the Bar in 18 months, if you forsake all semblance of a life."

Sam touched the scuffed leather bound law books with covers worn shiny, then blotted misting eyes on his sleeve. "Major Lemuel Montgomery's brains were blown out scaling the battlement above me. He actually fell dead on me -- I lowered him to the ground. It's ironic that he extends his hand from his watery grave in the Tallapoosa River to lift me upward now."

In June 1818 Sam began studying law, grasping precedent as quickly as he had *The Iliad.* Though his studies devoured his days and nights, he joined the dramatic club as lawyers Andrew Jackson and John Eaton had before him.

His creditors stopped growling when Sam tossed them tidbits from the $645.60 arriving from the War Department that summer. Sam fired more back pay demands at the government. He still owed people who'd helped when he was too weak to work. He'd pay them or die. But he needed comfort, so he rode a borrowed horse to Jackson's plantation near Nashville.

Rachel Jackson met Sam on the Hermitage terrace, her dress rustling loudly about her. Raising her hands to her cheeks the childless matron purred, "I declare Sam Houston -- I'd be so proud of a son like you! Sit and talk a spell!"

Truth be known, Sam much preferred warm Rachel to his stern Mother Elizabeth. An Indian boy about six brought Sam's lemonade. With a mischievous look, the boy sipped it, then set it before Sam. Saying nothing, the youngster with bright feathers in his black tresses ran off. Used to sharing with *Cherokees,* Sam savored his tart lemonade and waited for the Mistress of the Manor.

"See *Lyncoya* brought your lemonade, Sam. Where's my sweet little lad gotten to?"

"Must be close by. who is he?"

Rachel plopped her ponderous body into a chair across the table from him. "*Lyncoya's* the boy the General adopted as a baby on the battlefield during the Creek War. Boy's jealous cause of how I go on about you, Sam."

"Didn't meet *Lyncoya* when I was on the General's staff."

"Sam, much as I love my *Lyncoya*, wild blood makes him run away two -- three times a month -- usually after some Creek Chief has visited. Frightens me to a fare-thee-well." Rachel put her finger to her lips. The white haired Negro house-man puffed her pipe alive and brought it to her. She clamped it in her teeth and puffed away. "My solace," she muttered around the stem.

"How's the General?"

"That lovely man still writes to me more often than he has time to. Think he feels it keeps me with him. As always Andy has no trouble with the military side of his campaign -- just his horrid health and the political swamp he's floundering through -- going into Florida again with no declared war."

"Any specifics, dear Rachel?"

"I'll get his recent correspondence!" Rachel waddled into the house, returning with several letters.

The General wrote of a red pole in Fowltown's public square dangling 50 fresh scalps torn from the heads of American settlers. On April 8th Jackson hanged *Seminole* leaders Francis the Prophet and *Hoemallee Mecko*. He was angered by the attitudes of some of Washington D.C.'s champion hypocrites. Skipping the portions too private for his eyes, Sam eased the letters across the table to Rachel, "Thank you, dear Rachel."

"Sam you needn't pretend you're not as scared as I am. Andy's political opponents are honing their scalping knives. He's really done it this time, hasn't he?"

Houston took Rachel's hands, "Not enough in these cryptic missives to say. You restore his strength. Together, the Iron General and I will chastise and confound the pundits of the Potomac."

"Wonderfully put, Sam! You should be a lawyer!"

"God willing, I will be, dear Rachel. Must attend to my jealous law books. Write the General that I stand by him as I did at Horseshoe Bend." Sam strode from her terrace, certain the Genghis Khan of the age was about to be orated to death by Washington's word murderers.

Discharged by General Jackson with lavish praise in late summer 1818, Joel Walker reached home near Knoxville before the shimmering heat fled the shrinking days. Secretly wondering how Marm'd grayed all over, Joel asked, "Where's Joe?"

"Don't I get a hug, Joel?"

"Haven't washed off the trail dirt, Marm."

She opened her arms, "I'd love some, Joel."

Cautiously, Joel picked the delicate woman up and spun her around.

"General Jackson's taught you to pirouette," she laughed like tiny chimes in the wind.

Though Marm's linen dress felt cool in the heat, Joel put her down. "Not likely, Marm. Where's Joe?"

"Gone to Missouri to find us some fertile farm land. Abe McClellan --your sister Jane's husband -- has closed your father's estate. Abe's selling off land for our Scotch-Irish clans to finance moving all the families to Missouri."

"Don't know as I like that -- so sudden and all. What's Joe say about Missouri?"

"Nothing. Like you and your father before you -- huge men who can't lift a pen."

"This land go fallow?"

"Either that or Big John really can't farm."

"When's Joe coming back?"

"Likely when he has something to tell us, but if I were you, I'd sell what can't be wagoned to Missouri."

"Haven't sold all Papa's things have you?"

"No. By the way, how was Florida?"

"Tolerable."

"And how are you?"

"Bone tired."

"Going to tell me about the war down there?"

"No."

In 1818's early fall, Magistrate David Crockett was restin' on his front stoop amid buzzin' flies that wasn't goin' no place when Captain Matthews dropped by. "Davy, I am arunnin' fer Colonel of the Lawrence County Militia. Need yer support.

Figure if you's to run fer Major, we could pull us a strong vote. I'm ahavin' a frolic at my house Sattaday. Be obliged if you'd come speak on my behalf."

"Already bein' a Lieutenant, I don't much need bein' a Major, Mr. Matthews, but yer ideer's a good one. I'll be there."

As Matthews marched off down the road, Elizabeth Crockett burst onto the porch slappin' her thigh so hard she like to fell down.

"Jist what has thowed you into such a state o' joy, wife?"

She held up her plump hand, "Ole man Matthews thinks he's bamboozled Judge Crockett into supportin' him, whilst his wife done tole me their son Jeb will run fer Major agin you!"

David fumed, "Git ready fer Sattaday."

"You mean we're still goin' after what he's tryin' to pull?"

"Bet I do, darlin'. Mrs. Matthews is a fine cook!"

Come Saturday, all Crocketts, man, woman and child arrived at the Matthews' frolic and commenced eatin' like locusts.

Matthews asked David to speak. Crockett replied, "Give your talk, Captain. I'll go last."

"Last?"

"Last."

"Druther you go fust er second, Judge."

"Last."

Captain Matthews gave a speech extollin' his modest Militia service. The Captain concluded, "Next speaker's Judge David Crockett."

David rose, hooked his thumbs under his galluses and shouted, "Your son Jeb's a candidate. I'd like a sample o' what he's got to say, Captain. I consider honor a prime trait fer bein' in command o' the sons o' Lawrence County -- don't all you folks feel thataway?"

David's question brought "Yeas" and a host of nods, which prompted David to add, "The most honorable Captain asked me here today to run a joint campaign -- him fer Colonel and me fer Major. Trustin' Cap'n Matthews, I come here to campaign like he said. But under the blankets, I found he'd have me talk fer him -- then his son Jeb secretly runnin' fer Major -- was gonna talk agin me. You folks feel that's honorable, vote fer them. But fore that, I'm gonna speak as your Judge on behalf o' the best candidate fer Colonel -- me! Likely you think I'll ramble on bout my heroic exploits in the Creek War. Not so. And I did not foller General Jackson to Florida this summer, cause I figured the best way to git permoted from Lieutenant to Colonel was to stay the hell outa the war. So I done it. That's my talk."

His neighbors soon elected a smilin' David Crockett Colonel without a single Matthews on his staff. As he departed, David give ex-Captain Matthews a wave, quippin' "I think it was yer strategy that done it, *Mister* Matthews."

By the fall of 1818, Washington's bureaucracy bayed night and day over Andrew Jackson's unauthorized seizure of Florida. Having been in hiding at his private retreat for a month, President James Monroe had just returned to convene his cabinet at the White House.

In spite of the many letters Secretary of War Calhoun'd dispatched to Jackson during his 1818 campaign without demanding Jackson's withdrawal from Florida, Calhoun ended his diatribe, "I want this uncontrollable Jackson severely punished."

Treasury Secretary William Crawford, who now viewed Jackson as a serious contender for southern Presidential votes in 1824, added, "I concur."

Attorney General William Wirt nodded, "I agree with the Calhoun-Crawford position."

Pragmatic Secretary of State John Quincy Adams opposed. "Jackson's military action was necessary to protect our people from border raiders who could escape justice by jumping back across an artificial line into a lawless sanctuary. From the correspondence I've seen, I'm convinced Jackson was authorized by at least two men in this room to do exactly what he did. You both know who you are. In order to prevent renewed raids from Florida hideouts now, St. Marks and Pensacola must be retained. I've neutralized the British by negotiating the Anglo-American Convention of 1818, establishing the 49th parallel as the U.S. Canadian border from the Great Lakes to the western slope of the Rockies, disarming that border and agreeing to Joint Occupation of Oregon west of there till that boundary's settled. The British will not sacrifice the certainty and safety of their

Canadian border to save their tottering alliance with Spain."

"And what of Spain's ardent protests, Mr. Adams?" the President inquired dourly. "Jackson humbled them and left occupational forces on their soil when he returned to Tennessee."

"While you were -- vacationing in the country -- Mr. President, I responded vigorously on July 23, 1818 to the Spanish protest taking far stronger positions than I have here -- since I knew you did not want Florida handed back to these weaklings who can't keep their Indians and our runaway slaves from attacking us. If we stand pat with the hand we hold, the Spanish have little choice but to negotiate a sale of Florida."

Calhoun summarized, "Mr. President, you have two alternatives. Return Florida and censure Jackson or retain Florida and defend Jackson."

"I'll do neither. Mr. Adams, draft a note to the Spanish Minister accusing Jackson of exceeding his instructions, but insisting the General was compelled by military necessity to seize St. Marks and Pensacola to insure the safety of our people. Congress will attack Jackson. Stay out of the line of fire till we see who survives. This meeting is adjourned."

As 1818 drew to a close, Congressional hotheads wanted Jackson purged from the Army, but couldn't agree on exactly why. Some said he'd violated the Constitution. Others felt he was "a dangerous man." A few just wanted to black the Monroe administration's eyes. Many were furious at Monroe for conducting a war without Congressional approval. Behind boarding house doors, Congressmen decided to barrage Jackson with charges, but put off debate till after Christmas recess. Virulent political attacks on Jackson sprouted in the nation's newspapers.

To Judge Trimble's astonishment, Sam Houston finished his 18 month law course in six months and passed the Tennessee Bar. Desperate for money, Houston cast about for his best opportunity and settled in Lebanon, 30 miles from Nashville, where Isaac Halladay staked him to law books and an office rented for a pittance. Within the month, Sam became the Prosecutor for Nashville.

Locating a tailor with legal problems, Sam promptly

began to appear in Court as a tall military figure in a plum colored coat, tight breeches, fancy waistcoats, flamboyant ruffled collars and a bell-crowned beaver hat.

But Sam's sacred mission lay at the Hermitage. General Jackson wore his own death mask as he welcomed Houston into his study. "General, I rise or fall with you. Let's examine your correspondence with these Capitol jackals -- letter by letter."

Jackson chided, "Calhoun had a conniption when you appeared before him dressed as a savage. This get up would prompt him to launch another War Department investigation."

After perusing Jackson's correspondence with Monroe, Calhoun and others, Houston muttered, "Monroe's December 28, 1817 letter authorized you to do everything you did. His July 19, 1818 letter asking you to assume blame and seeking permission to alter your letters would make the Pope swear like a teamster. This Monroe you once lauded as a military man has thrown you naked to your accusers in a most cowardly civilian manner. You must repair to Washington at once, keeping these letters in reserve for your decisive counterattack."

Several days later, Sam received Tennessee Governor McMinn's appointment as Adjutant General of the Militia, a part time post with the rank of Colonel. Sam beamed, hoping his creditors would realize they could lie down and lick their lips.

After galloping wintry roads from Tennessee, General Jackson arrived in Washington January 23, 1819, a week after the House debate commenced on the broadside of censure resolutions introduced by Thomas W. Cobb of Georgia. Debate dragged into February -- longest in history on a single issue -- playing daily to packed galleries. Henry Clay crucified Andrew Jackson. Jackson supporters disseminated Clay's speech to newspapers in all 22 states to let Americans see his mad ravings. Jackson's House supporters rallied, portraying Clay as cynically deranged. They kept General Jackson closeted for fear he would "cut the ears off somebody." On February 8th the four final censure resolutions came to floor vote.

On #1, disapproving Jackson's hanging of Alexander Arbuthnot, ship master supplying the *Seminoles,* and shooting ex-British Marine Robert Ambrister as a spy, *Yes 54; No 90.*

On #2, prohibiting execution of U.S. captives without executive approval, *Yes 57; No 98.*

On #3, condemning seizure of Pensacola as unconstitutional, *Yes 65; No 91.*

On #4, for a law prohibiting invasion of foreign territory without authorization of Congress, *Yes 42, No 112.*

Thus Jackson triumphed on all four Resolutions, terrifying the Clerk that celebrating spectators bounding about the upper gallery would collapse it.

Every place Jackson went, he was mobbed by countrymen demonstrating their love and loyalty. Washington, New York City, Philadelphia and Baltimore exulted in Jackson's triumphs. Roaring mobs greeted his every appearance.

Furious at House failure to unhorse the "Napoleon of Tennessee," the Senate issued its scathing denunciation of Jackson's outrageous Florida excesses. Livid after reading their Report, General Jackson grated to John Quincy Adams, "I spent last year killing entirely the wrong people."

Adams grinned, "Politics is the art of the possible. Your supporters stalled the Senate Report's release long enough to prevent a vote, then tabled it to wither during adjournment. The Senate gives the appearance of having dealt with you. Now it's on to other wall-shadow fights for those windbags."

"You, sir are a master tactician."

"That's half my good tidings, General. The Adams-Onís Treaty ceding Florida to the United States for the assumption of up to $5 million in third party claims against Spain was signed February 22, 1819, burying your Congressional brawl with honors."

President Monroe invited General Jackson to a quiet conciliatory dinner in early March. "General, you are easily the most popular man in America."

Jackson raised his glass, but bit his tongue to refrain from repeating the popular press maxim that President Monroe, nick-named *Cocked Hat,* didn't have the brains to hold his hat up!

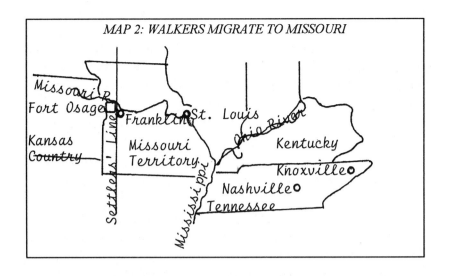

Missouri R.
Fort Osage
Kansas
Country
Settlers' Line
Franklin St. Louis
Missouri
Territory
Ohio River
Mississippi R.
Kentucky
Knoxville○
Nashville○
Tennessee

CHAPTER 9

MISSOURI'S OSAGE GROUND   SUMMER 1819 - SPRING 1820

By August 1819 Abraham McClellan had converted all the Walker Clan's land in Roane County Tennessee but his own to cash for their move to Missouri. A strong sandy haired man with the most direct blue-blazing gaze most people had ever felt, Abraham was twice as direct in his business dealings. His reputation for hard headedness cowed most men into accepting his deal.

But Joel Walker was not as easy as most men. Abraham and Joel often remembered they were kin by marriage just before they butted heads -- but not always. Joel growled, "Understand you're getting $2,000 for your place -- one house -- 170 acres. Near triple what you got for Marm's."

Abraham steeled his blue eyes. "Joel, you've been a hawk over my henhouse ever since you got home from the War. Unlike you and Joe, I'll never hunt for a living. I'm 10 years older, and a business man. I've done the best I could on all our properties with this country in a depression. You and Joe make meat. I'll handle our land deals. Where is Joe, anyway?"

"Standing behind you."

Abraham made himself wheel slowly, reaching out to shake Joe Walker's massive hand. A head taller and 40 pounds heavier, Joe bear-hugged Abraham's breath away, then put the dizzy businessman down, smiling through his black beard, "Man could buy all western Missouri and a spotted mule for $2,000. But I'd a site rather rent land from the heavens the way the *Osages* do."

Abraham groaned, "It'll take centuries to civilize you big Walker devils. Too bad Annis Carrick's husband died. He coulda done it in a whit."

Joe's smile faded, "Reverend Carrick's dead?"

Abraham nodded. "Apoplexy right in the middle o' running the devil outa Tennessee. Annis and the children are packed to leave. Are you?"

Joe grunted, "Mountain Man's packed when he slips a powder horn over his shoulder and shoves a spare pair o' socks in his possibles bag."

Joe, Joel and Big John Walker, now taller than his older brothers, trudged ahead of their three creaking Kentucky Turnpikers loaded gunnel deep behind four-horse teams. They left the old Walker home 50 miles west of Knoxville and rumbled over a rocky trace somebody'd called a road out of pity.

Marm Walker, her daughter Jane with husband Abraham McClellan and their two sons along with the widow Annis Carrick clung to their own wagon's side handrails stepping over stump butts and big rocks along the trail. Tiny William and Barbara Carrick watched over their wagon's tailgate as thickbodied slave Hardy and his boys herded the cattle and spare horses through the billowing dust behind them.

Abraham McClellan reread his inventory as he walked to be sure they had everything. Besides clothes and utensils, he'd made them bring tools to maintain the wagons, equipment for a blacksmithy and 12 baskets of straw-wrapped apple scions to plant an orchard when they got wherever they were going. It burned Abraham like drinking molten lead, that Joe Walker would not tell him where that was.

Like most Tennesseans heading west, the Walker Clan took the Ohio Valley route toward the Mississippi. Unlike the others, the Walker outfit never went hungry. One night as they ate venison around their fire, Abraham asked, "How do you Walkers always get our game?"

Joe shrugged, "We come from a long line of gunsmiths. Carry fine rifles cherished smooth by Walker hands. Mine's named *Gunstocker John Walker*. Any game animal strays into our sights straddles a spit. If it's a quiet hunt, Big John's lethal throwing his knife or tomahawk."

Abraham wiped meat juice from his mouth. "Why do you boys give your game kills to other travelers? Definitely not good business."

None of the Walkers spoke, but Joe's deep brown eyes glowing in the firelight said no man, woman or child would starve on the trail while he ate. Abraham McClellan suddenly realized Joe Walker's way might be wrong in the settlements, but it was right on the trail. When they reached St. Louis in mid-October, business would get back to business.

Pugnacious Thomas Hart Benton was happier writing articles for his *St. Louis Enquirer* newspaper than haggling in Court with some windbag. The article he was sculpting in his darkened shop would run September 25, 1819. It would herald his vision that each new state be formed with a central river for commerce in a pattern projecting beyond the Shining Mountains, known to the unimaginative as the Rockies.

Benton detested those *Little America* fools. Their party'd pressured Secretary of War John C. Calhoun into scribing a Settler's Line down the western frontier of the U. States and banning American settlement west of it. *Little Americans* wanted settlers prohibited from interfering with the American Factory system, those pathetic posts where the government traded with the Indians. The government also dumped uprooted eastern Indians west of the artificial Settler's Line cutting through Fort Osage near Missouri Territory's western border.

His article would alert Americans to their true destiny -- to flourish in a country reaching from sea to shining sea -- and *Little Americans* be damned!

Benton coughed hard. He daubed red flecks from his lips with his handkerchief. The consumptive curse that ate his father's lungs had attacked his chest before the War of 1812. He'd wanted to die in the war instead of rotting away, but Andrew Jackson had robbed him of a noble death as he had so many other honors.

After their 1813 gunfight, Jackson's minions forced Benton to forfeit command of the 39th Infantry that ascended to mythical stature at the Battle of Horseshoe Bend.

Jackson's New Orleans triumph had chased Benton and his mother from Tennessee to St. Louis. Though feverish with lung rot, Thomas Hart Benton would not relinquish another inch -- and neither would the settlers he championed in the West. He cast his bloody handkerchief aside.

Picking up his pen, he buttressed his budding article: *"The disposition which the children of Adam have always shown to follow the sun has never discovered itself more strongly than at present. Europe discharges her inhabitants upon America; America pours her population from east to west .... In a few years the Rocky Mountains will be passed, and these children of Adam will have completed the circumambulation of the globe, by marching to the west until they arrive at the Pacific Ocean, in sight of the eastern shore of that Asia in which their first parents were originally planted."*

In the fall of 1819 the exhausted Walker Clan arrived in Franklin -- Missouri Territory's thriving port on the Missouri River's writhing channel. As the largest U.S. settlement west of St. Louis, Franklin harbored 1,000 people, a spate of businesses, a brace of billiard parlors, a barbershop and bakery.

Abraham argued, "Franklin's a hub of commerce. We need to settle among its spokes."

Joe Walker pointed at Franklin's two story jail. "Too big for an honest town. I'll go west till I find a place where I can lean *Gunstocker John Walker* beside my front door and find him there when I come back."

Marm nodded her agreement with Joe. Big John rein-flicked her team and all three clanking wagons rolled west.

Twenty miles west of Franklin the road upped and died in a stand of hardwoods. They camped in their wagon tracks. Four plump turkeys discovered how well the Walkers could shoot. While the women dressed their kills around the flickering fire, Abraham asked the Walker men, "How far west you plan on going? We'll soon be beyond the Settler's Line where we can't legally settle."

Joe pointed to the dripping bee trees in the grove. "We oughta ask them. Bees keep about a hundred miles west o' the settlements, and nobody arrests 'em. I'll see if *the white man's fly* will tell me while I steal his honey for our biscuits."

After Joe eased soundlessly into the dusk, Abraham asked, "Doesn't Joe Walker ever get serious about anything?"

Marm blew away the tiny turkey feathers rising into her face on the fire's warmth. "Joe's the most serious Mountain Man you will ever meet, Abe. And the safest. How hungry are you?"

"If you ladies weren't here, we'd eat those turkeys raw," Abraham growled.

"If we weren't here, you'd be doing this," his handsome wife Jane quipped, tossing a handful of tail feathers at her husband.

By the time Joe Walker returned with a sweet-smelling bucket of honeycomb, the turkeys sizzled over the coals, two to a spit. That night the Walker Clan slept on full stomachs while Joe and Joel split night watch.

At dawn Joe Walker led the wagons onto the *Osage* Trace, a deep Indian and game trail along the Missouri's south bank. November's chill had etched the foliage with the river's frosty mists. Fiery oak and walnut leaves floated to earth about the wagons. Deer, elk and black bears, too unhunted to run, twitched their ears at the noisy wagons, then resumed their foraging.

The Walker wagons halted outside Fort Osage on a 70 foot bluff above the river landing. The fort consisted of four block houses connected with sharpened log palisades around a pentagonal parade ground. It seemed deserted.

Joe Walker said, "Fort Osage country is a place where we can raise the children. Ground's so fertile here, corn meal will sprout."

Big John asked, "Who's that?" nodding toward the man in an eastern suit grasping his head as he strode ever so deliberately toward them from Fort Osage.

"Major Sibley. He looks plenty mad at seeing us here with wagons beyond the Settler's Line. Sibley's a fine man. He helped General Clark build Fort Osage about ten years ago. He's still in charge. Major Sibley's plenty stern, but he's honest with a decent streak a yard wide."

Joe and Big John Walker strode toward Sibley like twin Gullivers meeting one of Jonathan Swift's Lilliputians. Sibley eyed them warily -- a dark bearded behemoth and an even larger fair-haired one. Joe said, "Good morning, sir. Looks like one of your headaches got here afore we did."

Sibley nodded, clutching his forehead. "No doubt you intend makin' it wuss. Whatevah ah you two doin' heah, Mistah Walkah?" he asked angrily in his Massachusetts accent.

"This is my brother Big John Walker. We came to hear your wife Mary play the piano. Only one I ever heard with a fife and drum attachment. Purely magical, Major."

Sibley let go of his head and stared. "Mistah Walkah, you know Fort Osage is beyond the Settlement Line for Whites. Ah you seriously thinkin' you fellas ah goin' to chaam me into lettin' you squat on Factory System Land?"

"Why no, Major. But I do know how lonesome Mary is. Big John, didn't our cousin Annis Carrick play the organ at her husband's church?"

"She did most worshipfully," Big John replied.

Major Sibley peered at Big John, "Plays the awgon?"

Joe added, "Annis could play a duet with Mary on your piano -- once she gets over seeing those splendid attachments."

"How fah would she have to come to play, Mistah Walkah?'

"I'd say that purely depends on you, Major."

"While we ah discussin' this treachery, if youah folks'd like a drink of watah they ah welcome. Just which one is cousin Annis?"

Joe pointed, "The lady clutching the handrail of that second wagon. Annis has just walked 800 miles, Major. We doubt she can play the piano today."

"I was thinkin' moah about tomorrah."

"So were we, Major."

After washing her clothes all night, Annis played shakily with Mary Easton Sibley, who'd given music recitals for European royalty. Afterward, Annis collapsed into a chair. Big

John congratulated her profusely, "Played angelically, Cousin Annis."

Though not overly impressed, Major Sibley proved his gentile upbringing by calling Joe aside. "Mistah Walkah, you cahnnot poochase gov'ment oah Indian land. Bah treaty, the gov'ment owns the six mile squaah around Foaht Osage -- called Six Mile Countrah. Youah family can -- rent as much of Six Mile as it needs to raise crops, build and the like -- in exchange foah youah soovices."

"Be just fine, Major."

"Don't you want to know about the soovices?"

"My guess is you'll describe them down to a gnat's eyebrow while my family's getting settled."

Sibley examined the ink on his fingers, wet them with his tongue and tried to rub them clean. "That is precisely coahrect, Mistah Walkah."

On November 1, 1819 with civilization squeezin' his soul, David Crockett resigned as Magistrate and retreated into Tennessee's backwoods. When their new cabin was up, David confided to Elizabeth, "I know you're gonna find this turble confusin' what with us runnin' away from civilization to git a little peace o' mind, but I'm fixin' to run fer the Tennessee Legislature."

"David, I would find it confusin' if you did somethin' that I did not find confusin'. Now while you're thinkin' on that, I'm gonna write yer first campaign talk and bring it to you on the stoop with some apple cobbler."

The Walker Clan built in a heavily timbered creek valley west of Fort Osage as snowflakes slipperied their hardwood logs. Because winter'd caught them in the open, they skipped clearing underbrush. Two cabins in the style favored by their southern Appalachian heritage rose 20 feet apart with a passageway between them. Construction ended with roofing of the passageway that would double as a kitchen for both dwellings.

A bit over a month after Christmas, the Sibleys came by in their buggy, but it wasn't entirely a social visit. While Mary watched the women prepare their apple shoots for spring planting, George spoke to Joe in the crisp cold outside.

"Youah help is needed with the *Osages*."

"Yes, sir, Major. What can I do?"

"Well, it's complicated."

Joe motioned for the Major to tell him more.

"Last yeah I tried to civilize the *Osages* so they'd be bettah able to soovive in ah society. I provided plows, rakes and othah implahments. Instead o' fahmin', they broke them into iron awnaments foah theah lodges. Instead o' becomin' useful wookahs, they kept makin' theah livin' by raidin' neahby tribes. They even used my tools to kill theah enemies. Thinkin' they might do bettah if I showed 'em the bounty of good fahmin', I had fahmahs raise a fine wheat crop and presented the field to them. Instead o' hahvistin' the wheat, they tunned theah ponies loose to feed, and they trampled it into the ground."

Joe choked back a smile. "Major, the *Osages* are God's own carnivores. How can I change that?"

"You will soon meet Mistah Bill Williams, who is moah *Osage* than White. He's writin' a book with 2,000 *Osage* woods in it. Want you to help him teach the *Osages* to fahm."

"I'll do my best Major, but I can't stand farming myself. Come spring thaw, I'll be trapping in New Mexico's mountains."

"What about youah brothahs?"

"Joel and Big John will be obliged to help you till they ride for Texas!"

George Sibley scooped up a handful of lush loam and showed it to Joe Walker. "Must be sumpthin' frightfully wild in this *Osage* ground."

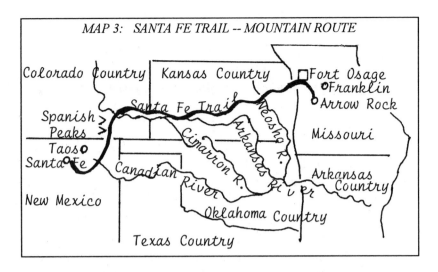

MAP 3: SANTA FE TRAIL -- MOUNTAIN ROUTE

Colorado Country | Kansas Country | □ Fort Osage
○ Franklin
○ Arrow Rock
Spanish Peaks
Santa Fe Trail
Taos ○
Santa Fe
New Mexico
Cimarron River
Neosho R.
Arkansas R.
Canadian River
Arkansas River
Missouri
Arkansas Country
Oklahoma Country
Texas Country

CHAPTER 10

OPENING THE SANTA FE TRAIL   FALL 1820 - JANUARY 1822

S hirtless and freezing in a filthy, vermin infested blanket, Joseph Walker faced another frigid fall dawn in his Santa Fe prison cell. The cell reeked from centuries of outhouse use by captives. Each day Joe awoke scratching his lice and flea bites on the dirt floor was more infuriating than the day before. No American could stand being imprisoned on a whim. *Antonio Bizet,* lying crumpled in the corner of Joe's rust-barred dungeon, had been sentenced to die. Joe had to get out! But how?

The prison's outer door clanged. Joe craned to see if they were bringing the salt-less bean slop in a gourd shell they usually spit in before shoving under the bars.

Bizet, expecting his execution every morning, asked in French accented words, "They coming for us?"

"I dunno," Joe muttered, trying to clear his throat. But he heard someone in the corridor.

A shaggy old rooster in rags shuffled up to the cell, dropped his wooden stool worn shiny, and plopped on it. "I'm James Baird," he croaked. "Know I look older'n Methuselah, but I'm 53. Eight years in these Spanish dungeons'll make a man look like he's died of old age. This stool's all I've got to show for near a decade o' pain. Who're you?"

"Joseph Rutherford Walker of Fort Osage, Missouri."

Joe's cell mate grated, "*Antonio Bizet.* Why you come?"

"Come to gitchu out if I can. What're you in fer?"

Joe said, "I was trapping beaver near Taos. Spanish soldiers stormed our camp one night. Took everything we had and hauled us here. Never said why and I've never seen the other trappers since."

"You on the floor -- whatchu do?"

"What is the difference?" *Bizet* asked, rubbing his eyes.

"Plenny. Whatchu in here fer?" the skinny man rasped.

Bizet replied, "I was captured with the *expédition* of *Auguste Chouteau* and *Jules De Mun* about three years ago for not having the licenses that pleased the Spanish."

"Guard says yer under a death sentence. Kill somebody?"

"Do I look like the assassin?"

"Why then?"

"*Monsieur* -- you will not believe why."

"I ain't gonna corkscrew this outa you. Tell me outright er I'm leavin'. Stink o' this place'd make a pig puke."

Grasping the bars with filthy fists, *Bizet* whispered, "*Chouteau* and *De Mun* were from St. Louis's best families. *Monsieur De Mun* got the permission from Governor *Alberto Mainez* to trap in New Mexico. But when *Pedro María Allande* took over, he thought we'd built a fort on the Arkansas River. Though they saw we had no fort, the soldiers dragged us before *Allande.* Chained like brigands blinking in our leather coats, we were forced to kneel. When *De Mun* said we had a license from the American government as well as the former Spanish Governor, *Allande* flew into such a rage, he could not speak. *I laughed.* He ordered me shot and the others held. After 44 days, he forced *Chouteau* and *De Mun* to kiss the paper listing their crimes. *Allande* confiscated their property worth $30,000 then released all but me."

"That was three years ago?" Baird said, his voice rising to a squeal.

"Right! And I have not demanded my execution sooner!"

Joe Walker dodged a shaft of sunlight spearing his bearded face. "You're not a diplomat, Mr. Baird. Whatta you doing here?"

"In 1812, I partnered up with another Scotch-Irisher Robert McKnight. With Ben Shreve and Mike McDonough we hired five men and come to Santa Fe to trade. Governor *Jose Manrique* seized our property then jailed us in Chihuahua, loanin' us convicts out as slaves to anybody who had a favor comin'. Some become servants -- others went to the mines -- some rotted in filth like this."

"How'd you get free?" Joe probed suspiciously.

"Last May Spain's *Ferdinand VII* give Spaniards a Constitution and issued a decree liberatin' all Americans held in Mexico. So far they freed everybody that ain't under death sentence. I'm jist tryin' to git us all loose."

"When you tell 'em *Bizet* here's done three years for bad manners and how sorry he is, maybe he can go home."

"If I can gitchu boys out, you gotta swoop back to the U. States -- cause if you're nabbed agin in Mexico, they'll stand you agin a wall fer sure."

"We'll leave *pronto*, right *Bizet*?"

"Wrong! I am not sorry for laughing at that maniac. I'll die proudly with a smile my lips."

"No, *Bizet*," Joe Walker growled cupping his hand over the Frenchman's mouth, "Mr. Baird, tell his nibs you discovered two Americans ready to make a run for the border."

Joe Walker didn't reveal that he planned to rejoin the Ghost Trappers of Taos and smuggle out enough beaver to get even for his 42 days in jail.

Thomas Hart Benton sat exhausted in his empty *St. Louis Enquirer* office. In spite of having been a Missouri State Senator for a year, his fall 1820 election for the U.S. Senate had been a horsewhipping contest.

His opponent'd brandished both Benton's duels with young lawyer Charles Lucas, son of renowned Judge J.B.C. Lucas, like bloody banners. The 1816 duel at the gentleman's 30 feet was fought over insults in court. Lucas survived Benton's neck shot and Benton his knee contusion. But when Charles

Lucas claimed in '17 that Benton shirked his taxes and had no right to vote, Benton demanded satisfaction at 9 feet. Barely 25, Charles Lucas died on Bloody Island with Benton's ball in his brain.

Oddly enough, Benton's election opponent omitted his 1813 gunfight with Andrew Jackson, which might have brought Benton down. But even after winning the polemic election, Benton couldn't take his U.S. Senate seat.

Congress'd passed the Missouri Compromise in March 1820, admitting Maine as a free state and Missouri as a slave state. But Missouri's legislature'd strangled its own statehood with a State Constitution excluding free blacks from the state.

The articles surrounding Benton's harangues in the *St. Louis Enquirer* often dwarfed Missouri statehood. After Spain's King signed the treaty ceding Florida to the U. States, Andrew Jackson accepted President Monroe's offer to become its Governor on February 11, 1821. Benton found it bizarre that once legally flogged for seizing Florida, Jackson was now its virtual emperor.

Joe Walker scanned the June 25, 1821 *Missouri Intelligencer* while having locks of his wavy black hair shorn to the floor in Franklin's oldest barber shop. William Becknell advertised for "... *a company of men destined to the westward for the purpose of trading for Horses and Mules, and catching Wild Animals of every description....*" Interested men were to come to Ezekiel Williams's farm Thursday. Joe saw the ad as a clever ruse to raise men to trade and trap in New Mexico. The working conditions in New Mexico were fierce, but the money was magnificent. Joe decided to give it another go.

Ezekiel Williams, a haggard farmer with bed-pillow bags under his eyes, stood in the lantern light among the 17 roughest looking men ever assembled in one barn. "No doubt you heard I was tried fer murderin' my partner Champlain -- and acquitted. Musta heard I love Mammon more than God and got sued by another partner's widow fer his share. Gotta know I stand accused o' bigamy. So you'll be glad to hear I got nothin' to do with this venture besides bein' between court appearances and havin' the biggest barn in Franklin, Missouri."

William Becknell stepped in front of the farmer. A slender but muscular man with deepset eyes, Becknell said quietly, "Just wanta raise a outfit to trade in Santa Fe. Spent most o' my life runnin' a ferry boat. Some managin' the salt works at Boone's Lick. Got no mercantile experience and can't spell a lick, but I'm honest -- and don't plan to sue nobody."

Everybody laughed but Ezekiel.

Somebody asked, "What're your terms?"

Becknell thought a while. "Every man's gotta bring a horse, rifle, three-month supply o' powder n' shot, change o' clothes and at least $10 to buy merchandise -- mostly cotton goods. Every eight men gotta have a pack horse, tent and ax. Profits'll be split equally among us. Ever'body'll foller rules we make fore we go."

Joe Walker asked, "Anything else?"

Becknell grinned, "Helps if you're sick o' farmin', itchin' to stretch your pockets and willin' to risk stretchin' yer neck."

On September 1, 1821, three weeks after Missouri's admission to the Union, Becknell's outfit left Arrow Rock, Missouri headed west with full bellies and high hopes. They reached Fort Osage the second day, where Major Sibley let them camp.

Sibley confided to Joe Walker, "Mistah William Becknell's a man of good charactah -- great bravery and a hahdy and enterprisin' man -- but he knows nothin' about sellin' shirts."

"Becknell's been forthright on that Major. Your *Osages* civilized yet?"

"Not noticeably. Mistah Bill Williams has been helpin' me, but since the United Foahn Missionary Society's missionaries arrived, Mistah Williams has spent his time translatin' sehmons. I do believe Mistah Williams is fah wildah than eithah the *Osages* oh yoahself, suh, and I'm shuah those Missionaries have no idea what they ah sayin' in those praah meetin's."

"Look forward to meeting Bill Williams on my return, Major."

"I wondah if you'll evah really retun, Mistah Walkah. You ah a free spirit boahn to run with free spirits."

Becknell's pack train crossed an endless prairie, then followed the Arkansas River. Ever watchful for the *Osage,*

89

Kiowa, Pawnee, Comanche and *Apache* they trekked from one cold water spring to the next and posted guards every night.

Marm had regaled Joe and his brothers as boys with tales of Spanish *Conquistadors* searching for gold. Joe Walker communed with the spirits of those ancients as he walked in their unseen tracks southwest through tall grasses and glorious chest-high sunflowers. Pity the Spanish gold-seekers hadn't been satisfied finding these golden-petaled, pie-sized sunflowers with their gingerbread centers, for they never found their cities of gold. The sunflowers excelled any beauty man could create.

When they reached the blistering *Jornada de Muerte,* a waterless hell between the Arkansas and the Cimarron Rivers, Joe Walker took Becknell aside. "We'd be smart to follow the Arkansas river, veer into the mountains, then cut southeast o' Taos instead of taking off across this desert."

"Tried that afore?"

Joe grinned, "Last time I came down here -- but then I ended up getting jailed in Santa Fe for nothing. You get thrown in a cell, you might get out in a couple of months. I'm subject to be shot -- leastwise that's what they said when they let me go."

Becknell clucked his tongue, "Don't know as I'da made this trip if I's you. Since you been down this trail before, we'll try it yer way."

Traversing a high mountain pass, they sent boulders bounding down its scarps, then slipped and slid down the slopes through a snow storm to the Canadian River.

On November 13, 1821, Spanish cavalry surrounded them -- but with empty hands.

Joe listened as the Cavalry Captain pointed to their new red, white and green flag with its eagle, serpent and cactus, proclaiming in Spanish they were *Mexicanos* who welcomed *Americanos* to Santa Fe. Joe hadn't heard words like *feliz* and *bienvenidos* the last time he was here, but in spite of the snow, they warmed him through.

When the Mexicans rode off, Joe asked Becknell, "You understand all o' that?"

"Said it's their honeymoon of liberty. All men are brothers. We're welcome in Santa Fe -- their city of new happiness."

On November 16th, Becknell led his men into Santa Fe. Children scampered beside Walker's horse waving happily like their new flag above the palace. The marketplace stretched across a clearing from the west end of the palace.

Citizens in *serapes* thronged around venders sitting cross-legged at their mats displaying chili, beans, onions, milk, bread and cheese. *Indios* with *burros* overloaded into moving hills threaded the crowds. Mutton, kid, pork and venison dangled from lines stretched to the pillars of the palace portal.

Walker'd never seen a better place for business. After Becknell arranged a stall for them at the edge of the market, Joe Walker cautioned, "Don't sell too cheap. They're used to paying for a lotta freight from Vera Cruz."

"You can help, Joe!"

"I don't *habla Español* so good!"

"That smile's all you need! You'll have 'em all learnin' *Inglés.*"

William Becknell, Joe Walker and three other exhausted men rode into Franklin, Missouri on January 29, 1822 with a glow in their eyes. The rest of Becknell's outfit had remained to trap in New Mexico. A mild winter had left Franklin's streets dry, but still wagon-rutted from summer storms.

Not a show off by nature, William Becknell had a score to settle with skeptics in Franklin who'd sneered at his chances of leaving Santa Fe with more than leg iron scars. He yelled, "Let 'er go, boys!"

Joe Walker and the others released rawhide bundles from their saddle horns to burst on the street letting $10,000 in Mexican silver roll around downtown Franklin, Missouri -- at least till everybody got a good look at the money.

CHAPTER 11

THE NASHVILLE RAILROAD   SPRING 1822

avid Crockett was not a patron of "uppity waterin' holes," but he'd been invited to the Nashville Inn for dinner with Governor Billy Carroll and the Major General of Tennessee's Southern Militia Division, Sam Houston, so he come. Carroll and Houston already had their table. Governor Carroll'd growed a little hog jowl ahangin' over his collar, but to David's surprise, they both got up to greet him. Both had outdressed him sumpthin' awful.

"Have a seat, Colonel Crockett! Carroll said shaking his hand with one that felt near soft as a lady's. "You're probably wondering why I called the Fourteenth General Assembly back in session the 22nd of April."

Before Crockett could blink, Governor Carroll contin- ued, "We face the most important business of our time."

"What's that, Gov'nor?" Crockett blurted.

"Passing a resolution nominating Andrew Jackson to be the next President of our Union -- then building the machine that will elect him to that highest of high offices."

"You fellers ordered yer food?" Crockett asked.

They both shook their heads lookin' peeved at how David'd ducked reactin' to their announcement.

Hiding his dirty fingernails, Crockett replied, "I led yer Gov'nor campaign in my district, Gen'l Carroll. I seduced all the votes I could fer you fer Major Gen'l, Sam. I'd be crazier'n a corn-liguored coon to back off supportin' Gen'l Jackson whom I served under inna Creek War in Alabama and agin the *Seminoles* in Florida. I's plumb sorry to hear he'd resigned last fall as Florida's Gov'nor after Monroe's administration left him stranded and broke down nere. No man ever worked harder to git a Gov'nor job -- havin' to make his District outa a foreign country and all."

Houston interjected, "Of course we plan to send General Jackson to the U.S. Senate in the next election. It's no secret that I loathe our current Senator John Williams, my former Commanding Officer at Horseshoe Bend, who has devoted his political life to hoisting me on his lance."

"What's that he done to ya?" Crockett asked wide-eyed.

Billy Carroll motioned to their waiter and cautioned, "Let's not sink into that swamp! Colonel Crockett, can we count on your support for General Jackson for the U.S. Senate when it comes before us in legislative session?"

"If I'd support Gen'l Jackson fer the highest office in the land, I'd have no hesitation bout turnin' him in with them fellers in the Senate. Be interestin' to see how the Gen'l handles them ole boys that give him such a fierce goin' over after the House found him free o' blame fer grabbin' Florida."

Carroll eyed Crockett like he was the town fool. "So much political water will have gone under the bridge by October 1823 Florida will be thought of only as a good place to fish."

As the waiter handed out the supper lists, Sam Houston said snidely, "Be a might more tense than that when General Jackson takes the Senate seat next to Missouri's Thomas Hart Benton, since he still carries a Benton bullet in his shoulder."

"Like as not Gen'l Jackson and Tom Benton'll be packin' pistols the first day o' that session!" Crockett cackled.

"Please try to be discreet, Colonel," Governor Carroll said nervously. "We still need to talk about electing General Houston to the U.S. House of Representatives."

"Say they's no end to the sweetmeats afore this meal, is they? I sure hope you ain't espectin' me to pick up the check on top o' layin' a hunnert miles o' track fer the Nashville Railroad!" Only Crockett's guffaws startled those at the tables around them.

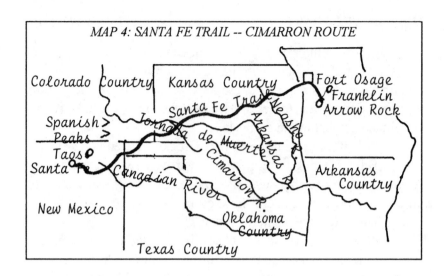

MAP 4: SANTA FE TRAIL -- CIMARRON ROUTE

Colorado Country   Kansas Country   Fort Osage
                                       Franklin
Spanish   Arrow Rock
Peaks
Taos
Santa Fe   Arkansas
                                       Country
New Mexico

                    Oklahoma
                    Country

        Texas Country

CHAPTER 12

WAGONS TO SANTA FE   SPRING 1822 - FALL 1823

Williamm Becknell'd asked men wanting to join his second trip to Santa Fe to meet in Arrow Rock, Missouri's big grove on May 10, 1822. When two dozen showed up, he climbed into his wagon bed. Becknell saw men with the bark on -- unfinished and eager to turn a profit, whatever the risk. He told them, "After our *peso* stunt three months ago in Franklin, we got investors changin' from sheep to wolves. One woman put up $60 and got $900 back last trip. Don't mean we couldn't come back broke this time -- er mebbe not come back. Only thing sure in this world is pain -- your mother's when yer born and yer own when you die."

A curious neighbor asked, "Bill, you really takin' wagons to Santa Fe?"

"Takin' this one, soon's I get it rigged. Hope they'll be more."

"How you gonna rig the wagon?"

"Hickory hoops, double canvas toppin' with heavy Mackinaw blankets in between to pertect merchandise from rain -- and

94

Mexican customs charges on the blankets!"

"Oxen er mules?"

Becknell scratched his head. "Oxen are steady pullers. Nobody's tried wagons. Trail's rough n' rocky. Oxen'd hafta be special shod. Good ole Missouri Mules'll pull my wagon."

"What about food, Bill?"

"Depends how many we gotta feed, but I'd say each wagon needs 50 pounds o' flour, 50 bacon, 10 coffee, 20 sugar, couple handfuls o' salt and a bushel o' beans. We'll leave the 22nd o' this month. Talked too much. I'm done." Becknell climbed down, but the men ganged him with questions.

"How old are you, Bill?"

"By birthdays I'm 24. By fool's years, I'm a hunderd. I'll try anything that'll make an honest dollar. If it don't kill me, I'm fool enough to keep tryin' it till it does."

At the crowd's edge Joe Walker tapped a balding man on the shoulder who was nearly tall as his own 6'4". "You a Young from Tennessee's Emery River-Caney Creek settlements?"

Looking about 30, the smooth-featured balding man offered his hand, "Ewing Young. How'd you know?"

Walker grinned, "We're shirttail cousins. I'm Joe Walker. Our clan migrated from Virginia to Tennessee with the Youngs, Houstons and McClellans and the Linams from South Carolina."

Young smiled, "And the other White Savages." releasing his grip that left Joe's hand feeling stepped on by a draft horse.

"You heard the Ben Franklin yarn too?"

"Every Scotch-Irishman's felt that lecherous old lout's brand," Ewing grinned.

The square-faced, powerful man in his mid-20's beside Ewing Young offered his hand to Walker. "William Wolfskill. I'm not your kin. My folks are Germans from Howard County Kentucky."

Wolfskill's handshake was gentler than Young's, but his ice-blue eyes weren't. Wolfskill confided, "Colonel Benjamin Cooper's outfit's leaving pretty soon without wagons. Likely beat Becknell to Santa Fe."

Walker mused, "Becknell's solid as a hardwood stump. I went to Santa Fe with him last year. Made good money trading, but some of his men strayed to trap those crystal beaver streams on the way home. Trapped those mountains myself. Take some traps if you're coming along. Furs oughta be worth plenty since the U. States shut down its Factory System and left the fur business to the trappers."

Ewing Young muttered, "I'll give it a try, Cousin. Tom Gage and I are selling our farm in Chariton. My share's going into Becknell's Santa Fe adventure."

On a misty May 22nd, Becknell's three wagons and 21 men assembled in Arrow Rock, Missouri, the first bold enough ever to try wagons on the Santa Fe Trail.

"All's set!" Becknell yelled.

"All's set!" the teamsters echoed back.

"Move out!" Becknell ordered.

Whips cracking started wheels creaking and men shouting over the rumble of the wagons. Joe Walker felt wildly alive. These 800 miles to Santa Fe could lead to his fortune -- or his grave. As days wore on, Joe watched the men's exuberance surrender to swirling dust. He found himself losing patience with mules that stalled to eat waving grasses they were forced to trample on the roadless prairies.

Not a people to permit free passage across their lands, over a hundred *Osages* drifted like wraiths from behind the rolling hills, surrounding Becknell's badly outnumbered men.

"You trade with 'em all the time, *Chouteau*. Whatta they want?" Becknell yelled over braying mules, disturbed by the *Osages'* odd odors.

"Horses!" *Auguste Chouteau* yelled back.

"How do ya know? " Becknell challenged.

"They always want horses."

"What're we gonna do? Brawl'll be bloody and brief at this range."

"Promise 'em horses on our way back," *Chouteau* replied, signing to one of the *Osage* Chiefs called *Shin-gawassa* [Handsome Bird] that Becknell liked to eat *Osage* legs raw and was looking right at him.

At the Chief's angry sign, the *Osages* thundered off on their ponies, while Joe Walker smothered his laughter.

"Fer God sake, how many horses did ya promise that

Indian, *Chouteau?*" Becknell yelled, but *Chouteau* was too busy watching the *Osages* to make sure they didn't double back.

Once out of Missouri, Becknell headed for the Neosho River in Kansas country about 150 miles across the waving prairie grasses. Before long, the sunflowers Joe Walker adored rose like an army of golden haired giants nodding in the winds, their chocolate faces tracking the sun across the columbine blue heavens.

Trekking to the Arkansas River in *Kanza* Indian country, Becknell held to the north bank until he found a ford for the wagons. When Becknell's wagon floated and began to yaw in the current, Joe Walker rode up and slid onto the tailgate, his horse swimming easily behind him. Once the wagon's wheels hit solid gravel under Walker's weight, Becknell pointed to the cloud crowned Spanish Peaks. "Some Indians call them the *Wah-to-Yah* -- Breasts to the World."

Dripping water from the fording, Joe Walker asked Becknell, "You gonna cross the *Jornada de Muerte* from here to the Cimarron River? You know that's the devil's own chunk o' the Santa Fe Trail."

"Last time we rode the mountain route up through Colorado Country, I seen that a mouse had to hold his breath to squeeze through *Raton* Pass north o' Taos. Never get through there with wagons. Gotta take this flat Cimarron route."

"Frying's not the way I wanna die," Walker grumbled.

"Few men choose how they die."

Becknell's wagons popped rocks with their wheels till the rocky trace crumbled to sand. They tied blankets on the wheel rims, but the wheels sank deep in the sand. Shimmering heat fried their hands on the wagons and baked their tongues in their mouths. They yanked on the stalled wagons until they collapsed.

After days without water, Joe Walker saw shimmering silver ponds in the shifting sand. He sucked rocks and swallowed his own spit, while others drank their dogs' blood or cut the ears off their mules to suck the salty red fluid that could not quench the thirst of madness.

Finding a foundered buffalo with a bellyful of water, they slashed its throat. Gregg plunged his knife into its swollen paunch then gorged on its stinking green water. Others ran to suckle the gash. One man groaned, "Nothing's ever passed my lips that delighted me like this filthy beverage."

After straining the buffalo's bilge through his hat, Joe Walker drank it, garnering enough strength to reach the Cimarron River and return with filled water skins for the others. He was astounded to find everybody still alive in this furnace. They freed their wagons at dusk and lumbered all night through the *Jornada* amid scurrying scorpions and sidewinders.

Santa Fe soon lay below them across a valley so majestic it put the past weeks' horrors from their minds. Having never seen *Americano* wagons before, the Mexicans rejoiced at the thought of exciting new goods to be laid before them. Most goods sold during the unloading.

As Becknell prepared to leave Santa Fe, he warned brash Ewing Young and William Wolfskill, "Keep them traps well hid. Mexicans welcomes commerce, but trappin' openly will make you boys the next things to git trapped. Joe Walker kin tell ya how bad Mexican jail beans is."

"Got enough men to handle the wagons?" Ewing asked.

"Will have if you and Wolfskill don't lure Walker with ya into the hills."

"Been a splendid trip for us, Bill. But Wolfskill and I are gonna dream away this Santa Fe summer till the beavers pelt-up on the Pecos. Put our share o' the money in the Franklin Bank. We'll see you on the far side of the *Jornada de Muerte* before Christmas. *Buena suerte*, Billy Becknell!"

Though Benjamin Cooper's pack train also got through to Santa Fe and back to Missouri in 1822, making themselves a fair return, they never bumped into Becknell's outfit. The October 8, 1822 *Missouri Intelligencer* noted the return of Colonel Cooper's men as casually as if they'd been on a picnic.

But when Becknell's wagons rolled into the Missouri settlements, news articles saluted William Becknell as the *"Father of the Santa Fe Trail"* and *"Commodore of the Commerce of the Prairies,"* leaving Colonel Cooper irked, although he knew Becknell'd been first with a pack train and with wagons on the Santa Fe Trail. William Becknell cared little for flowery words because they could not be entered in his bank book.

Joe Walker rode into Fort Osage's Six Mile Country. He stopped by the ample Sibley home they modestly called Fountain Cottage to check on the Major before riding on home. The Major said Mary was in the East visiting relatives.

Major Sibley sat fiddling aimlessly with his hands "Guess you know I'm unemployed since the Factorah System's abolishment."

"Major, I've come into some money that has no place to go. This bag would like to stay here. I mean that, sir."

"I know you do, Mistah Walkah. Will ask you for a loan if I have to," he added unconvincingly.

"That Bill Williams you wanted me to meet. He must be outa work too."

"Strange man Mistah Williams. Lost his gov'mint job as interpretah with the Factorah System's death. Got fahd as translatah when the Missionaries found out about his three wives and got an inklin' of what he had them sayin' in church. But Mistah Williams landed like a dropped cat. He's interpretah foah General Henry Atkinson and General Edmund Gaines. Theah heah to soothe disputes between the *Osages* and those *Cherokees* the gov'mint keeps herdin' in heah."

"Major Sibley, I haven't been home since Noah built the boat, but you've got your own miracle right here in Six Mile country. This money was lying right in your front yard."

"Mistah Walkah, the days of miracles ah ovah."

"Every new day is a miracle, Major."

"Pahaps, but I cahn't take chahity -- though I deahly appreciate yoah blessed ruse." He thrust Walker's money away and averted his eyes.

But Joe Walker didn't want this proud man to see the tears welling in his own eyes, so he just kept walking with his hand out to touch the mist.

As Walker mounted his horse, shadowy figures on horseback danced past in the fog, then he heard an unmistakable voice. Heeling his horse in the flanks, Walker galloped along the ghostly pack train till he reached its head. "Anybody got a stool a man might rest up on?"

"Thatchu Walker?"

Walker grabbed the bony hand sticking out of the vapor,

"Baird -- you shaggy old rooster! Where you boys headed?"

"Santa Fe," Baird cackled. "Come along -- jail lice ain't et right since you slipped away."

"Hold on," Walker gasped. "You realize that by leaving Missouri in November, you boys could be the first white men ever to freeze to death in the *Jornada?*"

James Baird showed his bad teeth in the fog. "Joe Walker, this's my ole partner Sam Chambers I tole you bout. Got this trip financed by American Fur Company. Gonna make money and have ourselves a helluva time. Play yer cards right, we'll even learn you *pocito Español.*"

"Always wanted to travel with linguists. I'll do it!" Joe yelled. "Somebody sell me a blanket?"

"I'd give you mine," Baird brayed, but they's a squaw in it!"

After buying three blankets and a kit from them at their first night stop, Joe Walker dozed off realizing how truly crazy he was to hook up with Baird. A Mountain Man could do anything without a woman to nag some sense into him.

Walker wasn't surprised when blizzards turned *Kanza* Country to tundra, but when the mules froze to death, he knew this might be his last trip. They built fires to unfreeze the ground, then dug deep caches for their goods, before setting out for Taos on foot. Friendships froze to death in the snow. Baird and Chambers dropped out of their firm, selling out to the Anderson brothers, Foughlin and McGunnegle.

Reaching Taos February 2, 1823, McGunnegle and the Andersons left Walker and Baird's group guzzling Taos Lightning around a friendly fireplace. They braved blizzards with several Spaniards and fresh horses to find their supply caches. But in early spring, they returned empty handed.

"What become of our caches?" Baird spat suspiciously.

"When the weather broke, the *Pawnees* joined *Miguel's* ear holes with an arrow and rustled our horses before we got to the caches," McGunnegle growled. "We had to walk to Taos -- again!!"

Having made friends with a *Comanche* named *Francisco Largo*, Walker rose and stretched. "*Francisco*, we oughta do something besides squaw work. Let's go raise their caches."

As spring wild flowers set the prairies of Colorado and Kansas Countries ablaze in columbine blue and paintbrush red, Walker suffered the ugly words between Baird and his former partners. After unearthing the Kansas country caches, Walker said, "Gentlemen, the only thing we've done here is give travelers some big holes in the ground to gawk at -- and the only Spanish I learned was from the *Comanche*. I'm through here. Leave my money with Major George Sibley at Fort Osage."

Back from Texas, Joel Walker joined Stephen Cooper's 30 man outfit in Boonslick County Missouri to go trading in Santa Fe. Their pack train snaked through Kansas country till they camped June 1, 1823 on the Little Arkansas River to hunt buffalo. At dawn next day *Pawnees* stampeded their stock.

Jerked from a sound sleep, Joel Walker found himself sprinting across the prairie after their stock. Soon outdistanced, Joel stalked angrily back into his camp.

Throwing wood on the feeble fire, the cook asked wryly, "Joel, aintchu forgot sumpthin?"

"Yes. I was in Texas, and I forgot to stay there!"

"Thinkin' more along the lines that you's plumb necked."

Ignoring the obvious, Joel yelled, "Steve, feel like jack-rabbitting back to Missouri for remounts?"

"Will if you'll quit showin' off."

Riding 800 miles in 22 days, Joel Walker, Steve Cooper and two others brought back a new *remuda*. But their renewed hope soon boiled away in the hundred miles of hell Mexicans called the *Jornada de Muerte*. Joel could see his men were faltering in air hot as a cooking fire and earth fiery as a frying pan. Riding up beside Cooper, who was choking his saddle horn with both hands, Joel said, "I'll take a dozen men and bring back water for everybody."

Steve Cooper just nodded.

Joel and his men espied a pond of wallowing buffalo. Joel shot a mangy bull. Skinning its thigh, Joel sewed it into a water bag with sinew, then gurgled it full of the pond's putrid water. Joel sent men back with the greenish water, while he and the others barricaded the buffalo herd from the water. They shot one stubborn old cow eight times before her madness ran out on

the sand. Joel knew they didn't have powder and shot to kill all
the buffalo.The bulls bellered, rousing the other shaggy monsters
from their heat stupor. Joel waded into the tepid slime with his
men and their horses. They waited for the stampede with loaded
rifles.

As buffalo bore down on them, Joel dropped the lead
bull. Grape sized raindrops mixed with hail burst from the sky.
Men caught rain in their hats, open maws and cupped hands.

But Joel heard new hoofbeats. Shading his eyes, he spied
a large party of horsemen closing on them. With the cloudburst
deluging his rifle's powder pan, he knew it wouldn't fire. Joel
leaped aboard his horse bareback and headed for the oncoming
riders, not wanting to pull his big knife until he had to.

As the two bands neared each other, Joel's mouth gaped
in astonishment. The leader he'd been sure was an Indian with
hair flying -- was his brother Joe Walker. Thank God it'd rained
too hard to shoot! His shock easing, Joel grinned. It wouldn't
do to shoot the Best Man for his upcoming wedding to Ewing
Young's cousin Mary.

"Economics govern the way men must be killed."
Ewing Young

CHAPTER 13

LEGEND OF THE GUN **FALL 1823 - WINTER 1824**

J oe and Joel Walker leaped from their horses dripping rain, grappling like the young bears they once were. Joel exploded, "What possessed you to ride down on us like that, Joe? Hadn't been for the downpour, I'da shot my own brother."

"Heard gunshots. Saw meandering tracks o' Whites in trouble. Thought you needed help in a hurry."

"How about coming to Santa Fe with us, Joe? We've cut a lot of Indian sign."

"My horse'll think I'm crazy."

"Why?"

"Every time we head for Missouri, we end up in Santa Fe."

Merging into a party of 55 men with 200 mules and horses, they set out across the desert. In half a day every vestige of the cloudburst was fried. Empty water skins turned board stiff. *Francisco Largo* scouted for water, but failed to return.

Joe muttered, "You've got trouble when your *Comanche* gets lost."

At Lower Cimarron Springs, they found *Largo* astride his dead horse. Shielding his eyes from the sun with a filthy hand, *Largo* groaned, "Horse smell water. Run hisself dead."

Joe eyed the dead horse, twisted grotesquely, eyes leathery and lolling tongue bitten bloody. "Water my horse, *Francisco*. I'm gonna bury yours. Horses give us everything -- no matter how we treat 'em. Buzzards'll not strip this dead friend."

Joel's men gawked with pursed mouths, saying mutely Joel's brother was a lunatic. Joel grunted, "That's the way Joe Walker is -- kind to a fault." He yelled, "Soon's I grab a shovel off a pack mule, I'll help, Joe."

One by one, sweating men came with shovels. *Largo's* horse soon lay beneath hot ground as buzzards circled futilely.

Sleeving the sweat from his eyes, Joel asked, "Gonna say anything over him, Joe?"

Joe gazed at once scoffing men now resting on their shovels. "They have said it all."

As their caravan entered Santa Fe, a squinting hag motioned to leader Joel Walker. He dismounted. Garbed in black and lisping English through snaggle teeth, she whispered, "You are among a bad people. A council is being held to decide if they should imprison you."

Joel asked, "Can I give you something for your risk?"

"Tobacco."

She clawed the twist from Joel's hand.

Riding ahead, Joe Walker assessed the *pueblo* founded by *Don Pedro de Peralta* in the arms of the Sangre de Cristo Mountains in 1609. Like any city of 5,000 Joe saw plenty wrong with it -- but it possessed the charm of a woman who'd forgiven herself her wild youth -- though she hadn't forgotten it.

Some Americans disliked Santa Fe because the *gente principal* treated the *peones* like *burros*. They saw the *adobe* brick houses smeared with flaking plaster as wretched mud huts.

But Joe Walker admired her *hogares* and her *gente*. With wooden tools, her farmers forced unyielding earth to surrender life to them. They heaped their marketplace with melons, slicing some open to show bright orange and red innards. Roasting *piñon* nuts perfumed the air with their pine heritage. Mexicans flashed smiles around corn husk cigarettes. Religious processions trailed wooden Christs past saloons where men gambled and became *boracho* on *mescal*.

After days of brisk trading without threat of jail, Joel Walker realized the old hag had worked him for tobacco, but he still wrote in his journal "*The women were all friendly, and told us what was going on. We had two bales of bleached domestic which we sold for Forty five Dollars a bale. We could have sold Calicoes and Cotton for any price asked. A little looking glass worth about ten cents was easily sold for a dollar.*"

After his goods were gone, Joel Walker headed for

Missouri with enough money to wed and support sweet Mary Young.

Unable to tear himself from the embrace of mystical New Mexico, Joe Walker surrendered to a winter in Taos.

Though Andrew Jackson gripped the pistol in his boot through the morning Senate session, the brute Thomas Hart Benton never gave him a glance. Jackson let go of his pistol grip awash in relief.

For a fortnight in the Senate Chamber, neither Jackson nor Benton uttered a word to each other. But when seated side by side in their Committee on Military Affairs, Jackson said, "I venture upon shaky ground here, but would you like some coffee, Senator?"

Benton nodded, grudgingly extending his cup. Still, they didn't address each other during the meeting.

Hearing a colleague's offhand remark that Tom's wife Elizabeth suffered some malady, Andrew Jackson lay in wait at the Senate's portal. Finally, he spied Benton swaggering down the hall like the overweening hero in a very bad play. What he was about to do required twice the courage he'd needed to turn the British charge at Chalmette. Palms sweating, he blocked Benton's path. "May I inquire on the health of Mrs. Benton?"

Benton eyed him dourly muttering, "Touch o' colic, but it was no match for Elizabeth. Few things are -- including me." Benton trudged past wearing a mild smirk.

Aware of the ego-ridden Benton's power over their peers, Jackson knew a thaw could float his Presidential aspirations from the doldrums. He called on Benton's lodgings, but Missouri's answer to war, famine, plague and pestilence was not in. Jackson left his card.

The following day they met outside the Senate. Benton stepped up to Jackson and bowed. Jackson shot his hand out to be crushed warmly by Benton, thawing a decade of acrimony. Jackson wheedled, "Wonder if we might share a toddy at the Sociable?"

"Just one? That's like revoking the second raindrop after a drought!"

"*¿Julian Joon?*" the fat Mexican innkeeper yelled. "*Su*

primo es aquí."

Ewing Young left the fireplace's friendly warmth to peer around the rough wooden beam at the desk. "Joe Walker! The Taos Lightning's in here!"

Joe trudged to the fireplace, his clinging cold air chilling William Wolfskill and Ewing Young. "Rather have hot food than whiskey. Who's *Julian Joon?*"

Ewing muttered, "My name doesn't translate. Mexicans have tried a dozen names on me. My favorite's *Joaquín Joven.*"

William Wolfskill rose offering his hand, "*Guillermo Guisquiel a sus ordenes.*"

Walker accepted Wolfskill's warm hand in his freezing palm answering, "*José Andarado acquí.*"

Young bowed. "Your *Español's* a lot better'n last year."

Joe bowed back. "A *gift* from the gracious *señoritas* of Santa Fe. You boys giving Sierra Madre beavers Christmas off?"

"God is. Ten feet o' snow up there," Young laughed, pointing for Walker to take his cowhide-seated chair by the fire.

While Joe wriggled from his snowy *capote*, Ewing said, "*Mais, tortillas y frijoles calientes* are coming. Billy Wolfskill came in here a half hour ago and told me how he got killed."

Sitting cross-legged on the bearskin in front of the fireplace, Joe stopped ladling delicious greasy food from his terra-cotta bowl. "Killed?"

"Killed," Wolfskill yelled, startling the prim *madre y dos hijas* with scarves over their heads eating across the room. Wolfskill hunkered on the bearskin and spoke softly. "In early 1823, I trapped the Rio Grande with an *hombre* I met here in Taos. Snow drove us into a brush hut. Bout the 27th of January, I woke with a fire hissing the snow outside our hut door. Figured my partner was getting warm and laid back down. Minute later, rifle blast hit my chest. Room was fulla powder smoke. Reached for my rifle, but it was gone. Stumbled out searching for my partner."

Wolfskill saw he had the people wide-eyed. "Staggered through a snowstorm to Val Verde near Devil's River."

"Texas?" Walker asked.

Billy nodded. "While I'm bleeding on the *Alcalde's* floor with a bullet in my breastbone, my partner runs in. Tells the

Alcalde Indians attacked, and I was *killed.* I yelled at the soldier to grab him. Soldiers marched him back to our camp. Only footprints in the snow were his and mine. Brought 'im back and locked him in a cold hut till he remembered where he'd left my worthless rifle. Said he'd shot me by accident cause of its hair trigger. Took 'im to Santa Fe for trial, then turned him loose."

Walker sleeved his mouth. "Must've been a worthless rifle if it wouldn't bust through your breastbone."

Young said, "Billy, show Joe how you sleep."

Wolfskill crossed his arms on his chest.

Young bent over Billy. "Look here. Bullet got slowed down going through his right arm then his left hand. But for crossing his arms, Billy woulda been killed."

"Who was the *hombre*, Billy?" Joe asked.

"Ain't worth remembering," Wolfskill snapped. "*Julian* here's been reading bout guns all winter. Took us one whole mule to carry the books he borrowed in Missouri."

Having made himself a beer foam mustache, Ewing figured Billy wanted to change the subject. He squatted beside Billy. "Story starts with a 13th Century Franciscan Friar named Roger Bacon -- an alchemist. Bacon wrote the first known formula for gunpowder listing the measures of saltpeter, charcoal and sulphur. Gunpowder use spread across Europe, mostly in barrel-sized cannon, spawning our term *gun barrel.*

"That would be in the 1200s?" Joe verified.

Ewing nodded. "First used hundredweight stones to batter castle walls. Exploding cannons killed more cannoneers than castle dwellers, but the noise panicked people who thought it was the devil."

"Cannons are the devil," Walker muttered recalling flying arms, legs and guts from his boyhood soldier days.

"In the 14th Century somebody designed a miniature cannon on a long stick to protect the gunner from being blown up by a mistake. A pikesman applied lighted punk to the touch hole to fire this *hand cannon.* Lucky shot occasionally punched through a breastplate, causing knights to die at the hands of infantrymen they used to chase like chickens. Just before 1500, the *matchlock* was invented -- a stock-mounted tube fired from the shoulder with a chance of actually hitting somebody."

"How'd that work?" Billy asked.

"Powder was poured down the smooth tube's muzzle. Ball was rodded in. Gunner stuck a snippet of smoldering rope soaked in saltpeter into the gun's lock. Pulling the trigger dropped the burning rope into a pan of gunpowder on the barrel. Pan's explosion blew through a hole in the side of the barrel, setting off the main charge shooting the ball down the tube toward the target -- now in real danger if closer than 50 yards."

"Musta taken a lotta time lighting that rope before every shot," Joe observed.

"Rope matches were lit before battle and stuck between the fingers, into a hat band or left smoldering in the gun's lock. They smoked by day, glowed by night and stunk enough to give away the shooter. Fizzled out in snow or rain. Worse, soldiers wore powder charges and balls in bandoleers and often blew themselves all over the battlefield."

"Why'd they use the matchlocks?" Billy asked.

"They terrified knights. Smiths doubled armor's thickness. Knights wouldn't buy armor without a dent to show it'd turned a bullet. Made armor so heavy neither man nor horse could outmove cold molasses. Changed the balance of military power in Europe. Training bowmen took years. But a hayseed peasant trained on a matchlock in two weeks could kill a knight that had honed sword and lance skills since before he shaved."

Joe Walker tossed pine knots on the fire. "Why is man's history always tied to killing?"

"Man's real enemy is man," Ewing retorted. "Had enough guns, Joe?"

"Go ahead. I'm sure to learn something."

"Gun wounds were beyond doctors' skills, so priests went into battle as Chaplains to serve beyond medicine's meager realm. Matchlocks allowed armies to maim each other in good weather and remained popular into the 1600s. Then gun designers devised the *wheellock*. With 50 working parts inside the gun, the shooter wound it with a key. He loaded it like the matchlock and fired it with his trigger snow, rain or shine."

Joe grinned, "Sounds like shooting somebody with your watch. How'd they do that?"

"Pulling the trigger spun a spring loaded wheel so the

hammer holding a piece of iron pyrites fell against it, knocking sparks off the softer pyrites. Sparks ignited the powder in a sheltered pan, firing the main charge down the gun barrel."

"Lucky my brother Joel didn't have a wheellock that worked in the rain!"

"Your brother was gonna shoot you?" Billy asked incredulously.

"Joel thought I was an Indian. So why don't we shoot wheellocks now, Ewing?"

"They cost a fortune. Economics govern how a man must be killed. Took a watchmaker to fix one, and men constantly lost their keys in battle. Besides, the *flintlock* made it a relic. About 1615 poor Dutch chicken thieves, who didn't want the farmer alerted with the matchlock's glowing match or his dog by its smell and couldn't afford the wheel, replaced the wheel's 50 parts with a simple sear. When their trigger was pulled, it released a spring-loaded hammer. The hammer rammed its clutched flint against the steel wall leading to the pan. Sparks hit the pan's gunpowder that ignited the main charge through a hole in the side of the barrel. The hammer reminded these rooster snatchers of the pecking action of their prey -- the cock -- hence they called it *cocking* the gun when they pulled the hammer back. Others say a Frenchman invented the *flintlock*."

"What's the difference between the rooster baggers' gun and what we have?" Billy asked.

"That is what we have, but not for long," Ewing replied.

"Why?" Walker inquired eagerly.

"Brainchild of a frustrated Scottish Vicar's on the way."

"First the Franciscan Friar. Now a Vicar. What ever happened to Christian charity?" Joe groaned.

"Guns sell better than Bibles," Billy cracked.

"Maybe, but this started with ducks."

"Ducks?" Billy repeated.

"Reverend Alexander Forsythe is an ardent duck hunter. Bothered him no end that every time he pulled his flintlock's trigger, the exploding powder in the pan put his duck to flight before the main charge fired bird shot down the barrel. He found that fulminate of mercury exploded the instant it's struck. In 1807 Forsythe patented his gun lock with a metal nipple on top of its barrel. A copper cap loaded with fulminate of mercury is slipped over the nipple which has a fine hole leading down into the barrel. The main charge in the barrel detonates the instant the hammer hits the cap. The Vicar's percussion cap eliminates the need for a powder pan. By the time the Vicar's duck hears the shot, he's dead -- rain or shine."

"Why don't we have those?" Billy asked, amazed this miracle had bypassed America for 16 years.

"Economics," Ewing replied. "When the Vicar's guns are made cheap enough, everybody'll have guns with his cap lock. But I won't give up Sweet Lips for anything."

Joe grinned at Ewing. "My Pa said you made an eagle feel blind."

"They say I have to salt my bullets so my kills don't spoil before I get there, but Sweet Lips doesn't like salt, so I don't. My grandpa Robert carried her during the Revolution. The British came over here with their .75 calibre smooth bore Brown Bess lobbing irregular bullets like a rock fight. Sweet Lips took out more British soldiers than all the French ladies of the night in Paris. Then British Major Patrick Ferguson's outfit landed with 100 breach loading rifles he'd designed. Some said they were the best rifles in the world, firing six to eight rounds per minute while ours fired one or two. My grandpa knew Sweet Lips would never settle for second best. On October 7, 1780 at the Battle of King's Mountain in South Carolina, he let Sweet Lips shoot Major Ferguson between the eyes. British brass blamed their King's Mountain defeat on the Ferguson rifle instead of admitting their Tory irregulars had lost the battle. They exchanged their fine Ferguson Rifles for the Brown Bess and forfeited the Revolutionary War. Rest assured, Sweet Lips will never be traded for some cap snapper."

"Heard a half-mile shot downed Ferguson," Billy tested.

"Sweet Lips made grandpa promise never to tell. He said a gentleman never betrays a lady."

Joe Walker stood, motioning the others to rise. "Let's drink to that." They drained their glasses.

"I'll not sink to the gutter to rise to the Presidency."

Andrew Jackson

CHAPTER 14

THE SKINNING   FEBRUARY 1824 - FEBRUARY 1825

n bundlesome bearskin coats Joe Walker, Ewing Young and Billy Wolfskill watched dawn tint the snows of Taos rose and gold. Joe pointed up at the blue mists of the Sangre de Cristos, "Beaver up there are itching to be trapped."

Ewing smiled, "Patience is a virtue everywhere. But in the Taos Valley, it's the law. Been that way since old *Don Fernando de Taos* founded the town in 1615. We're standing in the dream of every Mountain Man. They all come here once before they die."

Billy nodded, "Like buffalo to a salt lick. Taos women and Taos Lightning. I heard about them on every stream I ever trapped. If the mountains have a soul, it's likely right here."

Joe Walker mused, "Robert Burns wrote how we feel:
My heart's in the Highlands, my heart is not here;
My heart's in the Highlands, a chasing the deer.
Chasing the wild deer and following the roe;
My heart's in the Highlands, wherever I go."

Jostled by men bursting from the Congressional Caucus's February 14, 1824 Nominating Convention, Andrew Jackson ranted, "Everything's done by intrigue at this foul place!"

Huge General John Coffee gasped, "Keep your voice down, Andy. Temper's what they'll use agin you. You got one vote for President, so they conceded you're alive."

"You're right, John. I must show these Washington fops I'm a man of reason. But how can I be reasonable when my party nominates William Crawford of Georgia for President with 64 votes? He's crippled as a one-legged possum and couldn't carry a northern state in a basket!"

"Forget him. John Quincy Adams is your real opponent."

"They only gave Adams two votes!"

"He's a Federalist, Andy."

"Not any more. Federalist party's dead."

"These Democratic-Republicans of yours are in the hearse and headed for the graveyard," Coffee growled.

"I'd do better cadging support from the *Seminoles!"* Jackson shrilled. *"*Let's see who the people want."

"Tell you what I want, Andy."

"What?"

"Dinner. Listenin' to lunatics makes me hungry."

"Why?"

"Everthin' does. You can be jist as outraged at O'Neale's Sociable as you can out here starvin' in the snow."

Once Jackson and Coffee shouldered into the Sociable Tavern's smoky warmth, they overheard insiders narrowing viable Presidential candidates down to four.

Henry Clay, the 47 year old Kentucky Congressman who authored the Missouri Compromise, was strong

William Crawford, twice a cabinet member, was sickly at 52, but just got hand-picked by his party.

At 57, John Quincy Adams, scion of the second President, had proved history's most effective Secretary of State, demilitarizing the Canadian border and buying Florida. Adams was the biggest dog in this fight.

The bulldog who'd bitten the British, flushed Florida's *Dons* and chased off the Creeks was 57 year old Andrew Jackson. Not the biggest dog, but hands down the meanest.

Ewing Young and William Wolfskill trapped west along the San Juan River. But Joe Walker'd harvested so many pelts in the high country he kept climbing higher. It wasn't just that Ewing and Billy'd fallen in with Isaac Slover, who irked Joe. Walker'd become a Mountain Man to escape crowds. New Mexico's valleys teemed with noisy trappers. Mountain snow-packs were icy, but soothingly silent except for the winds strumming the harps of Angels. Joe wondered if his four pack mules could haul his enormous harvest down the mountain.

William Becknell's Santa Fe successes allowed him to assemble the biggest trading outfit anybody'd ever taken down there. Joining Becknell was Colonel Meredith Marmaduke, a whang-leather little man who meant business and had the money to prove it. Becknell's most notable venturer was Augustus Storrs, who feared nothing but being broke. Together, they rounded up 78 more men who had a rifle, a pistol, four pounds of powder, eight pounds of lead and 20 days provisions.

On May 15, 1824 their 25 wagons loaded with $30,000 in goods left Franklin. Next day they forded the Missouri River six miles above Franklin with their 150 horses and mules.

As they rolled across the flowery prairies, their formidable size scattered tribes from their path without firing the small cannon bouncing behind their last wagon. Water barrels sloshing at their tailgates said they were ready to spit in the eye of the *Jornada*.

With the Mexican government incensed over the throngs of beaver stripped from its streams, Ewing Young, William Wolfskill and Isaac Slover slipped into Taos by night in June 1824 with $10,000 worth of furs.

Ewing scratched his balding head. "Don't know what you boys're gonna do, but I'm gonna haul my furs to Missouri and cash out before Governor *Baca* changes the fur game down here to Cutthroat."

By the time Becknell's 25 wagons rumbled into Santa Fe on July 28th word of the Mexican central government's June 26, 1824 order prohibiting foreigner trapping in *Nuevo Mexico* scattered American trappers like a summer avalanche.

After furious trading, converting their $30,000 in merchandise to $180,000 in gold and silver, Becknell was elated to welcome renowned marksman Ewing Young with his haul of furs for their return to Missouri. But first, they had to celebrate. Since working men in the States earned $2 a week, it didn't take much ciphering to figure how much money they'd made.

While their younger men prowled the *cantinas*, Augustus Storrs answered a nobler calling. Having joined Senator Thomas Hart Benton's fight against the *Little Americans* who wanted no part of frontier expansion or trade with foreigners, Storrs memorialized his epic journey here to Santa Fe for Benton's upcoming fight in Congress. First describing the splendor of the prairies and his pleasant wagon travel across them, Storrs wrote: *"... The New Mexico fur trade is a business exclusively enjoyed by American citizens....American trappers have worked the Rio Grande and nearby mountains the previous winter when some descended the western slope of our continent. During the present season the number of trappers in New Mexico has tripled....Commerce of preposterous proportions awaits those who venture into this most ancient and lucrative city in our modern realm....I must therefore recommend that a road be surveyed from Fort Osage to the Arkansas river and thence to Santa Fe."*

Thomas Hart Benton was one of the few western politicians who'd been able to pull his huge head out of the fall 1824 Presidential fight long enough to urge passage of his legislation. After yelling till blood spattered his handkerchief, Benton closed his Senate floor plea for his bill to survey a road to Santa Fe, "No road to Santa Fe will be a boulevard for weaklings. But Americans will tread upon it unafraid. Danger, privation, heat and cold will be equally ineffectual in checking their careers of enterprise and adventure."

To the dismay of the *Little Americans*, the Senate passed Benton's Santa Fe Road Bill, and sent it on to the House.

At his boardinghouse Benton defended his Santa Fe Road Bill to congressional colleagues, "My Bill is the smallest of the political upheavals to befall us and the nation this fall. Chaos -- perhaps revolution -- embroils us. We suspected letting the people elect our President was a mistake. When the popular vote's translated to electoral votes, Jackson got 99, Adams 84, Crawford 41 and Clay but 37. With no majority, the House of Representatives must elect the President of this nation."

"You doubt the House is up to the task, Senator?" an

annoyed Congressman inquired.

"You can, but the consummate conniving of our century -- even by Congressional standards -- is coming. Gentlemen, just don't lose my Santa Fe Road Bill among all the conspiracies!"

The irritated Congressman asked, "With costs what they be, how can an 800 mile road be built for only $30,000?"

Sweat beaded out on Benton's forehead as he replied casually, "The road will be surveyed, not built. We expect Mexico to pay for the portion extending into their nation."

"The critical Congressman exclaimed, "Beyond Fort O-sage, your road's all in Mexican territory infested by hostile Indians. Why should we survey a road through another country with American money?"

Daubing his forehead dry with his napkin, Benton smiled, "My approach may be devious, sir, but it's in the best interests of this nation. Isn't that enough?"

Congressman Sam Houston accosted Henry Clay outside The Sociable after a muddled caucus unleashed frustrated men into the night. Tall and whip thin, Clay's mean eyes lanced him. "Mr. Clay, if you swing your electoral votes to Mr. Jackson, you can have any position you desire in his administration, sir."

Clay's eyes narrowed. He spat, "And you sir are drunk."

"Drunk?" the sober Houston repeated incredulously.

"Drunk or suffering a want of integrity. I prefer to say you are drunk and wish you a safe journey to your quarters."

Clay shouldered past him into the night. Perhaps Sam had sullied his honor, but he'd never served a more noble cause than General Jackson's quest for the White House. Still he must never mention this conversation to his mentor. Jackson would've given the hated Clay only the back of his hand.

Having sent their fortunes in money and furs home in the 25 Missouri bound wagons under the watchful eyes of Augustus Storrs and Ewing Young, William Becknell and Joe Walker set out to winter on the Green River together. Stopping for the night in Santa Cruz on the way north from Santa Fe to Taos, Becknell said, "Gotta do something fore we leave New Mexico."

"What?" Joe inquired.

"Governor *Baca's* got a bad stomach. Gotta finish my letter to him. Heard you know bout treatin' such things. Read this and tell me the medicines I oughta add to it."

Walker held Becknell's letter close to the candle on their table, and read it. Choking his grin, Joe asked, "Want me to write this letter for you?"

"No. You think it's funny ta help the Governor o' New Mexico. I say it's good business."

"Right. Put October 29, 1824 at the top."

"I know that. Git ta the medicines."

So Walker told him and Becknell finished his letter with:

"The Rubarbe you can take at ny time what will Ly on the pinte of apocket Knif sum shuger and a spunful of cold warter you may Eaeght or drinke any thing Hot or Cold. The Best time to take it is of aneight When you go to Bed it is not apecke agental purge and wil creteefy the stomack when in Bad order The Campor you can desolve in whiskey put a few drops in a dram of whiskey in the morning will Help the stomake very much. I send you A few of the qusawit Barks put them in to abotel of whisky 1 quart and ...stand in the sun for one or 2 days and then drink them...."

"How should I send this letter to Santa Fe, Joe?"

"Send it by a *Padre*. Governor *Baca* may need the Last Rites after he reads it."

Henry Clay turned up the collar of his fashionable coat and eyed his frozen city. Like the ice that paralyzed the Potomac, the Presidential stalemate imprisoned his nation. Clay wished to be remembered as the man who freed his country.

He considered Jackson a rash military chieftain, unsuited by temper or ability to govern a nation. Because of Clay's fierce denunciation of Jackson on the House floor after his vile incursion into Florida, the thought of serving in Jackson's administration was unthinkable.

He watched children in red woolen caps skating on the Potomac. Two crashed and fell, emphasizing his need for calm deliberation to protect his people -- even from themselves. He dismissed Crawford, the shaky Secretary of the Treasury, because of his ill health and his radical southern principles.

Perhaps there was wisdom in Houston's treacherous offer after the failed Caucus. Henry Clay must shunt his votes to a man who'd appoint him Secretary of State. That left John Quincy Adams, who currently held that post and realized it was the stairway to the White House. Above all, this nation needed a Clay Presidency. Adams could insure that for the future.

Returning to Washington in January 1825, Jackson declared on the Senate floor, "Having heard much talk about the Presidency being bargained and sold, I can but say I envy not the man who may climb into the Presidential chair in any other way, but by the free suffrage of the people."

Even as Jackson's naive words echoed in the Senate chamber, Clay conspired with House delegations from several states behind boardinghouse doors.

Moments after the Senate session adjourned James Buchanan of Pennsylvania braced Jackson on the icy street. Because of Buchanan's nervous tick in one eye when stressed, he kept winking at Old Hickory as he confided, "Clay's votes will go to Adams unless you declare your intention of dismissing Adams as Secretary of State."

Everything Jackson hated about this foul mess stood winking inanely before him. "Tell the gentleman I'll not sink to the gutter to rise to the Presidency."

On January 9, 1825 Henry Clay met John Quincy Adams at his lodgings in the evening. They parted certain Clay would swing his Presidential votes to Adams to be Secretary of State.

January 24th found Kentucky's delegation announcing for Adams with the Ohio delegation swinging in behind Clay's move to Adams.

When Jackson heard of these crucial defections, he fell down the Senate steps, suffering internal hemorrhages. Many said Clay's treachery would be the death of Old Hickory.

While Jackson lay bleeding to death both internally and politically, the House went into session at noon February 9, 1825 to choose the sixth President of the United States. Blustering raged throughout the afternoon in its freezing chamber.

Sam Houston got the floor and shouted, "The delegation from Kentucky has assigned itself to the asylum for the insane!

Easterner John Quincy Adams received not a single popular vote in Kentucky. The Kentucky Legislature sent explicit instructions to vote for western candidate Jackson -- and now they vote for Adams. Better we skin a live skunk here than suffer the far more noxious odor of this foul liaison!"

But New York jumped to Adams on the first ballot in spite of Van Buren's skillful opposition. Other Jackson desertions followed.

Having swung his support to Andrew Jackson when it became clear Clay was no longer a viable nominee, Thomas Hart Benton was aghast in the House Gallery as Missouri's lone vote was cast by John Scott for New Englander Adams. Benton bellowed, "Nine tenths of Missouri's people voted for Jackson!" Benton began to hemorrhage at the mouth.

Benton's bull roar rattled John Scott, who feared what would happen if Benton found out Adams had bought Missouri's vote by promising to keep Scott's brother in office.

From his bed, Andrew Jackson wrote John Overton:
"I weep for the liberty of my country. The rights of the people have been bartered for promises of office. The election is over and Mr. Adams prevailed on the first Ballot after the western states were bartered away by Clay."

Five days after being elected President, John Quincy Adams offered Henry Clay the cabinet office of Secretary of State. Though Clay knew he now risked assassination of his own Presidential aspirations since his vote swap was suspected by everyone, he accepted, telling himself, "In four years they will surely forget."

"... ruthless men have stolen the Presidency of this country with a corrupt bargain. Liberty has lost her way."   Andrew Jackson

CHAPTER 15

THE LOST ROAD   **MARCH 1825 - OCTOBER 1825**

When Andrew Jackson heard John Quincy Adams had appointed Henry Clay Secretary of State, he sat bolt upright in his Washington hotel deathbed. He raged, "The *Judas* of the West has received his 30 pieces of silver! His end will be the same. I'll see to that!"

Rachel Jackson smiled, making no effort to calm her beloved. She knew his fury would wrest him from the grip of the grim reaper as it had a decade ago in a Nashville hotel room upon news of the Fort Mims massacre. She abandoned her vigil and waddled to the hotel's clothes rack for her husband's pants.

Next day, Andrew Jackson assembled all the political allies his hotel room would hold. Thin and wobbly, he leaned on the table for support. "Friends, we have witnessed the theft of government! Blatantly scornful of the popular will, a small cabal of ruthless men have stolen the Presidency of this country with a corrupt bargain. Liberty has lost her way. I'm announcing for President of the United States of America in 1828. When elected I will root out corruption and create a new era of clean government. Are you with me?"

The room blowing up could not have brought louder shouts from Congressman Sam Houston, Senator Thomas Hart Benton and the others.

Rachel yanked the sitting room door ajar, holding her pipe behind her. She wanted to yell at the hooting, backslapping men to be quiet, but the joy in Andrew's face wouldn't let her.

As his final act as President of the United States, James Monroe signed Senator Thomas Hart Benton's Road Bill into law on March 3, 1825. It appropriated $10,000 for surveying and marking a wagon route along the Santa Fe Trail and

$20,000 for buying right-of-ways through tribal treaties. He rose from the desk he'd cherished for 8 years and walked into history -- proud of what he'd accomplished and brooding over what he hadn't.

Enraged at Missouri Congressman John Scott's role in the "corrupt bargain" roiling the newspapers, Thomas Hart Benton wrote Scott denouncing his vote for Adams and prophesying Scott would never hold office again. His anger exhausted, Benton penned a note to President Adams suggesting men to superintend the survey.

In mid-March embattled President John Quincy Adams appointed Pierre Menard, Lieutenant Governor of Illinois, Ben Reeves, former Lieutenant Governor of Missouri and George C. Sibley, once Fort Osage's Indian Factory Agent as Santa Fe Road Superintendents with Joseph Brown as Surveyor. Hoping to garner Senator Thomas Hart Benton's good will, Adams sent the powerful westerner a congratulatory note.

Chin deep in his financial swamp, the Santa Fe Road appointment came as a Godsend to Major George Sibley. His initial task was to hire 35 men for the field survey party. Many applicants had politicians pressure Sibley. Bravely, Sibley announced to the assembled job seekers, "We ah not lookin' foah gentlemen coffee drinkahs who cahnnot cook oah sahddle a hoase. Every man must be an expuht rifleman. In fact I do not see several men I considah vital to this entahprise -- and will now do some huntin' on my own."

Sibley invited Joe, Joel and Big John Walker to his Fountain Cottage. Except for their height and powerful builds, he would not have taken them for brothers. Joe was bearded, dark and swarthy. Big John blond and blue eyed with the face of a giant child. Joel's sandy hair was short, and he wore settlement clothes, looking tamer than his two brothers in buckskins.

Sibley seated the Walkers on his front porch. "Want to hiah you to suhvey the Santa Fe Trail. Pays $20 a month stahtin' at Franklin in July. Lotta men eagah to sign on. You willin'?"

The Walkers eyed each other then nodded.

"Anybody seen William S. Williams?"

Big John said, "Talked to two of Bill's *Osage* wives."

"What did they say?"

"Said they call him *Old* Bill Williams since he outfoxed the Blackfeet."

"Old? Man isn't foahty."

Joe Walker mused, "We're in our mid-20s, Major. Most Mountain Men never see 40."

"Please tell his wives I need to see *Old* Bill."

Joel muttered, "Tell 'im yourself, Major," pointing at the big gangly man in buckskins riding toward them with his elbows out. Drop reining his horse, Williams slid off and lumbered up the path in huge strides, kicking his legs outward.

The closer he drew, the redder his long hair and the deeper his pockmarks grew around his fierce blue eyes. "Looking for me, Big John?"

Big John thumbed at Sibley, "He is. This is my middle brother, Joe. You've met Joel." The Walkers shook hands around. Big John added, "Corn Woman says you are called *Old*. How old are you, Bill?"

"Be 38 June 3rd. What's on your mind, Major?"

"Need an interpretah and huntah foah my suhvey crew on the Santa Fe Trail stahtin' in July."

"What's it pay?"

"$20 puh month."

"When's the job over?"

"Only God and the Mexicans know. We need Mexican consent to suhvey pahst the Ahkansas Rivah."

"What about the tribes?" They'll resist a road across their lands."

"Negotiatin' treaties will be youah job."

Old Bill frowned. "Remember those five *Osages* tried in Little Rock for the murder of Major Welborn last fall?"

Major Sibley nodded.

"Only Bad Tempered Buffalo and Little Eagle got convicted. I interpreted at trial, then helped their lawyer prepare their appeals. Their lawyer's seeking a Presidential pardon. They have first call on me."

"I must know yoah price and intentions soon."

"Gonna pay the tribes for crossing their land? Job's over now if you won't."

"We will."

"See you Walkers Up The Mountain." Old Bill Williams took several short steps then leaped astride his horse. Heel-thumping it's flanks, he blurred into the road's dust.

Joe Walker declared, "There goes a man who knows exactly what he's doing."

Major Sibley nodded, "When he's sobah. Lived with the *Osages* foah ovah a decade. Likkah tuhns him from a civilized intellectual to a sahdistic sahvage -- some say a cahnnibal."

Flanked by Commissioners Ben Reeves and Thomas Mather, who'd replaced Pierre Menard, Major Sibley lead his Santa Fe survey expedition through the July 4th shooting and shouting in Franklin, Missouri. The three Walkers and Old Bill Williams joined them at serene Fort Osage for their epic march west. Old Bill Williams galloped off to palaver with the *Osages*.

Chaining went smoothly across Kansas Country's wood-less prairies. Surveyor Brown directed them to mark the Trail with dirt mounds. By the time they'd surveyed the 150 miles to the Neosho River, Old Bill Williams awaited them with the wildest *Osages* any of Sibley's party had ever seen.

Tilting and swaying aboard their fine steeds, the *Osages* tore in and out of camp in bright ceremonial adornments. They bristled with weaponry from ornate stone headed maces to feath-ered spears with jagged iron heads. These Red Cossacks of the plains, appeared more at home on a horse than their own feet.

Major Sibley handed Bill Williams a handwritten treaty.

Bill muttered, "Beside *Chief* being misspelled along with a few other words throughout, it's got a problem."

Sibley grated, "Indians cahnt read. What's wrong?"

"*Osages* want $300 parley money just to talk."

"Won't pay it. They could walk off with ouah money."

Old Bill showed big tan teeth. "See that war paint? If you want a spear through your belly, I'll tell 'em you won't pay parley money."

"The Walkahs can shoot a quatah at 100 yahds and a dollah at 300. Tell youah friends if they'll take the $300 pahley money and $500 right-of-way money in goods, we'll do it. Remembah Mistah Williams, I've traded with Indians foah 13 yeahs. These wahyahs came foah money and a good time, not woah."

As Old Bill argued with the *Osages* in their tongue, Major Sibley retired to his tent with a headache to write the $300 parley money in merchandise into Article 6th.

Next day all 16 Great and Little *Osage* Chiefs grunted their assent as their tribal names like Foolish Chief, Without Ears, Handsome Bird, Good Walker and White Hair were signed for them phonetically in *Osage* and duplicated in English by Old Bill on the Treaty allowing a road across their lands forever. Joseph R. Walker and William S. Williams signed as witnesses.

After the $500 in merchandise was distributed among the *Osage* Chiefs, Major Sibley called Big John Walker aside. "I undahstand you ah a sculptah with youah knife and tomahawk."

Big John grinned sheepishly, "Marm says so, but you might not."

"We ah shuly goin' to find out."

After describing the job, Major Sibley wrote in his day-book: "*I employed a young man of the party known to be remarkably expert in lettering with his knife and tomahawk, by name John Walker, commonly called in camp 'Big John,' in reference to his gigantic size, to memorialize this first grand treaty of our venture.*"

After seeing Big John's rendition, Major Sibley made the huge man blush. "You ah an ahtist as youah mothah said. Restoahs my faith in mankind to find that instruments fashioned foah muhduh can create such beauty."

Major Sibley finished his daybook: "*Big John executed the order very neatly and substantially incising a venerable white oak with the message 'Council Grove, Aug. 10, 1825'. Likely that will become the name for this notable place.*"

David Crockett slouched on his front stoop. Flies swarmed the peach cobbler he hadn't tasted.

Elizabeth put her hands on her hefty hips. "Colonel Alexander only beatchu by two votes, David. May seem like the end o' yer road, but it ain't."

"Member what I tole ever'body when they begged me to run for the U. S. Congress?"

"I do."

"What'd I say?"

"You said it was a step above your knowledge and you knowed nothin' about Congress matters. And I said that's the natural state of men runnin' fer Congress the first time -- and some runnin' fer re-election. If I counted our chickens the way them votes was tallied in the August election, we'd not have eggs with our bacon."

"I shoulda staid in the Tennessee Legislature. I don't belong up in Washington."

"You had a time of it in the Legislature, Davy! Member in '23 when you run agin Dr. Butler?"

David grunted, "Butler give the identical speech ever place we went."

Elizabeth cackled, "Never forgit his face the time you spoke first and give his speech word for word, leavin' him with nothin' to say. You whupped ole Doc Butler good, Davy."

"Feller cain't live on what he done."

"Yore gonna run agin Alexander in '27! This election he tole people they was gittin' $25 a hunderd fer their cotton cause o' his high tariff law. Kept sayin' his cotton price'd lift profits fer other Tennessee goods. You might as well have sung *Psalms* to a dead horse after that. But jist wait. Cotton prices will drop, and ole Colonel Alexander will go down with 'em."

"And it might start rainin' winnin' votes any minute. I'm goin' ba'r huntin' an' I don't know when I'll be back."

Elizabeth sobbed, "Sounds like a fine idee to me, Davy."

Surveying west from Council Grove, Major Sibley suffered more crippling headaches. One September dawn he lay in his tent his eyes clenched shut in pain.

Hearing the Major's groans as he passed the tent, Big John Walker fetched crystal spring water into Sibley's tent in a wooden bucket. Big John brimmed the Major's tin cup with the icy water. While Sibley sipped the soothing water, Big John soaked a towel in the bucket, then wrung it half-dry. "When we were little, Marm stopped our headaches like this." He laid the cool towel on the Major's hot forehead.

After several minutes Major Sibley moaned, "It's

wookin'. Tuhn around Big John."

"Why?"

"You ah no doubt the biggest Angel on ooth but youah wings don't show. I want you to cahve 'Big John's Spring' wheah you got this watah."

"I will, Major."

The following week, Old Bill brought the *Kanza* Indian Chiefs into camp smelling to the heavens. The first of two *Kanza* Chiefs to enter Sibley's Council tent was the oldest man he'd ever seen. Stooped, blind, sparse snowy hair with weals of wrinkles, the Chief said in a grinding voice, "*Je m'appele Vieil. Bon jour, mon ami,*" showing his two teeth. He offered a giant sunflower in his gnarled fist. "*Tournesol de mon coeur.*"

Sibley replied, "I speak no French, but youah flowah says moah than my woods evah could. Mistah Williams, will you find out from the young Chief how old this gentleman is."

Williams made the *question* sign holding his open right hand upward at shoulder height, rotating it on his wrist several times. He signed *how many* with his left hand palm down at a 45° angle across his chest, then starting with his left little finger, he folded each left finger down with his right hand. He finished with the *winter* sign by holding his fists a few inches apart in front of him and jiggling them as if shivering.

The young Chief answered in perfect English. "My great, great grandfather is 97."

Old Bill snapped, "Why didn't you say you spoke English?"

The Indian signed, "His winters are the only words of the Whites I know. All Whites ask about the old one's winters."

The *Kanza* Treaty was soon signed, and the survey party moved on to the Arkansas River, where Surveyor Brown said, "By my calculations we've reached 100° west longitude or in plain terms -- the border of Mexico."

Speaking with Commissioners Reeves and Mather after their buffalo hump dinner on October 1st, Sibley confided, "Diplomahtic inquahry foah puhmission to continue ouah suhvey into Mexico was made through ouah ambassadoah in Mexico City befoah we left Missourah. I expected someone heah to welcome us. We should mahch to Santa Fe and wrest

125

puhmission from the Mexicans."

Reeves grumbled, "The wind's cold with approaching winter and no approaching Mexicans. I'm going home."

Mather nodded. "Me too. Accost Santa Fe if you must Major, but as I see it, our grandiose road ends right here."

Next morning, Major Sibley galloped angrily into Mexico with Old Bill Williams and Big John Walker riding shotgun.

Commissioners Reeves and Mather commandeered the remaining Walkers and the other men. With provisions dismally low, the Commissioners urged the Walker brothers to hasten along the trail. But Surveyor Brown wanted them to tarry so he could recheck computations for the copious notes he'd soon dispatch to Washington. The Walkers simply kept their regular pace, using each afternoon to hunt.

While the Walkers were hunting, camp guards failed to hobble the horses and mules "because it was too early." But it was not too early for stampeding buffalo to scatter their stock. Returning after dark, the astounded Walkers, dumped two deer at the cook tent and spent the rest of the night rounding up four horses and one mule.

With their party afoot, they did not reach Council Grove until October 10th. Joe and Joel strayed to look at Big John's carving, wondering if their easygoing brother was all right. Their night hunt netted three rabbits and four grouse, a few bites each for 30 angry men.

Hunting on the plains, William Becknell rode up with two well provisioned pack mules. After the backslapping was over with his old pal Joe Walker, they agreed that Tom Mather, Becknell and both Walkers would ride back to Missouri to retrieve mounts and supplies, while the rest remained in camp.

On the way, Joe Walker asked his brother, "Notice anything wrong here, Joel?"

"Should I? I don't see anything."

"Neither do I. All those dirt mounds we made to mark the Santa Fe Trail have scattered to the winds."

CHAPTER 16

NEW BEGINNINGS   **FALL 1825 - FALL 1826**

After sending to Taos for mules, Major George Sibley's 13 man party trudged into Taos around the 1st of November 1825. Sibley wheezed, "Big John. Find my old pahtnah Paul Baillio. Tell him we need lodgin's."

Within the hour, Paul Baillio, looking like a grim, bearded child beside giant Big John Walker, joined Major Sibley at the edge of town.

"Thank you, Paul. We ah retuhnin' youah mules."

Old Bill Williams put his forefinger against the back of Baillio's head. "Pray for deliverance."

Turning quickly, Baillio shook hands with Old Bill.

Old Bill asked. "What's this I hear about the Mexican government stealing furs?"

On the way to his *hacienda*, Paul Baillio confided, "Time was when all you had to hide from in these mountains was *Apaches*. Now Governor *Narbona* takes bribes from Americans for trapping permits, then has his minions arrest 'em. If you have a trial, he'll overrule every *Alcalde* verdict in your favor."

"What's the answer?" Old Bill asked.

"Make a run for Missouri with your peltry."

After the *Osage* treaty, Abraham McClellan filed claims for himself, his son Mike, the three Walker brothers and the widow Annis Carrick amassing 1,500 prime acres of the Six Mile Country around Fort Osage. McClellan erected a blacksmith shop, a tavern and a distillery on his new parcels.

Shortly after Joel Walker returned from the stalled Santa Fe Trail survey, McClellan sat down with him outside the new smithy. Over hammer clangs and forge roars, the steely eyed McClellan barked, "Franklin's washed down the Missouri. Now that your firstborn has entered the Walker Clan, time's come for you to settle down and be somebody around here."

"You think land's better west of Fort Osage, Abe?"

McClellan replied, "Fine place for a new township about 15 miles west of the fort. Grand building sites on the bluff a-bove the Missouri."

It seemed to Joel Walker ever since he'd come to Mis-souri, he'd started buildings too late in the year, but he went ahead anyway. He and brother-in-law John Young cut timber for the first house on the town site Abe fancied. It didn't even have a name yet. Between rains, they really put their backs into their new buildings.

Infuriated by Mexican stalling on his Santa Fe survey, George Sibley's head hurt so fiercely on November 14, 1825 he saw a blue ring around Old Bill Williams. Major Sibley moaned, "What is on youah mind?"

Williams grated, "Mexicans have figured out that it's less work taking furs off Americans than beavers."

"So nahtchahally you want to get into the game."

"Better'n sitting around Taos turning to stone, Major!" Williams bellowed, knowing the Major's head couldn't take it.

"Official leave is granted until I recall you."

Old Bill's eyes narrowed, "*Soldados* drink with you by night and rob you by day! Just gimme time to get even, Major."

"Soldyahs follow theah oahdahs, suh. Shuhly you know the dangerous paht of a snake is its head."

"Seems to be yours too, Major."

Sibley's survey team disintegrated. Men slipped away daily till only Big John Walker remained, carving figurines of *padres*, crosses and *burros* and selling them in Taos. Boyish Benjamin Robinson begged to go trapping with Ewing Young. Sibley consented on November 27th, but the boy coughed him-self to death before clearing Taos.

Major Sibley felt the Catholic Mexicans would give his survey a rebirth in the spirit of the 1825 Christmas, but they didn't. He could no longer remember how many official letters he'd written or received about the Santa Fe Trail survey.

Rumors of Mexican patrols being ambushed to "liberate" American furs drifted into Taos, inflaming Mexican officials.

Around January 22, 1826, Ewing Young retreated to Taos with a stomach so tormented he couldn't straighten up. During Sibley's commiserations with Young over their illnesses, Old Bill Williams turned up in Taos on February 24th brimming with cash.

Sibley braced Old Bill in the *pueblo plaza*, "Wheah did you come by all that money, Mistah Williams?"

"Either got it trapping or trapping trapper trappers, Major. Difference lies only in the skinning. But now's the time for raising pluperfect hell." With that, Old Bill's leg-kicking gait seesawed him into a *cantina* infamous for gamblers who skinned trappers.

In the second week of March 1826, Sibley sidled into the smoky *Cantina del Jugar*. The Bill Williams he unearthed at a tilted table was a drunken wolf surrounded by foul smelling Mexican coyotes. "Mistah Williams, it is time to retuhn to the suhvice. Come with me now, suh."

Old Bill's red eyes rolled up into his head, then came back down wild. "You drag your pitiful little bureaucratic butt outa here, or your prim little missy won't be able to identify what's left o' you."

"You suh, ah fahd!"

Old Bill Williams exploded in riotous guffaws, joined by the coyotes around him. Soon everybody in the *cantina* laughed deafeningly. Impaled by a thrusting head pain, Sibley stumbled into the cold stormy night clutching his temples.

Needing supplies, money and Mary's comforting to continue his vigil, Sibley set out through the spring thaw with Ewing Young for Missouri with the ghastly laughter of the *cantina* echoing from every lofty crag. Each man had to learn what he feared most, and George Sibley had.

On August 29, 1826 Old Bill Williams and *Ceran St. Vrain* received a passport for themselves "*& their 35 servants*" from *Gobernador Antonio Narbona* "*to pass to the State of Sonora [Arizona] for private trade*" which did not include *"lingering to trap beavers."*

On the trail, Old Bill Williams conversed with the boyish 24 year old *St. Vrain* as they rode across the sweltering desert.

"You French?"

"Totally."

"Your Spanish was better than that official's."

"One tiptoes from *Français* to *Español* but it is a giant leap to English."

"Would it surprise you to learn we'll be trapping the *Apache* country north of the Gila?"

"French is not another word for *stupid* in any of the languages I speak."

Unable to tolerate *St. Vrain*, Bill Williams trapped alone. In September 1826 Old Bill was wading from the water with a 40 pound female beaver in a trap. Though in a torpor, she'd managed to avoid the usual drowning. Awakening, she buried her two yellow sabre teeth in his forearm startling a yell from Old Bill. He thrashed toward the bank for a rock to smash her brain, but found a band of glowering *Apaches* on feather-festooned ponies.

The Chief signed that Bill had no right to fish *Apache* streams or walk *Apache* land. He must pay with all his possessions.

Before Old Bill could sign back, the *Apaches* rode him down in the shallow water, freeing his beaver to swim away with his trap on her foreleg.

Snaring Bill's neck in a rope, they dragged him ashore fighting like a wet bobcat.

Holding a knife to his throat, they stripped him naked. The Chief pointed to the desert and signed for Bill to go back where he came from. Having never seen a man white as a fish's belly before, they snickered and pointed as he hobbled into the blistering desert with no more on than the day he was born.

"One cent reward will be paid to any person who will bring back the said boy [Christopher Carson]. *Missouri Intelligencer*

CHAPTER 17

POWER   **FALL 1826 - SUMMER 1827**

Old Bill Williams'd scavenged off the land for years in the mountains. But he'd never tried it stark naked without even a butcher knife. A fall wind stung him with blowing sand where he'd never been stung before.

Any other tribe would've killed him outright. But the *Apache* cherished the tortures the desert could inflict on a man with no food, water, clothing or weapons. The one thing they had not counted on was that William Sherley Williams was more of a savage than any *Apache* ever born.

Bill knew barrel cactus stored water. Yucca leaves'd weave into sandals once he'd bitten off their points for needles to use with thread stripped from their edges. He'd burrow under the sand like a lizard or find a cave by day. By night he'd hunt sidewinders and other night foragers with a yucca stalk sharpened to a spear with obsidian.

After licking the nasty beaver bite in his forearm clean like a wolf would, he began to trot. Trotting riled his blood, spurring him to run. Suddenly he was shouting -- his long red hair flying in the wind like a mustang's mane -- as he bounded across rocky ground that bit his feet.

When he could run no more, he lay panting on a warm slab of rock. Taos was about 200 miles northeast through the White Mountains. All he had to do now was avoid capture by the *Zuni* and cultivate a taste for raw rattlesnake, scorpion and Gila Monster.

Standing on the bluff overlooking the Missouri River, Abraham McClellan's blue eyes pierced Joel Walker. "Only way to be sure the government's fair to you, is to be the government."

"How you gonna do that?"

"Why you think I wanted you to build this first house in Independence? The 500 new settlers here see you as their founder. Lilburn Boggs and I are running for the Missouri Legislature this fall. Independence is young and strong. Got to have its own new county to grow like it should."

"We can't all run for the legislature, Abe."

"Course not! Government's got legislative, judicial and executive branches. You help get me and Boggs elected. We appoint you Judge and Joe the Sheriff."

Joel waved his arm at Independence. "Don't these people have anything to say about it?"

"Sure, they'll elect us. You'll see to that."

"Abe, you talk this over with Joe?"

"He's your brother."

Joel chuckled. "Ever since we could walk, Joe riled if I bossed 'im. Even told me not to boss him in the battle at Horseshoe Bend."

"Any man alive you'd rather see as Sheriff of your town than your brother?"

"Joe's way too kind to be sheriff."

"Better than some wild card we don't know. He's 6'4" and goes -- 220?"

"Probably 235 since he's filled out."

"Joe fight at Horseshoe Bend?"

"Like Samson slaying the thousand Philistines, but that was 12 years ago."

"With Franklin washed out and Fort Osage decommissioned, Independence will be the gateway to the West. Every drunken drover and hammer-fisted Mountain Man will want to knock this frontier town flat. We put Joe Walker in against the Philistines, he'll have to fight."

Becoming a Mexican citizen in 1824, made it easy for James Baird to get a license for distilling his famous Taos Lightning with partners Thomas L. Smith, Sam Chambers and a man named Stevens. Having served as interpreter for *Gobernador Narbona*, Baird reveled in his power over his old American friends.

On October 26, 1826 Baird unleashed that power in a letter to *Alejandro Ramirez, Comandante del Distrito El Paso,* writing: *"...not moved so much by personal interest as by the honor and general welfare of the nation...I have heartily joined, I must report that over the last year and a half small illegal groups have taken $100,000 worth of furs from New Mexico. I have learned that over a hundred Anglo-Americans plan to trap ... in New Mexico and Sonora [Arizona] along the Gila River. They ... are armed and arrogant. They have openly said that in spite of the Mexicans, they will hunt beaver wherever they please.... I ask that action be taken to enforce the law, so that we Mexicans can peacefully profit."*

Baird's letter incited the Mexican version of Spain's dreaded Inquisition against American trappers, but did Baird little good. He died in bed in El Paso. Mountain Men always said he drank more of his "rot gut panther fizz" than he sold.

Reaching the mesa country of the *Zuni*, Old Bill Williams wondered if he had a prayer of making it to Taos. Even with yucca sandals, his feet bled. Bushes had raked him bloody. Cholla cactus'd pincushioned his legs, leaving festering sores. He'd walked half-frozen almost entirely at night, but his fair skin still got sunburnt. His belly growled, and his cracked lips lusted for one good drink. Then things got worse.

He spied the *Zuni* warriors closing on him. He pitched his fragile spear in a bush, stripped away his primitive wraps and walked naked through the rough brush. When the *Zuni* were upon him, he tipped his head back, raised his arms to the weary fall sun and chanted his *Osage* Death Song.

The *Zuni* watched, letting Old Bill learn how to sweat through goose pimples. He danced a sacred *Osage* wolf ritual, expecting a tomahawk in his brain. Then came the shock. A blanket settled around his shoulders.

Old Bill clutched it, then accepted the tattered moccasins a *Zuni* elder held out to him. The elder signed that the *Zuni* had never before seen *the child of the desert*.

Astounded at the worshipful way the *Zuni* eyed him, Old Bill leaped on the paint horse they held for him. Seeing no chance of escape, he decided to ride to their village. His new feeling of being divine was almost worth dying for.

A winter of careful eating brought Ewing Young a healed spring stomach. Ewing watched silvery zephyrs dancing over the snowpacks of the majestic Sangre de Cristos above Taos. Around him bright wild flowers awakened in the sunny snow. He couldn't imagine a more magnificent place on earth.

He'd put out the word he needed Mountain Men and saw a short, stocky one in buckskins striding toward his cabin. The stoop-shouldered fellow with plastered down reddish hair, freckled face and pale blue eyes couldn't be over 17.

"You Mr. Young?"

Ewing nodded. "You looking for work?"

"Yup. I'm Christopher Carson. That there's a jawful. Most call me Kit."

They shook hands.

"Where you from, Kit?"

"Howard County, Missoura."

"C'mon in, Kit." Entering Ewing's warm cabin, they waited for their eyes to work in the dimness. "Have a seat."

Kit sat gawking at Ewing's book cases on three walls. "Never seed so many books."

"Like books?"

"Would if I could read."

"You one o' the Scotch-Irish Carsons that settled around Franklin township?"

"That'd be us."

"My people're Scotch-Irish too. Mine came to Tennessee from Virginia. I recollect Carsons in Tennessee from the Shenandoah Valley in Virginia."

"My Pa Lindsay landed in North Carolina, but married my Ma in Kentucky. We moved to Missoura and lived there through the war."

"You remember the war?"

"Not good. Too little. But one thing."

"What's that?"

"We forted up in Hempstead agin the Indians. They was seven widders innat fort. Any sentry found asleep had ta grind a peck o' corn by hand fer every widder."

"Folks still live in Howard County?"

"Fallin' tree limb killed Pa. Ma remarried an' bound me out to a saddler."

"Why'd you quit?"

"Saddler was a kind feller, but bond servantin' didn't suit my likin' so I left fer the mountains."

"They looking for you?"

Kit dug a ragged *Missouri Intelligencer* clipping from his possibles bag, handing it to Ewing. It read: " ... *Christopher Carson, a boy about sixteen years old, small of his age, but thick set, light hair, ran away from the subscriber ... to whom he had been bound to learn the saddler's trade, on or about the first day of September last. He is supposed to have made his way to the upper part of the state. All persons are notified not to harbor, support or subsist said boy under penalty of the law. One cent reward will be given to any person who will bring back the said boy. David Workman. Franklin, Oct. 6, 1826.*"

"Know what this says, Kit?"

"Been read to me a time er two, but I'm worth more'n one cent. Got a dollar a day fer drivin' a wagon to El Paso."

"Took sand to let me see that. Cook's only job I got left. My stomach can go wrong over nothing, so I'm crazy to turn a greenhorn loose on it."

"What's it pay?"

"Board and room."

"Want the job?"

"Reckon so. Will I git ta be a Mountain Man?"

"You will if my stomach doesn't give out first."

As 1827's spring grew short, Ewing Young's 40 man party trapped down the Gila to the Colorado where they met friendly *Yumas.*Trapper James Ohio Pattie wrote:"[*They are*] *the stoutest men, with the finest forms I ever saw, well proportioned ... straight as an arrow ... and as naked as Adam and Eve....*" After a brief rest Ewing's men swung north up the Colorado, trapping as they went.

The Colorado yielded many beaver, often 30 a night, until they entered *Mojave* country. Old tracks said a large party of Whites had come through there. Ewing knew his outfit was saddled with whatever happened between the *Mojaves* and the previous White outfit, because most Indians thought all Whites belonged to one tribe.

On a hunch, Young had his men build a cottonwood breastwork. Right after they forted up, a *Mojave* speared one of their grazing horses then died, shot by four trappers.

To show his might, the *Mojave* Chief launched an arrow arching a great distance to sprong in a cottonwood 50 yards from Ewing's barricade. Ewing raised Sweet Lips to his shoulder and snipped off the arrow, bringing gasps from his men.

The *Mojaves* slunk away, but Ewing knew they'd be back at dawn, so he had every man on the wall with rifles and pistols loaded and primed at 3 AM. As the stars died, 16 charging *Mojaves* did too, riddled by orange and yellow rifle fire.

Leaving the *Mojaves* where they fell, Ewing's outfit scurried up the Colorado on high alert for four days, posting guards in hidden vantage points and keeping the stock protected. Convinced the *Mojaves* had given up, Ewing let his guards rest.

The *Mojaves* attacked, killing two men, wounding two others and infuriating Young at them and himself. Ewing led 17 trappers thundering through cottonwood saplings on horseback after the *Mojaves*. Tomahawking four Indians to death, they hung their bodies in the trees to warn against more ambushes.

Ewing growled, "Let that be the last of this!"

But it wasn't. *Mojaves* brained three trappers scouting for beaver. Instead of hanging their bodies with no meaning, they roasted them in a show of great power that would bar them from the spirit world. As the *Mojaves* prepared to devour them, Young's men fired from the darkness but some *Mojaves* escaped. Speaking over the burial of his grisly trapper corpses, Ewing wanted to shout that revenge only spawns revenge, but he didn't.

David Crockett told wife Elizabeth, "You was right to goad me back inta this fight to go to Congress."

"Didn't have no choice. Losin's stuck in your craw fer

two years. Your boy John Wesley's gonna hold yer coat."

In the spring of 1827 David announced he was runnin' for the 9th U.S. Congressional District, then tried to live up to his Biblical namesake. But stead o' one *Goliath*, he faced two and another mere mortal like himself called Colonel Cook.

David's first *Goliath* was Colonel Adam Alexander who'd beat Crockett by two votes in 1825. The other *Goliath* was William Arnold, Tennessee's Western District Major General and Attorney General. David told 19 year old John Wesley, "Arnold's comin' after me with war work and law trick. What chance has a backwoodsman got agin them things?"

John Wesley said, "Election oughta be decided by a turkey shoot. Them speeches on what a feller kin do sounds good, but lead don't lie."

Early in the campaign David Crockett and Colonel Cook couldn't get invited to big doin's, so they "squared off in a mouse fight." Cook told whoppers about Crockett's "lack of decency," so Crockett told bigger lies about Cook. Cook brung witnesses to their biggest speech ready to prove Crockett was lyin'. John Wesley found out they was there and told his father, but David flung false charges agin Cook anyway.

His speech give, David headed for the wings, then halted. Eyein' Cook's witnesses, David quipped, "I know you folks been brung ta prove I tole lies bout Colonel Cook. If you'd asked me, I woulda admitted it and saved ya the trouble." While the crowd gasped, Crockett added, "But sure nuff, I got as much right to lie bout him as he does lyin' all this time bout me."

The crowd roared its approval of Crockett.

Colonel Cook folded and David's newspaper write-ups got him invited to the last big outdoor speech afore the election. David said, "In 1825, ever place I went, Colonel Alexander bragged bout cotton bein' $25 a hunderd cause o' his high tariff law. I said he jist as well take credit fer fat cattle, 14 shoats in a litter and Christmas. He beat me by two votes. Now cotton is *$6 a hunderd*. Tother feller Arnold's war record'd make a old maid yawn."

Spectators chortled, then muttered to each other durin' Congressman Alexander's talk that never mentioned Crockett, but attacked General Arnold. Polite applause follered.

General Arnold broadsided Alexander without mentionin' Crockett. A flock o' chatterin' guinea fowl landed. Arnold sent men to shoo 'em. Losin' his train o' thought, Arnold sat down.

Crockett leaped up yellin', "General, yer the first man sides myself who understands bird talk."

General Arnold shouted, "What foolishness is that?"

Crockett howled, "Since you didn't mention me in yer talk, them birds was cryin' *Crockett, Crockett, Crockett!*"

The audience shouted, "*Crockett, Crockett, Crockett,*"

General Arnold seemed powerful plagued.

Abraham McClellan and Lilburn Boggs barely had their bags unpacked for the spring 1827 session of the Missouri Legislature before lining up enough votes to lift Independence from sprawling Lafayette County and lay it in fresh new Jackson County "named for the man who should be in the White House."

After creating their fiefdom, McClellan and Boggs showed seasoned lawmakers how Scotch-Irish cronyism worked, appointing Joel Walker, Richard Fristoe and Henry Burris Justices of the Peace and Joseph R. Walker Sheriff of Jackson County. It was no coincidence that both Walkers and Fristoe had served under Jackson at the Battle of Horseshoe Bend. Bonds of battle and blood were not soon forgotten among White Savages.

On May 23, 1827, Major George Sibley invited Joe and Big John Walker to Fountain Cottage. Sibley looked haggard, but yelled, "Gentlemen, the Mexicans finally hahtched ouah egg! The suhvey cahn continue. Will you?"

Joe grated, "Big John and I'll sign on, but I have to tell you our marker mounds all the way to the Arkansas River blew away. With the surveyor's notes, we could pile rocks in their place."

"Mistah Brown's notes've been foahwadded to Washington. We'll pile rocks from the Ahkansas to Santa Fe, then remock the othahs on the way back -- if we have the money."

Joe saw how the survey'd addled Major Sibley. Leaving the first half unmarked -- to mark the last half? How would a newcomer find his way to the last half?

Big John felt sorry for Sibley too. "When do we leave?"

"Tomorrah befoah some fool figuahs a way to stall two moah yeahs!" Sibley's face reflected the desperation in his words.

Next day, his old survey team, salted with new faces, left Fountain Cottage, but Mary Sibley lay abed, too ill to wave.

Their caravan was two days out when Joel Walker overtook them on his lathered bay stallion. "Joe, you gotta go back," Joel panted.

"Why?"

"Remember when we named that town where I live?"

"Independence. What about it?"

"You're their new Sheriff."

"*What?*"

"Congratulations, Joe! Get your badge from Abe McClellan and tell 'im where you want your jail."

"Why not you, Joel?"

"I been made Judge."

Joe dug a cloth from his pack and rubbed the lather from Joel's chilling horse. "How about Big John for Sheriff?"

Joel got his horse rag from his saddlebag and helped Joe dry his stallion. "Came from the Legislature, Joe. *You* are the Sheriff of Jackson County."

Big John snorted, "I told the Major I'd go to Santa Fe with him, and I'm going. Joe, can you just abandon a fine man like him? He's a second father to us."

Joel nodded, "You're right, Big John. I'll work the survey to Santa Fe in Joe's place."

Big John muttered, "Thought you were the Judge, Joel."

"Judge without a courthouse. We all feel the same about the Major. I just sentenced myself to the Major's road gang!"

David Crockett confided to wife Elizabeth after his August 1827 election, "Me an John Wesley beat both them windbags -- who was too good to mention us -- by 2,748 votes! People don't want palaver. They want somebody ta roll up their sleeves an' clean house up there in Washington!"

"Aw Davy," Elizabeth shook her finger at him, "If'n that's what they wanted, they'da sent a woman!"

Old Bill Williams strode through Taos's summer heat in his *Zuni* Shaman's raiments without being recognized. Sauntering into his favorite gambling den, he pulled back a chair to sit in a card game. "You crazy? Gitta hell outa here," a flustered player yelled, shoving Bill away from the table.

Bill showed his big tan teeth."It's me! Old Bill Williams!"

One muttered, "Couldn't be! *St. Vrain* said *Apaches* killed Old Bill Williams."

"You idiots, I'm William S. Williams and I'm sittin' in this game. Now deal me a hand or I'll put a damn curse on you!"

Trapper Tom Smith huddled with *Señor Trujillo* and an *Alcalde Menor* in a *Trujillo Rancho* stable 12 miles north of Albuquerque."Why we be hidin' on your own ranch?" Smith asked.

"*Mi amigo* here says *mi casa* ees watched by hees own men for de goberment," *Trujillo* explained.

"Ees true," the *Alcalde* confirmed. "Thees James Baird has ruin de fur beezness for *Americanos*.

Irish Tom Smith grunted, "I ran a whiskey still with Baird. All he could ruin was a man's stomach."

The *Alcalde* shook his head. "Baird's letter got *Gobernador Narbona* fired and replace by thees madman -- *Don Manuel Armijo*. As we talk, *Jewing Jong's* furs *es en captura!*"

Smith put a calming hand on *Trujillo's* shoulder. "Ewing Young's a law abidin' man. Likely went in to talk it over, he did."

Trujillo snapped, "*Jong* heed hees skeens *en la casa de Don Louis Cabeza de Vaca in Peñablanca. En Junio*, many *soldados matan* -- killed -- *Don Luis* to get thees skeens. *Armijo* ees a keeler as de *Alcalde* say."

"Where might them skins be?"

"Seeting on *la Guardia* in Santa Fe. *Soldados* weel come for jour skeens. Jew most go queeck."

Ewing Young eyed the 29 bales of furs worth $20,000 drying in the Santa Fe plaza. Afternoon *siesta* time made a man connive. Hearing a noise behind him, Ewing turned to see 6'4" Milton Sublette slide off his buckskin horse with two pack mules behind him.

"Ewing you know which two o' them fur bales is mine?"

"One by the Armory and that one bear your brands."

Hobbled by his heel wound, handsome Milt Sublette seized the furthest bale, then lashed it on his mule's pack saddle.

"What the hell are you doing, Milt? Wanta get us shot?"

Sublette headed for his other bale with a small Mexican soldier jabbing the rusty bayonet on his musket at him. Sublette hoisted the bale as the soldier aimed his musket.

Realizing the fur bale would block a rifle bullet, let alone a load from a rusty old musket, grinning Milt Sublette kept the bale between him and the soldier, asking "*¿ Se habla Inglés?*"

"*Mas o menos.*"

"Then you know them ole muskets misfires. When it don't shoot, I'm gonna bust it over yer face."

The soldier's finger took the slack out of his trigger.

Ewing yelled, "Milt, a bale of furs isn't worth dying for."

Sublette's white teeth gleaming through his curly beard, he stalked toward the shaking soldier, "Pull that trigger, leave a widder. Step aside and spend *siesta en la cantina con su amor.*"

The soldier lowered his musket and ran into the barracks for help as Sublette lashed the second bale on the same mule. Seizing the mules' lead ropes, Sublette mounted his horse.

Ewing asked, "Why'd you bring two mules?"

Milton kicked his horse, charging into the Armory door's noise of running boots. "Thought it'd be worth a good mule to see how them *soldados* handle a Trappers' *Fandango.*" Milt released the unladen mule's lead rope, launching her to knock soldiers down like ten pins.

"What'll I do now, Sublette?"

"Ask one o' them Greeks you're always readin' about," Milt hollered as he dragged his loaded mule through the dust.

The officer of the guard charged Ewing Young, waving several squads of troops to surround the giant. They grappled him to the ground and bound him hand and foot. The furious officer spat, "Jew weel die for thees so beeg man!"

CHAPTER 18

SHERIFF JOE WALKER   **SUMMER - FALL 1827**

y the time Joe Walker reached Independence, he'd made up his mind to become Sheriff, depending on what Abraham McClellan had to say.

Joe found Abraham at his distillery in Fort Osage township. Having just fired his foreman for being soused, Abraham was still ruffled. "Sure you wanta talk about this Sheriff business today, Joe?"

"I do unless you can't."

Abe rubbed his face. "I can. Let's go outside, so I can cool off."

Joe followed him to a bench under a shade tree. Joe made the bench groan, while Abe paced, mopping his face with his handkerchief.

"Before you ask, you'll be the highest paid Sheriff in Missouri, right after the Sheriff of St. Louis County. Job won't take all your time at first, so you can earn some money on your own."

Joseph Rutherford Walker
by Alfred Jacob Miller

"Money's not my main concern."

"What is?"

"Who will I answer to?

"People of Jackson County and its three Judges, Fristoe, Burris and your brother Joel. That a problem?"

"What about you?"

"I'm to get a jail built for you, give you a badge and stand back."

Joe put his hand out.

"Whatta you want?"

"The badge."

"Where you want the jail?"

"Where you can get the best price on land and logs. Just don't make it big like Franklin's. Won't be many in it most o' the time."

"Won't be big, cause I only got $150 to build it. What're you gonna do when those big Trapper outfits and drunken drovers start tearing up the town?"

"Ask 'em to stop."

"Joe, you sure you want this badge?"

"Thought you were gonna stand back, Abe."

"I am. Take it."

Twenty-eight year old Joe Walker spent his first two weeks introducing himself as Sheriff to Jackson County's people and business owners while his jail was built. Joe nailed a board along the half built jail for posting wanted circulars on criminals, runaway slaves and indentured servants. One was for a young fellow named Carson who'd run away from a saddler in Franklin.

It was Joe's first chance to explore Independence. She was shaping into quite a boisterous lady. She lay on a high bluff overlooking the Missouri with a strong stand of log houses surrounding half a dozen stores, several warehouses and tippling taverns. Steamers bypassed Lexington and Franklin to tie-up at her wharves that still had the bark on. She'd come of age, though she was inexperienced. She was already the outfitter for Rocky Mountain fur traders, Santa Fe traders and Indians who hated White settlements too much to venture east of her.

The greasy, bathless men of the pack trains returning from the mountains would stop to the west of her and make the welkin ring with rifle fire to let the merchants and shippers know they were coming and get ready. Once in town with their spavin legged mules and old wagons with rawhide wrapped spokes, these savage men prowled her streets and taverns whooping and shooting into the air, giving her high carnival whether she wanted it or not.

Joe Walker would step out of the shadows, a brawny smiling giant with his hand out to shake theirs. He said much the same to all, "Friends, Independence's glad to have you. Want you to have a good time, eat plenty and enjoy being in business with us."

After Joe's hand-crumpling handshake, most would ask, "Who might you be?"

"I'm the Sheriff, and I need your help."

"What?"

"Gunfire in town makes our babies cry. I know you don't want that."

"Plumb right about that. That all?"

"I'm asking you to treat this town just like she's your mother."

Most were stumped and said something like, "Not used to Sheriffs askin' fer anythin', but glad to oblige."

Joe Walker didn't meet the man, however wild or sodden in galore of drink, who wanted to make babies cry or to rough up their mother.

Businessmen were astounded how well Joe Walker handled their customers and townsfolk. Samuel C. Owens, who was both the first clerk of the Circuit Court and a trader in partnership with John Aull, opined that it was Joe's commanding presence. A historian of Jackson County chronicled, "[*Sheriff Joe Walker] was never a braggart, soft spoken, yet capable of maintaining discipline.*"

Joe told Judge Fristoe, "Treat a man well and don't humiliate him, he'll be your friend."

Keeping order at trials was itself a trying task. Most of the participants had hide-out guns or knives, and the spectators came to see a circus -- or create one.

When a political adversary of Thomas Hart Benton sued for slander because the Senator'd said he "was *no better* than a sheep killing cur dog," Benton testified that truth was a complete defense and he could have said the fellow was "*worse* than a sheep killing cur dog" and still have been within his rights.

Benton's defense lawyer, the renowned orator Waldo Johnson, waxed poetic about Senator Benton's standing as a bulwark of liberty for free speech, freedom of the press and the Manifest Destiny of America, inciting a tipsy spectator to rise and beller, "Go to it, my little Johnson! Rise and shine honey! Live in the milk and die in the cream!"

The Judge's rulings in another trial provoked a burly bystander to challenge the Court shouting, "Hell's afloat and the river's risin'. I'm the yaller flower o' the forest -- a flash and a half o' lightning -- a perfect thunder gust! You wants to fight?"

The Sheriff simply pointed to the man, then the door, and the man left before the Judge could decide if he was in contempt.

Sheriff Walker's regular jail client was Joe O'Connor who fished in the horse troughs and sang to the moon when he was drunk. Walker liked the drunken O'Connor, but the man made his life hell. O'Connor regularly infested the small jail, where Joe Walker usually slept, with fleas. Then Sheriff Walker would have to drive sheep through his jail so O'Connor's fleas would jump on them. It got so, Sheriff Walker would soak O'Connor in a horse trough to get the fleas off, then just leave him there to sober up.

The few arrests Joe made in his first term were for assaults or riotous drunkenness. Though Jackson County hosted the most barbaric men on the frontier, it had not a single killing. Even with arrests, Joe had his own methods.

On a humid summer evening, half a dozen young sons of good Scotch-Irish families sold ten gallons of whiskey to a dozen *Osages*, then proceeded to outdrink them. By midnight all were snot-flying drunk, and a brawl erupted in the grove where they were spilling more whiskey than they drank.

Joe thundered up to the lodge of Owl, an *Osage* Chief, east of Independence. "*Wah-lo-gah!*" he yelled in the darkness. "Need you to prevent a Indian war. Hightail it to the grove by Independence!"

Then Joe galloped to the grove and thundered his 17 hand, bull-chested bay stallion through the melee. Once the flying bodies landed, Joe bellered, "White Savages line up in the crick and Red Savages on the bank!"

The scion of a prominent family turned to bludgeon Joe

Walker's snorting stallion with a whiskey jug, but his cohort yanked him into the brook, mumbling, "Paulie, Joe Walker'll rip your head off and feed it to the hogs."

Half-dressed, Owl galloped his chestnut mare into the grove and began shouting in *Osage*. He demanded that his *Osages* poison the fish with the rest of their whiskey -- save for one jug which Owl would keep in case of snakebite. Capturing his jug, Owl told the *Osages* to go to their lodges or get locked up in the White Jail. The Indians straggled from the grove. *Wah-lo-gah* herded them toward their village, cursing them imaginatively in their native tongue.

Walker yelled to his White Savages, "Drop your trousers and wade ashore! You're going to march to Independence with your pants around your ankles singing *Rock of Ages*. Those too drunk to sing every verse will sleep it off in jail. *Let's go!!*"

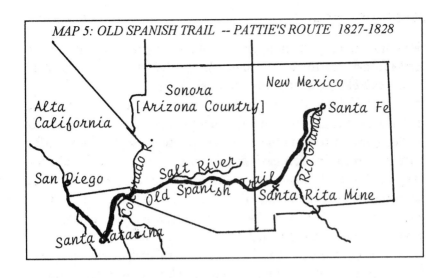

New Mexico

Sonora
[Arizona Country]

Alta
California

San Diego

Santa Fe

Salt River

Old Spanish Trail

Rio Grande

Colorado R.

Santa Rita Mine

Santa Catarina

CHAPTER 19

THE OLD SPANISH TRAIL   FALL 1827 - SPRING 1828

As the result of Ewing Young's "*open defiance*" and "*assistance of his fellow citizen the bandito Soblet in the robbery committed by the latter of a load of beaver skins*," "*Ewing Joon*" was literally thrown into the same filthy Santa Fe jail cell Joe Walker'd languished in seven years before. Though Mexican troops searched northern New Mexico, no trace of Milton Sublette or his "stolen" peltry was ever found.

Though "*Ewing Joon*" showed his license to trap beaver in New Mexico at his trial, he was convicted instantly of "disobeying *el Jefe Politico del Distrito*" and "robbery of beaver skins."

After months of wrangling, Governor *Armijo* decided to confiscate Ewing Young's $20,000 in beaver in lieu of his long jail sentence -- some of which he'd served while getting officially robbed of his peltry. Ewing was thrust from prison penniless and shaking his head. Justice was as hard to find in New Mexico -- as Milton Sublette.

Seeking shelter in a Santa Fe Inn where he'd stayed before, Ewing was arguing to pay for his lodging next week, when James Ohio Pattie, a muscular young trapper who'd served under Ewing earlier in the year, entered the Inn. Overhearing the dispute, Pattie handed Ewing the money, whispering, "After you get the bath you need so desperately, I must speak with you about my father's tragedy."

While smashing the insect feasting under his tattered pants, Ewing said, "Let's talk at supper here tonight."

Pattie agreed and rented his own quarters at the Inn.

After scrubbing in mescal-laced cold water to kill his vermin, Ewing met James Ohio Pattie in the Inn's chilly dining room. During dinner, Ewing mentioned being imprisoned and fined $20,000 for watching Milt Sublette steal his own furs, but he could see the 23 year old Pattie had to talk or explode. "What about your father, James."

"He's Sylvester Pattie. He's been leasing the Santa Rita Copper mines 60 miles southwest of here. His copper flakes were so pure most could be hammered into metal without smelting. He and his miners dug like badgers in that desert. He befriended a grizzled *viejo* called only *Señor,* who'd fled Vera Cruz after an *Alcalde's* murder, and said he had been *padre y profesor* before sinking to the *pico y pala* in the Santa Rita mines. *Señor* became his foreman."

"I don't mean to interrupt, but is your father hurt?"

"Not the way you'd expect in a mine. Let me explain."

"Of Course," Ewing agreed motioning to the waiter for *mas café.*

"*Señor* entranced my father with the tale of how *Juan María de Rivera* blazed the Old Spanish Trail along the San Juan River and across the Uncompagre Plateau to the Grand [Colorado] River basin and finally to California in 1765. *Señor* said Spanish friars, *Fra Francisco Anastasio Domínguez* and *Fra Silvester Valez Escalante* traversed the Old Spanish Trail again in 1776 from Santa Fe to California by a route so obscure most could only imagine it -- but they made it for they returned with objects fashioned from seashells."

"Did *Señor* talk your father to death?"

"In a manner of speaking."

"So tell me what happened."

"Precisely what I'm doing."

"My father became obsessed by the lure of the Old Spanish Trail the way a man craves a lost love -- or worse -- an enchanting love that never was. Meanwhile, father and his crew worked feverishly, piling up $30,000, exhausting the mine's tools and supplies. While I was trapping with you, he sent *Señor* to Santa Fe with his $30,000 to buy tools and supplies to return in a fortnight."

"So you're here in Santa Fe pursuing a thief."

"Exactly. Without working capital, supplies or tools, father's copper mine operation collapsed. Armed with a vague description of an anonymous swindler I sit here without a prayer of apprehending him."

"What can I do, James?"

"I'm certain *Señor* never came to Santa Fe. Unless I can console my father with clues to finding the Old Spanish Trail to California, I'm afraid the news that he's financially hamstrung will kill him."

"The Old Spanish Trail is less of a myth than the Seven Cities of Gold that drove the *Conquistadores* mad. Surely he will trap beaver while trying to cut this trail that's lain cold for half a century."

"Trapping's my father's only chance to regain his fortune and resurrect his self respect."

"Then we must lay out a trail that will enable the trapping of real beaver to leaven the myths."

In Ewing's icy room, they sketched a map of the few known segments of the Old Spanish Trail, leaving blank vast stretches where putting the pen to the paper would have been criminal. Near dawn, Ewing said, "We can do no more, James. I'll send you money for my room if you'll tell me where."

"Don't bother. I'll be off prowling the Old Spanish Trail with my father."

"Its lure is infectious, James -- like the meal you can never eat and the wine you can never drink. Fear I'll be forced to grope for it myself -- one day."

Obtaining a *guía* for hunting in Mexican territory, 45 year old Sylvester Pattie and his son James recruited 26 trappers in Santa Fe without revealing their obsession to unveil the Old Spanish Trail. As fate would have it, their party split at the mouth of the Gila where 20 men shunted off to the Colorado under Englishman William Workman.

Silversmith Nathaniel Pryor, Richard Laughlin, Jesse Ferguson, William Pope, Isaac Slover and Edmund Russell sided with the Patties. Their small band ventured west into the land of the *Yumas*, who'd become hostile to Whites since James Ohio'd seen them in the spring.

Skirting trouble, Sylvester camped miles from the *Yuma* village. A thunderstorm struck in the darkness, lashing them with winds and rains. *Yumas* crawled among the stock cutting tethers, then stampeded their horses.

When skies cleared, Sylvester's trappers were afoot and desperate. They set about hollowing out cottonwood logs for one-man canoes. As they chopped, Sylvester Pattie, secretly hoping to capture *Señor* with his money, said, "Gentlemen, this be the time to find the Old Spanish Trail to California."

Isaac Slover grated, "Doesn't sound any more far fetched than what we've tried so far."

The others grumbled acceptance, and soon set off down the muddy, raging Colorado River in cottonwood canoes laden with furs, traps and troubled men.

Tennessee's Governor Billy Carroll could not succeed himself, so Sam Houston agreed in 1827's spring to be a one term candidate for Governor so Billy could succeed him. Jackson protégé, James K. Polk, agreed to take Houston's place in the U.S. House of Representatives should Houston be elected.

Sam Houston campaigned fiercely through the sultry summer, appearing at log rollings, barbecues, horse races, camp meetings and fashionable ladies' boarding schools.

His named opponent was Newt Cannon, but his real adversary was his former Commandant of the old 39th, Colonel John Williams. Williams, who sought the State Senate, had reviled Sam for years. Cannon and Williams smeared Houston as a cocksure canebrake jackadandy no respectable woman would have anything to do with -- asking snidely, "Why's Houston still unmarried at 34?"

Needing to be seen with eligible young women, Sam courted South Carolina debutante Julia Ann Connor. Julia had heard Sam Houston was "God-like" and "Herculean." But after their meeting, she scrawled, "*[I] could not discern that superiority ... which has gained him such universal popularity. ...Unfortunately, too many people take his flattery at face value ... & seldom question it.*"

Though Miss Connor declined further engagements, Sam pretended she was indisposed on election day, personally appearing at all Nashville's polling places on a stately dapple gray.

Dressed to impress, Sam greeted voters in his bell-crowned black beaver hat, his ruffled shirt set off by a black satin vest and black trousers snug to the ankles. It angered Houston that his Horseshoe Bend thigh wound still drained, requiring a bandage to keep its pus from staining his fine pants. He sported a spectacular Indian hunting shirt caped around his shoulders in place of a coat. His black shoes had burnished silver buckles.

For all Houston's elegance, Newt Cannon still received 44% of the vote. Even as Sam gave his flamboyant Inaugural Address as Tennessee Governor on October 1, 1827, he wondered how to find that elegant first lady everybody hounded him about. When would she ride at his side down his road to glory?

The leaping canoe ride down the Colorado did not end in California as Sylvester Pattie'd prayed. The Old Spanish Trail was elusive. What kept Sylvester going in the shimmering desert wilderness was his hope he'd catch *Señor* with his $30,000.

When Sylvester was sure they'd die in a desolate wasteland, the river fanned into a marsh laced by beaver dams. They began taking 30 to 60 skins a night. Perhaps he'd recover his fortune even if he couldn't catch his faithless *Señor*.

James Ohio Pattie pointed to two *Yuma* bowmen stashed in lofty cottonwoods primed to kill them when they drifted underneath. Everyone checked rifle loads and powder pans as the canoes drifted into danger. Sylvester yelled, "Isaac and I'll take the tree vipers. Watch the river banks. Spend your lead wisely."

Sylvester and Slover shot the treed *Yumas,* who crackled through tree branches to thump to the ground like dead turkeys. Then they paddled like madmen, but no more *Yumas* attacked.

Instead of *Yumas* they next saw small Indians dashing from the Colorado River. Hoping to replenish their food, they paddled ashore. James Ohio Pattie knelt, motioning for the Indians to come back. Finally they did, then mistook the trapper request for food to be for their favorite delicacy, roast dog.

Pointing to themselves, they said, *"Cocopa."* Though shorter than *Yumas,* they were well proportioned and unused to clothing. They kept motioning for the trappers' clothes to be taken off. James Ohio Pattie wrote, *"[Our night] passed pleasantly in the village to the satisfaction of all parties."*

Met by a wondrous morning, Sylvester bought squash and fresh water with bullets that silversmith Pryor rolled into pointed sticks to mark with. By Sylvester's calculations, it was New Years Day, so he showed the Chief how to write "January 1, 1828" on a rock with one of the lead sticks. The Chief fled the marked rock on the beach like it was a devil and made his people bury their pointed lead sticks.

Drifting south on the Colorado's lazy current, the trappers found angry Indians screaming, *"Pipi,"* from the shore. They shot cane arrows with six foot bows. Some Arrows stuck in their cottonwood log canoes. Most missed altogether.

Several trappers fired, flattening the flimsy fish-drying table near the water. The *Pipi* fled, kicking sand behind them. James Ohio Pattie examined an arrow stuck in his fur bale. A hardwood stick tipped by flint had been shoved into the hollow cane shaft and fletched with what appeared to be gull feathers. He yelled excitedly, "California and the Pacific cannot be far!"

Eighty miles below the Gila River's junction with the Colorado on the 18th of January, the boaters smashed into the [Gulf of California] tide bore racing north up the river. Swamped, they floundered ashore. They flipped their boats and dried their wet furs in the sun's lonely desert splendor.

When the Colorado's tide swelling departed, they relaunched their canoes, hugging the bank to duck the next tidal surge. Learning tidal rhythms, they dodged enormous upsurges for over a week drifting south. Then on January 28th murderous savages on either shore forced them midstream to face a tumultuous tide they could not abide without capsizing. They paddled downstream smashing their blunt prows through huge billows flooding them gunnel deep in the Colorado. Paddling furiously, they reached an empty bank.

On February 16th they buried their furs some distance from the Colorado and headed west on foot for California.

Carrying two blankets and packs laden with dried beaver meat, they made good headway till reaching an Indian settlement near a salty lake. One Indian fugitive from Santa Catarina Mission spoke Spanish. Naked Indians were fascinated by the trappers' red shirts. Indian women bribed men to remove their prized shirts. Hungry trappers tore several shirts in strips, trading them for dried fish. Intoxicated by the crimson bands, Indian women fastened them around their arms, legs, and heads. James Ohio Pattie's journal celebrated it as *The Red Shirt Festival.*

Two Indians led Sylvester Pattie's party west, but the glaring heat of the desert sand brought Sylvester to his knees. Isaac Slover slumped down to die with him. Son James found a stream, where he and others dumped their powder, rushing back with horns of water to revive their black-lipped compatriots.

Once the trappers reached the Santa Catarina Mission, they were treated like spies by clerics and civil authorities. Marched by stages through other missions along *El Camino Real*, they landed at San Diego in early April 1828. James Ohio Pattie's journal complained of being given *"measles"* by *"ingenious lancets of legions of Spanish fleas."*

Hauled before *Gobernador José María Echeandia,* the trappers were stunned by the man's fury. Only Sylvester could understand his rapid-fire Spanish.

Sylvester said, "He's infuriated by recent dealings with one Jedediah Smith, whom he calls a faithless liar. He says we're spies, worse than thieves and murderers." Before them, *Echeandia* ripped up their passports, flinging the pieces at them. He ordered them stripped of possessions and thrown into cells.

James Ohio Pattie wrote, "*My prison is a cell eight or ten feet square, with walls and floor of stone. A door with iron bars an inch square crossed over each other ... grated on its iron hinges....On the front of this prison is inscribed ...*

Destinación de la Cautivo."

Religious Mexican Sergeant *Pico* and his pretty sister encouraged James Ohio to trust in God. One night *Pico* smuggled James to the iron door of his father Sylvester's cell.

Reeling from the stench, he whispered, "It's James Ohio. Are you all right?"

Sylvester gasped, "I'm still suffering from my desert collapse. I cannot survive in this dungeon."

"Be strong, father. I'll get us out of here."

Sylvester knew his son's fingers were through the grating, but his fumbling hand could not find them. He slipped down the door to the cold stone. Though awake, he couldn't move.

It dawned on Sylvester that *Señor* had worked the mines as a convict, aching for freedom, just as Sylvester now ached to flee the horrors of this place. Having tasted desperation's very essence, he wanted to forgive *Señor*. But he was too confused.

His agony was replaced by a numbing calm at first light, Sylvester yearned to wish his son -- whom he now thought of as a small boy -- farewell. Having no ink, he bit through his lip, scratching in blood on a shard of his passport, "*I am very ill -- without hope of recovery.*" Before he could write *Good-bye*, the note fell from his fingers. Sylvester Pattie of Kentucky lay dead with a cockroach walking across his open eye.

At sunrise on April 24, 1828, Sergeant *Pico* handed James Ohio his father's note in blood. "*Su padre es muerto.*"

Sergeant *Pico's* sister brought James Ohio a black suit to wear to the funeral. Six soldiers escorted father and son to the burial. Tears flooded James Ohio's face as they dumped his father in rags into the shallow grave. He rasped, "I shall soon be with you in the ground, beloved father. The Old Spanish Trail is the road to hell."

"The sole difference between a political and a military campaign is gunfire."   Andrew Jackson

 **CHAPTER 20**

THE COST OF VICTORY   **SUMMER - WINTER 1828**

With balloting for President commencing in September in some states, Andrew Jackson held a midsummer strategy session of his Nashville Central Committee in the Hermitage library. Still wearing black in mourning over the June 1st death of his adopted Creek son *Lyncoya* from tuberculosis, Jackson cautioned, "Lyncoya's death has dear Rachel bedridden. He was but a lad of 16."

Rising to his feet in the library where the leather-bound wisdom of the ages adorned the walls, Tennessee Governor Sam Houston said, "General, every man here feels Mrs. Jackson's unendurable loss. We know how delicate her health is, and how sensitive that dear lady is to life's vicissitudes. Please convey our wishes for God's comfort in her recovery."

John Overton, Hugh Lawson White, William B. Lewis, John H. Eaton, Felix Grundy and G.W. Campbell seated at the library table each nodded, said "Aye," then looked left in turn as they would voting on a measure.

Few men appreciated formal niceties like Andrew Jackson. He rose and rasped, "Thank you for recognizing Rachel's grief, for she is surely the most softhearted woman alive. Now we must assess our efforts to expel those alley cats from the White House! The sole difference between a political and a military campaign is gunfire. Organization must be at the core of each, or failure's certain to follow."

John Eaton effervesced, "Our organized frolics punctuate summer. *Hurra Boys* are holding parades, barbecues, dinners, street rallies and hog calling contests. They're affixing hickory sticks, brooms and canes on steeples, steamboats and signposts.

Old Hickory tree plantings follow many church services."

"Fine, John. Americans appreciate wholesome reminders. Let's retrace our steps to see if we missed anything before we target objectives for our final assaults." Jackson said.

Judge John Overton slid notes from a leather case. "I've chronicled key events to date. The first was the most important -- getting the sitting Vice President John C. Calhoun to rally to our side against his own President in October 1825."

Jackson said, "A fine Vice President Calhoun will make for our administration!"

After the polite applause, Judge Overton added, "General Jackson's resignation from the U.S. Senate on October 12, 1825 showed everyone he was committed to the Presidency."

"Early formation of the new Democratic Party was equally important," G.W. Campbell interjected.

Judge Overton smiled tightly, "Agreed, but the new party didn't coalesce until December of '25."

"A high point for me was Henry Clay's duel with Senator John Randolph of Virginia before Christmas '25," General Jackson opined.

"I don't have that in my notes, General. What's the importance?" Judge Overton asked.

"Proved Henry Clay can't shoot any straighter than he talks! Men don't walk away from a duel with Andrew Jackson with a hole in their coat! Frontier people put more stock in shooting a pistol than flowery talk!"

Governor Houston chimed in, "We must forgive Senator Randolph's miss. He's not from Tennessee where men hit what they shoot at!"

General Jackson groaned, "I still carry the bullets of Charles Dickinson and Jesse Benton as proof of that!"

Judge Overton persevered, "Our most notable victory was handed to us by Adams himself in his December 6, 1825 State of the Union message when he invited Congress to 'disregard the will of the people and do what needs to be done'."

Hugh Lawson White pushed back from the table, "How could Adams have better framed the great contest between the Adams aristocrats that tell the people what to do, and the Jackson Democrats who ask them?"

"That colossal blunder's got to be what swung Martin Van Buren and the southern Radicals in behind us after the Adams speech," Felix Grundy agreed.

General Jackson mused, "The Little Magician [Van Buren] gave us a harp we had best strum loudly in our finale -- that Adams' one party system spawned the 1824 theft of the election -- and that a two party system is our only salvation."

G.W. Campbell opined nasally, "The *Two Party* battle cry's likely why our fledgling party perfected a majority in both houses of Congress in 1827 -- only time in history a new party's done that in its first election!"

Judge Overton resumed his recitation. "While Jacksonian Democrats held the high moral ground, condemning flaunting of the electorate's will, never before in the history of this land has an opposing political party dipped so deeply into the sewer for its smear campaign. Maliciously attacking General Jackson's relationship with Rachel as adulterous and his marriage as bigamous is the basest of libels and slanders!"

Jackson leaped to his feet, flaming, "Understand this, gentlemen. *Lyncoya's* death may have been sent by the Almighty to distract dear Rachel from the horrors of this campaign. No one must ever mention these filthy lies to Rachel, for they would surely maim this most virtuous of females. For similar defamations I sent Charles Dickinson to the devil's domain. I have married Rachel twice, removing all doubt of legality or holiness of our wedlock before God and man. Whatever this Committee says about such filth shall be kept from her at all costs."

Sam Houston rushed to Jackson. "Pray calm yourself, General. I will shoot the next villain dead who repeats such a foul lie."

Judge Overton stood. "You must both take charge of yourselves. Governor, shooting someone over slanders only gets them restated in the newspapers. We have rebutted them with facts in our counter-pamphlets. The way to fight an old lie is to let it die. Please sit down before you have a stroke, Andy."

"I want this understood. When the *Cincinnati Gazette* or other venomous rag might reach Nashville bearing such vile trash, all copies shall be bought and burned before dear Rachel sees them, if I have to sell the Hermitage to finance those fires."

Abraham McClellan invited Judge Joel Walker and Sheriff Joe Walker to his distillery to discuss the upcoming summer elections. He poured each a sample of the belly burn he was making. Both declined.

Joe Walker said, "I read in the St. Louie paper the yearly per capita consumption of liquor in Missouri is 5 gallons."

Abe nodded, "Business couldn't be better."

"That's just it, Abe, it shouldn't be better," Joe snapped. "The women, children, slaves and preachers aren't swilling liquor. That means men are guzzling 20 gallons apiece. It's not just riffraff, Mountain Men or pig herders. I see lawyers, store-keepers, drummers, clerks and undertakers so drunk every day they don't know if they're afoot or horseback. Drunken Judges fall off the bench."

"Not me," Joel shot.

"Not you, but where does it stop, Abe?"

"Never, Sheriff. Don't so much as think of making Jackson a dry County! That's why you're a Sheriff instead of stimulating commerce to keep this County from a depression!"

"Dollars don't mean decency, Abe! Do you care about the women and children who are beaten by these men you get drunk?"

"Sheriff Walker, with God as my witness, "I don't get anybody drunk! I make a product for pleasure. I can't help it if some people have too much fun."

Joel said, "Joe, look at this logically. White men do the drinking. White men do the voting. You don't have the chance of a chicken in a frying pan that they'll vote themselves sober."

Abe argued, "Before you go off half-cocked, Joe, you gotta realize booze rules the whole country."

"Well I'll campaign on something I believe in."

"What do you believe in, Joe?"

"Decency."

"What's wrong with decency, Abe?" Joel asked.

"Absolutely nothing -- if he don't try to turn us all into preachers. There's such a thing as moderation, isn't there Joe? If I'm not mistaken, you've even owned some interest in a distillery or two."

"And children grow out of wetting their beds!" Joe snarled. "I'm in the horse business now because they don't get drunk, they don't turn on us and they don't lie about everything."

"I've heard about your fine horses, Joe. If they're not too good to pull our beer wagons, we could use some -- and we wouldn't mind you getting them shod at our smithy."

"I never mix horses with morality, Mr. McClellan!" Joe stalked from the distillery, leaving the other two members of his clan gaping.

"You better get hold of him, Joel. This Sheriff job's gone to his head."

Joel said, "No Abe, it's gone to his heart. And as I told you before -- Joe Walker can't be bossed."

"Being big hearted doesn't make him a shoo-in in his election. People want a two fisted Sheriff, who'll belly up to the bar with them."

"Abe, Joe Walker could beat Christ and the Devil for Sheriff on successive Sundays."

"We'll see about that, Joel. By the way, you're running for re-election too!"

"Like you are, Abe. And like you, I'm going to keep my head and not shoot my clansman under the kilt."

"No shooting, but spanking may be on tap."

On election day, Abraham McClellan doled out distillery samples, garnering 42 of the 43 votes for the State Legislature in his home township of Osage. But an equally ambitious tavern keeper beat Abe two to one in Independence, allowing Abe to win countywide by one lonely vote.

Having campaigned for decency to family and neighbors, Joe Walker was re-elected Sheriff by 150 of the 179 votes cast.

Since Jackson County's polling place was on Judge Joel Walker's farm where voters cast ballots by stating their name and votes to a clerk, Joel's landslide was not overly surprising.

Sam Houston, Robert Allen and his brother John had served together as officers under General Jackson during the war. Robert and Sam spent two terms in the U.S. Congress together before Sam's rise to Governor of Tennessee.

While Sam and Robert sought government office after

the war, John Allen'd become a plantation potentate in a mansion crowning the bluffs above the Cumberland River, at Gallatin, 20 miles from Nashville. All revering horse races, Sam, Robert and renowned horse breeder John often attended together.

Sam remembered the first time he'd seen John's oldest daughter Eliza humbling a fiery stallion with her quirt when she was a slender blonde of 14 in 1824. Eliza's horse skills and "vicious charm" kept her in the back of his mind as Eliza rounded into a stunning young woman. The Allen fortune made Eliza no less alluring.

As balloting began in Jackson's election, Sam Houston joined John Allen at his estate to show Sam's importance in the national election and to test John's future plans for Eliza. They walked to a white-fenced corral where Eliza trained a spirited bay thoroughbred to longe, making him circle her on a 25 foot rope at different gaits as she cracked her whip. John yelled, "Eliza, the Governor is here to assess your performance."

Pivoting with the circling stallion, Eliza sauced, "The Governor better mind his manners or I'll have him on this rope!"

Sam guffawed politely, then turned to her father. "John, Old Hickory's chances have slipped since we spoke last."

"Perhaps I could help if I understood the elective process better. Let's retire to the tack room so I can hear over Eliza's exuberance with that whip."

The immaculate tack room was perfumed by horse sweat and aging saddles. John spicketed each a glass of wine from an oak barrel. "Explain how the election works, Governor."

"Voting varies across the 24 states. State Legislatures choose electors in some states. In most states the electorate consists of adult white males selecting electors from a district ticket. Some states allow their electoral vote to be split; some do not. Since 1824 New York, Vermont, Georgia and Louisiana enacted popular selection of the President, increasing eligible voting rolls by hundreds of thousands of people."

"Increased popular voting should enhance Jackson's prospects rather than hurting them, Governor."

"True, but the Adams-Clay contingent is attacking the General personally, because it's now their only chance with the voters."

"What about?"

"His alleged adultery and bigamous marriage to Rachel."

John Allen smashed his wineglass on the wall, "That's so foul, words fail me!"

"Americans see marriage as fundamental to our way of life," Governor Houston observed.

"You're an odd one to be wreathed as the champion of marriage, Governor."

"Nothing against it. Just haven't found the right woman yet."

"Where are you looking, Sam?"

"Everywhere."

"But under your nose, Sam."

Having learned exactly what he wanted to know, Sam Houston pretended he hadn't by changing the subject. "As you know some say there was a tacit agreement between myself and former Governor Billy Carroll that I would step aside after one term so Billy could resume the Governorship of Tennessee."

"I hadn't heard that, Sam."

"Nor I, so I'm thinking of running for Governor again."

John said slowly, "Might be a sound idea for your future, Sam -- yours and those around you."

Though both knew of Sam's commitment to step down, so Carroll could be Governor again, they ignored Sam's pledge. Sam wondered if a man's honor was too high a price to pay for a prestigious wife that might befit him for higher office someday."

"Glad you see it my way, John. I've got to get back to Nashville. I'm speaking on behalf of General Jackson at a dinner tonight where I'm living at the Nashville Inn. I may also an-nounce my candidacy for re-election as Governor."

"Surely, stumping for Old Hickory in Nashville is like preaching to the choir. Why not seek converts up there in Ohio, where Adams' sin is more than the first syllable of Cincinnati?"

"As ever, John -- a sound suggestion. Could you have my horse brought up?"

Allen clapped his hands at a liveried servant. The immac-ulate Negro conferred in whispers with his Master then ran. "Governor, what can I do about this slander they're heaping on General Jackson?"

"Condemn it to every man you meet and pray we free the country's government so brazenly stolen after the last election."

Sam looked up to see Eliza spurring his dapple gray right at him. Stepping aside at the last instant, he escaped death under his own horse. "What was that about, Eliza," Sam said angrily, trying to appear casual.

She whirled the dapple gray on his hind legs. "I knew your old horse could move. I just wanted to see if you could."

General Jackson ran breathlessly through the Hermitage, yelling "Dear Rachel, come here!"

"By the heavens, what's the matter?" she hugged him to her, so rattled she'd forgotten to remove her pipe from her lips.

Jackson panted, then read the early December newspaper in his high shrill voice, "When the votes for President were tallied, Andrew Jackson took 647,276 popular votes and 178 electoral votes. Adams registered a mere 508,064 popular and a puny 83 electoral votes. John C. Calhoun was re-elected Vice President, and will serve under General Jackson."

Instead of the joy Jackson had hoped for, Rachel looked wistful. "You realize this means I will be flogged by the fashion mongers."

"What of it? A woman more beautiful than you has never trod this earth!"

She puffed her pipe. "Well, for your sake I'm glad. For my sake I never wished it. Perhaps I could feel the good of it more if *Lyncoya* were here. Sixteen's too young for a fine boy to leave this earth."

"Darling Rachel, you shall be the best dressed First Lady of this century. Go to Nashville and purchase the gowns that please you!"

Forcing herself to leave the Hermitage, Rachel shopped one Nashville store after the next till she grew weary of the fawning and the falseness. Retreating to the private office of an Editor distantly related to her, she sprawled on his couch. She wondered if she dared risk smoking her pipe with no ashtrays or spittoons about. Her eye strayed to a pamphlet on his desk with her name in large letters.

She seized it. The words defended her conduct before

her marriage to Andrew and other vile charges leveled at her since. Though meant to protect her, each defense was a knife in her breast. Never before had she known the ghastly lies leveled at her and her beloved Andrew. What was this horrid practice the men called "politics?" Rachel collapsed to the floor, weeping hysterically.

She refused to leave the newspaper office until her wonderful Hannah came for her with other slaves.

It was the 18th of December before Rachel could even pretend to resume her household duties. She'd barely begun her inspection of the Hermitage when pain pierced her chest and set her left arm ablaze. Screaming and clutching her heart, she sank into a chair and fought for breath.

Seated at his writing desk, Andrew Jackson heard her cries and rushed to her. He shrilled, "Hannah, come here now!"

When Rachel's beloved Hannah came, Rachel fell forward into her arms. Hannah and other servants carried their loving mistress to her room. Rachel cried herself to sleep as Andrew knelt at her bedside mumbling, "Now there, darling Rachel. I've sent for the doctors."

For two and a half days after the doctors arrived, Jackson refused to leave Rachel's side. Visiting Doctor Henry Heiskell had no hope of making the President elect of the United States leave his wife's room. But Doctor Samuel Hogg, their regular physician, convinced Andrew to retire to the next room, so they could treat Rachel.

"What procedure do you plan to employ?" Doctor Heiskell asked.

"Mercy, Doctor. I plan to let her die in peace. For her ailment there are no balms nor ointments. Her heart's bled white with grief."

"What will you put on her death certificate?"

"Pleuritic symptoms," Doctor Hogg replied sadly.

"Shouldn't I try something?" Heiskell asked desperately. "She is the wife of the 7th President of this nation."

"Pray for this gentle loving spirit who never knowingly hurt another creature on this earth, Doctor."

Rachel screamed and died.

Jackson bolted in, followed by all the servants of the

household who fell to the floor sobbing.

"Bleed her!" Jackson yelled.

Doctor Hogg sliced the inside of her elbow, but no blood flowed.

"Try her temple, Doctor," Jackson begged.

The Doctor obeyed, drawing but two ruby tears.

Andrew held her hand and put his cheek to her face. "Get out. Leave her alone on her stairway to God." Once they left he begged his dear dead Rachel, "Before you stands the loathsome creature who killed you with his ravenous ambition. Forgive me for ever wanting this pitiful Presidency, for in seizing it, I have sacrificed the life of the only person who ever truly loved me."

"Man's built like a ship. First timber's the keel -- straight and strong it supports all else."　　　　　　　　　　Captain John Bradshaw

CHAPTER 21

THE PRICE OF FREEDOM　　　　　　**WINTER 1828 -1829**

In dark blue seafaring regalia with his Captain's cap cocked to one side, square-shouldered John Bradshaw stood back from James Ohio Pattie's San Diego prison cell. In the dim light, the graying Captain resembled his dead father. Pattie entreated, "Come closer."

"No."

"Why?"

"The *Franklin* doesn't need fleas. "

"That the name of your ship?"

Bradshaw nodded. "Whatta you want?"

"Freedom. I've committed no crime. My father Sylvester Pattie and six other men of our party were imprisoned without trial last spring. They let my father die! I've been locked in this stone coffin with my own filth nearly a year. I'm going mad!"

"You're held as an illegal alien without passport."

"We had passports till *Echeandia* ripped them up and flung them in our faces."

"You have Jedediah Smith to thank for that."

"Who's he?"

"New Yorker who blundered into California with no passport to trap beaver in '26. Captain Cunnin'ham and three others gave Governor *Echeandia* their solemn word as Captains o' the open sea Smith'd leave and never come back."

"So?"

"So, *Echeandia* freed Jedediah Smith in January o' '27, but instead o' leavin' him and his crew trapped beaver up through central California. *Echeandia* got wind of it in April and sent troops. Smith fled, leavin' his crew hid out in the mountains."

"What happened?"

"Rash fool came back for 'em. When he hove to at the Mission San Jose, soldiers jailed him in Monterey. Captain John Cooper and three other Captains persuaded *Echeandia* to free Jedediah Smith a second time on a $30,000 bond. I paid $2.50 a pound for his beaver. Smith bought horses and drove them north outa California."

"We had no part o' Jedediah Smith. We trapped out of Santa Fe with a legal Mexican license. Decided at the Colorado River to rediscover the Old Spanish Trail to California."

"Looks like you found it."

"Don't be flippant, Captain -- sitting in prison for nothing while your father dies is hardly worthy of jest."

"True, but I understand why Mexicans lock up Americans."

"For God's sake tell me!"

"You're all alike to them. Beside bein' liars like Smith, Americans plot to seize their land like Jackson took Florida."

"You British?"

"New Englander."

"You're American. Why aren't you in jail?"

"I don't lie to them and the *Franklin* freights in everythin' they need from nails to champagne. Mexicans recently seized m' vessel on a trumped up smugglin' charge."

"But you're still free?"

"Bought back m' cargo with two cases o' champagne."

"I have no money to ransom myself from this dungeon. Lies are my only currency. Most arrogant of you to fault Jedediah Smith for lying. Man's real enemy in prison is himself. My fury's subsided into insane desperation. I'll say or do anything to gain my freedom."

"Exactly what you mustn't do, lad. Man's built just like a ship. First timber laid in a ship's the keel -- straight and strong, it supports all else -- like a man's conscience or backbone. Stempost and sternpost are pegged into the keel, so the ship can move to fore or aft without fear -- like truth to a man. Frames rise from the keel like ribs from a backbone. Frames support beams spannin' the ship for plankin' to make her hull seaworthy and her decks sound to walk. If her keel's crooked, she'll sink in her first squall. Don't lie your way out o' here, no matter what happens."

"Easy to be noble from your side of these wretched bars. You're worried about a few fleas. These cells abound with every bloodsucking vermin known to man."

"I'm no stranger to the maladies that madden ye. As a cabin boy, I supped on biscuits seethin' with weevils -- rotten horsemeat that caught in m' throat -- wormy potatoes that turned m' dreams to nightmares of worms seethin' in m' nose. Slept below the bos'n's bunk. He didn't rise to relieve himself. But I didn't lie my way out. With an unveerin' keel 18 hours a day, I worked m' way aft from the fo'c's'le to the freedom of a Captain's Cabin. Just like you will, lad -- if you don't flounder in foul lies that will sink you -- and the men who sail in your wake."

"Maybe *Echeandia'd* take our furs to free us."

"First smart thin' you've said. Where are they?"

"Furs are buried near the Colorado River. Gotta be dug up before the spring thaw or they'll wash away."

"I'll approach Governor *Echeandia* about your furs."

"Will you smuggle out my letter to John Coffin Jones, our American Consul in the Sandwich Islands?"

"Slide it 'neath the door. Keep talkin' while I stow it in m' boot."

James Ohio Pattie wanted to thank the departing Captain Bradshaw, but couldn't through his inner screams for freedom.

During the following month *Echeandia* asked James Ohio Pattie to translate several letters from English, and a ray of hope bloomed in him. Between Bradshaw and Pattie they convinced the Governor to take the furs for the release of Pattie and his men. But *Echeandia* held Pattie hostage while the other six prisoners under light guard scrambled to reach the cached furs before the Colorado River did.

While Pattie's men were away, smallpox struck Monterey, slaying hundreds of *Indios y Mejicanos* as it swept southward toward *Echeandia's* San Diego headquarters.

James Ohio knew Sylvester Pattie'd been a student of the recently deceased English physician Edward Jenner's vaccinations for smallpox. His father'd mentioned carrying plenty of vaccine in his medicine kit. James Ohio asked Sergeant *Pico* to bring him the packet of vials. After reading his father's inoculation instructions, James Ohio sent Governor *Echeandia* a letter about halting the plague of smallpox.

By the time Pattie's people reached the Colorado, spring floods'd scattered their furs. Fearing they'd die in jail like Sylvester, Isaac Slover and William Pope slipped away leaving the others to bear the grim tidings to San Diego.

After *Echeandia's* rage subsided, James Ohio Pattie begged an audience. In the Governor's office, he told a horror story in *Español* -- how *viruelas* fevered its victims then fed on them for a fortnight. Upon finishing, James Ohio examined the vain little man's forehead, face and wrists for *ronchas rojas* that would gouge pus holes in a man's face leaving him with hideous pockmarks if it didn't kill him. James prolonged his examination till he saw *Echeandia's* sweat glisten before giving his diagnosis of no *viruelas* -- yet.

James Ohio Pattie struck a bargain with the anxious *José María Echeandia* to vaccinate California's citizens for $1 per head, commencing with the Governor, as Priests recorded each inoculation. On January 18, 1829, Pattie walked free of his father's tomb with his honor intact, having used Sylvester's knowledge as his key to California's splendid sunshine.

Thanks to Captain John Bradshaw, James Ohio Pattie knew he would vaccinate every man, woman and child he could until the vaccine ran out. As precious as his freedom, his promise must be honored.

"I'm trying to decide if I can abide the sudden death of my youth."
Eliza Allen

CHAPTER 22

MAGNIFICENT DISASTER   JANUARY - APRIL 1829

ike much of the nation, Governor Sam Houston saw the end of 1828 through the bottom of a whiskey glass. He'd never been so sad as when he'd carried a corner of dear soul Rachel's coffin. He cherished her more than his own austere mother. His fondest memory was of Rachel calling him, "Son." On Christmas Eve, they'd buried Rachel in the Hermitage garden. Her beloved Hannah collapsed at the grave, and Andrew Jackson wept bitterly like the lonely orphan boy he was again.

That night, Sam'd been summoned to his bereft benefactor's bed chambers. Looking most frail, Jackson'd said, "My heart is nearly broke. My loss is so great, becoming President means little to me at this moment."

Kneeling by Jackson's bed, Sam was astounded to hear his mentor say, "I know you want to run for re-election as Governor. Go ahead. I'll back you. You know you are my heir apparent for the Presidency. Get married and take life in hand."

Gliding home in his carriage from the Hermitage in a downy Christmas Eve snow flurry, Sam'd mused how marvelous that a lowly White Savage like Jackson had become President -- but to have another as his successor! Old Ben Franklin's kidney stones would be striking lightning off each other in his grave!

As the New Year 1829 toddled in, Sam received an invitation from the Allens. His heart hammering and hat in hand, he appeared at their mansion door. Eliza answered his pull on the bell in a fluffy dress that added sophistication to her 18 years. "My father hints we are soon to be wed. Don't you think he's the wrong person to deliver such shocking news?"

"Let's sit over there on the sunny side of the veranda."

"No, we'll retire to the tack room. That's where all the

169

Allen Empire's decisions are made," Eliza grated.

Her full gown's whispers were the only sounds on their crisp winter walk to the tack room. Sam straddled a saddle on the rack. Eliza plopped on a boot stool.

"Shouldn't I pick my husband?"

"Assuredly, Eliza -- I --"

"Ever think I might find other men more exciting than you?"

"Your father never intimated --"

"He wouldn't! He sees me joining in holy matrimony with the sovereign state of Tennessee."

"Since you find our marriage repugnant, I'll leave." Sam lowered his boot to step off his racked saddle.

"Our marriage merits more than one minute of floor time before you vote."

"It's your tone, Eliza. I want a wife to love and respect me -- as I will love and respect her."

"How old are you?"

"I'll be 36 on the second of March."

"You're twice my age!"

"Did you think I was the boy Governor of Tennessee?"

Eliza shook her yellow hair violently, "No. I'm trying to decide if I can abide the sudden death of my youth!"

"President Jackson's lovely departed wife Rachel gifted her prized sterling silver flatware for my nuptials. I was her pallbearer."

"Isn't that impressive?"

"Eliza, Rachel Jackson was dear as my own mother. Her memory shall *not* be bandied in sarcasm!"

"That's what I wanted to see!"

"What?"

"A man beneath your fluff and flattery."

"My age may be fair game for sassy quips. My man-hood's not. I've proved it in battle."

"Don't you see? This is a battle! If you want my hand in marriage, fight for it!"

"Eliza, I demand your hand in marriage."

"Yell it!"

"Like hell! I'll not become a lout to prove my love."

"How kind of you to mention love, Governor."

"This tender tryst is over, Eliza. Give your family my best. Tell them I had to leave on official business."

"I will not. We're getting married. Now kiss me."

Sam leapt off the saddle. Seizing Eliza from her stool, he kissed her hard to seal their bargain, but wasn't sure she kissed him back.

Eliza's jubilant parents selected January 22, 1829 for the wedding in their Gallatin mansion. Eliza was the final requirement for his political future, but Sam still felt uneasy.

Just before the wedding, a notice in the *Nashville Banner and Whig* read: "*We are requested to announce the present Governor of Tennessee, Honourable Samuel Houston, is a candidate for re-election.*"

Right Reverend William Hume conducted their candlelight ceremony before a cavalcade of distinguished guests worthy of a monarch. The bride was reserved, but striking in her glorious gown. The groom was garbed in a black velvet suit with a crimson satin lined Spanish cloak. Whiskey flowed like the rain rivering down the windows. Near midnight the bride and drunken groom retired -- to separate rooms in the Allen mansion.

The newlyweds' carriage left for Nashville next morning. Tumultuous storms forced them to shelter in the Martin mansion. Governor Houston tippled with Robert Martin through the evening. Martin collected political insider stories, so Sam spun them as long as he could before passing out in his chair. Eliza exploded to Mrs. Martin, "I hate my husband!"

The Nashville Inn seemed the place to consummate the marriage, but Sam's cronies converted their first night there to a riotous wedding celebration. Political strategists beat on their door before noon to launch Houston's re-election campaign.

When finally left to themselves, Eliza was repulsed by her husband's running thigh sore, his souvenir of Horseshoe Bend. He was dismayed by her coldness -- and his other discovery.

President Elect Andrew Jackson turned up his lamp wick to write the draft of his Inaugural Address before retiring to his unbearably lonely bed. Rachel'd been the first casualty of his Presidency. He was the second, wondering each dawn if he could live one more day without her.

Jackson's brief address outlined his reform program. It championed strict economy in governmental disbursements, elimination of the national debt, judicious tariffs and distribution of surplus to promote education and improvements within the states. He would purge the nation's corrupt officials and show a just respect for states' rights.

With his address approved by advisors, the President Elect left by steamer for the Capitol on January 19th to complete his cabinet. Garbed in black, he wore a black arm band and a "weeper" band encircling his ebony beaver, hanging down his back to reflect his profound mourning.

Arriving on February 11th, Jackson registered at the National Hotel. He chose Martin Van Buren as Secretary of State for the Little Magician's diplomatic skills. John H. Eaton was to be his Secretary of War because he was a surrogate son.

Eaton's nomination was tainted by his recent scandalous marriage to Margaret (Peggy) O'Neal. Peggy was the libertine daughter of the proprietor of O'Neal's Sociable Tavern, where the 29 year old beauty'd been courted by every rake of her time. Hardly society's ideal of a Cabinet wife, she adored wielding influence over important men. Peggy's first husband, Lieutenant John Timberlake, had ended his career as a Naval Purser with his pistol after embezzling enough funds to cover her debts.

Washington gossips whispered, "Eaton has just married his mistress -- and that of a dozen others!"

Jackson's own pious wife having been murdered by the mouths of these people, he served notice with Eaton's appointment that gossipmongers would make no policies for him.

Meanwhile the city abounded with people come to the coronation of the man who'd rescued their nation. Washington regulars compared them to the barbarians overrunning Rome.

Believing Adams' vile slanders responsible for Rachel's death, Jackson refused to make the traditional final visit to the White House. So Adams decided to boycott Jackson's Inaugural.

After a late supper on March 3, 1829, John Quincy Adams and his family abdicated the White House. Concerned for their safety, they sought refuge in a rented house on Meridian Hill rather than facing Jackson's raucous hordes.

Wednesday March 4, 1829 dawned warmly. As Andrew Jackson left Gadsby's Hotel at 11:00 AM, old soldiers from the Revolution and the War of 1812 surrounded him in a loving brigade. With Jackson striding as a stately white haired figure in black, they escorted him through the cheering throngs lining Pennsylvania Avenue to the Senate Chamber where he witnessed John C. Calhoun's swearing in as Vice President.

At noon, Jackson's prodigious procession wended into the Capitol's east portico before 30,000 applauding Americans. Grand rotunda doors swung wide for Supreme Court Justices heralded by trumpets. Soldiers formed around them. The Marine Band played silently for all but those nearest in the hullabaloo.

Jackson bowed to the people roaring his triumph, then spoke shrilly. Though the crowd stilled, few heard Andrew Jackson deliver the briefest Inaugural Address in history. Chief Justice John Marshall administered Jackson's oath of office.

Moments later the crowd broke restraining chains to swarm lovingly about their hero. At first, U.S. Marshals barred people from shaking hands with the President, so Jackson simply walked around them and shook hands while other adoring Americans knelt to kiss the hem of his long black coat.

Concerned that Jackson would be killed by adulation, Marshals rushed the Seventh President of the United States to the White House to find the lower floor jammed with people of every conceivable race, color and social status.

With Jackson's arrival, the White House Reception went berserk. Barrels of orange punch toppled and burst. Pails of liquor sloshed the floors. Shattered glass raining from walls and ceilings kept waiters from taking ice creams to the ladies. Priceless china plates pitched high exploded among the revelers.

Men in muddy boots trampled damask tablecloths to glimpse the President. Valiants surrounded Jackson and took him in one badly ruffled piece to the Gadsby. Later Jackson, and Calhoun dined with confidants on sirloins from a prize ox, while revelers damaged Washington almost as badly as the British when they sacked and burned the place 15 years before.

Sam Houston took time from his political brawl with Billy Carroll, who'd expected to be unopposed for the Governorship, to wrangle with Eliza at the Nashville Inn. Convinced she was not as virtuous as he'd expected, Sam pressed her, "Who is Billy T?"

"No one you'd know."

"Well isn't he someone you've -- known?"

"I was mortified when you locked me in this pathetic room because of your insane jealousy. You're demented! I'm leaving you, Governor!"

"Not mid-campaign! You'll kill me surely as using a pistol -- perhaps bar me from Presidency of the United States!"

"You wanted an object to flaunt on your arm. Use your bottle. That's what you love!"

Unimpressed that she was changing the course of American history, on April 9, 1829 Eliza left Sam Houston and flounced home to her horrified parents.

Quite drunk, Sam penned a letter to John Allen hours after Eliza fled. The maudlin letter mentioned Sam's unhappiness and his former belief in Eliza's virtue. He swore not to pursue that issue, adding "*I would have perished first & if mortal man had dared to charge my wife or say ought against her virtue, I would have slain him. That I have & do love Eliza none can doubt -- that she is the only earthly object dear to me God will witness.*" Houston went on to say disjointedly that all must pretend no rupture in relations had occurred and keep the world ignorant of these things, adding "*She was cold to me & I thought did not love me.... that Mrs. Allen & you may rest assured that nothing on my part shall be wanting to restore our lost peace. Let me know what is to be done.*"

As if nothing had happened Houston thrashed Billy Carroll in their April 11, 1829 gubernatorial debate.

The following day Sam Houston had a wrathful meeting with the outraged John Allen. He saw Eliza briefly, begging her on bended knee to return to Nashville, but she refused with fire flashing from her eyes.

Sam thundered back to Nashville, nearly killing his dapple gray, while the Allen family made public announcements that their chaste daughter had been wronged.

Tennesseans could tolerate glaring faults in their public officials, but dishonoring marriage was not one of them. Sam

Houston was burned in effigy by a screaming mob in Gallatin.

When Nashville mobs threatened to horsewhip Houston in the public square, he called out the local militia to restore order. Sam's drinking cronies, Sheriff Willoughby Williams and Dr. John Shelby, barricaded themselves in his rooms at the Inn, where they paced the floors and drank themselves incoherent. Houston awoke from their debacle convinced he must resign as Governor. After the others recovered, they spent the morning burning stacks of personal papers in the fireplace, relegating Sam Houston's history to the ghosts of the flue.

Sam summoned Reverend William Hume, who'd officiated at his wedding, and implored Hume to baptize him in the Christian faith. After conferring with Presbyterian Pastor Obadiah Jennings, Hume refused, hinting that Houston stood accused of being a drunken heathen more interested in *Cherokee* salvation than Christ's.

On April 16, 1829 Sam Houston wrote out his resignation as Governor of Tennessee reciting how badly he felt about resigning because of "*private afflictions ... & ... sudden calamities that kept him from serving the people and the state.*" Sheriff Williams delivered it.

Amid the chaos, Sam Houston departed the Nashville Inn disguised as an Indian on April 23rd with the Sheriff and Dr. Shelby. At the Nashville levee, Houston hugged his friends then boarded the steamer *Red Rover* for the frontier.

Two burly men claiming to be Eliza's relatives boarded *Red Rover* at Clarksville, and came to Houston's compartment with the Captain. One demanded, "You will give us a written statement that Eliza had no guilt in this matter."

Reasonably sober, Sam retorted, "You may publish in the Nashville newspapers that if anyone dares utter a word against the purity of Mrs. Houston, I will return and write the denial of such libel in my heart's blood. However, I shall give you no written statement and but two minutes to clear this boat before I fling your flabby carcasses in the Cumberland River!"

"Man fights his enemies, not his friends."
Kit Carson

 CHAPTER 23

CAVALRY TO THE RESCUE   APRIL - AUGUST 1829

ransferring from one scabrous steamboat to another throughout April 1829, Sam Houston drank his way west. Sam's dedicated drinking companion asked, "See what Governor Billy Carroll said in this Tennessee newspaper?"

"Enlighten me, Sir."

"Says, *Poor Houston -- rose like a rocket -- fell like a stick.*"

"Nothing like an inflammatory boast to set a stick afire. You've made every steamer change with me. Who are you?"

"Call me a friend o' the family," Hugh Haralson muttered.

Having written a Congressman that he expected to "*...conquer ... Texas and be worth two million dollars in two years ...*" Sam Houston was not surprised to receive President Jackson's letter at Little Rock in Arkansas Territory in early May 1829.

Jackson's letter sounded like the rider of a runaway horse. " *... Indeed, my dear Sir, I cannot believe you have any such chimerical visionary scheme in view. Your pledge of honor to the contrary is a sufficient guarantee that you will never engage in any enterprise injurious to your country that would tarnish your fame....*"

Houston's May 11, 1829 letter to the President pledged patience before seizing Texas. He promised to advise Jackson of important observations. Then concluded with: "*In two hours I will leave here, for my old friend, Jollys of the Cherokees; and ... start on a Buffaloe hunt .... If ... you should feel ... the*

176

personal regard that would induce you to write to me, I will get it from [the] Cherokee Agency. You have much employment, and little time for private purposes, and I would not tax you with the labour of writing unless it is perfectly convenient -- tho' I will always be happy to hear from you. I need not tell how sincerely ... I wish you a successful and glorious administration of the Government of the U. States. May you live long, and may your days be as happy, as your life has been glorious and useful to your country. Farewell."

After climbing the gangway at Little Rock, Houston and Haralson descended the stairwell to the steamer's dingy saloon. Near the entry sat a nattily dressed gent with a healthy head of black hair and bushy sideburns. An unopened bottle stood beside a monstrous knife on his table. As they took seats nearby, Sam grinned, "You'll never get the cork out with that scimitar."

"Come join me, gentlemen."

The Arkansas River's lurching challenged their unsteady gaits, but they moved to the stranger's table. "Who might you be?" Houston asked, reading the vintage year on the untapped bottle of precious French wine.

"I was Jim Bowie of Texas when I boarded this river rat. And you gentlemen?"

"A homeless wanderer from Tennessee."

"Casual nomad," Haralson replied. "Who's your friend?"

Bowie touched the handle of his 15 inch, broad-bladed steel hunting knife lovingly. "My only child. In spite of his size, he thinks he's a razor. Havin' married above my station into the Veramendi family of Texas, I am now prayin' for the blessed addition of a baby girl to my family."

"You hail from Georgia, Mr. Bowie?"

"No Kentucky. But once you become a Texian, your heart will brook no other allegiance."

"We're interested in Texas," Sam said.

"Not a disinterested man livin' or dead. Texas is a religion that makes men see its vast plains greener, its waters bluer and its ties to Almighty God tighter. No dead man could do better than to have the warm soil o' Texas embrace his remains, for after Texas, Heaven will seem downright commonplace."

"That calls for a toast," Houston observed.

"If you gentlemen'll name your dog, I'll have it bite you."

"What about your fine wine?" Houston asked.

"Not mine, sir. The *St. Julian Medoc* belongs to him," tapping the enormous gleaming blade. "He'll not open it till Texas is a sovereign nation."

As Sam's surprised gaze met Hugh's, Hugh Haralson wondered how long it would be before Sam figured out that Hugh'd been assigned by a worried President to "stick like a tick" to Houston.

Ewing Young and William Wolfskill operated their store in Taos, New Mexico as partners, selling U.S. goods along with "Taos Lightning" and local produce. It was also headquarters for their "quiet" trapping operations.

Unable to get a Mexican trapping license after his imprisonment in Santa Fe, Ewing Young was left to subterfuge. His 40 man party, with Kit Carson and two others on their first hunt, left Taos in August 1829. They headed north for 50 miles. Once certain they'd eluded the Mexican constabulary, Ewing's outfit swung southwest through *Navajo*, then *Zuni* country to trap tributaries of the Gila River in Sonora [Arizona].

Discovering about 80 *Apaches* that had decimated a Young and Wolfskill party earlier in the year, Ewing told his men, "All but five of you crawl under packs and blankets or hide in the brush."

Unable to resist the five hated white invaders, *Apaches* attacked. Nineteen year old Kit Carson and his cohorts leaped from cover blasting, tomahawking and knifing 20 astounded *Apaches* to death before the surviving attackers scattered.

Ewing Young took Kit aside. "You've got a demon in you, Kit. I'd thought you mild mannered till this."

"Man fights his enemies, not his friends," Kit muttered.

Ewing grinned, "Glad to be your friend."

In the days following, they trapped down the Salt River to the San Francisco River with Indians occasionally stealing stock or traps by stealth.

The messenger bursting into camp with Wolfskill's message that Bent's party was under Indian attack on the Santa Fe

Trail faced half a dozen cocked rifles.

Ewing and his 40 men thundered through the mountains to rescue the Bent party on the trail. The Bent caravan's wagons lay in a square coralling their horses, mules and cattle with provisions piled in the gaps. Ewing said to Kit, "Bent's smart. See how he drove his stock around his wagons to flatten the grass, so these Indians couldn't burn him out?"

"When we gonna run nem Injuns off?"

"Kit, there's close to 2,000 Indians besieging those wagons. I'm sending a rider to Taos for reinforcements. You want that job?"

"Sure don't!" Kit Carson growled, "Charles Bent's down there gittin' whupped. Bent give me a job with his outfit in '26 when nobody else would. I'm goin' down nere an' help 'im."

Seeing he couldn't restrain the small man's rage, Ewing said, "Go down there and lie low till we attack."

"Lie low hell! Coulda done nat here. Goin' down nere and stomp ever Injun I kin." Kit sprinted to his horse.

Before nightfall 55 grim-faced Taos trappers led by short, wiry, gray-eyed William Bent arrived in Ewing's camp.

Heading nearly a hundred horsemen, Ewing strung them out in a great single rank, so they could shoot without hitting each other and seem five times their number to the Indians. Standing in his stirrups mid-rank, Ewing Young shouted, "*Charge!*" unleashing them as a vast thundering spectacle with booming rifles.

Though the terrified Indians vastly outnumbered the oncoming trappers, they fled these mad devil spirits exploding from the earth, and left their dead sprawled in the desert for the buzzards.

Ewing Young was surprised, but not surprised, to find Kit Carson crawling from under Charles Bent's wagon with his rifle so hot its wooden stock was smoking.

Short, husky Charles Bent and his men yelled "Huzzahs" for their rescuers. Glad to see his wild brother William unharmed, Charles told Ewing Young, "We're astounded that a force half our size put near 2,000 Indians to flight."

"Beside the fact that they already faced your 200, we had the advantage of surprise," Ewing replied quietly.

Charles countered, "But we had Kit Carson making us more like 300!"

Kit just kept spitting on his rifle barrel to see when it was cool enough to clean. Already sunburnt, Kit blushed scarlet when both Bent brothers hugged him. Clearly Kit Carson was better at battling than being hugged.

Ewing led Bent's caravan into Taos, where they reprovisioned with his partner Billy Wolfskill's help.

As Bent's wagons headed south for Santa Fe next day, Ewing Young and Kit Carson doffed their hats to the Bent brothers, then waved the dust from their faces.

Still plagued by memories of earnest young James Ohio Pattie and the beckoning of the phantom Old Spanish Trail, Ewing said, "Santa Fe's today. California's tomorrow. Wanta see it?"

Kit grinned, "Shoulda left yesterday."

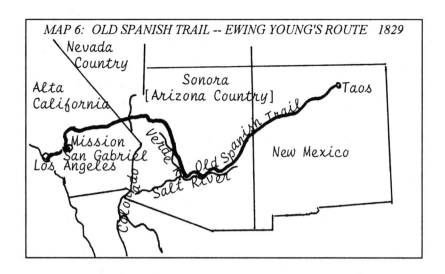

CHAPTER 24

ON THE TRAIL OF LEGENDS   AUGUST - DECEMBER 1829

Ewing Young provisioned his 17 trappers in the August mists wafting from the Sangre de Cristos to becloud his Taos store. His men received rations of salt, sugar, flour and coffee, but they'd have to hunt for their staples. With sunrise lighting the mist to clouds of tiny golden jewels, Ewing asked, "Anybody been to California?"

Silence.

"Anybody been on the Old Spanish Trail?"

A trapper asked, "Where is it?"

Ewing laughed, *"Rivera, Dominguez, Escalante.* They know, but their bones have turned to dust. James Ohio Pattie's outfit tried it last year and hasn't been heard of since."

Kit Carson asked, "Goes to Californy don't it?"

Ewing nodded.

Though Kit was greenest of the trappers, he said boldly, "All we gotta do is keep the mornin' sun agin our backs. We're bound ta hit it."

As men who'd spent most of their lives lost in the wilderness, the older trappers laughed till the tears came. Most were still grinning when Ewing led them and their mules into the mountain mists to seek the legendary Old Spanish Trail.

Game was scarce from the outset. Ewing made that worse by telling them he wanted head shots on their first three deer, so they could make the skins into water tanks. On their third gameless day, Ewing eased Sweet Lips from her doeskin cover, posted sentries and disappeared into the high country. Sweet Lips headshot two does at awesome distances while Kit Carson blasted a rutting buck that about ran him down.

While they dug the deer out of their skins ever so carefully to make water tanks, Kit Carson asked, "This some Scotch-Irish trick from the old country?"

Ewing Young shook his head, "*Apache.*"

"Why ain't we cooking this meat while we're doin' nis?"

"Cause the hills are full of *Apache* sign. We'll eat the tender cuts raw and cook the rest when we find a camp that's hard to find and easy to defend."

Biting into some raw neck meat, Kit asked, "Where is iss Old Spanish Trail?"

"Only God and the dead know, but like you said, Kit -- we're keeping the morning sun *agin* our backs!"

They filled the skins in a churning crystal stream. After letting the men and mules suck their fill of the brook, Ewing broached the barren lands.

For four days they trod fuming sand, risking small dead wood fires the first two nights to cook the rest of their venison. Ewing parsed water from the deer tanks, constantly guarded by trusted men like Kit.

Finding more fresh sign of a large band of *Apaches,* Ewing ordered cold camps. Since the men couldn't make hot coffee, most added a dab of sugar to mask the deerskin flavor of their water.

Their lead scout discovered an *Apache* warrior's mummified body at the bottom of a gorge. Ewing joined his men around the shriveled corpse, its skin dried black, eye sockets empty and lips turned to leather wearing parched buckskins.

Holding up the mummy's bow Ewing said, "One of man's

finest weapons. Sinew covering gives this bow its power. This arrow's a foot longer'n the plains Indians use for buffalo, and twice as cruel. The hardwood stick with its flint point is glued into this reed tube. If their victim pulls the arrow out, the hardwood shaft stays in the wound to bleed him to death. If he tries to shove the arrow through, the reed crumples. Warrior can shoot this arrow through a man's body at a hundred yards. He'll launch ten arrows a minute, while we get off two shots."

A trapper asked, "Whatta we do if'n we git shot with one o' them arrows?"

"Duck," Ewing muttered.

Kit said, "They's water down nis gorge."

"What makes you think so?"

"My mules twitchin' -- actin' like she smells water."

"Giver her head and we'll see."

In a few minutes, Kit's mule led the dusty pack train to a red cliff where clear water gushed from a break in the rocks, pooling into a lovely pond in the shade.

Before they made camp, every creature drank their fill -- and still the water warbled, happy to be free of its undergound dungeon. Somebody named the place, "Young's Spring," because Ewing stood watch till every man had his drink.

Ewing shot a great-horned mountain ram off a crag. They cooked it over twisted gray wood that burned clear at the firepit and barely tinged the air with stringy smoke. Guards watched from high ledges. After two days, they broke camp.

They pack-trained before dawn, waited out the scorching noons, then trekked west four more nights. Hunting for Verde and Gila River tributaries in the forenoon, they found fiery rocks and baking dirt instead. When it seemed they'd die of thirst or starvation, they heard Indians chattering in the canyon ahead. Ewing motioned for them to snug up their column and check the primes in their rifles. Pulling Sweet Lips from her doeskin case, Ewing forged ahead alone.

When his trappers heard Ewing yell, they charged into a clearing to find him trading trinkets to some nervous *Mojaves* for a half-dead mare swollen with foal. Ewing also conjured a peck of parched corn and a hatful of beans out of 19 glass beads.

To seal the bargain, Ewing gave the curious Indians the

red bead he'd been saving. The shapely *Mojave* squaw who got the red one, laughed and peeked at the sun through it, unconcerned that the trappers eyed her naked body.

Ewing motioned for his trappers to move on, then quick-marched to the Colorado River bank. Ewing posted men at every vantage point while their mules swilled the river's brown water. "Guess we know what happened to James Ohio Pattie's outfit."

"How?" Kit asked.

"Those *Mojaves* have massacred a party of Whites."

"Why ya say that?"

"White man doesn't trade his mother's gold wedding ring to a *Mojave* Indian."

"Depends on how bad off a man has got," Kit replied.

"What about his gold teeth and his scalp?"

"I never seen them things, Ewin'. None of us sees good as you."

"Why you think the *Mojaves* paraded that young squaw? You gotta look at what your enemy *doesn't* show you."

"Why din't they tack us?" Kit puzzled.

"Have to ask them."

"What we gonna do now, Ewin'? We're hungry nuff to gobble that stove-up mare raw," Kit groaned.

"Drive her to that sandbar under the outcropping, line up our mule packs as breastworks and cook the mare and her foal. Eat in messes of six while a dozen stand guard."

The mare and foal fed them for three eerie days. Well rested, they forded the Colorado River in bands of six under the guns of the others on the banks. One trapper found a flattened felt hat. Shoving his finger through the hole in the side of its rotting crown, he muttered, "Not likely this feller shot hisself."

Ewing added, "Or tossed his busted powder horn over there. Water the mules again before we tackle the desert. This place makes my hide crawl."

Ewing Young's trappers trudged into the torrid desert heading southwest for three days until they struck a faltering stream. They followed it northeast, boiling its alkaline water to kill the taste -- to no avail. Eventually the stream vanished in the sands of the Great Basin.

Gasping for water, they gorged on some foul desert runoff that nearly choked them.

Swinging west upward into the San Bernardino Mountains, they hiked, hauling their drenched mules through Cajon Pass in sheeting November rains that washed away most memories of the desert.

Descending into an idyllic green valley, they met Spanish speaking Indians working the fields of the Mission San Gabriel. The Indians told of Americans being seized from their beds by soldiers at the mission. But the starving trappers decided to risk contact, ready to fight the minute their freedom was threatened.

Reaching the glorious grounds of Mission San Gabriel, Ewing and his 17 men found Father *José Sanchez* and 15 soldiers. Wary that more soldiers might be in the outbuildings obscured by heavy fog, Ewing questioned the Priest in Spanish, "How many Indians live here?"

"About 1,000."

"In those buildings back there?"

"No. They prefer their primitive dwellings."

"Who resides in those buildings?"

"Priests, their aids and the staff to keep our mission immaculate for the sacraments."

"Mission keep cattle?"

"Perhaps 80,000."

"We are starving. Can we have a steer to eat?"

Father *Sanchez* answered, "Your mules haul goods. We have only the primitive cutlery the Indians forge. Perhaps we can help each other. We will trade one steer for four of your knives."

Ewing sent a man for the four knives, then observed, "Father, we hear of Americans being seized here and thrown into prison. We worry that we will be arrested any minute."

Father *Sanchez* confided, "Once that was so. Your Jedediah Smith was arrested here some time back, just as you and your men would have been, but that will not happen now, my son."

"Why?"

"We see Americans in a new light."

"I have applied in Taos to become a Mexican citizen, but I am still treated as a dangerous foreigner there. What has happened here, Father?"

"A few months ago, your James Ohio Pattie came here and saved every person at Mission San Gabriel from smallpox with his vaccinations. But for James, you might have found this mission empty of the living, and its Christian Indians reverted to heathens. Who could possibly ignore such holy deeds, my son?"

"To spare thee now is past my pow'r, Thou bonnie gem."
Robert Burns

CHAPTER 25

SHERIFF WALKER'S LAST CASE   DECEMBER 1829

Though Independence was touted in the East as the wildest town on the western frontier, Joe Walker had tamed it till it barely needed a Sheriff. Serving since the summer of '27, Joe was a friend to its townspeople, drovers and Mountain Men, and the town was yet to have it's first killing.

Still harboring his dread of daily routine from his dreary days on the Walker farm, Joe used every break in Jackson County's Court sessions to go horse trading. He knew breeds and the conformation each horse required to satisfy his buyer's needs. He bought horses on straight legs like a table's with noble arching necks and heads held high. They needn't be docile, but Joe left kicking, biting, screaming renegades on the lot. One thing Joe Walker was sure of -- it took horse sense to buy a horse.

Joe'd always known a horse was more than a dumb beast. As a boy in Tennessee, he'd learned their language. Horses signed like Indians. Extra white of eye said they were scared. Stomping meant nervous or hungry. Hungry or thirsty, their belly growled worse than a man's. They could also talk. A low whinny hailed a friend. Loud whinny cried outrage or fear. Next to wild grass, hay, grain and water, horses adored being curried and rubbed down. A carrot or an apple was their Christmas.

In early December, Joe rode into the Missouri Valley where breeding sound horses stretched back to the bloodline fires imported from Virginia and Kentucky.

At Lilburn Boggs' place, a freckle-nosed ten year old named Tommy with his neck wrapped in a cherry red woolen scarf trailed Joe through the horse corrals.

Joe asked, "What're you up to, boy?"

"Wanta know why horse buyers allas look in a horse's mouth. You tryin' ta see what he et last?"

"You ask your Grandpa?"

"He said I shoulda knowed that by now. Is it a secret?"

Joe smiled, "No. Unlike some owners, horses always tell you their real age with their teeth. Like boys, young horses sprout milk teeth first. A filly or colt with up to 24 milk teeth is saying they're under two and half."

"How many teeth they git when they're growed?"

"After two and a half, stallions will grow 40 permanent teeth and mares 36."

Tommy pulled a handkerchief and blew his nose noisily. "How come mares don't get 40?"

"Only the good Lord knows, but mares don't grow pointed dog teeth in top or bottom teeth."

"That all of it?" Tommy asked dragging his boot to scuff the frost off the rigid dirt.

"No. Horse's permanent front teeth come in with cups in the biting surfaces. Eating wears the cups away. The wear starts in the middle and gradually works to the sides. By age eight, the lower cups are worn flat. At nine, the upper front teeth's cups are gone, making the horse *smooth mouthed*."

"Why ya care about that?"

"With horses, their age figures into what they're worth. To a crooked seller, a *smooth mouthed* horse is nine forever. But a man really knows what he's up to can read the stars in a horse's teeth till the horse is 12. Since a horse's price falls after ten, buyer's gotta know the horse's real age."

"I'm ten. My price fallin'?"

"You're a boy. Your price'll never go down long as you are honest and work hard."

"You're Sheriff, ainchu?"

Joe nodded.

"That why you're tellin' me to be honest?"

"No, to keep you from being worthless -- like the horse nobody wants."

"Grandpa says ever'body wants your horses, cause you gentle 'em stead o' breakin' 'em. What's he mean Sheriff?"

"I don't break a horse. I want a partner, not a slave. I

rub and sweet talk an unbroke horse till it knows me. Next I spread a saddle blanket over its back, so they get used to the feel of it. Then I saddle the horse, but don't ride it. After that I add saddlebags fulla horseshoes behind the saddle."

"Here, they jist git on and ride. Ainchu wastin' time?"

"No. Horse doesn't know it, but he's being trained. After he's used to the saddle and saddlebags, I pull 'em off."

"When does he git rode, so he kin buck you off?"

"Never."

"Whatta you do?"

"Put the blanket back on, and lay belly-down over the horse's back while I sweet-talk him. By the end of a week, I ride the horse without a single buck."

"Sounds like you waste a lot o' time, Sheriff."

Missouri Congressman Lilburn W. Boggs walked up behind his grandson. "Time's not wasted, Tommy. High-spirited, Walker-broke horses are prized by Army officers at frontier posts in Missouri, Arkansas and Indian Territory. Joe sells high-stepping stallions for $150 that he's bought unbroke from me for $30 a head."

"That's a lot, Grandpa, but the Sheriff's makin' all the money!"

"Not quite, Tommy. The mare gives me the horse for nothing. We breed fine horses here. Mr. Walker does the hard work and deserves the most money."

"Your Grandpa's right, Tommy. The Army wants horses and mares with sound temperament for drilling and strong foals."

Joe didn't mention that he bought and sold geldings, but never gelded stallions because it was a betrayal of their trust.

After selecting three mares, Joe Walker went over them with Tommy, settled their prices with the elder Boggs, then drove them back to Independence in time for the Court's last Winter session.

The last case on the docket was against Hanna, a slave, charged with attempted murder of her master. A slender, even-featured young woman, Hanna sat at the defense table with the tears streaming down her cheeks, and her lip trembling. Her clothes were wretched and rumpled. She'd pulled her hair into a tight knot behind her head.

Because she ate and slept in his jail, Joe knew Hanna's story too well. She'd been promised by her master that he'd never sell any child they brought into the world. Hanna'd birthed him a baby boy. The minute the boy was weaned, her master'd grabbed him from her arms to sell him, inciting her to such a state of grief, she'd stabbed her master in the shoulder. Hanna knew the gallows awaited her.

The rotund prosecutor finished his opening statement by telling the jury, "Slaves got no right of self defense nor any other rights to speak of, so you need to find this wench guilty before it gits warm enough in here to pull our coats off."

The small balding defense lawyer retorted, "The prosecutor's told you Hanna has no legal rights. If that's so, why's he tryin' this case?"

Hanna's master testified she'd jumped him and gashed his shoulder with a butcher knife. He finished, "And the wench woulda murdered me, had I not knocked her flat."

There was really no need for Hanna to testify. The jury, like everybody else in the small town, knew what had happened and who'd bought Hanna's baby boy. They convicted her of attempted murder anyway.

Unfortunately, Joe Walker's brother Joel was not the Judge. As Joe Walker awaited Hanna's sentence, he began to sweat in the icy courtroom. If she went to the gallows, he knew he could not -- and would not hang her.

Finally the Judge read the order he'd been writing and rewriting since the trial began, "*The said Hanna to receive on her bare black ass Thirty Nine lashes well laid on, and it is Ordered that the Sheriff cause execution of this order immediately.*"

Hanna stiffened. The jury filed out, unable to meet her gaze. When only the Judge, Hanna and Joe remained in the frigid room, Sheriff Walker said solemnly, "Her master's the lying thief who oughta get these lashes. Taking a horsewhip to Hanna for trying to save her baby is barbaric."

"Sheriff you will remember yourself and carry out the sentence."

Joe muttered, "Your Honor, I can not carry out your Order."

The Judge glowered in disbelief. "You what?"

"Thirty-nine lashes will maim her for life. I can't do it."

"You well know she should be hanged, Sheriff."

"I resign, Judge."

"Your resignation's refused. You are the duly elected Sheriff of Jackson County, and you will do the job the taxpayers of this county pay you to do. We'll not hold another election to get one that can -- although it sounds to me like we should."

Hanna gazed at Joe Walker, her eyes brimming with tears. She put her small black hand on his huge white one. "You kin do it Sherf. You has to. Let's git it ovah with. Ah cain't stands to think on it."

"Judge, I don't own a horsewhip."

"You're a horse trader and you don't own a horsewhip?"

"I've never taken a whip to man nor beast -- let alone a woman."

"Buy one from the saddlery."

"It's not in me, Judge."

"Want me to change this order to have her hanged?"

"Oh God no!"

"Then do your duty, Sheriff!"

Hanna touched Joe's hand and pointed to the door. They left together.

Joe's deputy, Jacob Gregg, was not at the jail, so Joe left the sobbing Hanna locked up and went to the saddlery.

"A whip? Gonna work oxen?"

Joe shook his head and paid for the whip. He coiled it and walked back to the jail. A bloodthirsty crowd had gathered, and Hanna sat nude in her cell. He gave Hanna a pair of his huge pants and walked her out. He cleared his throat and told her, "Hold on to that bulletin board, till I get this over."

She couldn't reach across the bulletin board with its parched wanted posters and land sale notices, so she gripped one side of it and clamped her eyes shut.

He lashed her bare back with the whip, making her flinch, but Hanna did not yell.

Somebody in the crowd hollered, "That's one!"

The whip bit her bare back again, and the whole crowd counted, "Two."

As Joe Walker whipped Hanna, he heard himself reciting the Robert Burns ode *To a Mountain Daisy:*

> *"Wee modest crimson-tipped flow'r,*
> *Thou's met me in an evil hour;*
> *For I must crush among the dust*
> > *Thy slender stem:*
> *To spare thee now is past my pow'r,*
> > *Thou bonnie gem.*
> *There in thy scanty mantel clad,*
> *Thy snawy bosom sunward spread,*
> *Thou lifts thy unassuming head*
> > *In humble guise;*
> *But now the plow uptears thy bed,*
> > *And low thou lies!*
> *Such is the fate of artless Maid,*
> *Sweet flow'ret of the rural shade!*
> *By love's simplicity betray'd,*
> > *And guileless trust,*
> *Till she, like thee, all soil'd is laid*
> > *Low into the dust."*

When the crowd chanted, "Thirty-nine," Joe Walker hurled his whip to the ground rasping, "You're free Hanna! Now by God, I quit!"

"Be sure you're right, then go ahead."
David Crockett

 CHAPTER 26

SUICIDE FOR CHRISTMAS   DECEMBER 1829

I t was Christmas mornin' of 1829. David Crockett sprawled on his unmade bed in a cut-rate Washington boardin' house, but he felt like a feller laid out in his coffin. Back home in Tennessee, when a man decided to kill hisself, he jist put a pistol in his ear and pulled the trigger. Here in Washington, a Congressman could do it by sayin' the wrong thing to the newspapers, drinkin' outa the finger bowl at dinner er fightin' fer the wrong cause. How in the world had things got so God-awful fer him?

The tracks led back to when the Tennessee Vacant Land Bill first come up last year in 1828. Looked so simple then, like when God tuck Adam's rib to make Eve.

The Vacant Land Bill proposed to give all vacant federal lands in Tennessee to the state to sell to the highest bidders, so the money could be used for Tennessee schools.

Tennessee's Legislature'd sent instructions to James K. Polk to have all its Congressmen vote fer the Vacant Land Bill.

Right at first, Crockett'd supported the Bill, but then he seen what it was up to -- stealin' land from poor squatters o' his district to aid rich land speculators in east Tennessee. Them poverty-strick folk squattin' on them vacant lands was the advance guard o' the nation. They'd fought Indians, dry spells, floods, swamp fever, ba'rs an' whatever else'd come after 'em to keep them lands. Most'd never see the inside of a school.

On January 5, 1829, Crockett'd offered his ten line Amendment to give these federal lands directly to them poor folks without payment to state or federal governments.

193

With one ten line Amendment, David Crockett'd swapped all his friends fer enemies and visey versey. James K. Polk had charged up to him, callin' him a traitor for tryin' to rob money Tennessee needed to edicate its children -- and worse fer goin' agin the Jackson party machine. But big Whig Matthew St. Clair Clarke, crony o' Nicholas Biddle who run the U.S. Bank, had backed David's Amendment and even offered to help David write his autobiography. Men David'd publicly called "pap suckin' fops" was cozyin' up to him. This here was a lotta action fer ten lines on a piece o' paper that was still ahangin' fire.

On January 15, 1829 David'd put out a circular to the poor people o' his district, most written by them once "pap suckin' fop" Whigs. It said land surveyors charged more to lay out the land in west Tennessee than the land was worth to a poor man er anybody else. The circular charged Crockett's own party with fraudulent land practices.

Not about to forsake them poor folks in west Tennessee that needed their own little homesteads, David'd spoke fer his Amendment on the House Floor. He'd admitted that he run contrary to the call o' his home state's legislature because he answered a higher callin' -- his poor constituents. He'd read his speech that said, "*I propose my amendment on behalf of the hardy sons of the soil; men who entered the country when it lay in cane and opened in the wilderness a home for their wives and children. These folks had been run off other lands they'd improved by greedy men wantin' to make money. Now they've took land nobody else wants -- little fragments of soil where they've fixed their little homes. They have mingled the sweat of their brows with the soil and by perseverin' toil have earned the few comforts they possess.... Is it fair for the Gen'l Government to take these humble cottages from them to make a donation of the whole to the legislature of the State for the purpose of raising up schools for the children of the rich?... Will you take away their little and give it all to the legislature to speculate upon?...*"

In the speech for his Amendment, David also called his own party "a swindlin' machine." All for nothin' because the Bill and his Amendment had got tabled on January 14, 1829 by a vote of 103 to 63.

Suspectin' the Whigs was behind David, James K. Polk'd claimed David was a turncoat puppet o' the opposition party. Bein' called a renegade and gittin' threatened didn't scare David none.

Two days ago on December 23, 1829 David'd rose up again in the House to move for reconsideration of his tabled Land Bill Amendment and got swatted flat 86 to 74.

But when Polk'd moved to have the whole matter hustled into his standin' Committee on Public Lands, David had spear-headed the defeat of Polk's "slight o' land trick" 92 to 65.

This here was now open war agin his own party. It was bad enough, he was gittin' sued back home fer debts he couldn't pay cause he was allas up here in Washington stead o' workin' fer his own family back home.

Some o' the Whigs writin' his speeches an' offerin' to publish his life story was hintin' he might be their next candidate fer President of the United States -- agin Gen'l Andrew Jackson!

David Crockett remembered speakin' his motto a hunnert times, "Be sure you're right, then go ahead." But how could a feller go ahead when he was dead as a froze tater -- with his home state lookin' ta bury him? Why would a feller rig his own political suicide, jist to help a bunch o' penniless squatters who didn't even vote?

"There is a proud undying thought in man that bids his soul still upward look."   Sam Houston

CHAPTER 27

WHITE SHADOW   **JANUARY - MAY 1830**

After only eight months in political exile, Sam Houston checked into Brown's Indian Queen Hotel in Washington, D.C.on January 13, 1830 with three of his *Cherokee* brethren.

With his hair plaited into a queue down his back, a silk head-piece, a white doeskin shirt, yel low leather leggings up to his thighs and a breech-clout, Sam's blue eyes were the only clue to his White birth.

Unlike his trip to this caldron of intrigue garbed as an Indian in 1818, Sam had no rank nor money, but an invitation to the White House awaited him.

Recalling how former Secretary of War John C. Calhoun had become apoplectic at seeing Sam in *Cherokee* rai-

Sam Houston : Cherokee 1830

ment's a dozen years before, he hoped the sitting Vice President would not be among President Jackson's other guests.

Seeing no other carriages outside the White House, Sam wondered if he'd mistaken the date. The meeting was far smaller than expected. Only his old friend John H. Eaton, Secretary of War, awaited him in the President's quarters.

"Good to see you, John, but I was hoping to see the General."

"You will. He's penning a communiqué to Anthony Butler in Mexico City. They're trying to buy Texas for $5 million from Mexico. Talks are barely afloat. Slightest ripple could sink them. That's why the General's enraged by the slightest hint of an American plot to seize Texas."

"I've surely been misquoted in the past on the subject of taking Texas, John."

"Walk wide of it in the future, Sam. You must have plenty of other things on your mind, judging by your letters."

"Plenty, Sir."

"Sit down, Sam. Let's talk till the President joins us."

"Certainly," Sam replied, sinking into a leather overstuffed chair and pouring himself a whopping glass of whiskey from the crystal decanter on the President's desk.

"What have you been doing, since you left Tennessee?"

Houston smiled, "I have the feeling you and the General know far more about that than you'll let on."

"Hear you became a *Cherokee* citizen."

"Did it formally on October 21, 1829 -- with all privileges and immunities as though natural born. I say I am the Raven again. But my father *Oo-loo-te-ka* says that even though I appear *Cherokee* in all things, I still cast a white shadow."

"How are things with the *Cherokees*?"

"Abysmal."

"What's wrong?"

"*Cherokees* are scattered along the Texas Road -- near Cantonment Gibson in Oklahoma Country -- under siege from all sides."

"Surely, there's no trouble with the U.S. Army."

"None. Cantonment Gibson's Colonel Arbuckle tipples a bit with us, but he can't muster enough troops to protect a hen house let alone control the Hostiles. The *Pawnees, Osages* and the *Comanches* raid us *Cherokees* constantly without fear of reprisal."

"Can't you keep the tribes from warring?"

"No. *Pierre Aguste Chouteau* has accompanied me to *Osage* villages, where he's a virtual God. They respect him, and if ever a man deserved to be their Indian Agent, *Pierre* is that man. But the *Osages* are rampaging predators. *Cherokee* wigwams, livestock, slaves, fields, muskets and fine clothes turn the *Osages* to wolves. Can you help us, John?"

"Very little. Congress has abandoned the Indian cause. Senators grumble about the scores of expensive treaties with the tribes. They complain about $3,000 spent for Chiefs' portraits in three months. Senator made a floor speech about an exorbitant Indian Hotel bill for oysters on the half shell, gin slings and damaged furniture."

"Those are lost acorns! Let's talk of burnt forests."

"Let's do. What's the problem?"

"Five corrupt Indian agents." Sam handed Secretary Eaton his crumpled list.

As the Secretary read the names, Sam rasped, "That first man should be in irons."

Eaton read, "Major E. W. Duval. Why?"

"I went to Fort Smith in Arkansas Territory to witness the government's annual treaty payment to the *Cherokee* Nation of $50,000 in gold coin due for millions of acres of *Cherokee* land confiscated in Georgia and Tennessee. Fort Smith was agog with prostitutes and whiskey runners. But Duval and his sub-agent Hamtramck stole all the money before the other thieves even got there by issuing worthless *Certificates of Indebtedness* to the *Cherokees* and keeping the gold for themselves."

"Have that much on these other three Agents?"

Houston thought a moment then said, "Close."

"Put it in writing, and I'll tear them out by the roots!"

They adjourned to the dining room, where Andrew Jackson awaited, looking more cadaverous than ever. He rose, extending his claw of a hand into a handshake. He pretended Sam was properly attired to eat in the White House, and dinner was served.

"Sam, I asked John to advise you why there can be no more irresponsible talk of conquering Texas," the President said, stopping to suck a strand of roast beef from between his teeth.

"John told me, Mr. President. There will be none."

"What's come of your marriage, Sam?"

"From what I know of it sitting out in Oklahoma Country, I'd call it stalemated hatred."

"Any chance of reconciliation?"

"About as much as your ceding the Presidency of this nation back to John Quincy Adams, Sir."

Jackson scowled, "Not too likely, then?"

"No greater than yours with Mr. Adams."

The second mention of Adams irritated the President, who struggled to cut another slice of his roast beef.

"Mr. President, how are things between yourself and Senator Thomas Hart Benton?"

"I count Senator Benton a loyal supporter, although that assessment does not extend to his serpent of a brother Jesse."

"Senator Benton's been writing to me on the frontier. Wants me to promote western expansion with all of my being."

Jackson looked up angrily. "Well, if that includes a Texas takeover, you'll denounce that until we know if Mexico'll sell it."

"Rest assured, I'll merely exchange pleasantries on Texas with Senator Benton, Mr. President."

With his stomach paining him, President Jackson withdrew after a brusque handshake, retiring to his private quarters.

Sam asked, "What's eating the General, John?"

"Wolves ripped him bloody today."

"Am I one of them?"

"Not directly, Sam."

"How then?"

Eaton got up. Let's go back to the private office. Never know who's listening in the dining room."

John Eaton walked like a beaten man. Once cloistered, Eaton lighted his pipe. Blowing out the smoke, he muttered," The President's working on the Indian Removal Act of 1830."

"What's that entail, John?"

"$500,000 appropriation to remove 53,000 *Cherokees, Creeks, Choctaws & Chickasaws* into 33 million acres in the Trans-Mississippi southwest."

Houston shook his head. "Western tribes are already outraged by hordes of eastern Indians overrunning their lands. My peacemaking efforts are feeble as whispers into a cyclone. We can't control the situation now, let alone after 53,000 more are deluged upon us."

John Eaton poured Houston four fingers in his crystal water glass from the President's private bourbon decanter. "His spies told him this morning that Great Britain's also bargaining with Mexico to buy Texas."

"President have many spies?"

"You remember how many spies he had in the war? He has more now because he has countless enemies to spy on. He's got somebody in everybody's camp."

"How well I know. That all of it, John?"

"No, Congressman Crockett who served under the General in the Creek War's become the tool of the Whigs. He's trying to become a feudal land baron over the ragtag squatters of western Tennessee."

"I know Andrew Jackson prizes loyalty above all else."

"He's loyal to a fault himself.

"Is that directed at me, John?"

"No, myself. My wife Peggy's involved in the Petticoat Wars."

"What the hell's that?" Houston asked, gulping bourbon from his glass.

"Peggy -- has led a colorful life. Certain Cabinet wives have refused to attend any function where Peggy's present. The situation's been aggravated by bigots, busybodies and the President's strident protestations that Peggy's as chaste as the Virgin Mary."

"Sounds like the bard's *Much Ado About Nothing.*"

"It's gotten so bad the President's going to pick up the Dutch Ambassador's diplomatic visa unless his wife recants her boycott of Peggy."

"Looks like our marriages have jeopardized our standing with the President, John."

"You could read the *Washington Globe* through the thin ice upon which we stand, Sam."

During his Washington stay, Sam conceived a plan with New York financier John Van Fossen to bid for the government contract to supply the *Cherokees* in Indian Territory with rations mandated by their treaty with the United States.

On February 18, 1830 Houston's bid and Van Fossen's

money in a sealed envelope reached John H. Eaton's desk.

The following day Secretary Eaton fired five Indian Agents and Sub-agents on Sam Houston's written charges. No sooner had their official heads rolled than their countercharges exploded like artillery fire around Houston. They claimed Houston, Eaton and Jackson himself had conspired to obtain the *Cherokee* ration contract. Though their proof of conspiracy was nil, the ice under Houston and Eaton got gossamer thin.

An unsigned note addressed to Sam arrived at his hotel. It read, "*In 1818, you came to Washington and bullwhipped a coterie of crooked Indian Agents, who countered with malignant charges that nearly got you imprisoned. It appears that small minded men who make history never learn from it.*" Sam could visualize the absent signature of Vice President *John C. Calhoun* on the note.

Needless to say, Houston and Van Fossen did not win the contract to supply rations to the *Cherokees.* Apart from their flagrant conflicts of interest, the official reason advanced was that they had not submitted the lowest bid.

Not that Sam Houston needed an excuse to carouse, but he proceeded to drink Van Fossen into oblivion in the bar of Brown's Indian Queen Hotel. *Bon vivant* Dr. Robert Mayo, who joined them, matched Houston drink for drink as he recounted his endless exploits. But as the night wobbled into the wee hours, Mayo bled damning information from his loose-tongued *Cherokee* companion, who had no idea Mayo was emptying his own toddies into the ice pail.

Crestfallen and broke, Sam Houston departed Washington in early April 1830 without calling on the President, who was ramming the Indian Removal Act through Congress, or John Eaton whose wife Peggy continued to generate etiquette earthquakes among the social set.

By late May 1830 Houston reached the *Cherokees* in Oklahoma Country. Though Sam's adopted father *Oo-loo-te-ka* was 65, he still stood six feet with a courtly grace to his walk and greeted the Raven as the tribe's hero.

Oo-loo-te-ka asked Sam to negotiate peace with the *Osages* and the *Delawares* ravaging the *Cherokees* and scalping their children. Sam risked his life to implore the Chiefs of both tribes not to delight the Whites by killing other Indians. The ingenious argument did nothing to halt the killing.

One May evening in 1830 Sam met the stately daughter of Scotch-Irish trader Hell-Fire Jack Rogers and a *Cherokee* wife. Sam'd known the slender beauty since her carefree childhood in Tennessee, but now she seemed forlorn.

In *Cherokee* he asked her, "What saddens you?"

She replied, "Please speak English. My husband David was murdered by the *Osages*."

Sam recalled she'd been married to a large, prosperous, mixed-blood blacksmith named David Gerry.

"What do you call yourself now?"

"*Tiana* Rogers."

"Weren't you once *Talahina*?"

"That was my little girl name."

"I had forgotten that you are more beautiful than warm rain at sunset."

"My Anglo name is Diana."

"*Tiana* is perfect. How long have you mourned David?"

"In two days it will be a year."

"Has your heart healed?"

"It will never heal," *Tiana* whispered, "But I do not sit with the old women. My life cries out to be lived."

"I am the same blood as your father Hell-Fire Jack -- Scotch-Irish. Are you seeking a man of *Cherokee* blood?"

"No. Like my father, only your drinking saddens me, because you are so noble when you are sober, Raven."

He viewed her head to foot. She was a fully ripened woman in every sense.

She asked, "Do you have a Tennessee wife?"

"She fled my house after our wedding and refuses to return. She may be my wife to the Whites, but under *Cherokee* law, she is a stranger."

"Why do you look upon me?"

"Like you I'm lonely. Do you know any woman who favors me?"

"No." The wind gently mussed her long black hair and pressed her doeskin dress to her body. "I cannot say I know myself, for few ever do."

Sam Houston smiled, "Will you walk with me?"

They walked hand in hand into the setting sun until a short, burly *Osage* warrior leaped into their path with his lance raised high.

Sam shielded *Tiana*. In broken *Osage*, Sam said, "Your people killed this woman's man without reason. She wishes to live in peace."

The *Osage* snarled and pulled back his lance.

Sam Houston lurched forward, kicking the warrior in the gut with all the power his 6'5" frame could muster. The *Osage* lost his lance and sprawled on his back. Sam broke the lance over his knee, then whacked the warrior about the head and body with the shaft until the smaller man ran, leaving Sam and *Tiana* laughing.

"Place this broken *Osage* lance on David's grave as my tribute of peace to him and his lovely wife."

Tiana took the lance and murmured, "David sent you to fill my life and protect me. Why must we both be so lonely?"

"To end our loneliness, I must speak to your father."

"You can't."

"Why?"

"He's drunk. Let's speak to *Oo-loo-te-ka*."

The marriage of Sam Houston and *Tiana* Rogers was a traditional *Cherokee* ceremony amid great celebration in her father Hell-Fire Jack's large house. *Oo-loo-te-ka* smiled, "Now that you have taken your *Cherokee* wife, Raven, your white shadow has fled."

Sam and *Tiana* settled at Wigwam Neosho on the Texas Road near Cantonment Gibson. *Tiana* pointed to the road. "One day I will lose you to that road, if the whiskey does not steal you from me before then."

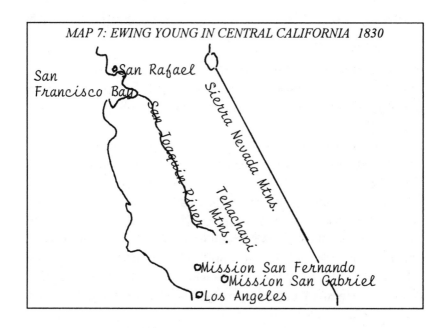

San
Francisco Bay

San Rafael

Sierra Nevada Mtns.

San Joaquin River

Tehachapi
Mtns.

oMission San Fernando
oMission San Gabriel
Los Angeles

CHAPTER 28

CALIFORNIA PARADISE   MAY - SEPTEMBER 1830

E wing Young and Father *José Sanchez* rested after breakfast on a bench of hand hewn planks rawhided together under a palm tree in Mission San Gabriel's courtyard. Ewing mused, "California is a paradise swathed in the world's most exquisite mysteries. Where does its name come from, Father?"

The Priest smiled, "Even that is a mystery. Romantics say it commemorates *Califia*, queen of the sea mists. Most believe *Hernan Cortes* christened California in 1536 for the fictional island of great wealth in his favorite novel by Spaniard *Garci Ordoñez de Montalvo*."

"Though California baffles me at every turn, I must see more of it. We leave within the hour. Thank you for your gracious hospitality, Father."

"*Vaya con Dios!*"

Ewing Young led his brigade from Mission San Gabriel to Mission San Fernando, a day's travel. Wary of being jailed, Young made his men eat their fresh vegetable meal in the

204

courtyard where only the mission's ghosts could have ambushed them. Ignoring Kit Carson's complaints that "...vegetables is goat fodder," Ewing headed northwest into the rugged Tehachapi Mountains. He camped high enough on a mountainside to see a long stretch of backtrail.

Reaching the San Joaquin River in early June, they trapped streams so beaver rich, they got three sets a day from some traps. But as suddenly as the bonanza'd bloomed, it died. Tracks and beaver guts said other trappers were hooping their plews. Several days later, Ewing found them.

Ewing cold-camped his trappers in a grove atop a small rise, standing six men on watch. At sunset, Ewing Young and Kit Carson crept up on 60 men camping under a fluttering flag emblazoned with stags and beavers. Ewing whispered, "The Old Lady of the North."

Frowning, Kit asked, "Where's a ole woman?"

"Their flag," Ewing chuckled, yelling, "Hello, the Camp!"

A sawed-off man about 35 stalked toward them on tree-thick legs with his rifle angled over his shoulder and an inquiring scowl. "Friend or foe?" he queried curtly.

Ewing countered, "Friend, or you'd have three eyes."

"Peter Skene Ogden of the Hudson's Bay Company," the dark stocky man growled through a grin, extending his hand.

"Ewing Young and Kit Carson," Ewing replied. "We're camped an easy rifle shot down your backtrail. Why not join us after supper? We'd be honored to host your wives as well."

Looking mystified, Ogden asked, "How did you know of our wives?"

"People mislead each other with their mouths, not their moccasins," Ewing smiled.

"We will come, Mr. Young."

As whining mosquitoes swarmed around Ewing Young's fire, Peter Skene Ogden trudged into the firelight with his Indian wife three paces behind him. Some trappers lavished lady lodge partners with hawk's bells and gewgaws, but Ogden's thickset wife was free of ornaments. Her buckskins were plain like her husband's. She even walked with his deliberate strides. Ewing said, "Somebody bring Mrs. Ogden a blanket."

Though he didn't introduce his stoic mate, the shine in

Ogden's eye said he appreciated Ewing's deference. "I had mis-givings about coming here, Mr. Young."

All sat snug to the fire to escape flying bloodsuckers. "Americans are not as boorish as their reputations." Ewing splashed Taos Lightning into the Ogdens' tin cups.

"You're older than I envisioned you, Mr. Ogden."

"This life turns a young man 60 overnight. Wading cold water all day to earn a few shillings per beaver -- a convict at Botany Bay is a gentleman at ease compared to a trapper."

"Been trapping that long?"

Ogden reminisced, "Served with the American Fur Company for a quail's flight 20 years ago. Went with the North West Company till she was devoured by HBC in 1821. I've met the run of Americans from the Johnson Gardeners who shout ultimatums to Methodist oracles like Jedediah Smith acutely interested in saving me from perdition."

"What's Jedediah like?"

"Educated -- courtly like yourself -- but openly devout."

Mrs. Ogden signed with her right forefinger pointed straight up, then raised her arm fully to say Ewing was "Taller."

Peter Ogden continued, "Met Jedediah at Fort Vancouv-er after his California debacle in 1828. Matter of fact we just followed the route Jedediah laid out past your big salty inland sea down to the Gulf of California. Jedediah cautioned us about the perils of ambush while fording the Colorado."

"Why's that?" Ewing asked.

"*Mojaves* massacred ten of his men there."

Kit Carson grunted, "We seen where it happened."

Ogden lamented, "Still got attacked there ourselves by the *Mojaves* this February past. Lost a friend of many years."

Ewing splashed the tin cups with whiskey. Peter's ex-pressionless wife whispered to her husband. He frowned.

"Our whiskey too raw?" Ewing inquired.

Ogden shook his head. "Urges me to recount her show-down with the Americans last year."

"Our trappers attacked her?"

"Not exactly, Ewing."

"What happened?"

Ogden's wife made the signs for her husband to talk fast.

"Joe Meek's outfit braced us in Ogden's Hole, a Utah Country valley among the Bear River Mountains. They bartered with our *Iroquois* trappers for furs, but didn't garner a pelt until they cracked their whiskey. Soon, a year of our men's peltry was squandered for a pittance. Before I could take them to task, several of our horses stampeded into the American camp -- her horse among them with our baby clinging to the saddle."

"Your baby hurt?" Kit asked.

"Wife stormed into the hostile camp, leaped on her horse and rescued our baby -- then saw another HBC fur laden horse held by Americans. She signed she wanted our horse and furs."

"What claim did Joe Meek's men make on the furs?"

"Claimed them as spoils of war!"

"She feigned riding off. Then with our child in one arm, she gave her tribal howl and charged back through the Americans. Seizing the HBC packhorse's rope, she wheeled to ride out. Trappers yelled, '*Shoot Her! Shoot Her!*' Clutching our baby to her breast, she hauled the packhorse through the raised rifles. She heard hammers cock, but galloped through them. Finally, some American trapper yelled, 'You boys fraid to admit we been bested by the Madonna and child?' "

As Ogden finished the tale, his wife rose and bowed sedately. Ewing's trappers clapped so loud they panicked the coyotes just beyond their firelight into yelping flight.

Following Ogden's outfit down the San Joaquin and its tributaries, Ewing's crew shared camps with HBC for ten nights, then parted in the delta of San Francisco Bay with fond farewells all around. Ogden trapped north along the Sacramento River while Young established a base camp in the San Joaquin Valley.

The Americans had never before seen elk, deer and antelope by the thousands. Since summer made beaver pelts unusable, they shot larger game till they had more than enough.

While lying about the resplendent countryside in mid-July, Young's men discovered the perennial feud between savage nomads of the Sierras and Missions near the Coast. Each time mountain tribes raided the Mission horse herds, the government retaliated with a punitive expedition.

Handsome Lieutenant *Francisco Jiménez* and eight *soldados* startled Young's outfit by prancing long-maned horses into their camp in grand style with sliding halts and leaping dismounts.

Displaying his empty hands *Jiménez* told Ewing Young in Spanish, "Deserting neophytes from the Mission San Jose have taken refuge with their horse-stealing kin in the mountains. We beg your help in retaking them. If these renegades escape, the whole Mission System is doomed!"

After polling his bored trappers, Ewing Young sent Kit Carson and 11 men with the *soldados*. Reaching the horse-stealer village, Kit Carson led an attack that degenerated into a day long sniper battle. The Indians were routed, losing a third of their warriors to the dead-shot trappers. Refusing to surrender the fugitives incensed the *soldados*, who burned the village.

Next morning Kit signed to the horse-stealers all would lie dead by noon if they did not yield the fugitives. The runaways marched out and were promptly returned to the grateful Priests.

Gathering the beaver they'd trapped in California, Ewing Young, Kit Carson and four trappers trekked to Mission San Rafael in the first week of August 1830. Young did not disclose his full plan to his men, but his first step was to sell his peltry.

Hide and tallow trader Captain John Cooper, who'd once befriended both Jedediah Smith and James Ohio Pattie, met Ewing at the Mission. Cooper was a proper, hatchet-faced New Englander in a ship's officer uniform. "Seems you've not alienated every Priest in California like some I've met here."

"We returned the Mission's runaways, pleasing them handsomely," Ewing replied.

"Must have. Soldiers are not collectin' duties on your beaver. I'll take your entire haul at $3 the pound."

"Make it $3.25 and I won't sell it all to *Don José Asero*."

Cooper laughed, "Wasn't for your Tennessee drawl, I'd make you for a Downeaster! $3.25 it'll be! My schooner'll be burstin' its hatches with musty beaver."

With Ewing's peltry money, he purchased a herd of carefully inspected horses from the Mission. Unable to ride with anything approaching the skill of the Mexicans, Ewing's men herded the horses clumsily back to camp. They planned to hobble the horses after supper. While venison sizzled over their fires, Indians stampeded 60 head into the growing darkness. Furious, Kit Carson saddled his horse. Kit would've taken after them alone if Ewing hadn't made him wait for the other 11 men.

Within a mile, Kit discovered 14 horses milling about in a draw. Two men herded them back to Ewing's camp.

Their other horses were being driven off at a gallop. Their herd's dust smeared the sunset two days running, but the unshod tracks never had horses in them. Pausing to wolf down cold venison, Kit muttered, "They git them horses into a large herd, we're whupped. Gotta catch 'em *pronto* er we're gonna come back with what the cross-eyed Injun shot at."

August's days chilled as Kit's men tracked the lost herd into the majestic Sierra Nevadas. About 100 miles into the mountains, the thieves slaughtered six horses. Kit could have attacked while they were gutting Ewing's mares, but badly out-numbered, he waited. Kit whispered, "Druther fight a feller with a full belly than somebody who's hungry-mean and wide awake."

"We're plenty hungry, Kit!"

"And yer plumb put out about it. That there's the point!"

As the horse-feast ended, Kit's men charged, killing eight Indians outright and recovering all stolen horses except those eaten. The rest fled, leaving three wide-eyed children among their dead kin. "Whatta we gonna do with these tikes, Kit?"

"Make sure they've et and take 'em with us. We leave 'em here, wolves and bears'll be feastin' here next."

On September 1, 1830, Ewing Young's outfit headed south. *Gobernador José Echeandia's* reputation as a jailer of foreigners caused Ewing to shy wide of the settlements.

Short of fresh water, Ewing broke his own rule and strayed into the Pueblo of Los Angeles. Mexican *soldados* de-manded their California passports, refusing to consider New Mexico licenses and papers valid.

When Mexican authorities started selling liquor to his men, Ewing called them aside. "They want to arrest us, but fear's holding 'em back. Get drunk and you're in jail."

Some grumbled, but Kit Carson snapped, "Anybody that

ain't got a pitch knot tween his ears kin see Ewin's right."

Ewing motioned Kit aside. "Take our three best men, all the loose animals, packs and the like and forge ahead. If I don't reach your camp by tomorrow, move on and report us as killed, for I'll not leave a man behind to rot in a dungeon."

In spite of Ewing's sage warnings, most of his dozen men got drunk on the way to the Mission San Gabriel. Mexican officials offered them more to drink at every step. Ewing knew once these Mexicans added the 15 San Gabriel *soldados* to their force, they'd seize everybody.

Before Ewing plotted his counter move, fate made it for him. Hideously drunk, James Higgins dismounted from his horse and joined the outfit's loudmouth bully "Big Jim" Lawrence at the side of the trail for a necessary stop. Big Jim doused Higgins' leg. Higgins pulled his pistol and blew away the right side of Big Jim's head from his eye back to his ear.

Higgins' unprovoked murder of his fellow American unnerved the Mexicans. They spurred their horses into the dusk.

Ewing knew the *soldados* would reinforce and come after them, so he left Big Jim sprawled in the dirt with his buckskins down and yelled, "Light out!"

While Ewing rode hard to catch Carson's crew in the desert, he couldn't help regretting how one drunken man had sullied paradise for them all with a single bullet. At least Eve'd had a serpent and a semblance of an excuse.

CHAPTER 29

THE BEAVER MINE   **SEPTEMBER - DECEMBER 1830**

After galloping his men past the Mission San Gabriel, Ewing Young located Kit Carson, his three stalwarts, the pack horses and loose animals at dusk.

Kit hailed, "Looks like them boys got sobered up."

Ewing snapped, "The hard way."

"How's zat?"

Reining in his lathered horse, Ewing spat, "Higgins blew Big Jim Lawrence's head off."

"Big Jim had it comin'. You got a Mexican escort?"

"Will have if we don't get outa here. Soon as we saddle new mounts, scatter these half-dead horses down our back trail while we break camp. Mexicans'll likely round up our spent horses and head back to their barracks *para comida*."

Cutting their old trail into California, they rode through the night, then cold-camped. With no sign of pursuit, they reached the Colorado River in eight days.

Deciding to rest his weary men and mounts for a couple of days, Ewing camped near the Colorado and led a trapping party. Minutes after Ewing and the trappers left, several hundred unarmed *Mojave* warriors swarmed the camp manned only by Kit Carson and four others. Having been tricked before by trappers leaving a few men as bait, the Chief had them hide their weapons and feign friendship until he explored the camp. Kit sent his four men to bring back the rest of the brigade.

While the *Mojaves* tried to solve the puzzle, Kit shadowed the Chief, loading his pistols so the Chief knew he'd be the first to die if a fight started.

Unable to find Ewing or the other trappers, Kit's scouts unearthed the *Mojave* weapons cache by the river. One legged it back to let Kit in on their find. Kit said, "Git back there and give them guns a swim."

Convinced the meek die before the brave, Kit stood beside the Chief and yelled, "*¿Habla Español?*"

A *Mojave* no bigger than Kit said, "*Yo hablo.*"

Kit told him in Spanish the trappers had tossed the *Mojaves'* weapons in the Colorado River. Glaring at the hundreds of Indians surrounding him, Kit Carson told the interpreter to order all *Mojaves* to leave inside of ten minutes. Kit added that if one *Mojave* was still in camp after that, he would be shot dead. Before ten minutes were up, Kit Carson stood alone, wiping his sweaty face on his sleeve.

Without further *Mojave* interference, Ewing's men trapped down the south side of the Colorado to tidewater, then up the north side to the mouth of the Gila River in Sonora [Arizona], amassing a gigantic haul of beaver.

Trapping up the Gila to its junction with the San Pedro River, they discovered a sprawling Indian village and a vast horse herd with feathers braided into mane and tail. Ewing called his men to council. "A mole could see these ponies are stolen."

A trapper smelling of beaver bait asked, "Whatta ya say, Ewin'?"

Ewing grinned, "Steal their horses. Since my herd's melted away, we need fresh mounts and pack horses to haul all this beaver."

Ewing's howling trappers thundered into the horsethief hamlet, putting the Indians to flight without firing a single ball. As the sun came to rest on the snow capped mountains, the hooting trappers restole scores of Indian ponies.

That night, ground-thunder rolled under Ewing's camp. Convinced the Indians were stealing their horses back, the trappers grabbed their guns, forked their horses bareback and galloped into the moonlight to thwart this foul injustice.

But the 200 horses bounding through the moonbeams with Mexican Sonora brands, were herded by a handful of *Utes*. Intoxicated by the moonlight spectacle, the trappers fired over the heads of the *Utes*, scattering them into the silvery hills.

Next morning, Ewing's men selected the finest riding horses and pack animals from their vast throng. They butchered ten for jerky, leaving the others wild-eyed and flighty.

Kit Carson squatted beside Ewing Young. Silently, they gorged on fresh brazed horse while burning pine knots spat hot pitch on their dirty buckskins. Kit sleeved meat juice off his face. "Ain't gonna herd all these horses back to Taos, are we?"

"Take ten times the men we have to do that."

"Whatcha gonna do with 'em?"

"Give 'em to God."

"What?"

"Everybody else's already had 'em."

Leaving several hundred horses wild and free to graze the sparse grasses, Ewing's party filed out riding the strongest and leading the sturdiest under bulging loads of beaver.

As they continued up the Gila River, Kit Carson spurred his horse up beside Ewing Young's. "Where we headed?"

"Rather get paid, or have Mexican troops take our furs?"

"That there's a real hard choice."

Ewing ordered an early camp. After dark, Young rode out alone. Returning around ten, he yelled, "Get the hard knots outa your beaver pack ropes, boys. Beaver are going to ground for a couple weeks."

In tribute to their trust in Ewing Young, not a man balked while Ewing, Kit and five others led pack animals piled high with beaver into the night.

Robert McKnight waited for them at the Santa Rita Copper Mines. Not sharing his dead partner James Baird's hatred of American trappers, McKnight helped them lower their beaver packs into a worked-out mining shaft.

"Mines are spooky at night. That somebody moving around over there in the dark?" Ewing panted.

The heavily muscled McKnight shook his head. "Not sposed to be anybody in nere now. Some say they seen old Sylvester Pattie searchin' these shafts for the thief *Señor.*"

"James Ohio Pattie's father?" Ewing asked.

"Smart feller too, but fool enough to send his *mayor-domo Señor* to Santa Fe with $30,000 to buy supplies. What'd you say your beaver's worth?"

"I didn't. There's over 2,000 pounds. My sentries'll bunk here with that beaver till I get back, so you won't have to worry about any pelts walking off."

McKnight nodded, "Fine, but don't let your men build fires. Once in a while these tunnels fills with sumpthin' like swamp gas and blows up. How long fore you're back, Ewin'?"

"Under a week."

Riding hard, Young and Carson covered the 60 miles to Santa Fe in two days. Ewing had no trouble procuring a license to trade with the Indians along the Gila River. He dispatched Kit Carson and several others to bring their beaver to Santa Fe.

Santa Fe fur traders were astounded at how Ewing Young could trade for a ton of furs between two deep snows. While paying Ewing, one Mexican fur buyer asked, "How do jew geet so much beaver so queeck?"

Ewing quipped, "The Indians had a beaver mine!"

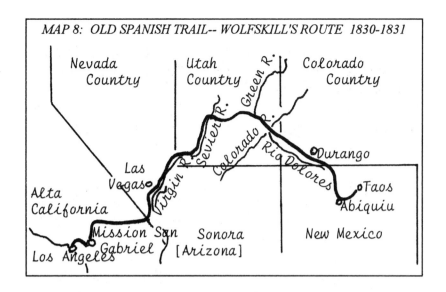

MAP 8: OLD SPANISH TRAIL-- WOLFSKILL'S ROUTE 1830-1831

Nevada Country

Utah Country

Green R.

Colorado Country

Las Vegas

Sevier R.

Colorado

Rio Dolores

Durango

Alta California

Virgin R.

Taos

Abiquiu

Mission San Gabriel

Los Angeles

Sonora [Arizona]

New Mexico

CHAPTER 30

WOLFSKILL'S OLD SPANISH TRAIL FALL 1830 - WINTER 1831

W illiam Wolfskill began to worry what had become of his partner Ewing Young in California. No matter what he did in Taos, the fear that Ewing might be rotting in jail out there gnawed at him.

Men Wolfskill tried to enlist for a fall beaver hunt in California told him it was too late in the year to travel the high country. He only had to ask himself, "Would Ewing do it to save me?"

He sought reckless men who would fight no matter the odds. Naturally the first man on that list was Old Bill Williams.

William Wolfskill

215

Deeply pockmarked with long red hair to the shoulders of his filthy buckskins, Old Bill Williams braced Wolfskill at his Taos store. "Hear you're looking for me."

Wolfskill nodded. "I'm signing trappers to go to California."

"In September?"

"Before the first fall snow."

"What'll you do out there?"

"Find Ewing Young and trap California's rivers with both our outfits.

"Happy to know I'm not the only madman in Taos."

"Know anybody else as wild as you?"

"Peg-leg Smith, if I can sober him up enough to strap his leg on. What's a trapper worth to you?"

"Pint of Taos Lightning for every man you sign, but you must drink it before we go. Whiskey'll not wreck our fall hunt."

"I'll shake out a few saloons to see who turns up."

Wolfskill watched Old Bill's wide strides, fascinated by how a man could walk like a gate with no hinges.

Having become a naturalized Mexican citizen on March 25, 1830, Wolfskill had no trouble getting Governor *Manuel Armijo* to issue a license in September to *José Guillermo Wolfskill* to hunt *nutria*, New Mexico's provincial word for beaver.

Somehow Wolfskill convinced Dutch George Yount to join his fall hunt along the Old Spanish Trail to California. Yount signed free trappers Zachariah Ham, namesake of Ham's Fork on the Green River, *Francisco LeFourri*, Alexander Branch, *Baptiste St. Germain* and *Bautista Guerra*.

In mid-September Wolfskill enrolled John Lewis, Ziba [Zebediah] Branch, John Rhea, Sam Shields and David Keller as trapper employees for his trip.

Wolfskill got wily trader *Ceran St. Vrain* to sign other trappers willing to work for wages. *Ceran* recruited Nathaniel Pryor, *José Archuleta, Manuel Mondragon*, Love Hardesty, *Blas Griego*, Martin Cooper and Lewis Burton. But the 28 year old *Ceran St. Vrain's* partnership with Charles Bent kept him too busy to leave Taos "on an errand of the insane."

A week before Wolfskill's expedition was set to leave,

Lemuel Carpenter, William Chard, Dan Sill and *Juan Lobar*, all dredged up by Old Bill Williams, entered Wolfskill's Taos store. Wolfskill told them of his fair wages and keep for employees.

What Wolfskill didn't say was that he had different wages for everybody. Employees'd get their food and $7 a month with some receiving $8 and others as much as $20. Free trappers would get $5 per beaver skin and pay for their food.

Wolfskill assured the men, "I'll haul flour and drive cattle for food. Free trappers who don't wanta buy my food, can hunt their own. They'll still get $5 a skin for beaver."

"What about trade goods for free trappers?" William Chard whined. "I'm too stove up to stand belly deep in ice water all day. Druther buy gewgaws to trade to Injuns for peltry."

The merchant in Wolfskill came to life. "Goods'll be priced fair to you boys. Tobacco and gunpowder at $1.50 the pound. Lead 50¢ the pound and gunflints 3¢ each. Knives $1. Awls 12½¢. Combs 50¢. Strands of sparkling beads and bright vermilion sticks 25¢. Shirts $3 and shoes $3 the pair. Jews harps 25¢. We'll carry the finest linen, calico and even real silk stockings!"

"I'll buy a pair o' them stockin's m'self jist to look at. Like havin' a lady along," Chard grinned.

The men muttered among themselves through a pint of Taos Lightning, then all signed on as employees or free trappers.

The night of September 28th, Wolfskill doled out five pints of whiskey to half-soused Old Bill Williams, who confessed, "Me and Peg-leg Smith don't mind shooting it out with *Apaches*, but being found froze black when the snow melts is way too respectable for a couple o' rowdies like us."

On September 29, 1830 William Wolfskill's 20 men left Taos on what he hoped would be the grand adventure of their lives. But he had no idea he'd never see his beloved Taos again.

Heading southwest in swirling rains for two days, Wolfskill's outfit reached the *pueblo* of Abiquiu as the downpour froze to sleet. There he purchased four bullocks to be driven along for meat. After drying their clothing, the trappers bought woven woolen *capotes, serapes* and *fresadas* to turn rain and snow and keep out the mountain cold that numbed a man.

Taking advantage of a warm foggy spell, they swung

north following the Chama River into what some called Colorado Country. When the sky cleared, they packed west to the San Juan River, eventually passing a few miles south of the hat-sized *pueblo* of Durango.

As the weather iced everything, they veered northwest. After fording the freezing Animas River, they camped to ponder the course of the legendary Old Spanish Trail while they dried out. Mexican *Manuel Mondragon* spoke reverently of *Juan de Oñate's* lost route of 1604, finishing, "I can feel een my bones that we walk in hees footsteps."

Gnawing half-frozen beef in face-numbing cold, *José Archuleta* told of his great grandfather's sojourn under *Juan Maria de Rivera* along the San Juan River across the Uncompagre Plateau to California in 1765. But *Archuleta* had no idea where their ancient tracks were.

Finally, Wolfskill said, "I'd settle for finding Ewing Young's trail from last year -- or better -- jist Ewing."

Laconic silversmith Nathaniel Pryor said, "On Pattie's 1828 expedition, we went hundreds of miles south of our current course -- and were ten times warmer."

Wolfskill muttered, "Our luck better beat Patties'. I don't relish dying in a California jail."

Pryor's misty eyes peered under grizzled brows. "I died each day in that filthy prison. Don't ask why I'm goin' back, cause I don't have the slightest inkling."

To quiet the rumbles Pryor set off, Wolfskill snapped, "This expedition's led by a Catholic citizen of Mexico with all proper papers and licenses."

Somebody growled, "That's plumb dandy if we don't hafta burn them papers to keep from freezin' to death."

Next day, they followed the Rio Dolores northwest, futilely trapping its icy banks as they headed for what some called Utah Country.

During a respite from the screaming winds, they forded the Colorado River, pressing west over Salt Wash to the Green River. Finding the Green too scant of beaver to trap, they turned due west. Freezing tree trunks split like rifle shots, making the men wild-horse-skittish -- rifles aimed with nobody to shoot at. Still they trooped on, great staggering bundles of furs with faces swathed in woolen scarves.

Emerging from the frosty pines at the edge of the Sevier River, Wolfskill's party suddenly faced a horde of *Utah* Indians. Before anyone could fire, Dutch George Yount recognized several Indians he'd met before in this awe inspiring valley and yelled, "Hold your fire!"

While talking with the *Utahs* in their tongue, Yount learned by accident that his party'd interrupted the burial ceremonies of a great *Utah* Chief.

Dutch George said in their language, "We are here to pay the respects of the Great Father in Washington to your honored Chief. Our Great Father, equipped with mighty rifles, big cabins and many braves is the son of the Great Spirit who rolls the sun; whose pipe makes the clouds; whose gun makes the thunder and whose rifle flashes the red lightning."

The *Utahs* bowed down before Yount. Seeing this, Yount gathered a handful of loose dirt from their fire pit and sprinkled some on each of their heads. Yount announced, "Chief Wolfskill, will bid each of you to kiss his rifle out of respect for the Great Father at Washington. Once that be done, the Great Father's gifts will ease your sorrow and insure peace between us while we trap your lands."

After the rifle kissing, Yount presented the Indians with knives, tobacco, beads, awls and vermilion -- as Wolfskill noted each precious item in a ledger that hinted at his bankruptcy.

The *Utahs* set the wood ablaze under their Chief's body. As the astonished trappers watched, three of the dead Chief's servants threw themselves onto his blazing funeral pyre to burn in silence with their patriarch.

Still shaken, the trappers followed the Sevier River until they found themselves slogging deep snow on a high plateau. There, blew the most fearsome blizzard any of them had ever suffered. While shrieking winds ripped at his paper, George Yount wrote: "*During several days no one ventures out of camp. Here we lay embedded in snow, very deep, animals and men huddled thick as possible together ....having spread our thick and heavy blankets, piled bark, brush wood and beaver skins around and over us....*"

Falling snow gave way to paralyzing rain, only to be

silenced by cold so intense it smothered everything with a crust of ice. When the storm subsided, the forest remained a brilliant crystal-glass wonderland against the dark blue sky.

Yount and Wolfskill scaled the nearest peak. Panting clouds around his face, Wolfskill confided, "I must abandon my plan to enter the north of California. The bitter cold, scarcity of food -- the demoralization and disorganization seizing this motley company -- leave me no choice but to turn south."

Yount nodded, pointing his bare trigger finger through the hole in his mitten at the frozen Sevier River. "There's our course if we live to follow it."

Descending the icy tableland into a canyon leading to the Little Salt Lake, they stopped to slaughter their last bullock as it shivered violently in the arctic cold.

Building a bounteous bonfire to hearten the men and roast the bullock through, Wolfskill decided to blaze an Old Spanish Trail others could follow by slash-axing the trees and placing rock piles atop the snow.

Rested and fed, Wolfskill's party struggled south to the Santa Clara River. They hugged its red rock banks to its junction with the Virgin River in Sonora [Arizona]. In freezing twilight, they camped among sheltering crimson crags that shaped the wind into the scream of a trapped cougar.

Continuing southwest, they braved cruel desert gales and searched for an Indian *pueblo* some called Las Vegas, but couldn't ferret it out of the blowing snow and swirling sands.

At the Colorado River, they swung south into the land of the *Mojaves*. Though reputed as a treacherous tribe among Mountain Men, the *Mojaves* of this small village gave Wolfskill's men bread kneaded from pounded corn and baked in ashes, dried pumpkins and small white beans in exchange for red cloth, knives and trade trinkets. Continually expecting to be murdered, the trappers rested two days before lurching into the desert to unearth the Mojave River.

Girded with food traded from the *Mojaves* and Colorado River water in every bottle, pan and canteen, they hiked the fuming desert. Reaching the San Bernardino Mountains, they threaded Cajon Pass to the *Rancho* of *Antonio Maria Lugo*. Thinking it was January at the latest, they marveled that it was

February 5, 1831 the day they arrived.

At a meager dinner for the expedition's leaders, *Antonio Lugo* said, "Your countrymen are not the scourge they were once thought to be by Californians."

But wary of meeting Mexican authorities and Priests, Yount muttered, "With our total ignorance of your customs, and our crude buckskins, we are filled with misgivings."

After eating their fill of savory beef and fresh vegetables at the crudely made table in *Lugo's* low-ceilinged dining room, Wolfskill said, "Let's try the Mission San Gabriel. We'll leave the men here till we test our reception."

William Wolfskill and Dutch George Yount got cordial greetings from Father *José Sanchez* at Mission San Gabriel even before Wolfskill revealed he was a naturalized Mexican citizen converted to the Catholic faith.

Father *Sanchez* related, "Your James Ohio Pattie did us a great service inoculating us against smallpox two years ago."

In Spanish, Wolfskill said, "I know and respect *Señor* Pattie. Have you by chance seen my partner Ewing Young?"

Smiling broadly, Father *Sanchez* answered in *Español*, "A truly intelligent fellow, Young. Arrived here in December 1829. We traded him a steer for four knives, and his men rested and dined well for many days as yours are welcome to."

"You know Ewing's whereabouts now?"

"I'm afraid not. One of his drunkards recklessly murdered another. The gracious *Señor* Young was forced to flee with his men past this very Mission last September. My surmise is that he has returned to New Mexico."

Wolfskill hung his head. "That means he was in New Mexico when I left there to look for him in California."

Father *Sanchez* placed his hand on Wolfskill's head, "God meant for you to come to this bountiful land, my son."

His hopes of finding Ewing Young dashed, he brought all his men down from *Lugo Rancho* to the Mission San Gabriel. Gradually recovering from the marrow-freezing cold of their trip, Wolfskill's men basked in California's glorious winter sun.

Father *Sanchez* confided in English that Californians seldom harvested beaver, preferring the lucrative capture of Sea Otters much prized by the Chinese and shipped by schooners across the Pacific. Reading Wolfskill's New Mexico License, Father *Sanchez* mused, "I am amazed that the New Mexico *Licenciar* knew of our Sea Otters."

"Where do you see that?" Wolfskill asked.

"There. *Nutria* is our word for otter. Such a license as this is priceless and is but rarely issued here."

Greatly heartened, Wolfskill released his men to retire to New Mexico with his equipment. Burton, Rhea, Cooper, Ham, Shields and Ziba Branch decided to remain in California. After squaring accounts with them, Wolfskill was destitute and desperate to salvage his barren trapping venture.

Before departing, Wolfskill's men reaped good profits trading their woolen *capotes* and *fresadas* for mules to drive to New Mexico, not realizing they were the forerunners of a decade of trade in such goods over Wolfskill's Old Spanish Trail.

Making the most of the "mistake" in his New Mexico trapping license, Wolfskill decided to build a vessel for hunting Sea Otters with George Yount, Samuel Prentice, Nathaniel Pryor and Richard Laughlin.

With Father *Sanchez's* Indian laborers, the guidance of Boston ship builder Joseph Chapman and timber hauled from the San Bernardino Mountains, California's first-built schooner began taking shape near *El Pueblo de Nuestra Señora la Reina de Los Angeles de Porclunicula*, a sleepy hamlet lying near the Pacific Ocean since its sleepy birth in 1781.

As Wolfskill lay exhausted in his blankets, he wondered if a ship with such humble beginnings would ever sail.

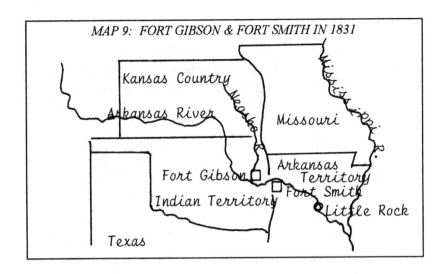

MAP 9: FORT GIBSON & FORT SMITH IN 1831

Kansas Country

Arkansas River

Neosho

Missouri

Mississippi R.

Fort Gibson

Arkansas Territory

Fort Smith

Indian Territory

Little Rock

Texas

CHAPTER 31

ESCAPE FROM FORT GIBSON   FEBRUARY 1831

Deep in Indian Territory with only eight thoroughbreds left in his string, Joe Walker'd roped them together one behind another to keep them from being stampeded by horsethieves. Astride his chesty 17 hand stallion, Joe watched for any sign of frontier renegades. Though he was not a violent man, the brace of .60 caliber pistols in his belt and his rifle *Gunstocker John Walker* across his pommel said he would fight to the death for his horses.

It was unseasonably warm for a winter morning in what some called Oklahoma Country. Bright patches of melting snow painted the rolling earth all the way to the horizon. Walker's horses, recently purchased from the *Cherokees*, knew the country's grasses well, stalling to nibble them. Intending to grain his horses at Fort Gibson, Walker kept the slack out of their lead rope, clucking his tongue to keep them moving.

223

Walker's bay thoroughbreds had been bred in the lush green meadows of Georgia. They'd been driven beyond the old frontier by *Cherokees* who were themselves driven here by a government that rewarded their war service against the *Muskogees* in 1814, by exiling both tribes out here together.

The most expensive mare in the string, a spirited seven year old with a reddish sheen to her coat, had cost Walker $44. She was spirited enough to draw a wise buyer's eye, but not wild enough to make him shy from her.

Joe knew he'd sell all eight glistening beauties at $150 a head to lonely Army Officers who called this grim outpost 100 miles north of the Texas frontier Cantonment Gibson and lavished all their affections on their horses.

Nearing the entrance to the fort beside the muddy Texas Road, Joe Walker reined up in alarm. A lone Indian woman in a heavy coat knelt over a fallen man in buckskins. The slender woman appeared to be trying to shove the huge man onto a travois behind her pony. She could be the decoy in a ruse to rob Walker.

Pulling his dented brass spyglass from his saddlebag, Walker stretched it, probing every shadow around her. Finding nothing wrong, he closed his glass and rode toward them with the eerie feeling he knew the fallen brute in the mud.

She shoved her man closer to the blanket stretched between the two trailing poles tied to her pony.

"Give you a hand?" Walker asked.

She shook her head without looking up.

Joe dismounted, drop-reining his stud. Shouldering her gently aside, he grasped the muddy man, larger than his own sturdy 6'4" frame, and rolled him onto the travois, gasping at sight of his face.

"Does he owe you money?" the *Cherokee* woman asked.

"No," Joe replied trying to conceal his shock.

"Never seen a drunk before?"

"Seen way too many."

"One drunk for a husband is way too many."

"Sam Houston's your husband?"

"You know him?"

"He's my kin. Taught all us Walkers in his Tennessee

school. Fought the Creeks at Horseshoe Bend with Sam."

She wiped her muddy hand down Houston's ornate war shirt, then offered it to Joe. "I am *Tiana* Rogers -- daughter of Hell-Fire Jack Rogers -- your countryman who taught me the care of drunken White Savages from childhood. Who would you be?"

"Joe Walker. What's brought Sam to this?"

"He's a whiskey merchant who's his own best customer. At our home, he has barrels of Monongahela Whiskey, corn liquor, cognac, gin, rum and wine. Once called the Raven by the *Cherokee*, he is now called *Oo-Tse-Tee-Ar-dee-tah-Skee.*"

"What's that in my tongue?"

"Big Drunk."

"Can you forgive his tippling?"

"Drinking's not the only reason the *Cherokee* nation has turned its back on Sam Houston."

"What else's he done?"

"Mindlessly struck his *Cherokee* father, *Oo-Loo-Te-Ka*, causing our Council to denounce him. His white wife in Tennessee ripped his heart out and kept it. Scorned by our people, Sam drinks here at the fort till they vomit him outside."

"He was Governor of Tennessee. Dont' give up on him!"

"Sam Houston has given up on himself."

"Let me help. *Osages* will cut his throat for those beaded buckskins."

Tiana laughed bitterly. "*Osages* believe Sam Houston's a Devil wolf. They will not come near till he's dead." Grabbing her horse's mane, *Tiana* swung easily onto its back. Digging her heels into its flanks, she dragged her drunken husband onto the Texas Road, his noble head lolling back and forth like the pendulum of a pitiful clock on the bouncing travois.

Feeling sick at what he'd seen, Joe leapt astride his stallion and led his string into Fort Gibson's well raked horse lot.

Walker recognized Lieutenant William Montgomery, a connoisseur of horseflesh who'd bought a stallion from Joe at Fort Leavenworth. "Fine mounts in that string!" the bearded Montgomery yelled.

"Interested, Bill?" Walker asked as he slid off his stallion.

"You won't keep these thoroughbreds long."

"From Georgia or Kentucky?"

"Georgia."

"God was feeling kindly when he fashioned these."

"Shouldn't worship openly, Bill. Price goes up."

"You gutted my pay account last time. I'll let the officers know you've got mounts even an Infantryman'd be proud to die on. Captain Bonneville's afoot. I'll find 'im."

"Thanks, Bill." Joe corralled his horses and pulled their ropes off. Opening the fragrant oat bin, he dragged a bucket for each horse, dumping them in feed boxes on the fence. He toweled off their trail dust to shine up their coats. With each rub, Walker tried to wipe away the sickening sight of Sam Houston sprawled on the Indian blanket with drool dripping from his chin.

Montgomery returned in stride with a stocky officer wearing a walrus mustache and an air of authority. "Meet Captain Benjamin Louis Eulalie Bonneville."

Shaking hands with Walker, Bonneville asked, "What're you asking for that Bay Mare with the chestnut tinge?"

"She'll fetch $150 easy, but to Bill's friend -- $125."

"Make out my Bill o' Sale in the Officers' Mess. Had a hard night with Sam Houston, former Governor of Tennessee and missed morning mess call. Isn't he your cousin?"

Joe nodded, wondering why Sam'd talked about him.

Bonneville turned to Montgomery. "Get somebody to stall my new mare."

As Bonneville led the way through the viscous mud to the Officers' Mess, Walker asked, "Could you have the mare's lip tattooed inside instead of branding her? Be a crime to scar a hide like hers."

"Put that in the Bill of Sale."

"An Officer's word's gospel to me, Captain."

After scraping clinging mud off their boots on the top step, they seated themselves on benches worn smooth at the head table in the Bachelor Officers' Mess. Walker made out Bonneville's Bill of Sale while they waited to eat. When their sidemeat came, Army tableware proved too dull. Walker handed his hunting knife to Bonneville, who razored his meat and returned it. Walker had cut the hides off a buffalo easier than carving his sidemeat. Having choked down enough to be polite,

Walker muttered "Thanks for the meal."

Ignoring the rest of his half-cooked cartilage, Bonneville said, "Something I'd like to talk to you about."

"Go ahead."

"Not here. Let's walk along the river."

"Fine. But I'll be selling my stock purty quick."

As Bonneville led the way out of Fort Gibson's gate, he suggested, "Ought to wait till the bidding for those fine horses heats up."

Walker replied, "Sounds like you've been in the horse business."

"Bought horses for the Army."

Bonneville and Walker hunkered down beside the Neosho River. Roiled brown waters with ice chunks clacking from an early thaw slid by.

"Governor Houston told me you served valiantly at Horseshoe Bend under General Jackson in the Creek War."

"My brother Joel and I both fought down there."

"Weren't you a frontier Sheriff?"

"Year and a half as Sheriff of Independence. Got re-elected after I quit, but I didn't want the job. Too confining. I had to get out. New country's food for the soul."

Bonneville laughed, "I feel exactly the same way. Any skeletons in your military closet?"

"Whatta ya mean?"

"Trouble in the Army?"

"My trouble came after I was mustered out. Had a lawyer trying to collect my Creek War Army pay ever since. What's that got to do with you buying a mare?"

"Nothing, but I'm looking to head up an expedition. I need an experienced frontiersman for my second in command."

Walker looked long and hard at Bonneville. "I'm a civilian."

"This would be a fur trade expedition."

"Not for me. I waded all the ice water I ever want to -- just like that right there. Walker thumbed toward the angry Neosho River.

"We'd be after bigger game."

"Bigger game -- buffalo, moose, elk?"

"Much bigger game, Mr. Walker. I'm a desperate man. I've been preparing for such a grand adventure all my life. I was born in Paris to an anti-monarchist *journaliste* living in the shadow of the gallows. When your revolutionary Thomas Paine moved in with us, dungeon doors swung wide. My father went into hiding and packed us off to New Rochelle, New York. We lived there with Mr. Paine. My father fled France and joined us the year before Mr. Paine died. I graduated from the Military Academy at West Point where I studied Latin, Greek, math and engineering. Served five pathetically boring years as a recruiting officer in New England. In 1820, I escaped to build a Military Road through Mississippi. Then I landed a frontier assignment at Fort Smith in Arkansas Territory where I languished until we built Cantonment Gibson in 1824. But nothing happened. I got loose again to escort the Marquis de Lafayette around the United States. Took a leave of absence for 18 months and went back to France with him. Returned here, and I've been stuck here in the Seventh Infantry ever since. With your help, I can escape again. Like to be gone by the time its name change to Fort Gibson becomes effective next year."

"To do what?"

"Every man has a touch of Lewis and Clark in his soul."

"I got more than a touch in mine!" Walker blurted. "Exploring the wild country's been my dream since I could walk. But who'll pay for it?"

"I believe I can persuade the Jackson Administration to outfit an expedition to explore the unexplored West -- to discover the undiscoverable. Will you go, Mr. Walker?"

Walker turned west where his dreams roamed among the clouds. "Here's my hand on it, Captain!"

CHAPTER 32

KIT CARSON'S GOLD

SPRING 1831

After selling his ton of beaver skins in Santa Fe, Ewing Young rejoined his men at the Santa Rita Copper Mines in early April 1831 and led them back to Taos to settle up with them.

Kit Carson entered Young's Taos store with the look of an eager boy, though he was all of 21. "When we gonna git paid, Ewin'?"

Young smiled, "Sent word around this morning that we'd settle up behind the store at noon."

"Guess I'm early," Kit said dejectedly.

"No you're not. You traveled 2,000 miles to California and back and waited 20 months." Ewing rummaged around in his musty storage room, then returned. "Here's your share, Kit."

Carson hefted the small buckskin bag with a gleesome look. "If you didn't cut my silver with sand, I'm rich!"

Ewing said, "No silver in that poke."

Kit's face went dark. "What is it?"

Ewing whispered, "$300 in Gold."

Tipping the pouch, Kit spread the cool golden coinage into his palm. "Never spected nuthin' like iss, Ewin'." He clamped his hand on the money. "Feels good!"

"If you're smart you'll skim $20 off for drinking bouts and bury the rest five miles from Taos right now."

"Why so far?"

"You'll have to saddle your horse to get to it. If you're real drunk, you won't be able to find it. By that time, you'll sober up enough to leave it be. Go start yourself a business, Kit."

"Sure won't be no saddlery. Thanks agin, Ewin'!"

Kit intended follerin' Ewin's advice, but couldn't walk past the laughter and squeals bubblin' from the *Buena Suerte*. He'd just dampen the dust inside his neck, then ride out and bury his poke. After six drinks, Kit's gold was so much dross.

By supper time, Kit'd had two fine fist fights and won 'em both against men half agin bigger'n him. He'd bought drinks for the losers -- and everybody at that saloon. By midnight he wasn't even sure which saloon he was guzzlin' in.

Kit woke at daylight with a mongrel pup lickin' dried blood from his gouged cheek. His head felt like somebody'd packed black powder in each ear, then sparked it, blowin' the top o' his head plumb off.

He sat up in pain, eyed his bootless feet and clawed $80 from his possibles bag. Like Ewin' had said, Kit'd start his own business. He'd sell *stupid*, for he surely had enough to dumfound ever man west o' St. Louis.

"Jackson himself is no longer a Jackson Man."
David Crockett per Thomas Chilton

 **CHAPTER 33**

CHILTON'S CROCKETT PUPPET   **SPRING - SUMMER 1831**

Kentucky Congressman Thomas Chilton met Tennessee Congressman David Crockett on the sly in the private salon of a posh Washington hotel, both entering by the back door. Their steaming coffee was poured from a silver teapot and served with ornate cookies, but their alliance was crude. Educated in the finest schools, Chilton was the political hatchet for the Whigs. Pitifully under-educated, Crockett's backwoods babble bothered Chilton like a boil on his backside. But this once prominent Jacksonian Democrat Crockett was the chink in the armor of Andrew Jackson's upcoming re-election campaign.

"What do you hear from Sam Houston?" Chilton asked, opening their clandestine meeting on a folksy note.

"Last time I seen Sam was two year ago in Nashville. He'd broke up with his wife and was goin' to live with the Injuns. Reckon he's havin' a high time without this backroom business."

"Nothing more recent on Houston?"

"Nope an' I don't expect nothin'."

Chilton sipped his coffee while he discarded Crockett's Houston information as ancient dirt compared to the lethal mud of last spring's *Cherokee* supply contract.

Chilton still hoarded Houston's drunken boasts to Dr. Robert Mayo in the Indian Queen Hotel Bar last May about conquering Texas. Houston's rantings would infuriate the Mexicans enough to abort negotiations with Jackson for the sale of Texas. That would keep Texas votes from re-electing Jackson. Chilton would spill Houston's slime on the press any day.

Smiling over his china cup, Chilton oozed, "Are you still planning to let me help you write your autobiography, David?"

"Ain't give that much thought. Been too set on gittin' myself re-elected to Congress to hanker fer the Presidency."

"Then let's consider your congressional re-election strategy paramount."

"What? All right."

"I've developed powerful messages for my constituents in my own campaign. We could adapt them for yours."

"Gotta be careful, Tom. Your folks is Whigs. Mine's Jackson supporters."

"Your dinner with President Adams in the White House is common knowledge. You didn't enhance your party affiliations with your stand on the Tennessee Vacant Land Bill in '29. Will it serve you now to pretend those things never happened? I recall your motto being 'Be sure you're right, then go ahead.' Now that you've set sail down Whig river, shouldn't you stay the course?"

Crockett stirred sugar into his cold coffee with his finger. "Wisht I never heard o' politickin'. Me an' my boy John Wesley could jist let them bear dogs loose and high tail it after their bayin'. That there was honest. This here ain't."

Isn't getting re-elected to Congress as a prelude to running for the Presidency against Andrew Jackson important? Can you not elevate your destitute Tennesseeans more as President than as a rollicking bear hunter in the backwoods?"

"Most likely. Didja bring them voter messages with ya?"

Chilton extracted a sheaf of papers from his satchel and slid them across the polished walnut table to Crockett.

"You sure don't suffer none from wonderin' what to say."

"These handwritten papers boil down to 16 pages of hand-set type. Everything in here is vital to the people who sent us to try to make sense out of this mess here in Washington."

"Looks like a heap more'n anybody wants ta read about politickin'."

"Let's isolate stanzas that strike a chord with you for your own message. You must appear to have a grasp of national issues, retaining local flavor to woo your District's electorate."

They hashed out each point in Chilton's papers well past supper time. Around nine, they had meat, bread and buttered corn brought to the salon. David got sleepy after the rich food, but Chilton bore down harder. Around midnight, David said, "My head's ringin'. Do my Circular like you think it orta be. You think it'll take longer'n this to write my life story?"

"Lots longer. National heroes aren't fabricated in a day."

"When'll this here Circular be printed up so I kin git it out afore the election?"

"You'll have your Circular Letters tomorrow."

"Ain't that kinda quick?" Crockett asked disgustedly, realizing their palaver had been squandered on circulars which had done been printed.

"Nothing's too quick when your nation needs it, Congressman Crockett."

The 16 page Circulars dated February 28,1831, addressed to "*Citizens and Voters of the Ninth Congressional District*" arrived at Crockett's boardinghouse. He read one, growin' more worried with each word. It attacked Jackson's increasing government expenses when he'd campaigned to lower them. It denounced Jackson's cruelty to Indians and complicity in Crawford's exiling them from their lush Georgia homelands to the barren West. It hammered Jackson's seeking re-election when he'd run as a one-term President vowing to get a Constitutional Amendment limiting Presidential tenure to four years.

The Circular concluded: "*I thought with him as he thought before he was President. He has altered his opinion -- I have not changed mine. I have not left the principles which led me to support General Jackson. He has left them and me; and I will not surrender my independence to follow his new opinions, taught by interested and selfish advisers, and which may again be remoulded under the influence of passion and cunning. In short Andrew Jackson himself is no longer a Jackson Man.*"

When Congress adjourned on March 3, 1831, David toted the Circulars home and handed 'em out in his district. It rattled David, but did not swerve him from distributin' the Circulars when his good wife Elizabeth opined, "I heard o' soldiers shootin' theirselves in the foot to git sent home, but I never knowed politicians done it too."

On the campaign circuit, Crockett's opponent William Fitzgerald often charged that Crockett was crooked. At Paris,

Tennessee, Fitzgerald spoke first. Mounting the speaker's stand, he laid something on the pine table with a handkerchief over it. Barely into his speech, Fitzgerald yelled, "I'm here to reassert the reports that I've said Crockett is a crook and to prove them!"

David Crockett rose to holler, "I'm present to hear them lies and to whup the little lawyer that would repeat 'em!"

Fitzgerald responded, "I'm going to tell you of the perfidy of Congressman David Crockett you've all come to hear."

Crockett charged toward the speaker's stand. When he was within three feet, Fitzgerald yanked the pistol from the handkerchief on the table, aimed it at Colonel Crockett's chest and said deliberately, "Another step and I'll fire."

Dumfounded, David turned around and resumed his seat.

It was never clear if it was the Circular Letter or the pistol in the hanky that killed Crockett's re-election to Congress. By one count of the 16,482 votes cast in August 1831, David lost by 586. A later one listed his losing margin as 807 votes.

When David sprawled on his front porch he expected Elizabeth to console him as she had in the past. Tirin' of lickin' his wounds alone, he shuffled through their cabin till he found her on the back stoop. "Bin waitin' to hear from you, Elizabeth."

She squinted up at him, tears welling in her blue eyes, "That's odd, cause I don't reckon I know zactly who you are."

"What's got into you, Elizabeth?"

"It's what's got into you, darlin'. Them big words them Whigs put in yer 16 page death warrant ain'tchu. You was once the warm, bold David Crockett that made folks laugh and like you. Where's the David that shoulda asked Fitzgerald with his pistol, 'How much are ye holdin' me up fer this time?' stead o' slinkin' back to yer chair? This feller I see now ain't my dear husband. He's Chilton's Crockett puppet."

Taking her chubby hand, he consoled, "You'll feel better bout all this here when I'm President."

Elizabeth Crockett pulled his head down to her bosom and hugged it, sobbing, "My poor, darlin' Davy."

"Our countrymen are daily becoming more desirous of understanding the true situation and resources of that portion of our territories lying to the north of Mexico and west of the Rocky Mountains."
Captain Benjamin L.E. Bonneville

CHAPTER 34

BONNEVILLE'S QUEST   SPRING - SUMMER 1831

N ow that Captain Benjamin Louis Eulalie Bonneville had Joe Walker's handshake on their pact to explore the West, he had to find a way to incarnate their divine vision in the secular world.

Obtaining Army leave to visit his mother in New Rochelle, New York, Captain Bonneville departed Fort Gibson.

Having been in the Army since entering West Point on his 17th birthday, 35 year old Bonneville understood the Army game and how to play it. But he'd never attempted anything so grandiose. He knew he had to lay the groundwork for his Washington quest in New York City's financial district.

After the City Hotel's minions pressed his Army uniform, Bonneville wore it proudly, striding through New York's high carnival streets. Buildings towered four stories high. All 250,000 New Yorkers seemed to throng its streets at once. Sidewalk venders hawked hot chestnuts. Young boys thrust newspapers at him like *petit* stickups. Painted women rolled their eyes. Carriages careened down the streets, running races in all directions. A beggar tugged his sleeve. Bonneville pulled free to find moments later he'd been fleeced of his gold sleeve button the same way Indians snatched them in the West.

Arriving at the building of John Jacob Astor, America's richest man, Bonneville was issued into a sumptuous suite. He had to run his fingers over the leather and polished cherry wood while he waited to see his boyhood friend Alfred Seton.

A clerk for Astor's ill-fated Astorians in his youth, the slender, graying Alfred Seton entered his office by a rear door and slipped into his leather chair with a nearly imperceptible shake of Bonneville's outstretched hand. "Good to see you again, Ben. How's your mother?"

"Know more when I've seen her. How's your family?"

"Dead and expensively buried. What brings you here?"

Reluctant to expose his bald pate, Bonneville leaned forward confidentially with his cap on. "The Army wants me to scout the West as a fur trapper, but I have to finance the venture through private sources."

"Money."

"What?"

"That's what New Yorkers talk about."

"There's far more involved in my mission than money, Alfred."

"Perhaps for you, but for John Jacob, it's money. Parsimony is his passion. Will your venture make money?"

"I thought Mr. Astor might relish a measure of revenge after what the British did to his Pacific Fur Company at Astoria during the last war."

Seton tipped his chair back and let his mind drift. "I can see the frothing Columbia River where Wilson Price Hunt led us in February of 1812 after our killing trek through the wilderness from St. Louis. We were skeletons. John Jacob's ship *Tonquin* had reached there before us; its crew built Fort Astoria on the south bank. The fort was intensely primitive, but it was heaven to us -- with salt pork in casks and biscuits without weevils. We set about accomplishing John Jacob's objective."

"What was that?"

"Owning all the fur business -- Atlantic to Pacific."

"When did John Jacob's Astoria plan go awry?"

"For the *Tonquin*, it was the day John Jacob crewed her with Canadians under an American Captain. After a disastrous cruise around the horn, they built Fort Astoria, then sailed to Nootka Sound. Captain Thorn enraged the Indians who massacred the crew, save three who escaped and Lewis the clerk. Mortally wounded, Lewis barricaded himself on the ship. At dawn, he beckoned the Indians back aboard, waited till they rushed him and tossed a lit fuse into the powder magazine."

"Fort Astoria didn't fall until later, did it?"

Alfred Seton's cheeks colored with reincarnated hatred.

"In October 1814, the Northwest Company's *voyagers* camped outside Fort Astoria, flaunting their arrogant British flag. Our leader McDougal refused to raise the Stars and Stripes. He read us a letter from his uncle warning of a British squadron tasked to destroy every American on the Northwest Coast. With that scheming knave in charge, we became pawns in a tug o' war over our fort's $100,000 in furs."

"How long did that charade take to play out?"

"Two months. Sloop-of-war *Raccoon* with 26 guns sailed in. Their Captain threatened to level Fort Astoria with a broadside. Our *surrendering* Captain was by then a *partner* in the *conquering* fur company. British flag went to the top of our flagpole December 12th. We had the choice of walking home or sailing to Russia on the brig *Pedler*. I walked home, vowing revenge against the British every step of the way."

Bonneville probed, "Since Hudson's Bay Company and the British presence in Oregon are two objects of my mission, this is your chance to avenge those unspeakable indignities."

Seeming to ignore the bait, Seton grunted, "John Jacob's devouring the world's fur trade. By sponsoring your fur expedition on the sly, he can bleed his Rocky Mountain competitors. He'll no doubt want your Army reports."

"Alfred, were you not irrevocably my friend, I would take umbrage at your suggestion. You know I could never give an official dispatch to Mr. Astor -- although no particular harm seems evident if you simply review my reports."

Seton's budding outrage dwindled to a wink. "We'll still have to tell John Jacob you're going to make money to separate him from any of his. You'll have to identify me beyond these walls as your sponsor, so other fur companies won't connect you to John Jacob Astor or his American Fur Company."

Bonneville lifted his cap to handkerchief beading sweat from his pink scalp. "I defer to your artifice, Alfred. I have a tendency to be fatally honest."

Rising from his chair, Seton offered his hand, "Better practice the art of deception, Ben. Spies who don't lie well die young. The struggle to dominate the fur trade's as fierce as any war between nations with bloodshed, treachery and unbelievably acute antagonism. What happened to your hair?"

"Lost it worrying about coming to see you!"

After a punishing stage ride to Philadelphia, Captain Bonneville slept the night away in the Congress Hall Hotel.

Next morning, he boarded a steamer to New Castle, then switched to the New Castle Railroad that bounded like a jack-rabbit along the Delaware River to Frenchtown, New Jersey.

He missed the Chesapeake Bay steamboat to Washington, spending the night in a quaint inn where a deranged guest played viola all night despite demands to desist shouted through the wall. At dawn, Bonneville beat on the offender's door, issuing a vociferous, but unanswered challenge to a duel. He boarded the steamboat to Washington where he took a smelly cab to Brown's Indian Queen Hotel.

Making forced marches from one staff officer's drab cubbyhole to another, availed Bonneville nothing. Most wanted his plan in writing, even after he'd explained it was not the sort of plan one should put in writing.

In mid-May 1831, Bonneville presented himself at the office of John H. Eaton, Secretary of War. To his amazement, he was issued into the Secretary's office, where John Eaton listened most attentively. Eaton said, "I like it, but President Jackson has the last word."

"I trust you will explain it to him, Mr. Secretary."

"He cherishes bold officers. You'll fare better than I."

Captain Bonneville's prearranged meeting with Major General Alexander Macomb was bizarre. General Macomb, who kept donning his eyeglasses, then taking them off said, "You will write me a letter using these notes." He handed Bonneville an envelope. "If we answer your said letter, our answer shall remain absolutely confidential. Communicate with me in writing through your most trusted men. If your situation goes awry with a foreign government, you will assert that you are a private citizen engaged in the business of fur trapping. Dismissed."

Mystified over why they needed a letter, Bonneville returned to his stuffy hotel room and meticulously prepared his letter exactly as directed.

"Washington City, May 21, 1831
Major General Alexander Macomb.

    Sir, observing that our countrymen are daily becoming more desirous of understanding the true situation and resources of that portion of our territories lying to the north of Mexico and west of the Rocky Mountains, has determined me to offer my services for the advancement of that object. I ask for no outfits, no presents for the indians, no command, want no protection, save passports from our and the Mexican authorities at this place, and leave of absence for that purpose.   Eleven years residence among the indians west of Arkansas Territory, has afforded me a good opportunity of becoming acquainted with the indian character and the command of several distant expeditions into their country, some qualifications for the proposed enterprise.   I would there, by observations, establish prominent points of that country, ascertain the general courses of the principal rivers, the location of the indian tribes and their habits, visit the American and British establishments, make myself acquainted with their manner of trade and intercourse with the Indians, finally endeavor to develop every advantage the country affords and by what means they may most readily be opened to the enterprise of our citizens. These, Sir, are the objects I propose accomplishing. Early next spring, I would leave the United States, with some of the companies trading there, and on my arrival, immediately begin my labours.   I have for a long time, had this object in contemplation, anticipating with great pleasure the moment that would place it within my reach.   I can conceive of no time more propitious than the present, while the attention of the country, generally, is directed towards it. You will therefore, I trust, excuse me if I indulge the hope of your approbation towards an enterprise likely to prove of so much importance.   I am now on my way to New York for the purpose of settling some private business, after which, if my application be favorably received, I shall earnestly turn my attention to such preparations as may be necessary to ensure its complete success. I am Sir, Most respectfully, Your very obedient Servant

                      BLEBonneville
                      Capt. 7th Regt Infantry"

Captain Benjamin Lewis Eulalie Bonneville stepped to the window to watch the lamps illuminate one window after another across the District of Columbia. Beginning tomorrow, he would commence carrying out his unwritten instructions until he heard back. His soul said his fascinating future lay far to the west of this strange place.

New York City's muggy July thrashed the weak from its crowds, making Captain Bonneville's walk from the City Hotel to Alfred Seton's office a pleasant stroll.

Forgetting formalities with his boyhood friend Seton, Bonneville wore the lightest tan cotton outfit he could buy in the sultry city topped with a broad-brimmed straw hat that etched screen shadows across his features.

Wearing his blue serge suit as nonchalantly as he would in winter, Seton smiled as they seated themselves in a deserted French cafe for lunch. "We've located your equipment through Harvard's supplier."

Bonneville napkinned his sweaty face. "That would be the sextant, barometer, thermometer and the Dolland reflecting telescope?"

"For some reason, the sextant won't focus, but the rest's ready at our warehouse. New sextant's due tomorrow."

"Excellent."

"Exactly what's a Dolland telescope do, Ben?"

"I need more training at West Point, but my understanding is that by observing Jupiter's moons, I can ascertain my longitudes during this grand adventure into the unknown."

"John Jacob says with what it cost, it *bettah verk*!"

Bonneville laughed, "Tell Mr. Astor that at *vorst* I'll be able to read the orders of the day at Fort Vancouver from the opposite bank of the Columbia."

"I want you to consider hiring a distinguished young Frenchman, *Michel Sylvestre Cerré*, for your expedition."

"In what capacity?"

"Same level as this Joseph Walker you've touted."

Bonneville frowned, "Have more information?"

Seton extracted a paper from his inside suit pocket. "*Cerré* was born May 6, 1802. Called *Lami* by his friends, his grandfather was old line St. Louis stock owning a lead mine, salt works and land interests. His father *Pascal* was a Lieutenant in the Spanish Army. His aunt *Marie* married *August Chouteau.* *Cerré's* been in the Santa Fe trade and was a partner in *P.D. Papin & Company* until that was acquired by John Jacob's American Fur Company last year. *Cerré* is quite well off, but as profoundly anxious to roam the wilderness as you are."

Bonneville knew instantly that *Cerré* would be Astor's spy, reporting when Bonneville coughed, but this wasn't the time to protest. "Sounds fine, but I'd like to meet him before he signs on formally."

Alfred Seton smiled, "There goes that fatal honesty again, Ben. *Cerré's* already signed on, and I have no doubt you know why. He's waiting for you in St. Louis."

Nodding, Bonneville managed a wink. They reminisced about their boyhood days through the rest of lunch. Afterward, the Captain retired to his sweltering room and wrote:

"New York City July 18, 1831

Major General Alexander Macomb.

Sir, I have the honor to report to you that I have now completed arrangements to enable me to collect information in the section of country lying west of the Rocky Mountains, as promised in my letter to you dated at Washington City the 21st May last. I have provided myself with a telescope, sextant & horizon, compass to determine the variation of the needle, thermometre, microscope, pocket-couple case of instruments & patent lever time piece to assist me in my observations. Barometers are so clumsy and so easily broken that I do not contemplate taking any. I have also examined every work that was likely to yield me any information respecting that country. Thumbed McKensie's and Clark's journals. Having now no further business to detain me here, I am, therefore, anxious to leave this city for the west as soon as possible. Taking Pittsburgh by the canals -- Cincinnati and St. Louis in my route to Fort Osage. As it is impossible for me to say where I shall be at any one time, you will, I hope, excuse me if I request instructions and passports may be sent to me at this place previous to my departure. Tomorrow I shall go to spend a few days at West Point in order to practice the taking of a few astronomical observations and I'll return to this city about the 27th next. My object in calling for passports is fearing that in some of my distant excursions I may meet with defeat or other misfortune and have to take refuge in the Mexican territories, I just dislike to create groundless suspicions -- If a passport from the United States State Department will prevent that, it is all I want. I have given to Lieut. S. Cooper, your aide de camp, a description of my person. I expect to leave Fort Osage [and be] 200 miles up the Missouri as soon as the spring opens sufficiently to supply horses with food and remain the full winter and spring in that country -- and return to St. Louis about the month of October following. I have the honor to be General, with perfect respect, your mo. obdt. Servt.

BLEBonneville Capt 7th Inf."

Upon his return to the City Hotel from practicing astronomical observations at West Point, Captain Bonneville received the reply of Major General Alexander Macomb, Commandant U.S. Army at the front desk and tried to rein in his rampant curiosity as he trotted to his room. With shaking fingers, he tore the end off the envelope. It read:

"Headquarters of the Army
Washington July 29th 1831

Sir;

The leave of absence which. you have asked, for the purpose of enabling you to carry into execution your designs of exploring the country to the Rocky Mountains and beyond, with a view of ascertaining the nature and character of the various tribes of Indians inhabiting those regions: the trade which might be profitably carried on with them, the quality of the soil; the productions, the minerals, the natural history, the climate, the geography and topography, as well as geology of the various parts of the country within the limits of the territories belonging to the United States, between our frontier and the Pacific; -- has been duly considered, and submitted to the War Dept. for approval and has been sanctioned.

You are therefore authorized to be absent from the army until October 1833. It is understood that the Govt. is to be at no expense, in reference to your proposed expedition it having originated with yourself; and all that you required was the permission from the proper authority to undertake the enterprise. You will naturally in providing yourself for the expedition provide suitable instruments and especially the best Maps of the interior to be found. It is desirable besides what is enumerated as the object of your enterprise, that you note particularly the number of Warriors that may be in each tribe or nation that you may meet with; their alliances with other tribes, and their relative position as to the state of peace or War, and whether their friendly or warlike dispositions towards each other are recent or of long standing. You will gratify us by discribing their manner of their making War, of the mode of subsisting themselves during a state of war, and a state of peace; their arms and the effect of them, whether they act on foot or on horseback, detailing the discipline and maneuvers of the War Parties, the power of their horses, size and general description, in short any information which you may conceive would be useful to the Govt. You will avail yourself of every opportunity of informing us of your position and progress, and at the expiration of your leave of absence, will join your proper station.

I have the honor to be, Sir
Your obt. servant,
Alexander Macomb,
Major General commanding the Army"

Upon completing the General's cumbersome correspondence, Captain Benjamin Lewis Eulalie Bonneville leaped to his feet and yelled, "So be it!" His inner vision of himself at that moment was of a great screaming eagle soaring into the sky ending a millennium of incarceration.

"All scoundrels whomsoever are hereby authorized to accuse, defame, slander, vilify and libel me..."   Sam Houston

CHAPTER 35

THE HOUSTON REDEMPTION   SUMMER - FALL 1831

r. Robert Mayo not only spied for the Whigs, he was a dubious confidante of President Andrew Jackson. After sharing a night of debauchery with Sam Houston in the bar of Washington's Indian Queen Hotel in late April 1830, Mayo had incensed Jackson with his December 1830 communiqué. Mayo confided that Houston had gone to live with the *Cherokees* *"to afford a cloak"* for his conspiracy to raise an army to invade Texas.

Fearing Houston's filibustering could scuttle his negotiations to buy Texas from Mexico, President Jackson wrote William S. Fulton, Secretary of Arkansas Territory: *"D'r Sir, it has been stated to me than an extensive expedition against Texas is organizing in the United States ... and that Genl. Houston is to be at the head of it ...I am skeptical, but since the issue is now so potentially dangerous to the interests of the United States, it must be looked into.... Recruits are allegedly gathering along the Mississippi, soon to clamber aboard steamboats already chartered. ... You are ordered to keep me truly and constantly advised of any movements which may serve to justify my suspicions... all with the utmost secrecy.... My office -- not the War Department -- will reimburse you for any expense you may incur in your investigation...."*

One of Jackson's spies sent him a secret dispatch that his envoy negotiating with Mexico, Anthony Butler, whom Martin Van Buren had recommended, was engaged in bribery and corruption of Mexican officials -- and worse that the British had leapfrogged the United States as the primary buyer of Texas.

Before Andrew Jackson could contact Anthony Butler in remote Mexico City, a Congressional Investigation ripped into his covert annexation of Texas, propelled by Congressman Thomas Chilton. Investigators seized papers and spewed vitriol that Jackson was trying to buy Texas voters with the people's trust funds just to re-elect himself.

Getting wind of the President's plight, Sam Houston sobered up enough to write him a letter encoded in their Masonic cipher. Sam said there was no truth to the vicious lies Dr. Robert Mayo had spread about him and Texas. Sam identified a freebooter named Hunter in his Mayo conversation who'd said he'd launch a filibuster into Texas in 1831. Once expelled from West Point, Hunter claimed to have signed thousands of men who were supposedly moving into Indian Territory -- though Sam had seen no evidence of such armed militia.

Shortly after Sam sent his encoded letter, William S. Fulton answered President Jackson's inquiry with a confidential report that read: "*I went myself to the western frontier and ascertained in person all the facts... getting satisfactory information from the Mississippi River at the various points, at which it would be likely that such an expedition could be prepared or fitted out....In short, I am satisfied...that no organized expedition was at that time in contemplation or on foot from any point within the Territory of Arkansas against Mexico, either on the part of Genl. Houston or any other person....*"

Sam resumed running his modest trading post at Wigwam Neosho. In early July 1831, he sold his interest in the Grand Saline salt works to John McLemore and M.H. Howard for the princely sum of $6,500. But before he could spend a dime of it, he received a morose letter from his brother in Tennessee that his mother, Elizabeth Paxton Houston, lay on her deathbed in Baker's Creek Valley and lit out to be at her bedside.

Upon reaching Tennessee, Sam Houston made the discovery no man seeks -- that while seemingly alive, he was still the butt of ridicule and vicious laughter over his treatment of his wife Eliza -- and was actually quite dead except for formalities with the shovels.

Infuriated, Sam spent some of his salt works money to chastise Tennessee's jeering populace. On July 13, 1831 he had an odd *Proclamation* printed and handed it out in the streets. As former Governor of Tennessee, Sam wrote, "...*all scoundrels whomsoever are hereby authorized to accuse, defame, slander, vilify and libel me...and that I will in no wise hold them responsible...in law or honor....*" He ended it vowing to reward the person who told "*the most elegant, refined and ingenious lie or calumny* with *a handsome gilt copy of the Kentucky Reporter Bound in Sheep or a snug plain copy of the United States Telegraph since its commencement Bound in Dog.*"

Kneeling at his mother's bedside, Sam saw death in her face and everything around her, it having seeped into her half finished knitting, her threadbare clothes, the murky glass of water on her bed table -- even her Bible with its leather binding flaking away where her hands had held it for decades.

Though he was sure she could not hear him in the depth of her dying, Sam asked, "Mother, does all mankind come to this -- ground into insignificant meal by the cruel stones of time?"

Astoundingly, she opened the misty eyes in her wrinkled gray face and said, "Most die miserably. Only the great among us have the strength to face both life and death unflinchingly. You have that strength, Sam Houston, if you have but the courage to use it." She clutched his arm with her bony hand that went limp in death.

Sam Houston felt that somehow she had infused him with the power to rise above himself and his pitiful failings. He rose and stood taller.

CHAPTER 36

CALIFORNIA BOUND   FALL 1831

ummer's bloom was off Santa Fe by the end of August 1831. Fickle winds howled in her narrow lanes, making her citizens lash their shutters and scorch the spider webs in their chimneys. Armed with letters to Captain John Cooper from Ewing Young and Henry Hook for Monterey mule buying, David Jackson assembled his men at dawn of August 25, 1831. Jackson's Negro slave Jim was flanked by Jedediah Smith's brother Peter, William Waldo, budding historian Jonathan Trumbull Warner, *Antoine Leroux* and five others.

Wrapped against the chill in his scarlet *serape*, Ewing Young covered the Old Spanish Trail's landmarks with David Jackson, then muttered, "I should be going with you. *Maria* knows I'll leave one day. Joy has fled *mi casa* like an uncaged canary."

"When will you follow, Ewing?"

"In about a month, but it'll be after our fall hunt. You'll beat us there by half a season. That young Kit Carson I told you about -- did he head for St. Louis with Sublette's caravan?"

"I found Kit, but he was going to Colorado Country to trap with Tom Fitzpatrick's outfit. Isn't Kit's older brother Moses still in Santa Fe?"

"He is, but he's a right respectable trapper, and he's signing with me."

"Gonna stay in California, Ewing?"

"Dunno. My partner Billy Wolfskill's building a ship from what his letter says. Wants me to help him capture sea otters. I've dreamt about embracing the sea since I was a child."

"What's California like?"

"A different Goddess to every man she enchants."

"You think the rest of us oughta unsaddle?" one of David Jackson's impatient voyagers hollered.

"Not unless you wanta ride to California bareback!" David Jackson retorted. "Ewing, I'll leave a letter for you with Captain Cooper, so we can keep track of each other."

They shook hands robustly as the dawn sky's rose streaks melted into flaming gold, and David's outfit raised dust on the dimmest horizon.

Ewing Young's parting with beloved *Maria Josepha Tafoya* for his October 1831 expedition was nothing like he'd dreaded. She kissed the palm of his huge hand tearfully, then looked into his eyes murmuring in Spanish, "I only wish you had left me the joy of a child to fill my empty heart while you are away, but I know you will come back. Destiny has entwined our souls."

Within minutes Ewing led 36 shaggy buckskinners into the fanning yellow light of day, but *Maria* was with him in spirit as she'd surely intended. Perhaps they would be together again.

Every outfit's trail sound was different to Ewing Young. This one clanked. He yelled, "Roast pots, soup pans, wash basins -- cookie tins? Next time we rest, find what's loose in those packs and tie 'em down or we'll scare off all the game within ten miles!"

Behind Ewing on clopping trail horses swayed Moses Carson, Job F. Dye, Sidney Cooper, Benjamin Day, Isaac Sparks, Joseph Gale, Joe Dofit, John Higans, Ike Williams, James Green, Tom Low, *Julian Bargas, José Teforia,* John Price, little Cambridge Green, Big Jim Anderson and 20 other rough men scraped off the corners of Santa Fe and Taos.

Ewing yelled back over his shoulder, "Only thing we can be sure of in God's wilderness is that heaven and hell await us -- with *Apaches*, bone fractures and grizzly bears. With luck we'll all be stretching $5 plews before the week is old!"

Most of Ewing's men shook with laughter, but some checked the primes in their guns. It was a long way to California, and they knew some of them would never live to see it.

"I've had 14 duels with a spate of war wounds in between."
Andrew Jackson

 CHAPTER 37

THE THINNEST VENEER

WINTER 1831-32

*A*ll *partenaires* of *P. D. Papin & Company* had gotten responsible positions in the American Fur Company after selling out to Astor's empire except for *Michel Sylvestre Cerré.*

Though he was well off, *Michel* had implored John Jacob Astor's staff for a worthy task. When it seemed beyond hope, suddenly it had come!

He reread Alfred Seton's letter. *Michel* was to begin assembly of a 110 man expedition

Michel Sylvestre Cerré

and 20 freight wagons in St. Louis! This grand land fleet would set out May 1, 1832 -- five days before *Michel's* 30th birthday. After being so long in the shadows of his prominent family, what more could a young man ask to show his worthiness?

Seton's letter said little about this Benjamin Bonneville. Though *Michel* was delighted Bonneville was born in France, only his Army career was mentioned. Who was he?

But Seton left no doubt that *Cerré* was to maintain the appearance of answering to Bonneville. All reports Bonneville made to his superiors were to first be reviewed for any commercial value they might have to AFC's fur interests.

Reports *Cerré* made to AFC about Captain Bonneville would be in strict confidence. Astor's personal instruction was that no convict nor sinister person be hired in the event the expedition's true sponsorship should ever surface.

Michel Cerré vowed to search St. Louis for men, mules, wagons and supplies immediately after the Blessed Christmas. Now his brother *Gabriel,* trading on the Missouri, and his sister *Catherine Louise,* married to his former *partinenaire P.D. Papin,* would grasp the magnitude of his stature, not from his words, but the funds that would fatten his personal account.

Every man had to grow into himself. With 30 staring him in the eyes like the black hearted bayou snake it was, *Michel Cerré* would don himself like a greatcoat and march proudly into a grand new life.

Few places in this world could feel colder than Washington, D.C. in the dead of winter. Captain Benjamin Bonneville was keen to learn what the New Year 1832 held for him. His task now was to hurdle bureaucratic barriers and keep his mission headed West.

After months of wrestling arcane instruments at West Point, he'd created the semblance of competence with them, though it might not stand the scrutiny of a scientist. He was a soldier -- not a bookworm.

He'd received word to report to the White House. The mere hint that some perverse change might bar his name from America's annals beside those of Lewis and Clark chilled him more than the winds off the Potomac.

Bonneville prayed Washington's internecine wars would not kill his expedition. The bloodbath over rechartering the United States Bank soaked the front page of every newspaper. Some sided with Jackson, demanding an end to the national menace. Others backed Bank President Nicholas Biddle. Bonneville knew Astor was a Biddle man and vowed to walk wide of that political bog.

The White House stood majestically in drifted snow. Bonneville knew he would always remember it this way like a painting by the masters. He entered and started through the armada paid to keep people from seeing the President -- even if they had an appointment.

Unbeknownst to Captain Bonneville, President Jackson had summoned a Philadelphia surgeon to the White House who arrived the same hour as the good Captain's appointment. Jackson's assistant directed Bonneville to the waiting area outside the President's private office where he sat readying answers for all contingencies that might hamstring his mission.

Inside the President's office the renowned Dr. Harris of Philadelphia examined the shirtless Andrew Jackson. "Mr. President, you are a mass of scars."

Jackson replied, "I've had 14 duels with a spate of war wounds in between."

"Which scar in your collection brings me here today?"

"As we discussed by letter, it won't be Charles Dickinson's ball lodged against my heart, though the Lord knows it pains me most. Today, Jesse Benton's ball must be removed. Was in my left shoulder, but it's settled lower."

"This scar is old."

"Nigh 20 years."

"I can't feel the bullet, Mr. President. Where is it?"

Jackson elevated his skinny arm. "Worked itself inside my arm to hang right there most painfully."

"Whiskey, Mr. President?"

Jackson's eyes flared. "Would you have me making decisions for the nation in a befuddled state?" Jackson gripped his walking stick and gritted, "Go ahead."

Dr. Harris made the incision, squeezed the President's arm and out popped a flattened ball. He staunched the wound, then began suturing it with gut.

"Let me see that ball," Jackson ordered, trying to feign that he didn't feel dizzy and weak.

Depositing the mangled bullet in Jackson's unsteady hand, the surgeon resumed stitching the wound.

Jackson mused, "Lead was a good deal flattened by striking my bone and looks somewhat hackled around the edges. See my secretary for your fee."

After Dr. Harris departed, President Jackson dressed, stifled his urge to kill the pain with a jolt of liquor and had the

Army officer ushered in as though nothing had happened. "Sit down, Captain."

Bonneville eyed the bloody towel on the floor by the President's desk, doffed his cap, inserted it under his arm and saluted, "Captain Benjamin Lewis Eulalie Bonneville, 7th Infantry Regiment reporting as ordered, Sir!"

Andrew Jackson couldn't resist returning the smart salute though himself clad as a civilian. There was something precious about military tradition and the men who practiced it. "Do sit down, Captain."

Bonneville sat erectly.

"The 1818 Joint Occupation Treaty of Oregon with Britain is an infernal nuisance, but it gives you the right to go where you wish up there. It's not enough to know where the British are or what they are doing. I want to know what they are *thinking*! I want your estimate of the force necessary to take Fort Vancouver. Are you remembering this, Captain?"

"Most assuredly, Sir! I've never conversed with another President."

"Find out how California is garrisoned and what it will take to reduce it. You going there soon?"

"Joseph Walker will go. He fought in your command at Horseshoe Bend with his brother Joel and Sam Houston. Joseph also served as Sheriff of Independence, Missouri, Sir."

"I remember Joel Walker. He served under me in Florida as well. I can't place the other Walker, though I remember Sam Houston most acutely."

"Joseph Walker is a black-bearded behemoth of a man, though he was but a boy of 15 when he served under you on the Tallapoosa River. Claims he still hasn't got his Army pay."

Jackson laughed at Bonneville's audacity in bringing that up. "Captain, you need to shield your thought of the moment with clever subterfuge if you're to succeed as an operative."

"I shall, Mr. President, but I shall never be less than candid with my Commanding Officers."

Andrew Jackson chortled, "Then you'll likely spend a long time in grade as a Captain!"

Bonneville reddened, "About California, Sir. I will get Walker's passport and visa before I leave Washington. What shall I do about Texas?"

"Absolutely nothing!" Jackson snapped.

"You'll do fur trapping to pay costs of this enterprise?"

"That's our intention, Mr. President."

"Do not ever contact me directly from the field. Channel your reports through the Commanding General of the Army or the Secretary of War -- and by all that's holy -- be careful with your reports. Stray paper is far more deadly than artillery and every bit as apt to hit that at which it is not aimed."

"I understand, Sir."

"Do you really. We shall see, Captain. Good day, Sir."

Joe Walker led his string of six handsome horses into the draw. They snorted and looked about, eyes wide, ears flicking. When they did not graze right away, Joe looked up and down the draw. He walked among them, patting them to quiet their stomping. He sensed somebody was watching, but saw no one.

His mission to find the *Delawares* just west of Fort Osage had turned to a hair shirt. The weak winter sun was sinking into the rolling hills. Tracks of eight ponies gouged the snow, but they'd circled again and fanned out. He decided to make camp before it got too dark to find the best place to sleep.

Walker hobbled his horses, then pounded the stakes for their 12 foot ropes deep into the hard ground. They could graze on the tan grasses spearing through the snow. He knew a man seeking company at night makes a fire, so he started one with dry wood off his pack horse. Then he collected branches shed from the cottonwood, ash and persimmon trees standing with slender mantles of snow along their limbs.He strung the branches out to dry by his fire. New moccasin tracks barely visible in the dark snow told him he was not alone. He waved toward his fire.

"Why you follow us, Blackbeard?" asked the smallest of the several *Delawares* in the shadows.

"Eat with me, and I'll tell you, "Joe replied, kicking his tree branches closer to the snap-popping fire to dry.

"We eat no white man's food, but we will sit."

Joe hunkered down beside the fire with three of the *Delawares* well aware of two more just beyond the firelight. He eyed their heads, shaved except for their scalplocks. "Don't your heads get cold?" he asked, watching their hands.

One Delaware replied, "Is your face cold?"

Joe said, "Not like the rest of me."

"We are all face," the *Delaware* grunted.

The smallest *Delaware* said, "I am called Joe. Why you want us?"

Walker smiled, "I am also Joe. Your tribe is prized by the fur companies. You have kept the faces that made you feared in the Appalachians and the strength that lets you wander from Mexico to the Arctic barrens. My friends will soon send an outfit to the big waters in the West. We want to hire you as trappers. How many are you?"

"You know there are eight from the tracks of our horses. We know you are one with six horses fit for Chiefs. Why should we not let your blood into the snow and take your horse people?"

The hair stood on Walker's neck, but he smiled. It was easy to see why *Delawares* terrified western Indians and struck Whites speechless. *Delawares* were wolves of the plains with the thinnest veneer of civilization. He said softly, "Because you are so different from me, I see you as a child looks in wonder at the night sky. I am peaceable in all my life's doings, but I have been the Sheriff of Missouri, and my killers will lie with me in my grave."

Delaware Joe rasped, "You speak like a squaw, but you are a true warrior of death -- like us. We will council, but my heart tells me we will run with you, Black Wolf of the Plains."

CHAPTER 38

CALIFORNIA CASH CROPS   **SPRING 1832**

wing Young's trapping trip to California suffered an *Apache* attack, then a charging grizzly. He ended both with Sweet Lips, giving the *Apache* Chief and the bear a third eye.

Then little Cambridge Green, called "Turkey" by the men, buried a trade tomahawk in the forehead of the outfit's bully, Big Jim Anderson. For the rest of the journey Ewing stewed over what to do about Anderson's murder. Reaching Los Angeles February 10, 1832, he turned "Turkey" over to the *Alcalde* and set out in search of Billy Wolfskill.

Ewing's friend Father *Sanchez* at the San Gabriel Mission shook his huge hand warmly. "*Señor* Wolfskill's men and our *Indios* built the 60 ton schooner with timbers from the San Bernardino Mountains. We christened her *Guadalupe* to invite the Sacred Virgin's good graces. Her sections were hauled by ox cart to San Pedro harbor, assembled and floated ever so valiantly. She sails now in quest of sea otters."

With romantic notions of the sea burgeoning in his breast, Ewing sent his men to trap beaver in San Joaquin Valley and hastened to San Pedro.

After Ewing Young and Billy Wolfskill quit slapping each other on the back, Wolfskill said, "Otter hunting's powerful odd."

"Why's that, Billy?"

"When you trap beaver, your feet never leave solid ground, even under water. Otter are smarter'n beaver and show no mercy to land critters in the ocean. You haven't learned how to feel totally helpless, but you will."

Ewing joined Billy Wolfskill, young Jonathan Warner who'd been left to look after property in Los Angeles by David Jackson, several *Kanakas* from the Sandwich Islands and a *Californeo* pilot who knew the rocks in the coastal kelp beds where otters cavorted in the seaweed.

Getting drenched launching the longboat through icy dawn surf to row to the schooner didn't start the hunt auspiciously for Ewing. Learning gunshots ran off every otter for miles was worse. He spotted an otter on its back, breaking a shellfish open against a rock on its belly, but by the time they paddled to the swirl, there was nothing to club or spear.

"What's a sea otter look like outa the water, or hasn't anybody caught one?" shivering Ewing asked blue-lipped Billy.

"Overgrown weasel. Round four feet long counting a foot of tail. Weigh up to 80 pounds. Webbed hind feet. Silky brown fur. While we freeze in these foggy swells, they doze on their backs like the ocean's warm broth."

"Only proves a shoemaker should stick to his lasts."

"You saying we oughta make otter shoes?"

"No, Billy. Beaver bait stinks, but it puts plews in your pack. Better put me ashore where I know what I'm up to."

While Ewing Young waited for the raging Salinas River to settle in its banks, David Jackson's mule herd arrived on the other side near the end of February. David's drovers finally forded the Salinas, and Ewing joined their drive of 600 mules and 100 horses to the Sierra Ranch on the Santa Ana River. This was only a fourth of the stock they'd expected to buy, but with Captain Cooper's help they'd paid under $8 a head. It'd cost more to feed and corral them than to move them east grazing free along the trail.

Ewing rounded up his beaver trappers, and joined forces with David Jackson. They started their herd under towering dust clouds for the Colorado River. When they arrived, the river's boiling red waters were swollen by spring floods. It took them 12 days to ford their entire herd below Yuma.

East of the Colorado at last, David and Ewing camped in an easily defended flat and plotted the balance of their journey. David gave Ewing $3,000 in cash to buy more mules in the area, then drive them eastward to meet again in Santa Fe. Young also received arms, powder and shot, tobacco and traps worth $7,000 belonging to the Jackson, Waldo & Young partnership.

Young transferred 6½ bales of beaver peltry to Jackson to be concealed near Santa Fe, until they could get trading permits to sell them in New Mexico. Young would sell their mules in Santa Fe if prices were good, or drive them on to the settlements in the states.

"Wolfskill still hunting otters?" David asked Ewing over their supper of stringy jackrabbit and burnt beans.

"Mountain Men make miserable sailors. Billy's planting wine grapes."

"Terrible awakening after building a 60 ton vessel."

"They were selling the *Guadalupe* to Captain William Hinckley who'll sail her to the Sandwich Islands."

David sipped his hot coffee. "Sounds like California's cash crops are beavers, mules, wine -- and schooners."

"Some day, somebody'll reap a rich harvest of otter."

"Won't be you, Ewing."

"I'll reap my reward in Taos -- if my *Maria* will have me back."

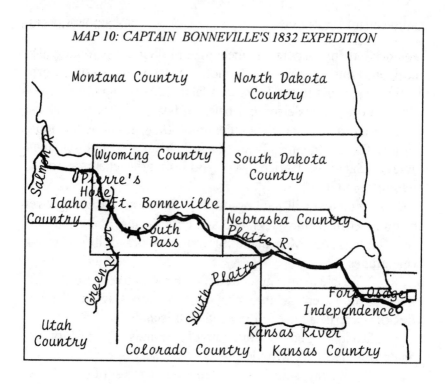

Montana Country

North Dakota Country

Wyoming Country

South Dakota Country

Salmon

Pierre's Hole

Idaho Country

Ft. Bonneville

South Pass

Nebraska Country

Platte R.

Green River

South Platte

Fort Osage

Independence

Utah Country

Colorado Country

Kansas River

Kansas Country

CHAPTER 39

FREE UPON THE PLAINS   SPRING - FALL 1832

aptain Benjamin Bonneville in buckskins turned in his saddle to view his 110 man army of exploration amassed in the rising sun on May 1st outside Fort Osage. No man had ever savored a prouder moment. "Move out!" he bellowed, pointing west, his bold command echoed by one muleskinner after another atop the freight wagons aligned in two columns of ten.

In all his life Joseph Walker had never witnessed a more spectacular sight -- men escaping civilization like an armada of freed spirits. Walker motioned his *Delaware* scouts out to the expedition's flanks.

Michel Cerré was too awed by the majesty of the moment to utter a word. He sat his horse like a knight of old, to his Captain's left with the black bearded giant Walker riding regally on the right. No man among them would ever forget this -- least of all a young Frenchman once accused of being nobody.

Freight wagons hauled by four-mule teams fought May's wheel-sucking mud. Frontiersmen bristling pistols, knives and rifles, rode with easy grace. A mixed herd of riding stock, mules and cattle brought up the rear where lusty curses and cracking whips slashed the morning mist. At dusk Bonneville directed the wagons into a square, five to a side. After herding the stock into the center, the 33 foot intervals between wagons were filled by evening messes, each with its own fire. The air grew rich with braising meat and the laughter of men free of civilization.

Still licking his fingers, Joe Walker posted the guard. He showed the drovers how Captain Bonneville wanted horses side-lined by hobbling the fore and hind foot on the same side 18 inches apart. Joe'd ask to change to a frontleg hobble, but not this first night when the Captain would brook no challenges.

Forging northwestward, they reached the Kansas River May 12th. Spring rains had swollen the normally fordable stream to 300 yards wide requiring a raft to float the wagons across.

By nightfall, they reached the *Kanza* village near General Marston Clark's agency. *Kanza* Chief White Plume and his subchiefs shared Captain Bonneville's fire. Bonneville found their tales of tribal wars with *Pawnees* interesting for his report to General Macomb. White Plume lamented White bee hunters invading *Kanza* land to steal honey.

Through May, they rolled west over undulating plains that seized wagon wheels but flogged tempers out of control. With heat rising to 90° game grew scant, forcing them to harvest the wild onion, Indian potato, prairie tomato and red root.

North of Red River vast sandstone slabs towered like gravestones in an old churchyard, causing Bonneville to write: *"One might almost fancy himself among the tombs of the pre-Adamites."*

On June 2nd, they arrived at Nebraska Country's Platte River. While men and mules rested, Captain Bonneville measured the Platte for his report to General Macomb. He wrote: *"...I found the River 3/4 mile wide, the banks 2 to 3 feet high, river about 4 feet deep, but full of quicksands; the plains upon the banks of the Platte are from 3 to 5 miles wide...."*

Passing the Platte's fork on June 11th, Bonneville tracked the south branch two days seeking a ford. Finally, he ordered wagon bodies dislodged from their wheels, covered with buffalo hides and besmeared with tallow and ashes to form crude boats. With three men per boat and others pushing, they braved 600 yards of strong currents before rebuilding them into wagons.

On June 21st they camped amid high cliffs of clay and sandstone at a place called Scotts Bluff. While they stood together at twilight, Walker pointed to the stone art stretching to the horizon, "Stones become towers, castles, churches -- fortified cities in a harsh scape they soften to a land of Angels."

Bonneville raised an eyebrow. "Are you a poet, or is it that these images would move any man?"

"Hard to say what moves a man. Robert Burns penned an ode to a louse at seeing one on a lady's bonnet at church!"

"Don't suppose you'd favor me with a bit of it?"

"Ye ugly, creepin blasted wonder,
Detested, shunned by Saint and sinner,
How dare ye set foot upon her,
*   Sae fine a Lady!*
Gae somewhere else and seek your dinner,
*   On someone shady.*

*   . . .*

O would some pow'r the giftie gie us
To see oursels as others see us!
It would from many a blunder free us
*   And foolish notion:*
What airs in dress and gait would lea'e us,
*   In pure Devotion."*

"You are a man of many faces, Joseph Walker!"

"As are you, Captain. Few fur trappers spend a forenoon measuring the Platte."

Sundown of June 24th found Bonneville's outfit camped for the night on the North Platte. Sixty Crows in war paint on horses smeared with bloody handprints rode out of the sun. Bonneville was ready to give the command to fire but Joe Walker whispered, "Wait. See how they stare at our cattle?"

Crows dismounted, surrounding a cow and calf. Bonneville told his interpreter. "Ask in *Absaroka* what they want."

In tortured English the *Absaroka* Chief replied, "Us not see tame buffalo people before. We want know how you take wild out. We rest from our chase of *Cheyenne* knifers."

Donning his uniform, Bonneville asked the Chiefs to dine with him while Crow braves wandered the camp touching wagon wheels and anything else the Mountain Men would allow. Near midnight, the Chiefs hugged Bonneville, *Cerré* and Bonneville's guards in a display of friendship before riding into the darkness.

Cerré sputtered angrily, "Captain, you know those Crows lifted our wallets, pocketknives and coat buttons?"

Bonneville nodded, "Just like New York City, *Michel*, but it's cheaper than war."

Before setting out next morning, Captain Bonneville shot altitudes of the sun with his sextant, ascertaining his latitude at 41° 47' North. He recorded temperatures of 59° at 6 AM, 92° at 2 PM and 70° at 6 PM.

On June 26th they camped at Laramie's Fork, a clear stream 20 yards wide wending through meadows rich in currants, gooseberries and tree groves. While his men fished and gathered berries, Bonneville observed Jupiter's satellites with his Dolland reflecting telescope, ascertaining his longitude to be 102° 57' west of Greenwich.

July 1st, the same 60 Crow warriors hove into their path, Cheyenne scalps on their lances. Their Chief asked Bonneville's soldiers to join in their scalp dance. Bonneville replied, "Our God will not let us join your dance. Go in peace." After the Crows filed down the rocky gorge, Bonneville directed, "Wrap your horses' feet with raw buffalo hide like the Crows did."

Joe Walker persuaded Bonneville to use front hobbles for the horses instead of side-lining them at their next camp.

On July 24, 1832 Bonneville lead the first wagons ever over South Pass, proclaiming in his journal the feasibility of this route for future emigration.

During the morning of July 26th, Bonneville's rear guard reported a dust cloud closing fast. Preparations to repel attack ensued. Joe Walker took scouts down their backtrail. Walker galloped back. "Dust's from an American Fur Company outfit."

Bonneville gave the order to stand down and waited.

Swarthy Lucien Fontenelle rode up with a sneer that deepened to disgust. "You've mindlessly driven all wild game before you since leaving the Platte. We've been on forced march to avoid starvation. If you'll step aside, we'll reach the Green River by nightfall, though it's unlikely you will with your rubbish haulers."

Having been insulted by real experts during his 19 years in the Army, Benjamin Bonneville replied, "May you be well down the road before the devil learns you're dead, sir."

Fontenelle wheeled his horse, and the American Fur Company pack train passed in great swirls of dust.

Bonneville waved AFC's dust from his face, then yelled, "Let's beat those goats to the Green River. Move out!"

Though they gave all they had, by 9 PM, the moon rose on mules crumpling in their harnesses and teamsters unable to close a fist on the reins. Bonneville's caravan camped askew on an open plain without water or pasturage. But by noon the following day, Bonneville reached the limpid Green River. Men and horses splashed into its icy water while jealous mules rang the welkin with their braying.

Just upstream, Fontenelle's men lay like corpses strewn after a battle. Their animals wandered, but were too tired to flee.

To Bonneville's astonishment, when Fontenelle moved his camp across the Green, Walker's highly prized *Delawares* packed their traps and moved into the AFC camp.

Joe Walker spoke to their leader. "Why Little Joe?"

"Fontenelle promises us each $400 for a year's trapping."

"Make Fontenelle pay $200 to each *Delaware* today, so you will not lose all if he lies."

"Thank you, Black Wolf."

When Walker returned, Bonneville asked, "How did Fontenelle lure the *Delawares* away?"

"Doubled their pay."

"Two times smoke is more smoke," Bonneville retorted.

"Not now," Walker grinned.

After AFC's caravan left for the 1832 Rendezvous at Pierre's Hole, Captain Bonneville revealed his plan to Walker and *Cerré* to build a fort adjacent to the Green River.

Walker argued, "Winter on the Green brings four feet of

snow, howling winds, no animals to hunt and no forage for stock. There is no worse place for a trading post."

Cerré sided with the Captain. Fort Bonneville was born about 300 yards from the Green with a commanding view of the open plain. Large enough to house 110 men, some horses and two blockhouses at its diagonal corners, its cottonwood palisade poles were dug-in to stand 15 feet above ground.

While fort walls went up, Joe Walker rode hard to reach the band of free trappers Fontenelle planned to hire. After a night of revelry, Walker returned with all of them, more than replacing the *Delawares* Fontenelle had purloined.

Bonneville's journal recited that his fort was centrally located among the most warlike plateau and plains tribes, controlling the Snake River plateau passes to Oregon and California. He deemed it an excellent base from which to launch an attack or repel a force coming from the Pacific side of the Rockies.

Walker's veteran trapper recruits told Bonneville he should call his post "Fort Nonsense," urging him to move 200 miles west to the Salmon River in the Columbia River basin. To Walker's surprise, the Captain agreed. Caching supplies at his fort, they set out for the Salmon to build again before the snows.

On September 3rd, Bonneville's column reached the summit of Teton Pass with a commanding view of the valley trappers called Pierre's Hole. Its streams wound through green meadows fringed by stands of willow and cottonwood stretching away to distant mountains and the lava plain of the Snake River.

Suddenly Captain Bonneville stretched his telescope, traversing over strewn bodies of men and horses in the willows, cold fire pits and empty lodge circles trampled into the grass. Handing the glass to Joe Walker, he muttered, "There is no trapper's Rendezvous. This is the valley of the shadow of death."

"Could he gain votes by it [Clay] would kiss the toe of the Pope and prostrate himself before the grand lama." The Hartford Times

CHAPTER 40

TURMOIL OVER TEXAS   FALL - WINTER 1832

am Houston crouched in the corner of his dark Indian Queen Hotel room, his head in his huge hands. He'd made every Homeric mistake one man could make in Washington. There had to be a way to salvage some vestige of a future.

Ohio Congressman William Stanberry had started it all last March in a maniacal House speech, charging Houston and Secretary of War Eaton with corruption over the 1830 *Cherokee* rations contract. Stanberry never mentioned that the contract was awarded to someone else or that his real aim was to assassinate Andrew Jackson's 1832 Presidential campaign.

Sam'd challenged Stanberry to a duel, but the Ohioan merely carried two pistols and tried to avoid Houston. On April 13th, while strolling with Tennessee Congressman Blair and a Missouri Senator, Houston glimpsed Stanberry. He charged across the street brandishing his cane as Stanberry fumbled for his pistols. In seconds Stanberry lay senseless and bleeding.

The House voted to arrest and try Houston. The House trial'd dragged on for months. By a 106 to 89 vote, the House'd found Houston guilty, but gave him a mere verbal reprimand.

Stanberry'd sworn out criminal charges in the city court where Houston was convicted and fined $500 on June 28, 1832.

Houston'd written President Jackson seeking a Presidential pardon. Jackson's reply on Houston's letter deemed the fine excessive, excusing it. But Houston felt damaged beyond repair.

Each time Sam was about to do a Texas land deal with New Yorker James Prentiss, the press skewered Houston, ruining his chances for fame and fortune below the Red River.

Of course Prentiss blamed land deal failures on the Cholera epidemic that'd driven the business elite from New York City while corpses of the poor littered its streets.

The 1832 Cholera Epidemic was interfering with everything. City dwellers across the nation were afraid to venture outside their homes. President Jackson had refused to designate a national day of mourning and atonement and been viciously attacked by Henry Clay. Duelist, drinker and gambler Clay seemed an unlikely symbol of national piety. The Hartford *Times* said, "*Could he gain votes by it, [Clay] would kiss the toe of the Pope and prostrate himself before the grand lama.*"

Sam Houston let go of his head, packed his only suitcase and left for Tennessee. In early September, Sam met President Jackson in the library of the Hermitage. More spectral than ever, Jackson slouched before the crackling fireplace in his black robe.

"Mr. President, this job weighs too mightily upon you."

Jackson grunted, "I've become numb to the punishment."

"I appreciate your seeing me.I know you ride the powder keg of Civil War with South Carolina's Nullifiers of your Tariff Act threatening open rebellion."

"I will negotiate an end to the Tariff crisis or double Charleston's population with U.S. Army troops. No doubt you are here because of Texas."

"Indubitably, Sir."

"Before you baffle me with your brilliance, I'm prepared to make you my agent to negotiate with the *Comanche* nation in Texas. Your passport awaits you at Fort Gibson. But by all that's Holy, do not start a war down there in Texas just now."

"Your Texas envoy in Mexico City -- Anthony Butler -- is inept and corrupt. If Texas is ever to escape Mexico's tyranny, it will be in a sea of blood."

"A revolution festers in South Carolina, and storm clouds of revolution darken the Texas sky. One revolution at a time, Sam. You'll have to get in line with yours."

In his riotous November travels to Fort Gibson, Sam shared steamboats and stagecoaches with notorious boozer U. S. Marshal Elias Rector. Mostly they celebrated President Jackson's re-election, but often drank because the bottle was uncorked.

Rector chortled in their bounding coach, "They say I get

drunk on whiskey and sober up on wine."

"To hell with the wine!" Houston shouted.

At Fort Gibson, Houston secured his passport, which listed him at only 6'2", three inches shy of his actual altitude. Washington Irving joined Sam in the Bachelor Officers' Mess, and they spun stories for an hour or so. When Irving retired for the night, he penned: "*Gov. Houston, tall, large, well formed, fascinating man -- low crowned large brimmed white beaver hat -- boots with brass eagle spurs -- given to grandiloquence. A large and military mode of expressing himself. Old General Nix used to say God made him two drinks scant.*"

At Wigwam Neosho Sam found tall and slender *Tiana*. Before he could speak, she said, "I know you are leaving me for good to conquer Texas."

He kissed her hand. "I'm deeding you our wigwam, the trading post, all livestock and our two slaves. I'm retaining one decrepit horse."

"You should have a fine animal to ride for your grand entry into the Texas tornado -- from which you may not escape."

Her ominous words startled him, but he remained the gentleman, "One old horse will suffice. May you live long, prosper and remarry a better man than I."

She rushed into the night to be alone with her tears.

On December 4th, as Sam prepared to head south on the Texas Road, he met Marshal Rector. "I know President Jackson sent you to protect me, but from here south, I must be a sober man -- shaping my own destiny before me."

"At least let me trade horses, so the crows don't eat your mount from under you. General, I wish to give you something else. All I have is my old razor."

"I accept the gift," Houston said sublimely, "And mark my words, if I have the least bit of luck, your razor will shave the chin of the President of a Republic."

"Just make sure your shave's not posthumous, General."

"... the snow lay spread in dazzling whiteness: and whenever the sun emerged in the morning above the giant peaks or burst forth from among clouds... mountain and dell, glazed rock and frosted tree, glowed and sparkled with surpassing lustre." Benjamin Bonneville

CHAPTER 41

BLACKFEET AND BLIZZARDS   WINTER 1832 - SUMMER 1833

Captain Bonneville had learned from the Nez Percé that Lucien Fontenelle's outfit missed the epic Battle of Pierre's Hole in mid-July 1832 between 200 Blackfeet and a like force of trappers, Nez Percé and Flatheads. William Sublette'd led the trappers and friendlies to rescue his brother Milt. Seven trappers, 25 friendlies, 27 Blackfoot warriors and one squaw died. Nearly 100 from both sides were wounded, William Sublette among them. It was the Blackfeet's untended dead that had been discovered on the battlefield by Bonneville's telescope.

Leaving Pierre's Hole as macabre as he 'd found it, Captain Bonneville had built his Salmon River Fort in Idaho Country, then dispatched three buffalo brigades to make meat for a brutal winter that had driven all game to ground.

After being caught in a Blackfoot ambush that killed William Vanderburgh and two other AFC trappers, Warren Ferris escaped with a shoulder wound to Bonneville's Salmon River fort. Though grateful for the Captain's aid, Ferris wrote: *"This miserable establishment consisted entirely of several log cabins, low, badly constructed, and admirably situated for besiegers only, who would be sheltered on every side, by timber, brush etc."*

Dwindling game drove Bonneville to erect even cruder shanties amid blizzards on the Salmon's North Fork. Unable to trap in the fierce gales, Bonneville detached Joe Walker and his men south to trap along the Snake with orders to meet Bonneville at the July 1833 Rendezvous at Fort Bonneville on the Green River near Horse Creek.

After Walker left, a detachment of Bonneville's trappers under Matthieu wandered aimlessly in Idaho Country's blinding snows. Bonneville led the searchers who snatched this doomed party from the Grim Reaper on the frozen Snake River.

After surviving the Rockies' wickedest blizzards, Bonneville mustered 28 torpid men for the spring hunt along the Malade River that some called the Big Wood. Just when it appeared his trappers might take their *first* beaver, Milt Sublette and *J.B. Gervais* of Rocky Mountain Fur gleaned the *last* beaver from the Malade's banks ahead of Bonneville's frustrated men.

1833's early spring ushered in arctic storms piling snow higher than Bonneville's horses near John Day's Creek. Shooting two foundering buffalo saved the lives of his men starving in the sub-zero snowfields. Barely able to walk in the icy gales, Bonneville and his men snowshoed on to Godin's River.

When survival seemed beyond any hope, Bonneville found himself awed by the majesty of their spectacular prison. He wrote: *"Far away over the vast plains, and up the steep sides of the lofty mountains, the snow lay spread in dazzling whiteness: and whenever the sun emerged in the morning above the giant peaks or burst forth from among clouds in its mid-day course, mountain and dell, glazed rock and frosted tree, glowed and sparkled with surpassing lustre. The tall pines seemed sprinkled with silver dust, and the willows, studded with minute icicles reflecting the prismatic rays, brought to mind the fairy trees conjured up by the caliph's story-teller to adorn his vale of diamonds."*

Then Bonneville's fortunes fell to the ice sheeting the drifted snow. Bonneville put a different horse in the lead every 100 yards to break the bloody trail through jagged drifts. When all mounts were too lacerated to go on, Bonneville ordered his men to camp amid breastworks of snow.

Still in Idaho Country in what seemed like March 1833, Bonneville's men hacked a freezing bison to death with axes on the banks of the icebound Malade River. Alternately gorging and curing the meat to jerky, they were suddenly surrounded by friendly Nez Percé, who called themselves the *Saapten.*

Bonneville shared his last cuts of buffalo with these noble warriors, who excitedly recounted their exploits in a recent battle with the Blackfeet.

Over 300 Blackfeet had ambushed the Nez Percé village as adopted Blackfoot renegade *Kosato* returned home with his wife. Only ten other Nez Percé were in their village, but they dug in and fired their fusees. Shot in the head, *Kosato* fell, but his wounded wife refused to abandon him. Bellying behind a log, a Blackfoot rolled it to the main lodge, but was killed when he sprang up. As another Nez Percé warrior fell wounded, his wife seized his bow, impaling a host of Blackfeet with her arrows. Having exhausted their arrows and powder, the Blackfeet skulked away. Merely stunned, *Kosato* awoke with his valiant wife shielding him. She and the valorous female archer were feted through the night by proud Nez Percé warriors who would long tell tales of how their women bested the Blackfeet.

On April 1, 1833, while trekking the Godin River, Bonneville's men found a swamp of muskrat dens. Nearly a year after his expedition's grand departure from Fort Osage, Captain Bonneville launched another effort to take his *first* skins. To get his men, Indians and free trappers into the spirit, he put a bounty on every muskrat, bringing joy to his camp.

But his scout galloped up shouting, "Lodge poles down the trail!" Bonneville suspended the hunt to reconnoiter. Like the plague, Milt Sublette's Rocky Mountain Fur Company infested Godin's River, dashing Bonneville's hopes of an unmolested hunt.

The following week brought axed trap chains, traps dangling from trees and rotting beaver entrails in his outfit's traps. Disgusted, Bonneville headed for his caches. He would replenish supplies, then set out for the summer Rendezvous at Fort Bonneville, hoping Joe Walker had trapped prime beaver -- or any beaver at all.

CHAPTER 42

REVELATION AT RENDEZVOUS JULY 1833

Captain Bonneville knew Mountain Men called his Green River citadel "Fort Nonsense," but he felt it should be "Fort Insanity" when his outfit arrived there July 15, 1833. Drunken trappers from American and Rocky Mountain Fur Companies, who'd torn up each other's traplines for years, staggered arm in arm, firing pistols in the air amid riotous laughter.

The crowd parted, allowing thundering horses under near-nude Whites and *Shoshones* to race across the meadow. Trading resumed on hoof-torn grass with men haggling for scarlet blankets, beads, trinkets, tiny mirrors and vermilion sticks, their currency to please *Shoshone* beauties in nearby lodges. Other trappers vied for rifles, pistols, powder, shot, butcher knives and traps, paying 400% of their cost in St. Louis.

Everywhere rowdies wrestled, foot-raced and tried to beat each other's heads off with gory fists.

Bonneville sent his men to erect the camp. Turning on his horse, he spied huge Joe Walker striding through the crowd, his black beard framing a dazzling smile. Sliding off his horse, Bonneville shook hands warmly with Walker, then asked, "Take any beaver?"

"Twenty-two and a half packs, Captain. You fare well?"

"Abominably. Yours is our outfit's whole catch for this season. Report to my lodge this afternoon."

"Where is it, Captain."

"It'll be in that glade. We have serious business."

"Keep watch for rabid wolves, Captain. They're racing through the camps ripping men and livestock bloody."

"Sounds as crazy as these trappers."

Soon after the American flag flew from the peak of Bonneville's lodge, Joe Walker yelled, "Hello the camp!" and ducked through its flap. Walker seldom spoke and said even less when he was worried. He sank to the buffalo-robe rug, squinting to accustom his eyes to the dimness.

Bonneville sat cross-legged with his eyes closed like a bald Buddha in buckskins. "It's time I revealed our mission."

Walker nodded.

"Britain, Russia, the Spanish, who yielded to the Mexicans, and hordes of Indians have craved sole ownership of all land west of the Mississippi longer than the mind of man runneth not to the contrary. All scheme to seize it -- just as we do. We're not the first Americans in this silent war. Lewis and Clark spied for Jefferson from 1804 to 1806. While they mapped the way to the Pacific, Zebulon Pike, a 25 year old Army Lieutenant, bought fort sites from the Indians on the upper Mississippi until becoming embroiled in the most convoluted spy intrigue of this or any other age."

Sweat inched down Joe Walker's temples. He was torn. He hated chicanery, but the lure of roaming beyond the horizons beckoned irresistibly. "My ear's yours, but my enthusiasm isn't."

Realizing he'd found another man with a streak of fatal honesty, Bonneville continued, "Unaware General James Wilkinson was a spy in the pay of Spain, President Jefferson appointed Wilkinson Governor of Louisiana Territory in 1805. Unbeknownst to Spain, Wilkinson conspired with Jefferson's Vice President Aaron Burr to create an independent nation on Spanish land. To ascertain Spain's vulnerability to invasion, Wilkinson sent Lt. Zebulon Pike to reach Santa Fe by any means he could to spy on the Spanish."

"Did Pike know Wilkinson's real stripe?"

"Unlikely. With Wilkinson's spying and counterspying, nobody's sure he knew his own stripe. In fact while Burr traveled to New Orleans, Wilkinson informed Jefferson of Burr's plot, getting Burr arrested and tried for treason. Meanwhile, Pike's orders from Wilkinson included locating the headwaters of the Red River. In what some call Colorado Country, Pike's expedition discovered a peak rising halfway to the sun -- which he named for himself -- though he could never climb to its top."

"How did Pike get to Santa Fe without being arrested like I was?" Walker yelled, over drunken shouts outside.

"Pike wanted to be arrested. He camped on the Rio Grande till Spanish soldiers captured him, hauling him and his men to Chihuahua while Pike noted everything in sight. Wilkinson used his covert Spanish connections to get Pike put back across the border at Natchitoches, Louisiana."

"You expect me to be enticed by this skullduggery?"

"Not even slightly, but look what's come of these spy missions. Lewis and Clark's maps and lore sustain us where we sit, enhancing our country's growth to the Pacific. Pike's 1810 published report still helps American men and women settle the wilderness where he traveled just as your ancestors tamed the Appalachians. Our observations will aid Americans yet unborn."

"And that's why you measure the rivers, map the trails, calculate latitudes and longitudes and interrogate Indians?"

"Along with my fierce urge for my country to reach from the Atlantic to the Pacific without foreign powers in the way."

"Does our government sanction this mission of yours?"

Bonneville opened his leather pouch. "Here's Passport #2567 issued January 23, 1832 to Joseph Walker with a Mexican Visa allowing you and your men legal entry into California, all aboveboard. Your task is to map the best emigrant route to California. Once there, to learn everything about the Mexicans, Russians, British and their forces. You'll be well equipped and permitted to explore all you wish. Will you proceed, or must I find an imposter to use Joseph Walker's Passport and Visa?"

Walker tipped his head back and groaned. Finally, he replied, "I'll do it."

"Then your first objective is to see if Zebulon Pike's theory was right about the Rio Buenaventura flowing west from the Great Salt Lake through the Rocky Mountains to the Pacific."

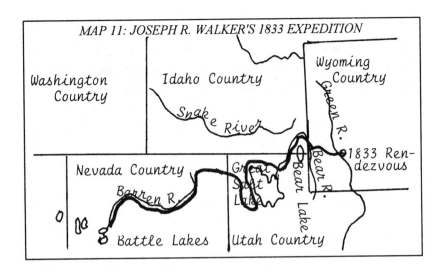

MAP 11: JOSEPH R. WALKER'S 1833 EXPEDITION

Washington Country

Idaho Country

Wyoming Country

Snake River

Green R.

Nevada Country

Barren R.

Great Salt Lake

Bear R.

Bear Lake

1833 Rendezvous

Battle Lakes

Utah Country

 CHAPTER 43

PROBING DESERT MYSTERIES   JULY - SEPTEMBER 1833

Joe Walker was eager to recruit men to explore Eden, but he couldn't resist the rough-and-tumble horse races at the 1833 Rendezvous. Joe's Herculean size made most trappers bet against him -- the first time. Then powerful bounding leaps fused Joe into his stud horse with his weight over each stride. That was the last other riders saw of him. By the third week of July, Joe Walker couldn't even get a race with blind drunks.

After eating a tough slab of roast buffalo, Walker strolled the camps telling likely looking men he was hiring trappers to go to California. A slender man said, "Like to hear more bout what you said to that other gent."

"What's your name?"

"Zenas Leonard."

"Right off the farm?"

Zenas laughed, "Might look that way, but three years ago on my 21st birthday I told my Pa I could make a living without picking up stones on the farm. He gave me liberty to try it. Walked from Clearfield County to Pittsburgh and worked in my uncle's store. Come west and clerked for Gantt & Blackwell till they went broke. Got into it with the Blackfeet at Pierre's Hole. Didn't run cause I was scared o' looking like a coward. Been a free trapper with a empty possibles bag ever since."

Impressed by the man's honesty, Joe said, "Be at Fort Bonneville first thing tomorrow."

"How many you hiring?"

"Forty."

"George Nidever hankers to see California. He's been cleaning up with his rifle like you have with that big bay stud.

Captain William Drummond Stewart, stocky British Army veteran of Waterloo, braced Mountain Man Joe Meek. "You know a rabid wolf ripped George Holmes' face, yet you were so drunk last night you couldn't walk. You're going to get bit."

Handsome bearded Joe Meek's grin lighted him head to foot. "Cap'n, if that wolf hadda bit me last night, it woulda killed 'im -- if it didn't cure the rascal!"

Feeling guilty because he'd put Holmes out of their bower so he could share it with a *Shoshone* lady, Captain Stewart said "Be sensible! Many men are barricaded in their shelters. I heard wolf howls ringing the timber at daylight."

Joe Meek retorted, "They best bite me quick, cause me an brother Steve is leavin' fer Californy tomorrow."

"Godspeed, Joe Meek!"

"John Barleycorn'll watch over this child all the way. Cap'n, them wolves plays the pious Vicar better'n you do!"

Benjamin Bonneville shook Joe Walker's hand after Walker's last mule was packed on July 24, 1833. "You are provisioned for a year. Each man has four horses, two blankets, buffalo robe and dry comestibles. Don't give up your Passport to a minor official. Trust your instincts, for they are remarkable."

"See you next year on the Bear River!" Walker rendered his first salute since 1814 and vaulted onto his bay stallion. He could barely contain his joy as he led his legion west into the delicious mystery reborn with every new horizon.

Bonneville's Army leave of absence was over in less than three months. As a West Pointer, Bonneville knew it was tantamount to career suicide to assume in his letter that his extension of leave would be granted. But he had no choice. He couldn't take time to report in at a post hundreds of miles away. And if his extension was refused? He only had Walker's 22½ packs of beaver. He would be disgraced with lifelong friend Alfred Seton unless his peltry production burgeoned before he returned to New York's crass realities. He'd send these pelts to St. Louis and goad his men to trap like fiends when beaver fur thickened in the fall. Dating his letter the day he expected to complete it, he wrote:

"Crow Country Wind River July 29, 1833
Major General Alexander Macomb.

Sir, I have the honor to report that on the 30th of April I left Independence with 120 men and 20 wagons. On the 12th of May crossed the Kansas, Kept up the left bank, moved up the Republican, which I headed, having at first gone through a rolling country upon the Republican. I marched upon an elevated plain, then struck it a little west and in one day fell on the Platte, the 2d June, here I found the River 3/4 mile wide, the banks 2 to 3 feet high, river about 4 feet deep, but full of quicksands; the plains upon the banks of the Platte are from 3 to 5 miles wide, and I marched to the forks 130 miles without a break or creek. I have visited only the heart of the Rockies, i.e. the headwater of the Yellowstone, Platte, Colorado of the West and Columbia. I will explore the Cottenais and the new Caledonia and winter on the lower Columbia ...going to the southwest towards California on my return which will certainly be in the course of next fall. I would not have presumed this much were I not aware how desirous you are of collecting certain information respecting this country. I have kept a journal. The information I have already obtained authorizes me to say this much; that if the government ever intend taking possession of Oregon, the sooner it shall be done, the better, the military force necessary to seize Oregon will require a full garrison. My list of forts and garrisons includes Vancouver and

Walla Walla and the forces necessary to reduce them; Vancouver's 180 men are generally scattered about trapping and trading and Walla Walla with only a few men can be easily reduced. The Willamette Valley is rich and fertile beyond all I have seen. Hudson's Bay Company is long entrenched with a network of co-opp'ing indians for trade and totally dominates the Columbia Valley to the exclusion of all others. American companies roam in and west of the Rocky Mountains often capturing rich harvests of furs -- weather permitting -- and the fact that the American Fur trade can support so many men indicates its richness in furs. I discribe many tribes and their habits and characteristics in my journal. I have never seen the Salt Lake, but have heard that five trappers attempted to coast it. On my return about the last of June (1834) I shall meet Mr. M.S. Cerré, and if you shall have any instructions for me, shall be glad to receive them either to join any party that might be sent, to comply with any other commands in this country, or to return to the States. I remain Sir, Your very Obt. Servt

BLEBonneville
Capt. 7th Inf "

Four days west of Rendezvous, Walker's party reached *Bannock* huts along Bear River. Having traded with them last spring, Joe was received with friendly shouts. After gifting the usual ornaments, Walker hand-signed with the Chief.

Returning to camp, Walker found Zenas Leonard. "*Bannocks* say Bear River Valley has buffalo shoulder to shoulder. Post five sentries here. Don't break off your hunt till every man has 60 pounds of jerky. Oughta take a week. Chief says Whites are camped on the Bear. I'm gonna talk to 'em."

Zenas nodded. "Most I ever heard you say at once."

Before sundown Walker hailed the White lodges. No doubt who the big redhead was walking toward him like a gate with no hinges. Old Bill Williams looked about the same as he had on Major Sibley's Santa Fe Trail survey.

"More Walker boys in that big gang down river?"

Joe shook his head. "Where you headed?"

"Where the fish bite and the women don't!"

"What's this outfit?"

"Twenty free trappers."

"Who's in charge?"

"The wind."

"I'd have a word with the trappers before dark."

"You're fresh money. They'll get you into a game of Old Sledge."

Joe headed for the camp. "How about a horse race?

Old Bill grinned, "I'm the only fool in this outfit, and I'm too smart for that!"

Trappers straggled in by twilight, several with deer and one with a bloody-headed, yearling elk buckling a pack mule's back. Joe recognized crazy Mark Head, big florid-faced redhead Levin Mitchell and ruddy red-haired Bill Craig. Joe said, "Even your elk's a redhead! We're 40 strong trapping to California. Welcome to join as free trappers. I'll stake each man to a horse, sugar and flour. Sign or make your mark on this paper to get the bounty. We're down river making meat for the trip."

Everybody signed or had Old Bill print their name beside their X, including Alex Godey, *Antoine Janise* and Bill Price.

By mid-August Walker's 60 men had ridden the Great Salt Lake's western desert shore seeing no sign of a tree or the Rio Buenaventura flowing from the briny inland sea. Joe noted on his crude map that another water passage west was a myth.

Thirst drove them northwest across fiery deserts toward snowy mountains. They chanced upon a milky stream shown as Ogden's River on Walker's map. It quenched their thirst, provided beaver and started an argument.

Old Bill said, "Anybody who's been away from home a week knows this is Mary's River."

Zenas Leonard settled it. "Man could walk its banks forever without finding stick enough for a walking cane. I'll call it Barren River [*since renamed the Humboldt*] in my journal."

Barren River beaver lived on poison parsnips, so their flesh sickened many Mountain Men, though none died nor even knew why they puked all night.

Ruddy Bill Craig sat chest deep in the Barren's milky swimming hole, three feet of water atop four feet of mud. Joe Walker leaped across the blistering sand like a buck deer.

"How is it?" Walker yelled.

"Joe -- it's just splendid," Craig replied choking his grin as Walker dived in head first. While Walker struggled to get his head out of the blue mud, Craig bolted into some briar bushes laughing hysterically. Walker dug mud from his eyes and ears, then splashed water over his head, listening to Craig's cackling.

Craig saw Walker squinting his way and slithered across the smoldering sand like a chortling sidewinder.

Walker burst from the water, sprinted to his lodge and seized *Gunstocker John Walker*. Half blind, he fired into the bushes. Reloading, he yelled, "Show yourself Craig and I'll dump a hunk o' lead in you!"

Still laughing, Craig clapped his hands over his mouth. After dark a shivering Craig slipped into camp asking for food.

Joe heard him and yelled, "Sit over here, Craig!"

Wrapped in a blanket, Craig sat down at the buffalo robe of Walker's mess across from Joe. But when he saw blue mud on Joe's nose, he laughed louder than before.

Joe exploded, "What the hell are you laughing at now?"

Craig pointed at the muddy nose gasping, "Gentlemen generally wash before supper."

Walker's mess roared till Joe got caught up in it. Wiping tears from his mud stained eyes, Walker howled, "That's your prank for this trip, Craig. You'll die laughing at your next one!"

Walker's outfit trapped the Barren River in early September, losing their traps to naked *Paiutes*. Reaching a *Paiute* village, Joe Walker got even for the stolen traps trading two awls and a fish hook to a *Paiute* for a robe of sewn beaver skins worth $40.

Joe made camp miles from the village. But skulking *Paiutes* purloined traps and anything else they could find. At Walker's campfire Old Bill Williams growled, "Those Diggers have taken their last trap from Old Bill. Next one'll cost them naked flea farms a bucket o' blood!"

Levin Mitchell yelled, "Make it a barrel!"

Others muttered agreement.

Joe Walker rose. "There are a thousand Diggers here.

Never lost a man from my outfit. We'll not go to war over rusty beaver traps. Tell Zenas how many you're out, and I'll make it good outa stores. These Diggers are from the stone age -- don't even have trade guns. Take what they see, cause that's how they were brought up. Leave 'em be."

Old Bill growled, "I take no charity and give none."

Joe said quietly, "Bill, I'm telling you plain. You wanta cut your string, go ahead but don't kill a *Paiute* and bring a thousand Indians down on our heads. *Paiutes* dip their arrows in sidewinder spit. Leave 'em be!"

Old Bill glowered, then strode into the darkness with Levin Mitchell behind him.

Zenas Leonard said softly, "I's you, Captain, I'd sleep in a different lodge tonight. Plenty room in mine."

Walker knew his clerk was right, but wouldn't be driven from his bed by Old Bill or the others who worked the wild side o' the river. "See you in the morning, Zenas."

Just before dawn a gunshot jerked Walker's camp awake. Zenas pounded up to Walker's lodge with his rifle. He yelled, "Helloo Captain!" and whipped the door flap back.

Bare chested and hairy, Joe burst past Zenas, "Shot came from the river."

Sprawled on the river bank lay two skinny *Paiutes,* one shot dead and the other with his throat slashed. Walker yelled, "Strike the camp and head down river."

Trotting down the Barren River, they reached the marshes on the 4th of September. Grazing their spent mounts, they rested their sore bodies.

Joe found Old Bill on his back with his fingers laced behind his head. "You kill those Diggers this morning?"

"As promised."

"Get out."

"This a trapper outfit or a quilting bee?"

"Don't you get it, Bill? They don't know any better."

"Maybe you don't either."

"You won't be here to find out. Pack up and move out!"

"Never kill a White man unless I have to."

"Bill, you better leave -- while you still can."

Old Bill sized Joe up, then headed for his lodge.

"Take Mitch with you, Bill."

Joe could see smoke rising from brittle grass on their backtrail. "Picket the horses. Build a breastwork around the camp with your packs."

Before their breastwork enclosed them, upwards of 900 naked *Paiutes* issued from the high grass. They signed they wanted to come in to smoke with the Whites. They edged closer. None were women, leaving no doubt they were a war party.

Walker said, "Been good riding with you boys. Load everything that will shoot. Put your knives where you can lay hands on 'em. Learned as a young soldier infantry's no match for cavalry, so get ready to mount up. Never fancied dying afoot."

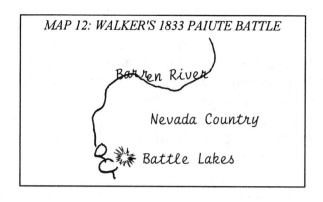

MAP 12: WALKER'S 1833 PAIUTE BATTLE

Barren River

Nevada Country

Battle Lakes

CHAPTER 44

DECISIVE BLOW AT BATTLE LAKES   FALL 1833

As Joe Walker and 30 of his men mounted to ride down upon the 900 naked surging *Paiutes* armed with sturdy bows and quivers of arrows, five of the Indians came forth signing that they were coming into Walker's camp. Ten trappers rose from behind their breastworks led by tall, handsome Joe Meek. Joe Meek, with his smaller brother Stephen at his side, signed that if the *Paiutes* came one step closer, they would be killed.

A naked *Paiute* in the delegation of five asked by sign, how so few could kill so many? Joe Meek signed it would be done with guns, causing the *Paiute* multitude to burst into tumultuous laughter like a theater audience enjoying a comedy.

The delegation's *Paiute* pointed to the ducks on the marshy lake behind the trappers' fort, signing that he wanted to see ducks killed with guns.

Joe Walker dismounted. He called, "George Nidever!" then turned to Joe and Stephen Meek. "Can you boys shoot a lick?"

"Can when we're sober," the older Stephen replied.

"Sober now?" Walker growled.

"Havin' the whole Digger nation ready ta kill us has sobered me tolerable," Joe Meek grunted.

Keen-eyed George Nidever stepped up on the breast-works, "Odd time for duck hunting, Captain."

"Beats shooting *Paiutes*. Fire!" Walker ordered.

Three rifles crashed together in a cannon blast, splattering duck feathers on the lake. The noise made the *Paiutes* lurch, some falling flat to the ground as the remaining ducks wing-slapped the air overhead.

Joe Walker nodded, "Reload and stand ready."

A big *Paiute* with long tousled hair strode forward to stretch a beaver skin on the river bank, signing he wanted to see his skin hit by White thunder.

Nidever muttered, "Must think we just spooked the ducks. I'll pop his pelt in the head." Nidever's ball made good on his word. The *Paiutes* nearest the headshot skin trotted off and the rest strung along behind.

Joe Meek grinned, "Make a right fine tall tale, George! You run off the whole damn *Paiute* nation with one shot."

Feeling relieved, Joe Walker posted 15 guards on three hour watches, to rotate throughout the night. "Don't bother to holler if we're attacked. Your rifles'll wake us up."

But the night passed peacefully. Before dawn Walker had his men riding along the marshy lakes strung like great waterbeads on a single strand of river with no sign of the *Paiutes*. At sunrise, Walker's force was suddenly surrounded by *Paiutes* surging from the high grass. Walker yelled, "Follow me!" He spurred his stallion through the startled Indians away from the marshes onto the hard ground of the desert plain in case they had to run their horses.

For several hours the *Paiutes* pursued them, staying to the brush. Several bunches showed themselves, signing they wanted Walker's men to stop and smoke with them. Each time Walker signed with them, he saw dust billowing from their following horde. Walker signed to the Diggers, "Go back or get what the ducks got." Diggers clustered into a hundred warriors waving bows with notched arrows tipped in rattlesnake venom.

After figuring what Andy Jackson would do against a force outnumbering his by 15 to one, Walker gathered his 58 men. "Diggers are stalling. Want us to fight their main force belly to belly, where their bows will beat our rifles. We must strike a decisive blow and take the fight out of 'em or they'll overrun us."

As Walker spoke, the *Paiute's* advance party surrounded his people. Angered, Walker shouted, "I want 30 men on fresh mounts. Rest o' you hold the horses. We won't last till sundown without 'em!"

With the main *Paiute* force launching dust on their back trail, Walker shouted, "Charge!" and bolted into the *Paiutes* with his pistols blazing, scattering them like partridges before a hawk. Pulling *Gunstocker John*, Walker shot a *Paiute* with a raised bow, then used the butt to flatten two more. Trapper horses ten-pinned *Paiutes* off their feet as muzzles flashed in the swirling dust. Howling *Paiutes* bolted, but their tribe kept coming.

Walker wheeled his stallion. "We're gonna leave their main party something to think about! Take their bows and finish off any downed *Paiute*!" Walker spurred his stallion toward the oncoming throng, but pulled up near his own reserve men. "Picket our horses. When you have a prayer of hitting somebody, fire. Gotta scare these fools bad enough to let us be before they get close enough to kill us all!"

After the first volley from the big bore rifles, the main force of *Paiutes* wheeled like stampeding buffalo, running over their followers.

Walker felt bad about what had happened here, but it seemed his men felt justified. He remembered the *Delaware* telling him he was a warrior of death -- maybe he was.

Their bloody encounter costing 39 *Pauites* their lives caused Zenas Leonard to name the marshes "Battle Lakes." Having left the main party of Diggers behind, Walker's men, sound except for minor wounds, met small bands of Diggers that seemed more friendly than the first bunch.

These *Paiutes* wore a shield of grass around their loins. Most were small, feeble and hairy. Walker watched them harvest grass seed by knocking the heads into a basket, much like Marm said the Hebrews did in the time of Christ.

Zenas wrote in his journal, "*Fish are very scarce -- their [Paiutes] manner of catching which is somewhat novel and singular. They take the leg-bone of a sandhill crane, which is generally about eighteen inches long, this is fastened in the end of a pole -- they then, by means of a raft made of rushes, which are very plenty -- float along the surface of these lakes and spear the fish. They exhibit great dexterity with this simple structure -- sometimes killing a fish with it at a distance. They also have a kind of hook by which they sometimes are very successful, but it does not afford them as much sport as the spear. This hook is formed of a small bone, ground down on a sand-stone, and a double beard cut in it with a flint -- they then have a line made of wild flax. This line is tied nearest the beard end of the hook, by pulling the line the sharp end with the beard, catches, and turns the bone crossways in its mouth."*

"In warm weather a fly about the size of a grain of wheat lands in the green slime on their lake in great numbers. When the wind rolls the waters onto the shore, flies are left on the beach. Female Indians carefully gather them into baskets made of willow branches and lay them in the sun till perfectly dry, then they are laid away for winter provender. Flies, grass seed and rabbits is their principal food during the winter season."

"Their habitations are formed of a round hole dug in the ground, over which sticks are placed, giving it the shape of a potato hole -- covered with grass and earth -- the door at one side and the fire at the other. They cook in a pot made of stiff mud, which they lay upon the fire and burn; after cooking a few times it falls to pieces, then they make a new one."

Unaware of the battle with their kinsmen, the Diggers, calling themselves *Shoshocoes*, built rafts of rushes and ferried Walker's men across the river.

Hunters left Walker's main party, surprising a few Diggers, who fled. In the brush the hunters found what looked like dried fish in two rabbitskin bags. Returning to the evening fire, they emptied the bags in their supper stew. They ate more stew for breakfast, but many vomited when Joe Walker dissected the "fish bits" identifying them as worms and insect larvae. Walker grimaced, "*Paiutes* won the last battle of this war. Moral is, you eat your enemy's food and it will beat you!"

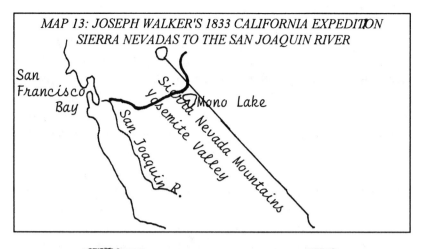

MAP 13: JOSEPH WALKER'S 1833 CALIFORNIA EXPEDITION
SIERRA NEVADAS TO THE SAN JOAQUIN RIVER

San
Francisco
Bay

Mono Lake

Sierra Nevada Mountains

Yosemite Valley

San Joaquin R.

CHAPTER 45

ICE, WONDERS AND SKYFIRE   LATE FALL 1833

hen Joe Walker scanned the majestic rampart of what some called the Sierra Nevada Mountains rising into the clouds, he felt this journey was his own beginning. He was Swift's Lemuel Gulliver going where others had never been. Would he meet six inch Lilliputians or 60 foot Brodingnagians, men with great intellects and no sense or civilized horses dictating to human brutes. Whatever was there, Joe Walker would see it, breaking trail for wagons full of children, spinet harpsichords and hope.

The lake they reached in early October did not disappoint Walker. Its water tasted like lye, suitable for washing clothes without soap. Pumice stone floated on it like dumplings.

He sent scouts to find game and a pass through the mountains. They returned with neither, finding only a frail colt that had to be killed and parsed out among his hungry legion.

Walker dispatched more scouts to find the path to the clouds, but none did. While he, Zenas Leonard and George Nidever searched for it, two Indians leaped up and ran at Nidever. He thought they were after him, so he fired, killing both as Walker had at Horseshoe Bend. Learning they were only frightened nomads, Nidever told Walker, "I am so very sorry," but they were dead.

So Nidever secreted their bodies in a rocky ravine and said, "May God bear them upward into the wonders above and spare the soul of this sinner."

Nobody had ever dreamt of mountains this steep, but Walker led them into the high country where the air knifed a man's lungs. The horses starved amid barren stones and the men ate gin berries picked from the junipers, staring at the everlasting snows awaiting them above.

As they broached the snows, Walker watched his beloved horses turn helpless. Floundering in drifts, they had to be lowered down cliffs on ropes and boosted like feeble old men.

The trappers' days grew into agonies of icy starvation, and still they climbed -- making less than ten miles per day. With supplies exhausted and no game in sight, Walker hunkered down in the snow with his freezing men. Some vowed to go back to buffalo country in spite of the majority vote to go on. "All we have is horses. Kill the weakest three." Their meat was black, stringy and tough, fit only for a dog, but it was eat that or die.

Once they reached the Sierra's icy summit, they became its hostages, for it was endless. Day after day, they inched west among drifts ranging from ten to 100 feet deep. Walker walked about them, determined no man should die, pointing west when they fell at his feet. The horses got stiff and stupid, and more had to die to feed their masters. Joe Walker couldn't watch these faithful creatures shot, willing to serve, but too weak to walk. And still they struggled west with each mile stretching into a continent and no earthly sign of man nor beast.

Small lakes bordered by lifeless grass teased the horses, affording scant nourishment while the men starved between horse murders. For the first time, Walker wondered if they would become frozen mummies for other explorers to marvel over.

Barely seeing the panoramic vistas that might be their last glorious visions on earth, they crept, staggered, crawled and dragged each other west. But all stared in wonder at the freshets shooting from under snowbanks to gather in a spectacular fall from a lofty precipice exploding into spray and mist in the glorious valley a mile below. They knew not that they were the first white men ever blessed to see the Yosemite Valley.

When all had lost hope, Joe Meek brought in a basket of acorns a fleeing Indian had dropped. An inch to three inches long, and an inch thick, the acorns were delectable roasted in the hot ashes of their otherwise barren fires.

Sight of the enchanting but unattainable valley below only heightened Walker's sense of imminent death atop towering perpendicular scarps. Then Nidever reported, "It's not much of a path, but it goes down, and there's deer and bear sign on it."

Walker led their zigzag descent from the giddy heights, so awed by the beauty below he hoped to have it as his last thought on this earth. In the midst of his idyllic pondering, somebody shot a small deer. He ordered it cooked, but by the time the coals were hot, it had been eaten raw as if by wolves.

After reaching a game rich area of oak bushes, two black tailed deer and a black bear fell to their rifles and were quickly roasted and eaten.

Having spent a month in the stark mountain crossing, Walker was delighted to see stands of white cedar, balsam and a strange tree with red wood showing through its lightning scars. Huge oaks spread to shelter elk, deer and antelope. Then they found Brobdingnag and stood in awe at its creatures towering to the clouds! Zenas Leonard wrote in his journal: "*In the last two days traveling we have found some trees of the red-wood species, incredibly large -- some of which would measure from sixteen to eighteen fathoms [96 to 108 feet] round the trunk at the height of a man's head from the ground.*"

They descended into lush country the likes of which neither Walker nor the rest had ever seen before. Beautiful plains laced by rivers and vigorous black walnut, oak, elm, mulberry, hackberry, alder and sumac. Fat wild horses of every color frolicked about, tantalizing the jaded expedition horses with noble brute appeal.

Around November 7th they found five huts populated by 15 or 20 Indians, that took time, and no small amount of smoking to calm. Though the Indians signed poorly, the symbol of friendship embodied in smoking their pipe said enough between them and Joe Walker. Naked except for skin shields on their loins, they lived in huts of logs and slept on beds of grass. They did not know where the Spanish were, but had two knives and a blanket with a Mexican design. They traded five fine horses with Spanish brands for a yard of scarlet cloth and two knives. Their scraps said they lived on horsemeat and acorns. Next morning they pointed west as Walker waved good-bye to them, a far finer thing than his bloody encounter with the *Paiutes*.

Next night Walker encamped them amid a pastoral painting by the greatest of all the masters. They supped on roast elk, posted one sentry and slept like hibernating bears -- until they were startled by repetitious thunder. Walker's men leapt up, shouting, "Earthquake!" Walker muttered, "Ground'd be shaking. It's the Pacific dashing her waves against a rocky shore."

Zenas Leonard didn't voice his beliefs, but wrote: "*The idea of being within hearing of the end of the Far West inspired the heart of every member of our company with a patriotic feeling for his country's honor, and all were eager to lose no time until they should behold what they heard.*"

Walker led his men toward the ever expanding roars, but made camp on November 12, 1833 in another glorious setting near the mouth of the San Joaquin River without reaching the ocean. Shortly after they entered their blankets, the sky burst into flaming streaks and cannon blasts with heavy bodies crashing to the ground around them. Their horses had to be roped and held by wild-eyed trappers. One yelled, "What is this mad place we've come to?"

Joe Walker, himself quite shaken, spoke calmly as he could, "Seen the stars fall before in Tennessee. It's the Leonid Meteor showers, apt to come in November from vicinity of the constellation Leo -- or so my mother said. She wasn't scared o' skyfire, so I don't think we oughta be. Besides, there's nothing you can do about it, so let's watch God show off."

"We have good reason to suppose the territory west of the mountains will some day be equally as important to our nation as that on the east."

Zenas Leonard

CHAPTER 46

ALTA CALIFORNIA   **WINTER 1833 -1834**

Joe Walker was anxious as every other Mountain Man in his outfit to catch his first sight of the Pacific Ocean. Following the San Joaquin River toward roars of crashing surf, they passed near naked Indians harvesting shad and salmon.

On November 20, 1833 the Pacific burst forth broad and brilliant. Joe expected his men to cheer, but like him they realized the magnitude of the moment and savored it reverently.

After their first camp by the sea, Walker led his men south, eager as boys to see gigantic curling waves roll through the mist to burst on the beach. Looming out of the fog was the shiny black body of a 90 foot beached whale. "Oh Lord God, would you look at that!" Zenas Leonard exploded.

Placing his hand on the dead beast, Joe Meek muttered, "Me and my brother Steve uses these for bait."

After the men got their fill of eyeing the monster, Joe Walker led them south. California was Gulliver's Brobdingnag.

Seeing a ship beyond the surf, Joe Walker had his men fasten two white blankets together and hoist them on a pole to hail it. The ship dropped anchor and put two longboats over the side. When the lead boat reached the booming surf, the man in the bow yelled, "What nation do ye serve?"

Joe Walker yelled, "The United States!"

The sailor shouted, "We be Americans too! Our ship's the 292 ton *Lagoda* outa Boston! Here's our salute!"

Signal flags from the longboats caused three ship's cannon to ring the welkin with smoky blasts. Walker and his men helped the boats beach.

A square shouldered man in blue with his cap cocked stepped onto the wet sand. "I'm Captain John Bradshaw of the tradin' ship *Lagoda* ready for business. Who's your Captain?"

"I am the Booshway -- Joe Walker from Independence, Missouri." They shook hands.

"What brings you to California, Joe Walker?"

"Wanderlust and beaver."

"Got papers?"

"U.S. Passport and a Mexican Visa for California. That enough?"

"Cut above most Americans landin' here, but the Mexicans are unpredictable. I meet most Americans in jail."

"Jailed me in Santa Fe 13 years ago for nothing. Bad place for a Missouri Sheriff. They got Americans in jail now?"

Bradshaw blinked in the salt spray. "Dunno. Come aboard m' ship. We can feed 45 with food n' cognac."

Walker's boat trip through exploding surf to the *Lagoda* was exhilarating, but the Tars served the first bread, butter and cheese the Mountain Men had tasted in two years. *Lagoda's* pitching deck greened Zenas Leonard, who retreated to shore, but the rest celebrated with the Jack Tars till dawn sent hungry gulls screeching round the ship.

Joe Walker asked Captain Bradshaw, "How bout coming ashore with all sailors your fair ship can spare?"

Starry-eyed with cognac, the Captain leered, "My Tars have eaten saltbeef rations so long they couldn't tell a steak from the Bos'n's hat. The beach it'll be!"

Walker was surprised how well drunken sailors could row a longboat. That none slipped under the raging swells was a miracle. Sobered by the icy surf they trooped noisily to his camp.

Recovered from mal de mer, Zenas had three fires going in the ground fog. George Nidever leaped astride a horse and headed inland with his rifle, returning in minutes with his first deer. While others dressed his kill, Nidever thundered back into the fog, returning shortly with another small buck over his horse.

Savoring his delicious roast venison, Bradshaw said, "First meat I ever had fresh enough to bound from m' plate."

As they shared aromatic meat and camaraderie, Bradshaw said, "San Francisco's 40 miles north o' here, but you'll do

better goin' directly to the capitol -- Monterey -- 70 miles south
to present your credentials. *Lagoda'll* make port there in two
days. I'll introduce you to Governor *José Figueroa.*"

"What manner of man is he?"

"Decide fer yourself. New in office. *Alta California* has
small garrisons and powerful British enemies comin' down from
the Columbia with the Russians a'ready dug in at Fort Ross."

Zenas asked, "What's *Alta?*"

"Upper. *Baja* or Lower California is the peninsula south
of San Diego," The sea Captain explained.

"Mexicans count Americans among their enemies?" Joe
Walker asked.

"Wouldn't you -- after what Jackson did to Florida?"

Joe Walker knew it was the kind of question that didn't
want an answer.

Zenas Leonard remained silent, but held sleep off long
enough that night to write: "*Most of this vast territory belongs
to ... the United States. ... Will the jurisdiction of the federal
government ever succeed in civilizing the thousands of savages
now roaming over these plains, and her hardy freeborn
population ... build their towns and cities, and say here shall the
arts and sciences of civilization take root and flourish?...Our
government should be vigilant. She should tak[e] possession of
the whole territory as soon as possible -- for we have good
reason to suppose the territory west of the mountains will some
day be equally as important to our nation as that on the east.*"

Next day *Lagoda* surrendered to the horizon. Walker led
his outfit south on the swampy shore only to be astounded again.
A 47 foot narwhal with a 12 foot ivory horn protruding from its
nose lay ashore with squawking seabirds diving on it.

Joe Meek announced, "Fore anybody asks, I gotta tellya
this here's a seagoin' moose that foolishly tried to outdrink me."

After shooting wild cattle with six foot horns for food
and moccasins, the Mountain Men met Mexicans who guided
them to John Gilroy's *rancho* 35 miles north of Monterey. The
ruddy Scot invited them to camp and share his liquor.

After camping, Joe Walker asked, "Been here long?"

"First foreigner ever to settle here, son," Gilroy replied,
rolling his Rs.

"How'd you happen onto this place, Mr. Gilroy?"

"British ship set me ashore to die o' scurvy at age 20 in 1814, but I prized this place so much I put off dyin'. I'm still doin' that -- even though I've suffered a dozen year marriage to *Ignacio Ortega's* daughter."

About to turn 35 on December 13th, Joe Walker tried to conceal his astonishment that old Gilroy was only 40. Walker asked, "Settlements between here and Monterey?"

"Mission San Juan Bautista with 20 priests and 700 Indians."

"Priests friendly?"

"Might rap your knuckles for sacrilege o' some kind, but tell 'em I sent you and they'll take that out on the Indians."

Next evening Walker's expedition camped near San Juan Bautista Mission, where Walker was well received despite his lame Spanish. Conferring with Leonard, Walker said, "I don't want our arrival in Monterey to resemble Barbarians falling on Rome. I'm taking but two men. You are in charge here. Build a breastwork. Fight off any attack then retreat east. Our mission was to blaze an emigrant trail. A goat couldn't climb the way we came in, so find a mountain pass on your way back."

"How'll we get you out of jail?"

"You won't. Meet Captain Bonneville on the Bear River in July of '34 right there on this map."

That evening, Walker and Leonard strolled San Juan Bautista's grounds, admiring its buildings, fields and vast vineyards in the quietude of twilight. Chants of evening devotionals seasoned the idyllic setting. Then a Priest asked in fractured English, "You go hunt wild cattle? You learn much."

Walker accepted, hoping it wasn't a ruse to separate him and Zenas from his men. Smiling *vaqueros* rode the mightiest saddles Walker'd ever seen, high in front and back with a huge flat horn and a leather rope tethered near it. Their stirrups were broad with ornamented leather shields hiding the men's boots so only their enormous spur rowels jutted from the back. Joe had never seen men more at one with their horses.

The Mexicans closed on a plunging range bull. One looped his *lasso* over the great horns, yanked it tight, wrapped the cord around his saddle horn and slid his horse to a stop, cartwheeling his prey. Another caught the bull's hind hoof with his noose. Between the one taunting the bull to charge and the other whipping him, they hauled the bull to the mission. Another rider looped a log and dragged it for firewood for the feast that lasted till midnight and fed all who brought a plate.

At dawn Walker left San Juan Bautista for Monterey with Joe and Stephen Meek. Outspoken Steve asked, "Bring us Meeks cause we're useless?"

Walker grinned. "Could say it's cause your mother Spicy Walker Meek's my relation, but I just like the way you fish."

As promised, Captain Bradshaw met Walker at Monterey Roads. "His Excellency *José Figueroa* expects us this afternoon. Have Passport and Visa at hand. All goes well, they'll issue local papers. If not, papers'll be the least o' your concerns."

Upon arriving at the palace, Walker said, "You Meeks wait out here. If I don't come out before dark, tell Zenas."

Joe Meek grinned, "You don't come out, we're comin' in. These boys ain't never seen nothin' like what'll happen next."

Walker knew the Meeks weren't men who walked away alive while a friend remained prisoner, so he entered the cool tiled hallway with rising confidence.

José Figueroa was pudgy and pleasant in a patrician way. He and Walker liked each other on sight. Satisfied with Walker's papers, *Figueroa* said in Spanish, "This man is law abiding. I will tell him our rules. Captain Bradshaw will explain." With Bradshaw translating, the Governor continued, "You and your men are welcome to stay the winter, to travel freely, to kill game for food and to trade with Mexicans. You must not permit your men to brawl or molest our residents. Trapping on Indian land or trading with Indians is forbidden."

Walker bowed deeply. "Your Excellency, your conditions are most reasonable. We will honor them."

Figueroa rose, and shook hands with Walker. He left the vaulted room, his bootheels echoing down the hall, without ever seeing Joe Meek's rifle aimed at his head from across the plaza.

Joe Walker conferred with Captain Bradshaw then returned to San Juan Bautista. Zenas Leonard and the others seemed relieved. After convincing them they must be fair and thoughtful in their dealings with the Mexicans, Walker relocated his men to a permanent winter camp near the Mission.

Following instructions from Bonneville, Walker reconnoitered, learning much. The Spanish built houses of sun dried mud bricks, making floors smooth by hammering the ground level and heating it with a fireplace in one corner. Most slept on the floor on a bed of blankets atop a cowhide, which they rolled up during the day. They ate beans and meat, often as soup with little bread, using crude utensils. They grew beans, corn and wheat. Vineyards produced their principal drink -- wine. To plow, they scored the ground with a sharpened tree branch dragged in wet weather behind ox teams.

Without barns or stables, when Mexicans wanted milk, they roped a cow, tied her and took it. Animals fended for themselves, but did not suffer as it appeared to be spring year round except in brutal mountain climes. They often drove wild mules and hauled hides to Santa Fe, where the mules fetched six to ten dollars.

Hide trading vessels plied their coast. When a vessel anchored, news wildfired across the *ranchos*. Wealthy Spaniards sent pairs of hunters on fleet horses, one with a noose to capture cattle, the other with a lance to sever hindleg sinews. They skinned, took tallow and choice cuts of meat, leaving the rest for wolves. Hides were pegged to the ground; tallow was shaped into cakes. Cowhides brought $1.50 and tallow 4¢ the pound from ship's buyers, often paid for in high priced merchandise.

Just before New Years 1834, Walker had his men pack beaver they'd taken on the San Joaquin, posted a light guard and left for Monterey. Walker noted that Monterey was made up of 40 houses, a church, a jail and courthouse, all situated beautifully on a deep navigable bay. A fort defended it with several artillery pieces aimed toward the sea.

After trading his peltry to Bradshaw for powder, lead and supplies, Walker and some of the Missourians attended the lavish New Years party on the *Lagoda* where they got on famously with colorfully clad *Gobernador Figueroa*, his top officials and their exquisite ladies.

Men wore blue velveteen breeches and jackets, often with scarlet collars and cuffs with pantlegs to the knees displaying white stockings. Some dressed in elegant black boots, with gigantic jangling spurs. Others wore fringed buskins to the calf, laced or strapped to their legs. Broad *sombreros* kept the winter sun from their eyes and brilliant *serapes* warmed one shoulder.

Not to be outdone, women sported bright silk and calico high-necked gowns, expensive shawls of lace or gossamer secured by a mother of pearl or jeweled *mantilla* in tresses ranging from blonde to ebony. Well formed with dark limpid eyes, they were admired by Mexicans and Mountain Men alike.

Most Mountain Men felt awkward in buckskins and moccasins, remembering their own finery in closets back in the States, but the Governor and other gracious Mexicans soon put them at ease. In appreciation, George Nidever and others offered to entertain the fine folks ashore with their rifles.

Once ashore, it was time for the Mexicans to admire sensational marksmanship in cutting *cigarillos* from each other's mouths and knocking branding irons over at 100 yards. Joe Meek borrowed a line from Ewing Young announcing, "George has to dip his bullets in brine for long shots so his game don't spile afore he gits there."

After the New Years celebration, the Governor summoned Joe Walker to a private meeting on horseback attended by one of his aides who translated. "I will give you outright title to 30,000 acres of the land you choose lying between here and the Russians if you will establish a colony of 50 American mechanics of different kinds. You may develop the land as you wish. In a few years you can amass a fortune and be the head of a rich and flourishing settlement."

Shocked to the soul, Walker's mind raced for answers. He had come here to spy upon this honorable man and his people. They offered to reward him with riches beyond comprehension -- but he could not betray so decent an enemy by accepting. "Your Excellency -- you have spoken the most generous words I have ever heard, but they give me pause. I've given my word to return to the wordly business of another far to the east this July. I'll never forget you." Walker wheeled his stallion and galloped into the afternoon sun.

CHAPTER 47

BONNEVILLE AND THE NEZ PERCÉ   FEBRUARY 1834

After 53 days battling ice-encrusted snow along the Snake River from the Blue Mountains to the Valley of the Imnaha in Oregon Country, the emaciated Benjamin Bonneville slipped into a sleep so profound, his men thought he lay dead. The Captain was startled, by the shocked looks his starving wraiths gave him when he emerged from his lodge alive.

It had been two months since the trappers had seen another human. They eagerly hailed a distant Indian on a fine horse, though he appeared reluctant to join them. He meant food, so they beckoned till he rode his high-mettled horse into their midst. With obvious dignity, the Indian invited them to his village and gave its location in the Nez Percé language, then left kicking snow. The trappers' spent mounts could barely move and were dragged rather than ridden to the village of some 12 families living under an ancient and venerable Chief.

Though heartily welcomed, a repast of mere roots was set before the trappers, doing nothing to deter their starvation. The Chief knew of Bonneville. He even addressed him as Captain, speaking in *Saapten*, which Bonneville had nearly mastered in his months of living among this tribe so much admired by Mountain Men for truth and fair dealings.

As he smoked their pipe of peace with them, Bonneville occasionally doffed his cap, causing a sensation among his hosts. Never having seen a bald head, some rose to examine it in wonder. The Chief asked if he had been scalped in battle.

Bonneville replied, "God has taken back my hair."

The Nez Percé spoke among themselves, announcing they had named him "Bald Chief." Bonneville entered his new title in his journal, adding,: "*A soubriquet for which I can find no parallel in history, since the days of Charles the Bald.*"

Though the trappers eventually begged their hosts for meat, the old Chief was reluctant to break in upon the tribe's winter stores, and only furnished them more roots.

Captain Bonneville devised a stratagem to avoid the embrace of death. He'd seen how his weather-beaten plaid cloak brightened the look of warriors and squaws. Pulling his sharpest knife, he sliced his cloak into strips, and with the talent of a Parisian milliner, he speedily made turbans *a la Turque* and other fanciful headgears of divers conformations. He offered to trade them to Nez Percé women for meat, instantly accumulating an abundance of dried salmon and deer's hearts on which he and his men dined sumptuously.

The Chief so appreciated Bonneville's ingenuity, he insisted the Captain sleep in his lodge. Next morning Bonneville awakened to a shocking surprise. At the Chief's signal, a beautiful young brown horse was led in prancing and snorting. Understanding that "Indian Giving" meant the gift could be subducted at any moment, the Captain placed a fine rifle in the Chief's hands to head off horse reclamation.

But suddenly a whimpering, leather-skinned squaw resembling an Egyptian mummy was pointing at the horse.

The Chief confessed, "This is my best wife. I love her nearly as much as she loves that horse. She cries for his loss. My heart is sore from comforting her."

Bonneville pondered that perhaps nothing but return of the exquisite horse would suffice. Then he remembered his set of glittering glass earbobs, wondering at what age personal vanity became extinct. The moment he placed the earbobs in her crone's hand, her whining ceased. Eagerly placing them in her ears, and still ugly as the Witch of Endor, she sidled out with a coquettish air, suddenly a perfect Semiramis ready as that legendary Assyrian queen to employ her wisdom and beauty to subjugate the unsuspecting men of the Nez Percé.

As Bonneville quickly saddled his prime steed, the Chief presented a young sulking Indian. "This is my son who raised this horse from an unsteady foal to the wonderful creature you have just saddled. The horse is a brother to his heart, which will be too heavy to survive when the horse leaves camp."

Though Bonneville's stores were nearly as bald as he

himself, he sent for a hatchet. Placing it in the hands of the youth, he was relieved to see his face brighten as his mother had with her earbobs.

Climbing into the saddle and about to depart, Bonneville saw the Chief's hand on the horse's mane with the gift rifle in the other. "This rifle will be great medicine, and I will love it for the sake of the Bald Chief, but it is dumb. I cannot make it speak. My family has lost its most prized horse, and without powder and shot, they will starve with me through the winter.

Captain Bonneville called for a supply of his coveted powder and ball and presented it to the Chief. While the old gentleman weighed it with his free hand, Bonneville heeled his spurs to his "gift-horse," and galloped off through the meadow's melting snow, welcoming its sweet silence.

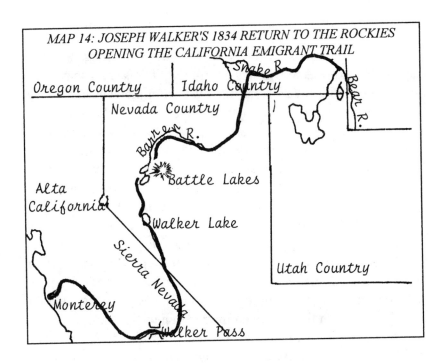

MAP 14: JOSEPH WALKER'S 1834 RETURN TO THE ROCKIES
OPENING THE CALIFORNIA EMIGRANT TRAIL

Oregon Country | Idaho Country

Snake R.

Bear R.

Nevada Country

Barren R.

Battle Lakes

Alta California

Walker Lake

Sierra Nevada

Utah Country

Monterey

Walker Pass

CHAPTER 48

CALIFORNIA EMIGRANT TRAIL FEBRUARY - JULY 1834

As Walker readied to leave for the Rockies on February 14, 1834 with 315 horses, 30 dogs, 47 beef and stores of flour, Indian corn and beans, George Nidever, John Price, Nathan Daily, George W. Frazier and two other men delayed him. Nidever said, "Captain, we are craftsmen. There's a future here in California where a rough table fetches $10 and a windmill $110. We ask your permission to remain."

Nodding, Walker said, "Being together this long, it will be like parting with brothers. May your future be as fine as your service has been to me." After shaking each man's hand, Walker mounted up and yelled, "Let's head for the Rockies!" Though some of his 52 men cheered, Walker didn't. And he didn't look back, for he felt a deep kinship to this bountiful land.

As the sun set on their second day's journey, two

caballeros rode into camp with 25 horses, asking for the Captain. Walker came with his interpreter. The largest man with the sad eyes said, "We've just run away from the Mexican Army for the second time. If we are captured, we will be shot. We want to sell you our fine horses for a pittance and join your expedition." Captain Walker merely nodded and smiled.

Riding down San Joaquin Valley, they saw many Indians, but most scattered. At the Kern River on March 10th, they met some 250 Indians calling themselves *Pagans*. Chief *Capetaine* welcomed the trappers. Since they were living on roots, parsley and cabbage, he gladly accepted beef and a dog from Walker.

Next morning Chief *Capetaine* brought a comely girl to Walker to trade her for an ox. Walker declined with a smile, "The ox will not grow lonesome and go home to its friends in a day or two," then they resumed their march to the south.

Zenas Leonard wrote of this journey: "*The country through which we passed still continued as charming as the heart of a man could desire. ...The prairies were most beautifully decorated with flowers and vegetation, interspersed with splendid groves of timber along the banks of the rivers -- giving a most romantic appearance to the whole face of nature.*"

They came to a village of 700 *Concoas*. Walker's Army deserters learned that years ago the *Concoas* had fled Santa Barbara Mission pillaging golden idols, candlesticks, and several thousand in gold. They traded with ships on the coast and nearby trading posts. Their women raised corn, pumpkins and melons. Raiding settlements, they stole many horses and ate them.

Posting triple guards, Walker prowled his perimeter, meeting two *Concoas* seeking tobacco. They told his interpreter they knew a pass to the east through their Tehachapi Mountains to the Mojave Desert, so Walker hired them as pilots.

In the morning Walker's guides led them along the Kern River to a gap in the mountains. After four days toil, reaching an elevation estimated at only 5,000 feet, they descended to a valley on the 1st of May. Walker gave his pilots a horse, tobacco and trinkets leaving them happy. Someone named the mountain gap Walker Pass. Following the base of the mountains, they found beautiful springs some knew as Indian Wells. Walker's party drank deeply before venturing deeper into the desert.

On May 2nd Walker elected to travel north along the eastern base of the Sierra till he found his earlier trail from Battle Lakes to the Walker River. They proceeded up what would one day be the Owens Valley between the Sierra Nevada on the west and the sun-broiled Inyo-White Mountains to the east.

The land turned grassless, tormented by icy mountain winds and merciless desert heat. Their only break in the forbidding terrain came from a steam cloud near a stream. Zenas Leonard described it, *"These springs are three in number and rise within a short distance of each other.... The water constantly boils as if it was in a kettle over a fire, and is so hot if a piece of meat is put under it at the fountain-head, it will cook in a few minutes, emitting a strong sulphurous smell."*

On May 10th Walker decided to shorten their trip by angling northeast across the desert. By the 11th every creature in their column was staggering. Two dogs died. Their only liquid to drink was cattle blood. The men confronted Walker. Old Stuttering Meritt stammered, "C-Captain, we've f-follered you p-plumb into hell. Now ya g-gotta head b-back to the b-base o' the mountains er share yer next d-drink o' b-blood with the d-devil."

Walker knew he'd lose if they took a vote, so he said simply, "We'll cut west toward the mountains tonight."

On the 13th, traveling by night in ragged formation the horses stampeded north. They followed the horse tracks to water. After drinking their fill of the foul fluid, their tally showed they'd lost 64 horses, 10 cows and 15 dogs.

Too little desert grass and too much wind-whipped sand slew more cattle, so they cut their hides into moccasins for those going lame and kept moving north. Dogs suffered horribly from thirst. When death threatened, they would look a man in the face and howl piteously till death took them.

Near May's end, they found sparse pasturage and rested the stock. Miraculously, their old trail welcomed them, causing the men to rejoice more than at any other time on their odyssey.

In early June they reached Battle Lakes in Nevada Country where they'd skirmished with the *Paiutes*. Suddenly the marshes swarmed with twice as many *Paiutes* as last time. Presents were tendered to the Chiefs, but the *Paiutes* prepared to fight.

Walker signed he would fight their tribal enemies, but the Indians only tightened their surround. Walker's men yelled in anger. Walker shouted, "Mount up! Charge!" Tired horses with their riders firing pistols and rifles smashed through the Indians. The *Paiutes* broke and ran.

In minutes, 14 *Paiutes* lay dead, and three trappers were wounded. Walker urged his trappers to move smartly up the Barren River, and they did without further Indian incidents.

On June 21st the Walker party veered north from the Barren River, finding deer, elk, beaver and bear aplenty with grass for the stock along the Lewis River and on into Idaho Country. July 3rd brought a grand discovery -- buffalo mingling with their Mexican cattle -- soon to satisfy long delayed cravings on the grand day of American Independence.

Walker made camp on the Bear River and waited. Soon Captain Bonneville's men were embracing Walker's trappers. A much thinner Bonneville strode up to Walker. "Got beaver?"

"No, traded my beaver for horses and cattle in California to support our trip back here, and the Buenaventura doesn't run west out of the Great Salt Lake."

Shaking hands, Bonneville muttered, "We've got to talk."

While Walker's men dazzled their old friends with tales of Bull-Bear fights, fandangos, great trees and fishes, Walker and Bonneville conferred over California maps and other details of the odyssey. Bonneville expected *Cerré* with supplies from St. Louis. *Cerré's* arrival set off a drunken revelry, but he brought no orders from the Army.

Unaware he'd been dropped from the rolls of the U.S. Army as a deserter on May 30, 1834, Bonneville split his force into three groups.

Cerré went to St. Louis with 45 men and a paltry supply of peltry to bring back supplies. Bonneville tasked Walker to cross the Rockies to the Missouri River with 55 men to hunt and trade with the Indians until June of 1835 when he was to meet Bonneville at the Bighorn and Popo Agie rivers. After affectionate handshakes around, Bonneville set out for the headwaters of the Columbia with 50 men. Walker headed out in grand spirits, ignorant of the vicious lies that would be told about him in days to come.

MAP 15: EWING YOUNG IN OREGON

Fort Vancouver

Columbia River

Willamette River

Umpqua R.

Oregon Country

CHAPTER 49

OREGON'S UNLIKELIEST HORSE THIEVES   SUMMER - WINTER 1834

aria Josepha Tafoya had joyously welcomed Ewing Young into their Taos cabin in the summer of 1832. But neither could shackle Ewing's wanderlust that soon parted them again. Ewing roamed the wilds of California while *Maria* birthed Joaquin Young on April 8, 1834, baptizing him in a lonely ceremony attended only by Father *Martinez* four days later.

John Turner was trapping California's San Joaquin Valley under Hudson's Bay Company's *Michael La Framboise* when he met Ewing Young in March 1833. Turner was a survivor of the 1827 massacre of Jedediah Smith's men on Oregon's Umpqua River, but still felt drawn to that gloriously fertile region. Turner transferred to Ewing's outfit and led him into Oregon. In Oregon's rich towering timber, Ewing saw a boundless fortune. Returning to Los Angeles, he struggled to buy or build sawmill equipment but failed and resumed trapping.

Disappointed with trapping, Ewing met Oregon enthusiast Hall J. Kelley near San Diego. Not easily influenced, Ewing was somehow captivated by this hollow-eyed zealot from Massachusetts, stranded en route to his Oregon paradise.

Ewing talked with the gaunt Hall J. Kelley over congealing food in a musty inn. The Boston Schoolmaster's white skin stretched dangerously around an oversized skull. He pounded the rough table, "By the living God, I will plant the vine of Christianity and the germ of Civil Freedom in the genial soil of Oregon!"

Ewing said, "I accept that Senator Thomas Hart Benton and others have plagiarized passages from your Oregon prose to spur Americans toward Oregon, but don't you feel somewhat -- eccentric?"

"*Eccentric*? Sir, you do not know what *eccentric* is. While I was promoting my Oregon Colonization Society in New England, I often tried to confer with Professor Thomas Nuttall of Harvard who lived on the second floor of a peculiar house near the Botanical Gardens. Entry was by rope ladder, which Professor Nuttall lowered only when the notion struck him -- a ladder I neither saw nor climbed. That Sir, is *eccentric*."

"Since you see Oregon as the paragon of horse markets, I'll buy horses and meet you in Monterey."

In early June 1834 Ewing tracked the destitute Hall J. Kelley to a Monterey garret. "Get up, Mr. Kelley!"

"I can't. I'm too feverish to consider moving as anything more than an unsubstantiated myth."

"Heading for Oregon with 40 horses and mules."

"Give my hand a modest yank, and I'll join you."

Buying horses in San Francisco and San Jose in July, Ewing amassed a total of 77 and his seven men drove 21 more, all fairly bought. Just north of San Jose, they encountered nine men with 56 horses. Two of the newcomers had served under Joe Walker, which put Ewing at ease as to the legitimacy of their herd. Merging herds, they set out for the Willamette Valley.

On September 9, 1834 at Santa Clara Mission, Governor *Jose Figueroa* wrote Dr. John McLoughlin, Chief Factor at Hudson's Bay Company's Fort Vancouver in Oregon Country, stating that Ewing Young, a rogue and a horsethief, with others of his ilk, were driving 200 stolen horses from California. He asked the Chief Factor's help in recovery of the horses and suggested he have no dealings with the rascal.

In Oregon's Umpqua Valley Young's party met the *La Framboise* brigade, and turned over the nearly comatose Hall J. Kelley for medical treatment at Fort Vancouver. Upon arrival at the palatial fort in October, Kelly was given medical treatment, but shunned and not allowed to table with the gentry.

In early November 1834, Ewing Young reached Fort Vancouver with the horses. A giant in a dark suit with white hair flowing from a beaver stovepipe hat confronted him at the entrance. "I'm Chief Factor McLoughlin. You shall not sully this fort with your presence nor your equine loot. For the Governor of California, I demand surrender of this herd for return to its rightful owners. We shelter Kelley because he's too ill to cast into the woods."

Choking back his fury, Young replied, "These horses are in the custody of their rightful owners. Don't you find the pedantic Mr. Kelley and myself, a long respected trapper, Oregon's unlikeliest horsethieves?"

"Surrender the horses. Sir!"

"You want three eyes?"

McLoughlin spat on the ground, then returned inside.

Unable to find anyone who hadn't branded him a horse thief, Ewing Young claimed 50 square miles of the Chehalem Valley, built his lonely cabin on a hillside and resumed trapping. Trading furs for supplies with American ships voyaging the Columbia, Young ignored local hostilities. Ewing prayed that *Maria* would never hear of his disgrace or his severe internal bleeding. He tended his horses and plotted how to even the score with "Emperor" McLoughlin.

"I told my constituents I was done with politics ... that they might all go to hell and I would go to Texas."   David Crockett

CHAPTER 50

TROUBLE AT THE TOP   JANUARY - AUGUST 1835

Basking in the glory of paying off the National Debt for the first time since America's birth, Andrew Jackson attended the funeral of South Carolina Representative Warren Davis in the House Chamber on January 30, 1835. Rites concluded, members of both Houses and the Cabinet followed by the President filed through the rotunda entrance where bearded 30 year old unemployed house painter Richard Lawrence lay in wait. Two yards from Andrew Jackson, he pulled his pistol, aimed it at the President's heart and fired.

Cane raised, Jackson lunged at Lawrence, who fired a second pistol at point blank range while being borne to the floor by Navy Lieutenant Gedney. Miraculously unharmed by two detonated caps that failed to fire their main charge, Jackson attacked until the cowering Lawrence was dragged away, then added, "That's a fool way to end a funeral."

Jackson had already sent the *Seminoles* his fierce message in October 1834 denouncing them for failing to abide by their 1832 Treaty of Payne's Landing and 1833 Treaty of Fort Gibson under which they agreed to leave Florida for the West. In February 1835, he had General Duncan Clinch read the *Seminole* Chiefs an even harsher threat if they did not keep their word and leave. Jackson's long-time friend and Florida Territorial Governor John Eaton warned the President that attempted removal of the *Seminoles* would result in fearsome resistance.

Jackson's response was that within a month the *Cherokees* would sign a treaty ceding all lands east of the Mississippi to the U. States, then would be removed to the West -- where they would meet the *Seminoles.*

306

On February 20, 1835, Representative David Crockett of Tennessee made his last impassioned speech in the House for his Tennessee Vacant Land Bill to grant free government lands to poverty stricken backwoods folks, but like all his previous efforts for this bill, it failed. Friends told him he'd been deserted as a captive of his eastern Whig masters.

In early March Crockett's *Autobiography,* written in part by Kentucky Congressman Thomas Chilton, reached the street in time for Crockett's re-election campaign, though much of the book denounced Jackson's presidency and sponsorship of his Vice President Martin Van Buren to be his successor.

On April 11, 1835 Jackson's attempted assassin Richard Lawrence came to trial. His defense was that Jackson had murdered his father and impeded Lawrence's succession to the British throne, resulting in his being found Not Guilty by Reason of Insanity and committed to an asylum. Newspapers called Lawrence's escape from the gallows *"a sign of the times."* Some said America had come through 40 years and six Presidents without such monstrous acts and decried the Presidency as a target for society's demented.

Osceola, a handsome, bold and dashing 35 year old mixed-blood *Seminole* Chief called Powell by the Whites, declared in early spring that he would kill any *Seminole* who obeyed the treaty. Federal troops clapped *Osceola* in irons.

After raging like an animal for hours, *Osceola* submitted, signing a paper certifying the validity of the Treaty of Payne's Landing, and they freed him.

To his War Chiefs *Osceola* bragged, "I broke free of their prison with a quill pen!" After *Seminole* Chief Charley Emathla sold his cattle in preparation for removal, *Osceola* shot him, left his body to rot and flung Charley's money to the winds. Florida's second *Seminole* War was on!

As agreed in July 1834, after Joe Walker's return from California, Captain Bonneville brought his men to the Wind River and the Popo Agie and met Joe Walker's brigade in time to celebrate 1835's Independence Day in rough hunters' style.

After recuperating from their revelry, the trappers got

down to business. Zenas Leonard wrote: "*We now set about packing and sorting our furs, & c., and making arrangements for the ensuing year -- such as paying off hands, hiring them for another term, and apportioning the different companies. Captain Walker with fifty-nine men, was to continue trapping in this country for one year from this time, and Captain Bonneville, with the remainder, taking all the peltries we had collected, and which were packed upon horses and mules, was to go to the States and return in the summer of 1836, with as strong a force as he could collect, and a large supply of merchandise, and meet Captain Walker in this neighborhood.*"

As Walker shook Bonneville's hand warmly, he had no idea Bonneville was not coming back nor of how the good Captain's tale of Joseph Rutherford Walker would be insidiously twisted by America's foremost writer, Washington Irving.

However, still held in high esteem in the fur trade in 1836, Joe Walker would become a respected Brigade Leader for the American Fur Company and a legendary figure of the West.

During the summer of 1835, David Crockett campaigned for re-election to the House against peg-legged lawyer Adam Huntsman. Both staying the night with a backwoods Tennessee farmer who favored Huntsman, Crockett waited until everyone was asleep. Selecting a straight-backed chair, he tip-toed to the door of the farmer's daughter and banged it with the chairleg till she screamed. Crockett then stepped on a rung of the chair and thumped away to his room. Then Crockett "rose from his slumbering" in time to keep the farmer from doing bodily harm to Huntsman.

But on August 11, 1835, after circulation of Andrew Jackson's virulent letter denouncing Crockett, Adam Huntsman bounced David Crockett from his chair in the House. After this loss Crockett wrote, "*I concluded my speech [to constituents] by telling them I was done with politics ... that they might all go to hell and I would go to Texas.*"

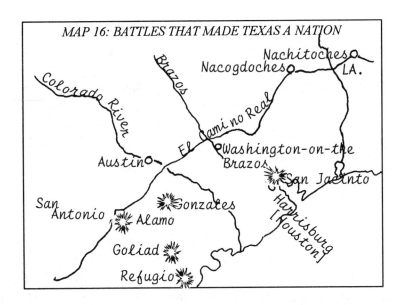

MAP 16: BATTLES THAT MADE TEXAS A NATION

CHAPTER 51

THE CAUSE OF TEXAS   SUMMER-WINTER 1835

Redheaded Thomas Jefferson Rusk asked his lawyer Sam Houston in a Georgia drawl, "Ever think you indulge too fully?"

Houston smiled at his 29 year old farmer client, recently arrived in Texas. He put his feet up on his rickety Nacogdoches law office desk, "You mean do I drink too much?"

"Yes, Sir."

"Indubitably," Houston admitted, knocking back three fingers of whiskey. "You serious about making a life in Texas?"

"How long you been a Texian?"

"Since December 1832, but I know the lay o' the land."

"Tell me about it, Sir."

"Texas has always been too big and too far from Mexico City for the Spanish -- then the Mexicans to manage. They've had a lotta trouble with foreigners and Indians up here."

"Whatta they do bout it?"

"Spain's armies were too embroiled in Venezuela, Bolivia and Peru in the early 1800s to do much, so renegade Americans

309

descended on Texas like weeds borne on the wind."

"What happened to 'em?"

"Spanish pulled up the weeds! When the Mexicans took over in 1821, they decided to bring colonists in to give the Indians somebody else to fight. Moses Austin brought 300 families from Connecticut under the first of many *Empresario* contracts made by Mexico. *Empresarios* received a huge tract of land. Moses died right off. Son Stephen Austin took over."

"Stephen's called the *Father o' Texas*. What's he like?"

"Plain man. Slender. Average height. Prematurely bald. Like most zealots, he's humorless. Shy -- a bachelor. Lives with his sister's family. Says Texas is his mistress. But he's not short on guts or vision. Led the Old Three Hundred through rough waters o' Mexican policies, and they've prospered. If there's a War Party and a Peace party among the 15,000 non-Mexicans in Texas, Stephen Austin used to head the Peace Party."

"Where's he stand now?"

"Hard to say. In 1827 Austin helped the Mexicans put down the revolt by the so-called outlaw State of Fredonia right here in Nacogdoches. He got Mexico to exempt Texas when it outlawed slavery in 1829, so Texian plantations still use slaves. Austin backed General *Antonio Lopez de Santa Anna's* successful popular revolt against President *Anastasio Bustamente* when the Centralists tried to collect taxes from us Texians in 1832. *Santa Anna* became President in 1833, but when Austin went to see his old ally to protest his policies, he got tossed in jail. Can't see Austin as a dove if he ever gits loose."

"Whatta you think'll happen to Texas?"

"Texas has roughly 15,000 anglos and 3,000 *Tejanos*. Most *Tejanos* are more anti-Mexican than the Americans. Think of us as a powder magazine. More American powder bags arrive every day. Half the deserted cabins in the American south have the letters *G.T.T.* on their door. Know what that means?"

"*Gone To Texas*. Painted it on my door in Georgia."

With rumors flapping about Texas like frightened quail, William Barret Travis, a militia leader from Alabama living in Texas since the 1820s, marched his ragtag unit to the customhouse at Anáhuac in late June and forced several bewildered Mexican soldiers to surrender before they could collect any taxes. Disarmed, the soldiers marched to San Antonio where General *Martin Perfecto de Cos,* brother-in-law of President *Santa Anna,* had just arrived with a sizable command.

While General *Cos* awaited orders to arrest Travis and his rebels at Gonzales, a disgruntled Stephen Austin was en route home from Mexico City's prison. He was aboard the *San Felipe,* an armed merchant vessel, when Mexico's war schooner *Correo de Mexico* was refused permission to board. After cannon salvos were exchanged, the badly mauled Mexican warship surrendered in what Austin dubbed "The first battle in the Texas War of Independence."

Consultations [conventions] were held by War Party advocates all over Texas. R.M. Williamson, Editor of the *Cotton Plant* proclaimed in his July 4, 1835 speech, "Liberty or death should be our determination, and let us one and all unite to protect our country from all invasion."

Cos ordered troops to Gonzales to capture their brass cannon and arrest agitators, including Editor Williamson. But when Mexican troops reached Gonzales, an aroused citizenry kept the cannon they needed to fight the Indians and thwarted all arrests. Mexican troops withdrew as heavily armed settlers converged on the defiant village. Someone hung a sign over their cannon that read, "Come and Take it"

Arriving home, Austin became a rebellion leader while vigilance committees met all over Texas. On September 14, 1835, the Nacogdoches Committee under Thomas J. Rusk appointed Sam Houston its Major General. They called a mass meeting of committees to decide if ties to Mexico should be cut.

No sooner had Sam Houston taken command of his tiny force than he learned that Texians had taken the Mexican fort at Goliad on the San Antonio River. Houston organized two 50 man companies then addressed his troops, "I offer to sell 4,000 acres on the Red River for $2,500, so I can get ready to fight and buy myself a uniform."

The Gonzales Consultation elected Stephen Austin, a man of no military experience, their Commander, begging him to attack San Antonio. Austin sent Colonels Jim Bowie and James Fannin to ready Gonzales forces.

A mass meeting at Columbia in mid-October elected Sam Houston commander of all Texian forces. Houston, still a U.S. Indian Agent, rose to say, "In a showdown with Mexico, the Indians could be the deciding factor. We must have them with us." But on November 3rd, the committee delegated Houston to draft a "*Declaration on the Causes of Texas Taking Up Arms.*"

When General Houston learned that Austin, Bowie and the Gonzales "army," were leaving to attack San Antonio, he rushed to Gonzales and called an assembly. "Gentlemen, I fought under General Jackson, our country's finest tactician, in the Creek War. We cannot flit like loose leaves in the wind. We have no supplies, no uniforms, no cannon and no training. We must form one strong, disciplined unit under one commander and pick objectives with care. Attacking San Antonio now is the purest folly. General *Santa Anna* marches to Texas with 10,000 trained soldiers under French, German and Italian field commanders. His banner's the Black Flag, which means he will take no prisoners."

As General Houston was hissed down by the volunteers, former U.S. Marine John Sowers Brooks yelled, "So much the better! We'll not be burdened with prisoners!"

On December 10th, after a five day battle, 300 Texians led by Stephen Austin, Colonel Ben Milam, General Edward Burleson Sr., James Fannin and "Deaf" Smith captured San Antonio, including the Alamo where Texian sharpshooters had driven their foe from the walls. General *Cos* lost 300 men, and the Texians but three -- one was Ben Milam, killed leading a charge. Instead of murdering their 1,400 Mexican captives, they accepted *Cos's* parole that he would march his soldiers out of Texas and fight no more. These brave Texans had defied Major General Sam Houston and proved triumphant as they questioned Houston's courage and his fitness to lead.

Between drinking bouts, on December 6th General Houston wrote Texas Governor Henry Smith begging for men to command and supplies to feed them. He ended, "*We must have an army or abandon all hope of defending the country.*"

From Washington-on-the-Brazos on December 12, 1835, Sam Houston, as ordered, issued his people's Proclamation:

"Your situation is peculiarly calculated to call forth all your manly energies. Under the Republican constitution of Mexico, you were invited to Texas, then a wilderness. You have reclaimed and rendered it a cultivated country. ...You have experienced in silent grief the expulsion of your members from the State Congress. You have realized the horrors of anarchy and the dictation of military rule. The promises made to you have not been fulfilled. ...the agents you have sent to Mexico have been imprisoned . ...Your constitutional executive has been deposed by bayonets of a mercenary soldiery while your State Congress has been dissolved by violence, its members fled or arrested by the military force of the country. The federation has been dissolved, the Constitution declared at an end and centralism established. ...the Dictator required surrender of arms of the civic militia that he might ... establish ... a policy which would forever enslave the people of Mexico.

The usurper dispatched a military force to invade the colonies and exact our arms. The citizens refused ... and the invading force was increased. ... Since our army has been in the field, a consultation of the people ... has met and established a provisional government. ... A regular army has been created. ...To all who will enlist for two years or during the war, a bounty of $24 and 800 acres of land will be given. ...The rights of citizenship are extended to all who will unite in defending the ... Constitution of 1824. Citizens of Texas, your rights must be defended. The oppressors must be driven from our soil. ...union among ourselves will render us invincible. ...Our invader has sworn to extinguish us or sweep us from the soil. He ... has ordered to Texas 10,000 men to enforce the unhallowed purposes of his ambition. His letters ... have been intercepted and his plans for our destruction ... disclosed. ...The services of 5,000 volunteers will be accepted. By the first of March next, we must meet the enemy with an army worthy of our cause. ...Liberal Mexicans will unite with us. ... Generous and brave hearts from a land of freedom have joined our standard before Bexar. They have, by their heroism and valor, called forth the admiration of their comrades in arms and have reflected honor upon the land of their birth.

Let the brave rally to our standard."

"Dissension will destroy Texas."
Sam Houston

CHAPTER 52

TEXAS WARLORDS   **WINTER 1835 - 1836**

hough desperate, General Sam Houston had to laugh at himself, an anachronistic Paul Revere riding from Nacogdoches to Washington-on-the-Brazos to Victoria, giving the alarm, "The Mexicans are coming!" But unlike his predecessor, no one heeded him. A General Council had seized power in a Texas *coup*, appointing Colonels to march off at random, leaving no one to combat General *Antonio Lopez de Santa Anna* marching inexorably north with 10,000 trained troops.

As the General of a non-existent Army, Houston sat down with Almanzon Huston, his designated Quartermaster of non-existent supplies, and presented lists of supplies for which there was non-existent money. Almanzon, a fierce eyed fellow who took things in their most serious light muttered, "Where the hell will I get a ton of lead, two tons of flour, 5,000 pairs of shoes, ¼ ton of soap, 500 pounds of tobacco, 4 barrels of whiskey, 1,000 butcher knives and 1,000 tomahawks *well tempered with handles*? What good's a tomahawk without a handle -- and what good's a list without a dime to buy a thing?"

"As Andrew Jackson would say, *Sir, you have an incredible grasp of the obvious. Now take care of it!*"

General Houston's spirits were buoyed, then sunk, by news from New Orleans that Commissioners Austin, William Wharton and Dr. Branch Archer had procured a loan, chartered five privateers to prey on Mexican shipping and recruited scalawags, to whom they promised such generous bounties that Houston's Regular Army offers to Texians paled into absurdity.

Houston was angered by the General Council's mindless suffocation of his attempt to raise a 5,000 man army. He was infuriated by their hare-brained scheme to invade Matamoros, Mexico, giving Colonel Fannin at Goliad the finest 500 volunteers yet to reach Texas. The 50 Red Rovers from Alabama under Captain Jack Shackleford even carried new muskets from their state's arsenal. The New Orleans Greys, equipped by Houston's friend Adolphus Sterne, would have been a trained nucleus to form his Regular Army around.

Before December's end, the General Council, still shunning its duly appointed Commander General Sam Houston, had half a dozen armies in the field and continued to badger Governor Smith to order invasion of Mexico.

Houston galloped to Goliad and assembled Colonel Fannin's troops, who were making ready to march on Matamoros. "I am the lawful Major General in charge of all Texas forces. I order and implore you not to leave Texas lying prostrate before the onslaught of *Santa Anna's* 10,000 trained assassins while you pursue this fool's errand. What good is victory afar if you return to the smoldering ruins of your homes and find your country enslaved? In order to win, we must act together. United we stand, divided we fall. Since our military power is weak, let our strength be in our unity!"

But the troops stood silent and unmoved until Colonel Fannin called them to attention and marched them out.

General Houston similarly failed to sway Dr. Grant and his band at Refugio.

Convinced the Alamo was indefensible without forces in the field to save it from bombardment, General Houston assembled Jim Bowie's volunteer company. "Your orders are to strip the Alamo of supplies and cannon, blow it up and return to Goliad." As Bowie's men marched off, Houston weighed Texas' chances. A third of its military was committed to the lunatic assault on Matamoros. His efforts to sign Regular Army recruits for the rewards in his Proclamation were abysmal, since warlords lured all the men away with licentious promises of plunder.

Houston got beastially drunk on New Years, and was still suffering when he wrote his January 2, 1836 letter to Colonel D.C. Barrett on the General Council:

" ... *I am most miserably cool and sober -- so you can say to all my friends. Instead of egg-nog I eat roasted eggs in my office. ... Union and harmony will make us everything that we could wish to be. Dissension will destroy Texas. ...*"

Houston had just expressed this letter to Barrett when a courier handed him a dispatch sealed with Colonel Barrett's wax signet. The wadded note inside was dated December 29, 1835, addressed to Barrett and signed by Henry Millard. "... *You must urge the government to abandon Washington-on-the- Brazos for San Felipe. ...The danger comes not from Santa Anna but from disaffected, power-hungry Texian officers forming their own mobs and planning to arrest the government -- or worse: Rest assured that the assassination of some of you and Gen. Houston is in contemplation. ...*"

While still enraged on January 2nd, Sam Houston received the December 26, 1835 missive of the General Council ordering him and experienced Indian agent John Forbes to negotiate critical treaties with the *Cherokees* and other tribes guaranteeing at least their neutrality and furloughing Houston from the Army until March 1, 1836.

While sparing Sam Houston the agony of ferreting potential assassins from Texian ranks, the Indian treaty assignment was another conundrum. His father *Oo-loo-te-ka* had died, but friendly *Cherokees* had kept Houston abreast of Mexican efforts to turn the Indians to their cause. Chief Bowl, his father's successor, Big Mush and other *Cherokees* had been to Mexico City and lavished with promises of land and gifts. Chief Bowl was a Lieutenant Colonel in the Mexican Army with a certificate of his rank. But the Mexicans did not speak *Cherokee*, and Sam Houston did.

With its military shattered into roving mercenary bands, Texians would have little chance if caught between Indian spears and *Santa Anna's* lances. Houston contacted Forbes, and they rode for Indian country hauling a string of gift laden pack horses and hoping they would not be dismembered for their trouble.

"We'll sell our lives at a high price."
David Crockett

CHAPTER 53

DARKEST DAY IN TEXAS   WINTER - SPRING 1836

avid Crockett donned his buckskins and coonskin cap. After tearful good-byes with dear wife Elizabeth, he turned to his eldest son. "John Wesley, you do what's gotta be done here, an' I'll do the same in Texas," then hit the trail with a lump in his throat big as his fist. By the time he made Memphis, he had hisself believin' he'd move his folks to Texas and go back into politics when Texas become a state.

Boardin' a Mississippi steamboat, Crockett found people gatherin'. He wrote: "*I drew nigh the cluster, and seated on a chest was a tall lank sea sarpent looking blackleg ... amusing the passengers with his skill at thimblerig ... picking up their shillings as a hungry gobbler would a pint of corn.*"

Seein' that the gambler in the broad Vicksburg hat let his mark find the first pea under the thimble, Crockett won and stopped, causin' the conjurer to quit. Crockett bought him a drink in the salon askin', "Whyncha gitcher self a rightful job?"

Thimblerig replied, "Being educated as a gentleman in Natchez, I was left unfit to perform any real work."

"Never seed Natchez, Mississippi. What's it like?"

Crockett wrote Thimblerig's words. "*Natchez is a land of fevers, alligators and cotton bales: where the sun shines with force sufficient to melt the diamond, and the word ice is expunged from the dictionary, ...where to refuse grog before breakfast would degrade you ... where the majestic magnolia tree ... calls forth admiration of every beholder; and dark moss festoons the trees like a funeral: where bears the size of young jackasses are fondled in lieu of pet dogs; and knives big as barber poles usurp the toothpick: ... and such is Natchez.*"

"Where's your place in Natchez?"

"Decent town's on the hill, but my den's under the hill where Satan looks with glee upon brothels and gaming taverns engaging in the Spanish Burial. Such is Natchez under the hill."

"What's the Spanish Burial?"

"Greenhorn's forced to join a funeral. Each person kisses the corpse's forehead, but the corpse seizes the greenhorn and mourners beat him until he agrees to buy drinks around."

By the time they docked in Natchitoches, Louisiana, Crockett had convinced Thimblerig to serve the cause of Texas. After praising the town of 800, Crockett wrote: "*... the low ground along the Red River will produce 40 bushels of frogs to the acre, and alligators enough to fence it.*" Takin' rooms in a tavern, they met a handsome hunter of 22 in ornamented buckskins. Crockett commented, "Never seed a hunter so clean."

The hunter doffed his fur cap, releasing curly clusters of black hair. "Clothes are new, but I'm a bee hunter. Their wax is worth more in Mexico for church candles, than the sweets."

Thimblerig slapped Bee Hunter's back, "His real sweets live in the towns! Come with us to Texas, Ned. World's biggest game's due to begin there any day!"

Next day, after buyin' Thimblerig a rifle and horses for all three, they headed for Nacogdoches 120 miles west. Crockett hoped to get his first buffalo, but found none between camps.

Nearin' Nacogdoches, they saw its flag flyin' and heard fifes and drums in patriotic tunes. Crockett wrote: "*...it is about 60 miles west of the river Sabine, in a romantic dell, surrounded by woody bluffs ... within whose borders ... flow the two forks of the Nana, a branch of the Naches. It is a flourishing town [of] 1,000 actual citizens, although it generally presents twice that number on account of trade, one half ... friendly Indians.*"

Bee Hunter made a beeline for the home of his beloved Kate, a splendid blonde lass with a mandolin. They finished the day singing ballads, often alternating verses. When Bee Hunter, Crockett and Thimblerig gathered January 8th, Kate said, "Here's a gourd I've slung for you that'll hold a gallon of water." Bee Hunter kissed her for the gift. Then she added, "Here are two books for you," tears forming in her large blue eyes.

"I'll take the Bible and leave the Bard with you."

"Where do you go now, Love?"

"The Alamo."

"Alamo means *poplar* or *cottonwood* in Spanish. When I hear of it, I'll see a tree -- leaves glinting in the sun -- tip rising to the heavens with you sitting under it."

Bee Hunter mounted his horse then sang to her:
"Saddled and bridled, and booted rode he,
a plume in his helmet, a sword at his knee."
Kate sang the next two lines of the ballad:
"But empty cam' the saddle, all bluidy to see,
And hame cam' the steed, by hame never cam' he."

Clearing the canebrakes, they saw three wolves runnin' out of rifle range. Bee Hunter said, "They put me in mind of us."

Lookin' for what flushed the wolves, Crockett pointed at two men, "My eye's not sharp as a lizard's but that bearded feller looks like he was hacked out of a gum log with a broad ax. Bull Injun's no peach neither. Check yer primes." As the men drew closer, Crockett read the cutlass scar on the bearded man's forehead and yet another on the back of his right hand. "Pirate."

Bee Hunter nodded, "*LaFitte's*. I know 'em from New Orleans. I'd say they're going to the Alamo."

The gravel voiced pirate confirmed their Alamo destination, endin', "Be wise to cluster. Never know what brigands be amang these ravines."

"Him right," the Indian grated.

Thimblerig and Bee Hunter doubled on their horses with the strangers, but rode in back until they reached the first cabin. The old woman there, gray hair waving wildly, had little food, but the Pirate said, "Thar be four rabbits in me friend's bag."

"Him Right," the Indian grunted.

Crockett asked Pirate, "That all the Injun ever says?"

Pirate grinned, "Only English I ever teached him."

All ate well with Kate's biscuits and Bee Hunter's honey. The old woman rasped, "See any hobbled mustangs, jist git right on. Men about here leaves 'em fer one another."

Separately mounted on mustangs, Crockett's party fired on a 15 man Mexican patrol about 20 miles from Bexar. The Mexicans fled when two soldiers flopped from their horses.

When Crockett's five rode into San Antonio on January

17th, people cheered. At the Alamo, they reported to young fire-brand Colonel William Travis. Only Crockett gave his name, but used to names being withheld in Texas, Travis said, "I've heard well of you, Colonel Crockett. Your force is welcome, but we're soon under siege and *Santa Anna* takes no prisoners."

"Then we best whup 'im!" Crockett snapped.

Travis replied, "Colonel Bowie will take care of you."

Thickset Colonel Bowie showed them to their billets. "How many men at the Alamo, Colonel Bowie?"

"'Bout 150. Hard to say the way they come 'n go. Near a dozen *Tejanos*, a freed slave and a passel o' Europeans."

"Live in Texas when you're not linin' up ta die?"

"Eight years, former Kentuckian. What's on your mind?"

"Like information fer my book." They sat on boxes. "Tell me whatchu know bout the Alamo?"

"They say Spaniards put a military outpost here in 1724, then Canary Island settlers arrived a decade later. We seized it before last Christmas. Gen'l Houston ordered the Alamo blown up, but Colonel Travis doesn't recognize Houston's authority."

"Whatta ya know bout *Santa Anna*?"

"'Bout 42. Spanish father. Mexican mother. Educated by Gen'l *Davila*, who made him a Major. Turned on Gen'l *Davila* at Vera Cruz. Led a revolt to be President. Calls himself *Napoleon of the West* and is more treacherous than a pet copperhead."

On February 22, 1836, Crockett wrote: "*The Mexicans about 1,600 strong with their President Santa Anna at their head, aided by Generals Almonte, Cos, Sesma and Castrillon are within two leagues of Bexar. General Cos ... has already forgot his parole of honor, and comes back to retrieve the credit he lost in this place December last.*"

Crockett wrote on February 23rd: "*Early this morning the enemy came in sight, marching in regular order ...in order to strike us with terror. But ... they'll find that they have to do with men who will never lay down their arms ...We have had a large national flag made; it is composed of 13 stripes, red and white, alternatively, on a blue ground with a large white star of 5 points in the centre and between points the letters TEXAS. ... The enemy marched into Bexar ... the Mexicans commenced firing grenades at us without doing mischief ...*"

On February 24th Crockett's Indian friend led 30 men from Gonzales. Mexicans woke the Alamo with cannon fired 350 yards from the fort. Thimblerig got hit by a glancing grapeshot. Crockett removed the big ball from his shallow chest wound. "You gonna drill this and use it fer a watch fob?"

"No. Recast it and lend it out at compound interest."

Colonel William B. Travis wrote and sent his February 24th plea for help to San Felipe: "*To the People of Texas and all Americans in the world. Am besieged by a thousand or more of the Mexicans under Santa Anna. I have sustained a continual bombardment and cannonade for 24 hours and have not lost a man. The enemy has demanded a surrender at discretion, otherwise, the garrison are to be put to the sword, if the fort is taken. I have answered the demand with a cannon shot and our flag still waves proudly from the wall. I shall never surrender or retreat. Then I call on you in the name of Liberty, of patriotism and everything dear to the American character, to come to our aid with all dispatch. The enemy is receiving reinforcements daily and will no doubt increase to three or four thousand in four or five days. If this is neglected, I am determined to sustain myself as long as possible. Victory or death.*"

On February 25th, Crockett rose to find Thimblerig firing alone from the battlement. "Whatchu doin' up there?"

"Paying my debts. I'll soon close the account." He fired. "That grapeshot poured four rounds, all deposited in Mexicans."

"*Santa Anna* may prevent our escape, but we'll still sell our lives at a high price," Crockett growled.

On February 26, 1826 Colonel Bowie fell abed with fever. Bee Hunter picked off 11 Mexicans at enormous distances before being sent out to hunt. Returning, he began reading his Bible and found a musket ball in it. He confided to Crockett, "I'm not the first sinner whose life has been saved by this book."

February 27th found Crockett noting: " *...Provisions are scarce, and the enemy are endeavoring to cut off our water. If they attempt to stop our grog, let them look out, for we shall become too wrathy for our shirts to hold us. ...*"

Crockett was enraged on February 28th: "*Last night our hunters brought in corn and hogs ...[and] accounts that settlers are flying in dismay, leaving possessions to the ... invader, who is literally engaged in a war of extermination, more brutal than the untutored savage of the desert ... Slaughter is indiscriminate, sparing neither age, sex nor condition ..."*

On February 29th Mexicans planted a cannon within easy reach of Crockett's Old Betsey, and he silenced it by shootin' five successive gunners who tried to lay a match to a single shot.

March 1st found Crockett noting the enemy had lost hundreds of men assaulting the walls. Texians were heartened by discovering 80 bushels of corn in a deserted house, and inspired by Col. Bowie crawlin' from his bed to direct the fightin'.

Colonel Travis addressed his men on March 3rd. "We have given up all hope of receiving assistance from Goliad or Refugio. If the Mexicans carry this fort, I expect each man to fight to his last gasp to render their victory more serious to them than to us." Three cheers from his men followed.

March 4th found shells hailing into the fort. Crockett and Bee Hunter saw a man running from Mexican Cavalry and knew it was Pirate back from Goliad. As Crockett and Bee Hunter rushed out, Pirate shot one of his pursuers from his horse, then clubbed his rifle and scattered the rest like sparrows. But 20 Cavalry cut all three off from the fort. Crockett led them in close combat, fighting furiously until a detachment from the Alamo drove the Mexicans off. Pirate and Bee Hunter had fallen. Crockett's forehead saber-cut matched Pirate's scar. Borne into the Alamo, Pirate bled to death and Bee Hunter lay gasping until death freed him. Crockett wondered if Kate could see the proud tree shinin' in the dark, as he could.

Crockett's final entry: *"March 5. Pop, pop, pop! Bom, bom, bom! throughout the day. -- No time for memorandums now. -- Go ahead! -- Liberty and Independence forever!"*

On Sunday March 6, 1836, Texas suffered its darkest day when 5,000 Mexicans came screaming over the Alamo's walls, the plain behind them strewn with their dead and wounded.

"And the leaves of the tree were for the healing of nations."
Revelations 22:2

CHAPTER 54

TOE HOLD IN OREGON   **SPRING 1836**

wing Young repeated, "Come in, Sol," but whoever'd rapped on his cabin door stood in silence. Ewing grabbed Sweet Lips, cocked her and yanked his door open.

"Hold your fire!" said the young uniformed Navy officer with his hands up. "Sir, I'd like to talk to you."

"Who are you and whatta you want?"

"I'm Lieutenant William A. Slacum of the United States Brig *Loriot* at anchor in the Columbia River 25 miles north of here -- sent by Andrew Jackson, President of the United States to see you."

Ewing lowered Sweet Lips. "Welcome to come in Lieutenant, but you're in the wrong pew. I'm not that important." Ewing gawked outside. "Where's your horse?"

"Came by longboat down the Willamette River. Walked from there."

"That's a good five miles!"

Slacum kerchiefed his sweat, then shoved his cap under his arm and crossed the threshold. "Mind if I sit down?"

"I'll pour us some coffee. What's the President want?"

Slacum spun one of Ewing's straight-backed chairs around and straddled it with his husky arms folded on the back. "The President knows you have a toe hold in Oregon. He wants you and other settlers to hang on in spite of British oppression."

Ewing set their steaming tin cups of coffee on the table. "How'd he know about Hudson's Bay Company?"

Slacum's coffee was too hot, so he blew on it while Ewing fidgeted. "May I speak in the strictest confidence Sir?"

"Certainly."

"President Jackson has operatives everywhere. Ever hear of Benjamin Bonneville?"

"Built that crazy fort over on the Green River?"

"Not all as crazy as some suppose. Bonneville's given the War Department a full report on McLoughlin and Fort Vancouver that has proved most useful."

"Leave your papers aboard ship?"

Slacum tapped his close-cropped blond head. "President doesn't allow those papers carried into enemy areas."

"We going to open fire on Fort Vancouver?"

"Economics work better than broadsides. Who's Sol?"

"Sol Smith. Came to Oregon two years ago with Nathaniel Wyeth, who's gone home. We're building a sawmill. People won't buy from me, but they might from Sol. McLoughlin's harsh treatment has been a cloud over me so long, it's nearly driven me mad. HBC controls everything. Won't even sell an American settler a cow -- though they might loan one if there's a child. Soon's I get the capital together, I'll set up a still and cook HBC's liquor monopoly in Oregon."

Slacum laid his jaw on his folded arms. "How's the Mill?"

"Be sawing lumber in another week."

"John McLoughlin presides like a feudal king over 670,000 square miles of wilderness -- twice the size of Texas. He's kindly one day and despotic the next, but an administrative genius. Did you know he was wrongfully accused of murder in 1816, tried and found not guilty?"

"No, but I get your logic. Perhaps if he's reminded, he'll recant his foolish accusations of horsethievery against me. Too bad I didn't know earlier before he hounded poor old Hall Kelley into fleeing to the Sandwich Islands in March of last year."

"Exactly. Don't know how your distillery'll do with no distribution system, but bringing cattle from California to breed and sell in Oregon would scuttle HBC's cattle monopoly."

"California Governor *Figueroa* will have me in irons. He fostered the bogus horsethief charges that doomed me here."

"Might fare better with his successor *Juan Alvarado*. You'll have to buy more cattle than you drive back, but as long as the *mordida's* not too stiff, it's feasible."

"Where's the U. States fit into this?"

"My orders are not to intervene militarily up here. Our troops are being humiliated in Florida's *Seminole* War, so the President keeps increasing those garrisons. Mexico's army's three times the size of ours. He's worried Mexican blood lust'll be so aroused after they've butchered the Texians, they'll keep on coming north. He's sent General Gaines to the Red River to block a Mexican invasion. He has no armies to send to Oregon. Except for information, you're on your own Mr. Young."

Ewing Young had no sooner entered his whiskey distillery partnership with Lawrence Carmichael and bought the copper cauldron from Wyeth's defunct trading post, than another stranger -- huge and black-bearded -- pounded on his door.

"What can I do for you, Sir?" Ewing asked.

"I'm Reverend Jason Lee. We just formed our temperance society on the 11th of February. We beg you not to open a liquor distillery. The settlements are overrun with men so sodden with drink they beat and starve their families. We hope to spare Oregon's children from sinful cruelty and privation. We've collected $51 from the families of the Chehalem Valley and we'll gladly pay it to you to halt completion of your still."

Ewing rubbed his painful stomach. "Hadn't seen it that way, but I'll ask my partner to cease. We won't take the $51. Think your prayers might stop the bleeding in my belly?"

"Kneel Mr. Young. Lord, bring health and prosperity to our Ewing Young, who cares more about Oregon's women and children than he does about money."

"Reverend, think the Lord could do something about Hudson's Bay Company?"

"Far too big -- even for our dear Lord. But somehow, I feel people all across our fair Oregon will see you in a new light. When I'm not serving the Lord, I'm in real estate. As John said in Revelations, '*And the leaves of the tree were for the healing of nations*.' I envision folks buying a lotta lumber from you, Mr. Young -- a whole lotta lumber."

"The victims of the Alamo and those who were murdered at Goliad call for cool, deliberate vengeance."   Order of General Sam Houston

CHAPTER 55

TEXAS TRANSCENDS   **SPRING - FALL 1836**

When Sam Houston returned to Washington-on-the-Brazos on February 28, 1836, the eve of the convention, he held drafts of treaties with eight *Cherokee* bands and five other nations, but felt no joy. The provisional government was dead. Texian units refusing his leadership were being exterminated all across Texas.

Constantly interrupted by wounded Texians staggering in from one rout after another to beg for troops, convention delegates devised a Declaration of Independence. It was approved and signed March 2, 1836 by many, including Sam Houston on his 43rd birthday. Provisional President elect David G. Burnet wrote, "*Gen. Houston was habitually drunk -- often to bestiality, during the convention.*" But able *Tejano* Vice President *Lorenzo de Zavala* defended Houston, and on March 4th the Convention appointed Sam Houston Commander in Chief of the Armies of the Republic of Texas. Armed only with his title, Houston searched for men to save the embattled Alamo.

On March 11th Houston ordered Fannin to blow up Goliad and retreat, but Fannin refused. At Gonzales Houston found 400 men to command. While he dispatched his spies, Mrs. Almaron Dickinson, her little girl and Colonel Travis's slave, stumbled in. "They're all dead at the Alamo! Mexicans swarmed over our walls -- killed my husband -- hacked Colonel Bowie to death in his bed -- murdered the last five men -- now 5,000 Mexicans are coming -- save yourselves!" she whimpered.

Writing to Captain Philip Dimmit, Houston declared, "*All our men are murdered! We must not depend on forts; the roads, and ravines suit us best.*" Jettisoning cannon in the river, Houston burned Gonzales and started the "Runaway Scrape" to put the Colorado River between him and the pursuing Mexicans outnumbering his men 12 to 1. Panicked civilians glutted roads and rivers, reducing his retreat to "molasses in January."

Learning of Dr. James Grant's annihilation at Refugio, Colonel Fannin abruptly abandoned Goliad. Fannin's aide, John Sowers Brooks, wrote: "*Our Colonel's plan is to sprint to San Antonio [80 miles northwest] and cut our way through the enemy's lines, to our Friends in the fort [Alamo].*"

Without cavalry or cover of darkness, Colonel Fannin's 420 men were pinned down on the plain by Mexican Cavalry, until General *Urrea's* 2,000 men swarmed them. Promised passage for all to New Orleans, Fannin yielded. Except for young Henry Ehrenberg who fled, all were shot and bayoneted, including John Sowers Brooks who once condoned the Black Flag because he would not "be burdened with prisoners."

As Houston's legions waded mud, shattered commands and recruits swelled his force to 1,000. Houston spied a blond giant slogging in with a compatriot and asked, "You men here to serve Texas?"

The smaller man asked, "You offering land to recruits?"

Houston nodded, "640 acres. You look familiar."

"Most likely you know my brother, Senator Thomas Hart Benton. I'm Jesse Benton, Jr.; hope you won't hold it against me that I shot Andrew Jackson. Big John Walker here don't."

"Not as long as you shoot straight in Texas."

The blond behemoth offered his massive hand, "You know my brother Joe Walker, former Sheriff of Independence. We woulda signed up without the land, General."

Nostalgically recalling meeting Big John Walker's brothers before the Battle of Horseshoe Bend 24 years ago, Houston grated, "Welcome to the crucible of Texas, Cousin!"

On the Colorado, Houston's scouts found General Sesma's 600 troops at hand. His men readied to charge, but Houston refused to order it. Petitions were circulated to have Houston "broke from command." He averted a coup by telling them, "This is not the time or place to strike a decisive blow. I promise to give you as much fighting as you can eat over."

By March 27th all the warlords, Fannin, Grant, Johnson, King, Morris, Travis and Ward had been assassinated with their men. Only Sam Houston stood between Texas and oblivion, and he was again in retreat with mass desertions. Houston halted in the timber on Mill Creek and sent spies out, learning that *Santa Anna* was leading 850 men toward Harrisburg, the new seat of the Texas government. Cincinnati, Ohio volunteers brought Houston the "twin sisters," a pair of brass six pound cannon.

Learning his only force was camped on the Brazos instead of fighting the Mexican Army menacing Harrisburg, President Burnet penned, "*April 1, 1836. Sir: the Enemy are laughing you to scorn. You must fight them. You must retreat no farther. The country expects you to fight. The Salvation of the country depends on you doing so.*"

Burnet called in Secretary of War, Thomas Rusk, and told him to deliver the scathing note to Houston. About April 13th, Rusk found Houston with his shoulder to the wheel of one of the twin sisters and dived in behind the other wheel. When the big brass cannon rolled from the bog, Rusk handed Houston the note. Houston read it. "Where's President Burnet?"

Beefy, red-haired, six foot Secretary Rusk growled, "Lit out for Galveston before the ink dried on this note!"

"Where are you headed now, Tom?"

"Wherever you are, Sam."

On April 18th, Houston's scouts captured a courier, who revealed that *Santa Anna* had torched Harrisburg and was marching 900 men to Lynch's Ferry on the San Jacinto. Next day Secretary Rusk wrote: "*To The People of Texas: Santa Anna is ... within sound of a drum. ... A few hours more will decide the fate of our army. What an astonishing fact it is that at the moment when the fate of your wives, your children, your homes, your country, and all that is dear to a free man, are suspended upon the issue of one battle, not one-fourth of the men of Texas are in the army. Are you American? Are you freemen? If you are, prove your blood and birth by rallying at once to your country's standard. Your general is at the head of a brave and chivalrous band, and throws himself, sword in hand, into the breach to save his country ...many, very many, whom I antici- pated would be first in the field are not here. What's life worth with the loss of liberty? May I never survive it.*"

Santa Anna's 900 troops attacked Houston on April

20th, firing cannon, but withdrew to the San Jacinto River when Houston's cannon blasted back. Estimating Texians at 750, *Santa Anna* sent for General *Cos's* column 20 miles away. Houston's scouts reported that the Mexicans were untenably positioned with bayou and swamp on three sides and Texians on the fourth.

After marching all night *Cos's* 540 men bedded down at dawn of April 21st, but the odds now favored the Mexicans.

Houston convened his officers. "We are well fortified. Is it attack or defend? How say you?"

All but two voted to wait for Mexican attack.

Houston cogitated, then sent Deaf Smith to blow up Vince's bridge over the San Jacinto. Once the smoking wood hissed out in the water, Houston said, "Now neither army can escape. Only death or a high place in history await."

The Mexicans dug firing pits till *siesta* time.

Sam Houston mounted his horse at 3:30 PM. "I want a thousand yard line of skirmishers with my battle flag in the middle. Cavalry, engage Mexican horsemen. As he marched his infantry doublequick across a meadow of bright grass, the twin sisters fired horseshoes and grapeshot, dismembering Mexicans and their breastworks. Four Texian musicians played *Will you come to the bower with me?*, but gunfire drowned them out.

Startled Mexicans fired raggedly with new English muskets, then dropped their weapons and ran. Lamar's cavalry charged through the Mexican horsemen, slashing men from their saddles and scattering the rest. Screaming, "Remember the Alamo!" and "Remember Goliad!" Texians slaughtered Mexicans with rifles, gunstocks, knives and tomahawks. Mexicans fell to their knees, shouting, "Me no Alamo!" General *Manuel Castrillón* fell dead, followed by four of 13 Colonels. Though he led his men bravely, Colonel *Juan Nepomuceno Almonte* was pulled from his horse and rifle-butted unconscious as hundreds of Mexicans flailed in the swamp with horses trampling them and bullets submerging their comrades.

Sam Houston toppled from his dead war horse and was carried to the surgeons' tent. A musket ball had pierced his boot, shattering his right ankle and both leg bones. While three surgeons plucked bone fragments, Houston gave orders for humane handling of prisoners and counting the dead. In a mere 18 minutes, the Battle of San Jacinto had altered world history.

A battlefield tally revealed 630 Mexicans dead and 208 mortally wounded. Corpses in the swamp were beyond counting, and 730 soldiers were prisoners, including General *Cos*. Six Texians died in battle, two died later, and 24 were wounded. Texians collected 900 muskets, 200 pistols, 300 sabers, 600 horses and mules and $12,000 in silver pesos. Wolves fought over the dead and made the wounded scream in the darkness.

While General Houston questioned Mexicans to locate *Santa Anna*, Margaret McCormick, an Irish widow owning the battlefield land, burst into his headquarters yelling, "Get those dead Mexicans off me land! Don't want 'em hauntin' it!"

As a surgeon inserted opium into his leg, Houston yelled, "Mexican corpses are Mexican business! Get her out o' here!"

On April 22nd, the self-styled *Napoleon of the West* disguised in a blue cotton smock and red felt slippers caused prisoners to yell, "*El Presidente!*" Darkly handsome, 5'10", pot-bellied *Antonio Lopez de Santa Anna*, said, "As President of Mexico, I place myself at the disposal of the brave General Houston. It remains for him to be generous to the vanquished."

Through the interpreter, Houston retorted, "You should have thought of that at the Alamo!" But Houston realized that dead, *Santa Anna* was 150 pounds of wolf bait. As a live hostage, he was the key to massive concessions for Texas.

Houston put *Santa Anna* under heavy guard of trusted officers who swore not to slit his gullet. He forced *Santa Anna* to draft and sign an order directing all Mexican troops to leave Texas. *Santa Anna* indicated his willingness to negotiate a permanent treaty recognizing Texas independence.

Houston distributed most of the spoils to his men, including the $12,000 cash. President Burnet and other Texas officials arriving after the shooting stopped were furious. Robert Potter suggested Houston's dismissal. Too weak to address his troops, Houston left them a written message of gratitude, then put Thomas Rusk in charge as a Brigadier General.

President Burnet and his cabinet boarded the steamer *Yellow Stone* for Galveston, denying Houston's request to be taken along. But the Captain refused to sail without Houston, who was penniless, having taken none of the spoils for himself. Dr. Alexander Ewing was ordered not to accompany the desperately ill Houston, went anyway and was dismissed from the service for it. At Galveston, General Houston asked to board the Texas warship heading for New Orleans, but was told to clear the boat, though he had to be carried off.

Houston got aboard the *Flora* promising later payment. He reached New Orleans near death on May 22, 1836 where a crowd cheered their emaciated hero limping feebly from the ship between two men. Wealthy William Christy had surgeons strip Houston's gangrenous flesh and sew torn muscle and sinews. Though Houston returned to Texas on crutches in June, his leg had to be treated repeatedly.

President Burnet rotated his cabinet by whim almost daily. The government of Texas stampeded to all points of the compass. The future of hostage *Santa Anna* changed daily, causing the Mexican government to seize Americans in Mexico in June, herding them into Tampico, other forts and jails.

President Burnet set a general election for September 5th. Though Stephen Austin and Henry Smith had declared their candidacy, Houston wrote Rusk that he would support Rusk for the Presidency. Rusk declined and implored Houston to take charge of the chaotic Army. Sam Houston did so in mid August, but on August 26th, 11 days before the election, Houston submitted himself for the Presidency. The Father of Texas, Stephen Austin, polled 587 votes; Smith garnered 743, and Houston made it a political San Jacinto with 5,199, representing 80 % of those voting. All but 92 also voted in favor of Texas seeking annexation to the United States.

As the first popularly elected President of the Republic of Texas, Sam Houston took his oath of office on October 22, 1836 at a crude table covered by an old blanket made ever so illustrious by the White Savage who stood tall when Texas called -- a stalwart American who would lead Texas to realize its rightful place of honor and greater glory.

EPILOGUE

RAILS OF THE WHITE SAVAGES is intended to end a century and a half of controversy among historians whether Benjamin Bonneville and Joe Walker were agents of the U.S. Government, where they went and what they did during their western explorations.

Letters of Bonneville and Macomb obtained from the National Archives [quoted in Chapter 34] framed Bonneville's mission. Bonneville's July 29, 1833 letter [pages 275-6] says in part: "... *if the government ever intend taking possession of Oregon, the sooner it shall be done, the better; the military force necessary to seize Oregon will require a full garrison. My list of forts and garrisons includes Vancouver and Walla Walla and the forces necessary to reduce them...*"

See also Walker's Passport and Mexican Visa [pages 252 & 272], the building of Fort Bonneville with only military uses [page 263], Bonneville's first trap in the water a year into his trip [page 269] and only Walker harvesting furs [page 270].

After Bonneville learned in autumn 1835 he'd been discharged as a deserter from the U.S. Army, he wrote two letters to Secretary of War Lewis Cass. His September 26, 1835 letter states:"... *I set out upon my tour with the consent of the War Department, and was charged by General Eaton, then Secretary of War,*[see page 238] *with instructions to guide me in collecting information with which he considered it advantageous for the Government to be possessed; ...*" His lengthy September 30, 1835 letter asserts: "... *Believing that I have now fully executed the order of the General in Chief and that from my maps, charts and diary I would be able to furnish the Dept of War with every information desired respecting the Rocky Mountains and the Oregon Territory...*"

When the Army balked at reinstating Bonneville, President Andrew Jackson intervened instantly, instructing the Senate on January 5, 1836 to reappoint Bonneville Captain at once [even though he'd been AWOL a year and a half]. Three days later on January 8, 1836 the Adjutant General's Office issued general Order No. 25, restoring Bonneville's rank and ordering him to Fort Gibson.

In 1991 the U.S. Bureau of Land Management issued *U.S. History on CD - ROM,* as approved by the U.S. Department of Justice [see Bibliography]. Under *"Exploring the Great American West,"* in Chapter 4 it expressly admits Joseph R. Walker was an agent of the U.S. Government. Case closed.

The defamation of Joe Walker by Washington Irving in his *Adventures of Captain Bonneville* [see Bibliography] since parroted by hosts of under informed historians requires redress.

How or why the facts were falsified is unclear. Did Bonneville need a scapegoat for his feeble fur production? Was this a "cover story" for his government mission? Or did Irving fabricate a villain? Irving's book said [1] Bonneville ordered Walker to explore only around the Great Salt Lake and return; [2] Walker wandered off to California squandering expedition assets; [3] Walker wantonly massacred the *Paiutes* twice, and [4] when profligate Walker returned in July 1834, Bonneville sent him packing to St. Louis in disgrace. Irving printed these uncorroborated lies with elaborate permutations.

The truth: [1] Bonneville is the named applicant for Walker's California Passport and Mexican Visa in January 1832; Bonneville's letter to Cass describes his maps and charts [quoted on page 332] which include California; [2] Zenas Leonard's journal, with no ax to grind, verifies his hiring by Walker to go to California, as does George Nidever's; [3] Leonard and Nidever, who fought in both *Paiute* battles, wrote Walker was justified as a leader of 60 men surrounded by 900 angry Indians in doing what he did. In fact, a respecter of human life, *WHITE SAVAGE* Joe Walker quite remarkably never lost a man from any of these expeditions. Did Irving, never west of Independence, know more about Indian fighting than the men who did it? [4] Although Bonneville's journal doesn't mention Walker's name after July 1834, it was *Cerré* he sent to St. Louis in the summer of 1834 as proved by Bonneville's September 30, 1835 letter to Secretary Cass; Walker not only ran Bonneville's northern fur brigade throughout 1835 [verified by repeated entries in unbiased Zenas Leonard's journal] but made a huge fur harvest [Leonard's share alone was worth $1,100] or Bonneville would have had even less to show for three and a half expensive years in fur country. Irving had access to Leonard's journal published serially in eastern newspapers and as a book before Irving finished Bonneville's saga. Please review the text of Chapters 43 and 44 based in the main on Zenas Leonard's daily journal entries. Then you decide who lied.

After the Death of *WHITE SAVAGE* David Crockett at the Alamo, his son John Wesley Crockett was elected to Congress and resumed his father's lifelong crusade for the Tennessee Vacant Land Bill for poor squatters. A forerunner of the Federal Homestead Act, Crockett's Bill became law well before Florida's second Seminole War [in which Captain Bonneville fought for three years] ended in 1842.

Jesse Benton [Thomas Hart Benton's brother] and Big John Walker [see page 327] each got 640 acres for fighting in the Battle of San Jacinto according to records furnished by the Daughters of the Republic of Texas Library at the Alamo.

In fall 1836 John Campbell wrote *WHITE SAVAGE* Sam Houston that his wife Eliza Houston was thrilled by his San Jacinto victory and awaited word from him. Cousin Robert McEwen wrote Sam that Eliza and her family welcomed a reconciliation. Sam didn't, but was pleased to hear how Andrew Jackson obtained the instantaneous release of all Mexico's American hostages [mentioned page 331] without firing a shot.

At an 1836 cabinet meeting, Secretary of the Navy Maholn Dickerson reported Mexican officials at Tampico had threatened to put all American prisoners to death in retaliation for the holding of *Santa Anna*. Enraged, *WHITE SAVAGE* Andrew Jackson ordered Commodore Dallas "*to blockade the harbor at Tampico, ... & tell them if they touch the hair of the head of one of our citizens, we will batter down & destroy their town & exterminate the inhabitants from the face of the earth!*"

BIBLIOGRAPHY
[169 References]
TRAILS OF THE WHITE SAVAGES
by Gary H. Wiles and Delores M. Brown

Note: "MM & FT" indicates the work is in *THE MOUNTAIN MEN and the Fur Trade of the Far West,* a superb 10 Volume set edited by Leroy Hafen. Arthur H. Clark Co. Glendale, CA 1965 - 1972.

*Arnold, Samuel P. *William W. Bent.* Volume VI, 61 - 84 MM & FT
Axelrod, Alan. *Art of the Golden West -- An Illustrated History.* Abbeville Press. New York 1990
*Bauer, John E. *Zacharias Ham.* Volume IX, 193-194 MM & FT
*Beckman, Margaret E. and Ellison, William H. *George Nidever.* Vol I, 337 - 354 MM & FT
Billington, Ray Allen and Ridge, Martin. *Westward Expansion -- A History of the American Frontier.* Macmillan. New York 1982
*Brandon, William. *Wilson Price Hunt.* Volume VI, 185 - 206 MM & FT
Burns, Robert. Editor Ricks, Christopher. *Selected Poems.* Penguin Books. London 1993
Buxbaum, Melvin H. *Benjamin Franklin and the Zealous Presbyterians.* Pennsylvania State University Press 1975
Carson, Kit. Editor Quaife, Milo Milton. *Kit Carson's Autobiography.* University of Nebraska Press 1966
*Carter, Harvey L. *Robert Campbell.* Volume VIII, 49 - 60 MM & FT
*Carter, Harvey L. *Kit Carson.* Volume VI, 105 - 131 MM & FT
*Carter, Harvey L. *Ewing Young.* Volume II, 379 - 401 MM & FT
Chittenden, Hiram Martin. *The American Fur Trade of the Far West.* Volumes I & II. University of Nebraska Press 1986
Cleland, Robert Glass. *This Reckless Breed of Men -- The Trappers and Fur Traders of the Southwest.* Alfred A. Knopf. New York 1963
Crockett, David. *The Autobiography of David Crockett.* Charles Scribner's Sons. New York 1923
DeBruhl, Marshall. *Sword of San Jacinto - Life of Sam Houston.* Random House. New York 1993
Dillon, Richard H. *North American Indian Wars.* Bison Books. Greenwich, CT 1983
Dufus, R. L. *The Santa Fe Trail.* Longmans, Green & Co. New York 1931
*Dunham, Harold H. *Charles Bent.* Volume II, 27- 48 MM & FT
*Dunham, Harold H. *Ceran St. Vrain.* Volume V, 297 - 316 MM & FT
Favour, Alpheus H. *Old Bill Williams -- Mountain Man.* University of North Carolina Press 1936
Ford, Henry Jones. *The Scotch-Irish in America.* Archon. Hamden, CT 1966
Franklin, Benjamin. Editor Smyth, Albert H. *The Writings of Ben Franklin.* Volume V. Haskell House Publishers Ltd. New York 1970
Gilbert, Bil. *The Trailblazers.* Time-Life Books. New York 1973

Gilbert, Bil. *Westering Man: The Life of Joseph Walker.* University of
Oklahoma Press 1985
Goetzmann, William H. *Exploration And Empire -- Explorer and Scientist
Winning the American West.* Alfred A. Knopf. New York 1966
Gowans, Fred R. *Rocky Mountain Rendezvous: A History of the Fur Trade
Rendezvous 1825-1840.* Peregrine Smith. Layton, UT 1985
*Hafen, Ann W. *James Ohio Pattie.* Volume IV, 231 - 250 MM & FT
*Hafen, Leroy R. and Hafen, Ann W. *Thomas Fitzpatrick.* Volume VII,
87-105 MM & FT
Hafen, Leroy R. *Broken Hand: The Life of Thomas Fitzpatrick: Mountain
Man.* Old West Publishing Co. Denver 1973
Hafen, Leroy R. and Hafen, Ann W. *Old Spanish Trail -- Santa Fé to Los
Angeles.* Arthur H. Clark. Glendale CA 1954
*Hanson, Charles E. Jr. *Michel Sylvestre Cerré.* Vol VIII 61 - 65 MM & FT
*Hays, Carl D. W. *David E. Jackson.* Volume IX, 215 - 244 MM & FT
*Holmes, Kenneth L. *John McLoughlin.* Volume VIII, 235 - 245 MM & FT
Houston, Sam. Editors Day, Donald & Ullom, Harry Herbert. *The Auto-
biography of Sam Houston.* University of Oklahoma Press 1954
Irving, Washington. Editors Rees, Robert & Sandy, Alan. *The Adventures
of Captain Bonneville.* Twayne Publishers. Boston 1977
*Lecompte, Janet. *Jules DeMun.* Volume VIII, 95 - 105 MM & FT
*Lecompte, Janet. *Levin Mitchell.* Volume V, 239 - 247 MM & FT
Leonard, Zenas. Editor Ewers, John C. *Adventures of Zenas Leonard.*
University of Oklahoma Press 1959
Leyburn, James G. *The Scotch-Irish -- A Social History.* University of North
Carolina Press 1962
*Mark, Frederick A. *William Craig.* Volume II, 99 - 116 MM & FT
Maughn, Ralph C. *Anatomy of the Snake River Plain.* Idaho State
University Press. Pocatello 1992
Meigs, William Montgomery. *The Life of Thomas Hart Benton.* Da Capo
Press. New York 1970
*Munnick, Harriet D. *Jean Baptiste Gervais.* Vol VII, 121 -129 MM & FT
*Nunis, Doyce B. Jr. *Milton G. Sublette.* Volume IV, 331 - 349
*Pedersen, Lyman C. Jr. *Warren Angus Ferris.* Vol. II, 135 - 155 MM & FT
Porter, Kenneth Wiggins. *John Jacob Astor -- Business Man.* Volume II.
Russell & Russell. New York 1966
Porter, Mae Reed and Davenport, Odessa. *Scotsman in Buckskins -- Sir
William Drummond Stewart.* Hastings House. New York 1963
Remini, Robert V. *Andrew Jackson and the Bank War - A Study in the
Growth of Presidential Power.* Norton & Co. New York 1967
Remini, Robert V. *Andrew Jackson and the Course of American Democ-
racy, 1833-1845.* Harper & Row. New York 1984
Remini, Robert V. *Andrew Jackson and the Course of American Empire,
1767-1821.* Harper & Row. New York 1977
Remini, Robert T. *Life of Andrew Jackson.* Harper & Row. New York 1988
Rosenberg, Charles E. *The Cholera Years -- The United States in 1832,
1849 and 1866.* University of Chicago Press 1962

Russell, Carl P. *Firearms, Traps and Tools of the Mountain Men.* Brand
Books. New York 1967

Shackford, James Atkins. Editor Shackford, John B. *David Crockett -- The
Man and The Legend.* Greenwood Press. Westport, CT 1956

*Strickland, Rex W. *James Baird.* Volume III 27-37 MM & FT

Sunder, John Edward. *Bill Sublettte Mountain Man.* University of
Oklahoma Press 1959

The Software Toolworks. *Illustrated Encyclopedia IBM Version 2.0.*
[13 of 21 Volumes] on CD-ROM. Grolier, Inc. Danbury, CT 1991

*Tobie, Harvey E. *Joseph L. Meek.* Volume I, 313 - 335 MM & FT

*Tobie, Harvey E. *Stephen Hall Meek.* Volume II, 225 - 240 MM & FT

Todd, Edgeley W. *Benjamin L.E. Bonneville.* Volume V, 45-63 MM & FT

Townsend, John Kirk. *Narrative of a Journey Across The Rocky Mountains.*
Henry Perkins. Philadelphia 1839

*Trottman, Alan C. *Lucien Fontenelle.* Volume V, 79 - 99 MM & FT

U. S. Bureau of Land Management with Department of Justice. *U.S. History
on CD-ROM.* [Using 66 of 102 Volumes] Washington D.C. 1991

Victor, Frances Fuller. Editor Blevins, Winfred. *River Of The West: Adventures of Joe Meek.* Volume I. Mountain Press. Missoula, MT 1983

*Voelker, Frederic E. *William Sherley (Old Bill) Williams.* Volume VIII,
365-394 MM & FT

*Walker, Ardis M. *Joseph R. Walker.* Volume V, 361-380 MM & FT

Walker, Joel P. *A Pioneer of Pioneers -- Narrative of Adventures Thro'
Alabama, Florida, New Mexico, Oregon, California & c.* Glen
Dawson. Los Angeles 1953

*Warner, Ted J. *Peter Skene Ogden.* Volume III, 213 - 238 MM & FT

Weber, David J. *The Taos Trappers -- The Fur Trade in the Far Southwest,
1540 - 1846.* University of Oklahoma Press 1971

Wiles, Gary H. & Brown, Delores M. *Behold The Shining Mountains.*
Photosensitive. Laguna Niguel, CA 1996

Wiles, Gary H. & Brown, Delores M. *Ponder The Path.* Photosensitive.
Laguna Niguel, CA 1996

Williams, John Hoyt. *Sam Houston -- A Biography of the Father of Texas.*
Simon & Schuster. New York 1993

*Wilson, Iris Higbie. *William Wolfskill.* Volume II, 351-362 MM & FT

Wilson, Iris Higbie. *William Wolfskill: Frontier Trapper to California
Ranchero.* Arthur H. Clark. Glendale, CA 1965

Articles: Reid, John Alden *Cannon at Enitachopco and Horseshoe Bend*
Reid, John Alden *The Thirty-Ninth Regiment of U.S. Infantry*
Reid, John Alden *Uniforms of the U.S. Regular Infantry - 1814*
Reid, John Alden *The Battle of the Horseshoe, March 27, 1814*

Horseshoe Bend Nat'l Military Pk, Rte 1 Bx 103, Daviston, AL 36256-9751

National Archives: 5 *Letters To & From Benjamin Bonneville - General
Alexander Macomb - Sec'y of War Lewis Cass -1831 and 1835*

Newspaper: *Cappers. Sunflowers in 1823.* Topeka KS Vol 119 - No. 2

PHOTOSENSITIVE™
DEPT. TWS
P.O. BOX 7408
LAGUNA NIGUEL, CA 92607
☎ OR FAX (7I4) 495-8897

BOOK ORDER FORM

Send To: _____
_____
_____
_____

Telephone _____ Fax _____

LIBRARIES, MUSEUMS & DEALERS CALL OR FAX FOR VOLUME DISCOUNTS.

DISREGARD SALES TAX UNLESS ORDERING FROM CALIFORNIA

BOOK & ½ SHIPPING COSTS	No.	PRICE EACH	SALES TAX CA ONLY	TOTAL
All Books are made like this one & are by Gary Wiles & Delores Brown **PONDER THE PATH** 279 Pages; 2 Page Map of Fur Country; 159 Vol Bibliography; 179 Person Index	____	$12.95	$ .99	$_____
BEHOLD THE SHINING MOUNTAINS 334 Pages; 2 Page Map of Fur Country & 2 other Maps; 223 Vol Biblio; 7 Pg Index	____	$14.95	$1.16	$_____
TRAILS OF THE WHITE SAVAGES 352 Pages; 16 Pinpoint Action Maps; 11 Portraits; 168 Ref Biblio; 8 Page Index	____	$16.95	$1.31	$_____
You pay ½ shipping at $1 per book; We package free & pay the other ½		$ 1.00 Shipping		$_____
		GRAND	**TOTAL**	$_____

_____ Check _____ Money Order   Payable to PHOTOSENSITIVE™

___ Visa ___ Mastercard No. _____ Expires _____

Signature of Ordering Party_____

[FREE] AUTOGRAPH TO: _____

[FREE] AUTHOR PHOTO BOOK MARKS _____ YES _____ NO

[FREE] REVIEWS OF BOOK[S] ORDERED _____ YES _____ NO

SPECIAL INSTRUCTIONS: _____
_____
_____

PHOTOCOPY AND MAIL TO THE ADDRESS AT THE TOP OF THIS PAGE